1917

1917

LENIN, WILSON, AND THE BIRTH OF

THE NEW WORLD DISORDER

ARTHUR
HERMAN

HARPER PERENNIAL

NEW YORK • LONDON • TORONTO • SYDNEY • NEW DELHI • AUCKLAND

HARPER ● PERENNIAL

FIRST HARPER PERENNIAL EDITION PUBLISHED 2018.

Designed by Fritz Metsch

The Library of Congress has catalogued the hardcover
edition as follows:

Names: Herman, Arthur, 1956– author.
Title: 1917 : Lenin, Wilson, and the birth of the new world disorder /
Arthur Herman.
Description: First edition. | New York, NY : Harper, 2017. |
Includes bibliographical references and index.
Identifiers: LCCN 2017021669 (print) | LCCN 2017039978 (ebook) |
ISBN 9780062570925 (ebk) | ISBN 9780062791467 (digaud) |
ISBN 9780062570888 (hc : alk. paper) | ISBN 9780062747365
(largeprint : alk. paper) | ISBN 9780062791498 (audio : alk. paper)
Subjects: LCSH: World War, 1914–1918—Influence. |
Wilson, Woodrow, 1856–1924—Influence. | Lenin, Vladimir Ilyich,
1870–1924—Influence. | Soviet Union—History—Revolution,
1917–1921—Influence. | United States—Foreign relations—1913–1921. |
Nineteen seventeen, A.D.
Classification: LCC D523 (ebook) | LCC D523 .H3478 2017 (print) |
DDC 940.3—dc23
LC record available at https://lccn.loc.gov/2017021669

ISBN 978-0-06-257089-5 (pbk.)

18 19 20 21 22   LSC   10 9 8 7 6 5 4 3 2 1

TO BETH, THE LOVE OF MY LIFE
AND MY GUIDING STAR

CONTENTS

CAST OF CHARACTERS

GERMANY

THEOBALD VON BETHMANN-HOLLWEG: chancellor, 1909–17

ERICH LUDENDORFF: quartermaster general

PAUL VON HINDENBURG: chief of the German General Staff

ARTHUR ZIMMERMANN: foreign secretary

JOHANN VON BERNSTORFF: ambassador to the United States

ERICH VON FALKENHAYN: general; former chief of the German General Staff (1914–16), then commander of German armies in Romania and Russia

BARON GISBERT VON ROMBERG: ambassador in Bern, Switzerland

MATTHIAS ERZBERGER: prominent member of Catholic Center Party in Reichstag; later Reich minister of finance, 1919–20

GREAT BRITAIN

DAVID LLOYD GEORGE: prime minister and leader of the Liberal Party

ARTHUR JAMES BALFOUR: foreign minister and former leader of the Conservative Party

WINSTON CHURCHILL: former first lord of the admiralty; later named minister of munitions (July 1917)

ANDREW BONAR LAW: leader of the Conservative Party and prominent member of the War Cabinet as chancellor of the exchequer

DOUGLAS HAIG: general; commander, British Expeditionary Force on the Western Front

WILLIAM HALL: admiral; director, British Naval Intelligence

EDMUND ALLENBY: general; commander, British Third Army during the Battle of Arras (March 1917) and later named commander of the Egyptian Expeditionary Force (May 1917)

CHAIM WEIZMANN: president, British Zionist Federation; later first president of the State of Israel

FRANCE

ARISTIDE BRIAND: prime minister (later succeeded by Georges Clemenceau, November 1917)

GEORGES CLEMENCEAU: leader of the Radical-Socialist Party in the Chamber of Deputies

JOSEPH JOFFRE: general; commander in chief of French armies on the Western Front, 1914–16 (replaced by Gen. Robert Nivelle, December 1916); later as field marshal served as French envoy to the United States, May 1917

ROBERT NIVELLE: general; commander in chief of French armies, December 1916–April 1917 (succeeded by Gen. Philippe Pétain)

PHILIPPE PÉTAIN: general; chief of the General Staff, April 1917 to November 1918

FERDINAND FOCH: general; supreme Allied commander on the Western Front

MAURICE PALÉOLOGUE: ambassador to Russia

INESSA ARMAND: mistress of Lenin

RUSSIA

NICHOLAS II (NIKOLAI ALEKSANDROVICH ROMANOV): "czar of all the Russias"

ALEXANDRA (ALEKSANDRA FYODOROVNA): czarina and wife of Nicholas II

NICHOLAS (NIKOLAI NIKOLAEVICH ROMANOV): grand duke; commander in chief of the Russian armies

MICHAEL (MIKHAIL) ROMANOV: grand duke; brother of Czar Nicholas II

ALEXANDER KERENSKY: lawyer; member of the Duma, Social Revolutionary Party; later minister of war and prime minister, Provisional Government

ALEKSEI BRUSILOV: general; commander of the Southwest Front; later commander in chief, Provisional Government

GRIGORI RASPUTIN: monk and mystic; adviser to Czarina Alexandra

NIKOLAI POKROVSKY: minister of foreign affairs

NIKOLAI CHKHEIDZE: member of the Duma, Social Revolutionary Party; later president of the Executive Committee of the Soviet of Petrograd or Ispolkom

PAVEL MILIUKOV: member of the Duma, Constitutional Democratic Party (or Kadets); later foreign minister, Provisional Government

MIKHAIL RODZIANKO: state councillor and president of the Duma

A. A. BOGDANOV: early member of the Bolshevik wing of the Social Democratic Labour Party of Russia and rival of Lenin; expelled from the party in 1909

LENIN (ORIGINALLY VLADIMIR ILYICH ULYANOV): leader of the Bolshevik wing of the Social Democratic Labour Party of Russia; later chairman of the Council of People's Commissars

NADEZHDA KRUPSKAYA: wife of Lenin

LEON TROTSKY (ORIGINALLY LEV DAVIDOVICH BRONSTEIN): early member of the Mezhraiontsy faction; then people's commissar for foreign affairs for the Russian Soviet Federative Socialist Republic (RSFSR) and the Soviet Union; later founder and commander of the Red Army

KARL RADEK (ORIGINALLY KAROL SOBELSOHN): Lenin's friend and fellow exile in Switzerland; later vice commissar for foreign affairs and key figure in the Communist International

LEV KAMENEV: editor of *Pravda* and brother-in-law of Leon Trotsky; later deputy chairman of the Council of People's Commissars of the Soviet Union

LAVR KORNILOV: general; named commander of Petrograd Military District in March 1917; later commander in chief under Provisional Government and then commander of the anti-Bolshevik Volunteer Army

ALEXANDER KOLCHAK: admiral; commander, Black Sea Fleet; later "Supreme Ruler and Commander-in-Chief of All Russian Land

and Sea Forces" for anti-Bolshevik (White) forces during Russian Civil War

ANTON DENIKIN: general; succeeded Lavr Kornilov as commander, anti-Bolshevik Volunteer Army

UNITED STATES

WOODROW WILSON: president (1913–21)

THEODORE ROOSEVELT: former U.S. president (1901–9)

WILLIAM HOWARD TAFT: former U.S. president (1909–13); later president, the League to Enforce Peace

HENRY CABOT LODGE: senator, Massachusetts (R); later chairman, Senate Foreign Relations Committee; and Senate majority leader

ROBERT LANSING: secretary of state

WALTER HINES PAGE: ambassador to Great Britain

WILLIAM MCADOO: secretary of the treasury

EDWARD HOUSE: colonel; special adviser to President Wilson

JOSEPH TUMULTY: private secretary to President Wilson

JOHN J. PERSHING: general; commander, American Expeditionary Force in France

GILBERT HITCHCOCK: senator, Nebraska (D)

WILLIAM SIMS: vice admiral; commander of all U.S. naval forces operating in Britain (named May 1917)

FRANKLIN D. ROOSEVELT: assistant secretary of the navy

GEORGE CREEL: former editor of the Progressive newspaper the *Independent*; later named by President Wilson as head of the Committee on Public Information

THOMAS GREGORY: attorney general (succeeded by A. Mitchell Palmer, 1919)

EUGENE V. DEBS: founding member of the Industrial Workers of the World and Socialist Party of America; presidential candidate in 1912 and 1920

1917

PROLOGUE:
A WORLD ON FIRE

The world is on fire. There is tinder everywhere. The
sparks are liable to drop anywhere, and somewhere
there may be material which we cannot prevent from
bursting into flame.
—WOODROW WILSON, JANUARY 1917

LONDON, JANUARY 17, 1917

HE WAS A small, narrow-faced man nicknamed the Door Mouse.
After coming up the steps of the Admiralty House, he quietly
made his way past the first sea lord's office and opened the door
to a dark, dingy room at the end of the corridor.

They called it Room 40. It was here that a handful of men and
women, many of them civilians, worked on decoding German military and diplomatic messages. This was wartime, and the decoded
information they'd passed on to their superiors had led to several
breakthroughs on the battlefield and in the war at sea. But no piece of
intelligence would be comparable to the message that dropped into
Room 40's wire basket that morning.

Nigel de Grey—that was the Door Mouse's real name—picked it
up and looked at it. He was joined by his colleague William Montgomery. They were an incongruous pair. Both were civilians,
although de Grey had done a stint in the Royal Naval Volunteer Reserve. Montgomery was a Presbyterian minister and an expert on the
works of Saint Augustine. De Grey was a junior editor on loan from
the publisher William Heinemann. But both men had the intellectual
skills that made code breaking an engaging and also highly successful
enterprise.

For example, de Grey saw at once, from the numbers at the top of the page, that this was a message in a diplomatic code used by the German Foreign Office. He and Montgomery pulled out the relevant notebooks that would provide the key for this particular message (an unusually long one, they noticed), derived from German Codebook No. 13040.[1]

Room 40 hadn't gotten hold of these diplomatic codes until the war was more than a year old. In the very beginning, in October 1914, as the British army was fighting for its life at the First Battle of Ypres, the director of naval intelligence had handed Alfred Ewing, who was director of naval education but also did ciphers as a hobby, a pile of intercepted German radio messages to decipher.[2] Ewing was delighted, and he summoned his friend William Montgomery to help make sense of the pile. That marked the start of a decoding industry based in Room 40 that would dramatically shift the odds for the Royal Navy in the war.

Ewing had started work there using a German naval codebook, *The Signal Book of the Imperial German Navy*, known by its German initials SKM, which Britain's ally Russia had found on a captured German cruiser, the SMS *Magdeburg*. The Russians kept one copy; the other they sent along to the British. Ewing and Montgomery quickly put it to good use, but it was just the start of a codebook treasure trove.

That same month, another codebook was captured, one that the Germans used for wireless or radio communication with naval warships, merchant ships, zeppelins, and U-boats. On November 30, came the codebook the German navy used to communicate with its naval attachés in foreign embassies.

Then, in March 1915—just as British and French troops were about to land at Gallipoli, in Turkey, in the hope of breaking the war wide open, and a British Cunard liner, the *Lusitania*, was taking on cargo in New York Harbor for the trip home—Ewing and Adm. William Hall received a suitcase captured from a German diplomat in Persia. Inside was a copy of the German diplomatic codebook known as No. 13040.

It was a code breaker's dream find. Of course, over a period of months, the Germans came to realize that their codes were being read, and they issued new ones. But ships or submarines far away at sea often didn't have access to the new codebooks, and had to send messages using the old ones; also, the new codes were often just variants on the old, which meant it was possible for the team in Room 40 to reconstruct a new code from its predecessors.

This was exactly what de Grey and Montgomery had done. The numbers at the top of the telegram, 13042, meant that the code was a 13040 variant, which was used for a message of more than one thousand coded groups. The men set to work. The first word they came up with, the signature at the end of the message, was "Zimmermann"—that was Arthur Zimmermann, the German foreign secretary. Then, at the top, came "Most Secret," followed by "For Your Excellency's Personal Information." The "Excellency" in this case was the German ambassador in Washington, DC, Count Johann von Bernstorff.

So far, no surprises. But the next word they decoded gave them pause. It was "Mexico." De Grey and Montgomery looked at each other. This was an odd country name to turn up in a wartime communication. For one thing, Mexico was neutral in this war, although its president was hardly a friend of the Allies and had good relations with Germany and Berlin. The next name they decoded was even more incongruous: "Japan." In fact, it popped up several times in this first part of the dispatch. Japan had been on the side of the Allies since August 23, 1914—but, alarmingly, the dispatch was worded as if Tokyo were about to become Germany's ally.

Thoroughly worried, the two code breakers worked with fierce determination for the next two hours. What emerged was a secret message from Berlin to Washington in two parts. The first contained what they knew was a diplomatic bombshell: on February 1, Berlin informed its ambassador in Washington, Germany would resume its unrestricted submarine warfare against neutral shipping.

This was an important warning to the German ambassador, because no neutral country's position was likely to change more as a result of that decision than that of the United States—and no leader's views more than those of U.S. president Thomas Woodrow Wilson.

The submarine was a new offensive weapon unleashed by this war, one of the most feared—and certainly the most controversial. From the start of the war in 1914, Germany had used its submarine fleet to strangle the Allies' maritime supply lines, especially Britain's. German submarines, known as U-boats, had sunk merchant ships without warning, and without picking up survivors—making no distinction between cargo ships of enemy combatants such as Britain, France, and Russia, and neutral ships such as those from Holland, Spain, and America. All those ships unloaded cargo, including industrial goods and sometimes even ammunition, in Allied ports; all were therefore fair targets, in the German view. This ruthless approach to war, one that didn't distinguish between combatant and neutral, or even between soldier and civilian, had brought down the collective wrath of the international community on Germany's head, particularly the wrath of American president Woodrow Wilson.

As 1917 began, Wilson was working hard to keep the United States officially neutral in the greatest war history had ever known. Most Americans thought he was right to do so. What did they care about a war being fought on the other side of the Atlantic, in Europe, or even farther away, in the Middle East and on the plains of Russia? Just that past November, Wilson had run for a second term as president with the slogan "He Kept Us Out of War," and voters had responded by sending him back to the White House for another four years.

It was true that some Americans thought their country should get into the war. Some, especially those of German descent, wanted to join with the Germans and Austrians. But those who pushed hardest for war, including former president Theodore Roosevelt, wanted the United States to join up with Britain and France. But Wilson had resisted their persistent calls for the United States to end its neutrality and choose a side in a conflict that, as the Allies kept insisting, defined the difference between civilization and barbarism—as witnessed by the all-out submarine warfare.

In Wilson's view, entering that war would irreparably damage his vision of what America was and should be to the world: the peacemaker, the symbol of a human future that turned its back on war— even though the United States was more than capable of fighting, and winning, the war if it had to. In Wilson's view, America's neutrality was a reflection of strength, moral strength, rather than weakness or timidity. His other slogan in 1916, besides "He Kept Us Out of War," was "Too Proud to Fight." While Europeans ruthlessly fought other nations for land and treasure, Americans did not—those holding this belief conveniently forgetting that, in the nineteenth century, the United States fought for land and treasure more than once: against various Native American tribes; against Mexico in 1844; and, that same year, very nearly against Britain over the Oregon Territory.

Yet Germany's submarine warfare strained even Wilson's patience. When a German U-boat sank the liner *Lusitania* on May 7, 1915, killing more than 1,100 civilian passengers, including 128 Americans, Wilson's wrath was palpable.

These moments tended to bring out the frustrated schoolmaster in Wilson. (In fact, he was a former college professor and onetime president of Princeton University.) He sat down at his typewriter in a small alcove near the Oval Office and set to work on an angry note to Bernstorff, the German ambassador. The note expressed Wilson's "growing concern, distress, and amazement" at Germany's conduct at sea, conduct that was "so absolutely contrary to the rules, the practices, and the spirit of modern warfare." Wilson added, "Expressions of regret and offers of reparation in case of the destruction of neutral ships sunk by mistake, while they may satisfy international obligations, if no loss of life results, cannot justify or excuse a practice, the natural and necessary effect of which is to subject neutral nations and neutral persons to new and immeasurable risks."

Therefore, Wilson concluded, "the Imperial German Government will not expect the Government of the United States to omit any word or any act necessary to the performance of its sacred duty of maintaining the rights of the United States and its citizens and of safeguarding their free exercise and enjoyment." It was a veiled threat that if the Germans persisted in sinking neutral ships without warning, the United States would be driven to take military action—to defend its ships at sea if necessary and to choose sides in the conflict if there was no other recourse.[3]

Berlin realized that Wilson meant what he said. Furthermore, if the United States did choose a side, it wouldn't choose Germany's. After a furious debate in Kaiser Wilhelm's War Cabinet, unrestricted submarine warfare came to an end. Ships were still sunk, but not unless they were in certain clearly demarcated combat zones and only after fair warning. Britain and France still lost vital supplies, and men at sea still died, but the German threat to American shipping was over, and Woodrow Wilson, and America, went back to diplomatic sleep.

This telegram would wake him up with a jolt, Montgomery and de Grey realized. Resuming unrestricted submarine attacks would be a direct challenge to the American president, the equivalent of throwing a gauntlet at his feet. Would Wilson pick it up? And if he did, could this finally be the tipping point? Could what the British and French governments had been praying for since more than a year ago actually happen: America's entry in the war on the side of the Allies?

At this point, an America joining the Allies would be an America coming to the rescue. The death and destruction wrought by two and a half years of war had brought Britain and France to the edge of economic collapse. They had seen their hopes of winning the war vanish in a continuous sea of blood, on battlefields such as Verdun and the Somme. Their ally Russia was even closer to collapse; more than a million and a half discouraged Russian soldiers had deserted in 1916. An America in the war would give the Allies a huge boost in supplies and manpower, and would certainly tip the balance of power in the conflict: Germany and its ally Austria-Hungary were just as close to the end of their respective tethers. On the other hand, America's remaining neutral could spell disaster for Britain, while a revived German submarine threat could bring Britain to the brink of starvation—and to defeat.

It was a powerful moment in history, a point of no return. Hence Room 40's intense interest in the contents of the telegram from Zimmermann. But the message was actually in two parts: the first was for the German ambassador in Washington, and the other part was "to be handed on to the Imperial Minister in Mexico by a safe route."

Unlocking all the secrets of that second part would require two weeks of eye-straining labor. But when the men in Room 40 got a first rough glimpse of the message the telegram contained, they realized it completely overshadowed the warning about renewing all-out submarine warfare.

De Grey scrambled down the corridor to the office of the director of naval intelligence, Adm. William "Blinker" Hall.

"Do you want to bring America into the war?" de Grey exclaimed.

"Yes, my boy," Hall answered. "Why?"

"I've got something here which"—the young man stammered—"well, it's a rather astonishing message which might do the trick if we could use it."[4]

The Door Mouse was right. If the first part of the telegram from Zimmermann set the detonator, the second set off the explosion that would change the world balance of power forever.

ZURICH, JANUARY 22, 1917

HE WAS A small, sturdily built man—"the neck of a bull," his landlord liked to say. Russian by birth, he was in his forties but already balding, with high cheekbones and what today we might call Asian eyes. He was an unusual sight on the streets of Zurich, the home of discreet bankers and mild German-speaking bourgeois citizens. Having lived outside Russia as an exile for more than a decade, Lenin—Vladimir Ilyich Ulyanov—spoke very good German, but he hated anything connected with the "bourgeoisie." In the nineteenth century, that word had become the symbol of everything Karl Marx's followers, including Lenin, were now dedicating their lives to discrediting and destroying in order to liberate Europe's working class, dubbed by Marx the "proletariat."

Before his death in 1883, Marx had had to limit his mission (that is, consigning Europe's bourgeoisie and its preferred economic system, capitalism, to the ash heap of history) to print only, in books such as *The Communist Manifesto* and *Das Kapital*. Lenin wanted more than anything else to translate Marx's theory into direct action. What he had heard that day made him think it might be more than a pipe dream.

The news had come from his native Russia, and it struck him like a thunderbolt. No fewer than 30,000 industrial workers had gone on strike in Moscow, while another 145,000 workers were on strike in Petrograd, the Russian capital. Workers in Baku, Nizhny Novgorod, Novocherkassk, Voronezh, Kharkov, Rostov-on-Don, the Donbass area, and other cities had joined in the one-day strike to commemorate the antigovernment riots that broke out that same day twelve years before, in 1905, when 500 people were killed. The current strikes were big news; many of them had been organized by friends and comrades of Lenin's, even while he was stuck in Zurich.

And he might be stuck there forever, he was thinking as he hurried through the streets of the working-class neighborhood where he and his wife, Nadezhda Krupskaya, were living. Their home there was a one-room apartment they'd sublet from a shoemaker, Titus Kammerer, whose shop was next door. The apartment was dark and dank; there was one table, a sofa, a couple of chairs, and no heating. Lenin had no job; everything had to be paid for from the slender income of his wife's mother's legacy. He and Nadezhda had been forced to economize to make ends meet. They hadn't bought any new clothes since arriving in Zurich; they ate horse meat instead of beef or chicken. Often there was only oatmeal for dinner. When Nadezhda, an indifferent cook, burned the oatmeal, Lenin would say jocularly to their landlady, "We live in grand style, you see. We have roasts every day."[5]

The Kammerers, however, liked their boarders. Titus Kammerer was impressed by Vladimir—"a good man," the shoemaker told visitors years later—and Frau Kammerer took a liking to Krupskaya, whom she let use her kitchen, as they often prepared meals together. The trust between the two women transcended politics, for Krupskaya was as committed as her husband to Marxism and revolution. But then, it seemed unlikely that anything would disturb the domestic calm in the Kammerer household, since Switzerland seemed far away from the upheavals in Russia that had sent Lenin scrambling back home that evening.

For nearly thirty years, Russian Marxists had tried to translate Marx's economic and political principles into revolutionary action in Russia—without success. It mostly got them prison sentences in Siberia, including one for Lenin in 1902–3, or exile in cities such as London, Paris, and Zurich—much better than Siberia, even on a slender pension. Still, it was a grim existence: being a permanent stranger to one's neighbors, suffering bad relations with fellow exiles, being occasionally spied on by government agents, and above all having no money. Lenin's mother-in-law used to say, "He'll kill Nadyusha and himself with that life"—and all for nothing.

But the coming of war in 1914 had changed everything. As Russia joined its Entente Cordiale partners, France and Britain, in fighting Germany and Austria-Hungary, Lenin sensed that the demands of modern war would stretch Russia's fragile political system—indeed, stretch all capitalist powers—to the breaking point.

He was right. Already by 1915, shortages of food and other supplies, after just a year of war, were commonplace in Russia, even for soldiers at the front. By 1916, the government's capacity simply to feed and supply its population, including its army, had broken down. More than one million Russian soldiers deserted their posts that year. By January 1917, the capital, Petrograd, was facing starvation. There was only a ten-day supply of flour in the city. Meat and other foodstuffs were almost completely gone. People were standing in line for hours, in painfully cold temperatures, hoping for a loaf of bread or two, or a couple of strips of bacon. One of the czar's own counselors of state, Mikhail Rodzianko, had told Nicholas II himself that unless there were a drastic change in government, the country could face massive upheaval.

When he heard the news of the strikes in Moscow and elsewhere, Lenin concluded that "the mood of the masses" was "a good one." He was excited. What better moment for a man whose mission in life was triggering revolution not just in Russia but around the world?

The next day, Lenin was addressing a circle of young socialists on the lessons of the 1905 Revolution. He spoke of the events of Bloody Sunday; of the series of momentous strikes that nearly brought the government to its knees; and of how, despite the failure of the revolution, it heralded the workers' revolutions to come. He stressed that the war now engulfing Europe would be what made those revolutions possible. "In Europe, the coming years, precisely because of this predatory war, will lead to popular uprisings under the leadership of the proletariat against the power of finance capital, against the big banks, against the capitalists; and these upheavals cannot end otherwise than with the expropriation of the bourgeoisie, with the victory of socialism."

He added at the end: "We of the older generation may not live to see the decisive battles of this coming revolution," but he was confident that the young socialists in the audience would "be fortunate enough not only to fight, but also to win, in the coming proletarian revolution."[6]

But how? "Life was astir," his wife remembered, "but it was all so far away."[7]

Here, both Lenin and his wife were wrong. Not only would he live long enough to be a witness to Marxist revolution and worldwide upheaval, but he would be at the center of them.

PREFACE

T HIS IS A book about two men who set in motion two momentous events in a single world-shattering year, two men who were
very different and yet very much alike. Today we still live in the
shadow of (and, in some cases, the rubble from) the events they set in
motion that year, and the legacy they both left as they launched the
world into a state of perpetual disorder and upheaval—the world we
still live with today.

The year was 1917, and the two men were Woodrow Wilson and
Vladimir Lenin. In April, Wilson thrust the United States into the
greatest war in history up to that time, the First World War. Seven
months later, Lenin overthrew a Russian democratic revolution and
imposed his own Bolshevik Revolution in its place. Together, these
two events changed history in ways that make the world as it existed before 1917 seem strange and alien, and the world afterward
very much *our* world and age, the modern age. It's an age that's been
shaped as much by what Lenin and Wilson aimed and failed to do as
by what they succeeded in doing.

How did they change history? President Woodrow Wilson's decision to thrust America into the First World War marked the emergence of the United States as a global hegemonic power—or, rather,
put the final stamp on the power that, as this book will show, had
been evident for some time. Likewise, Lenin's Bolshevik Revolution

in November 1917 triggered the emergence of a world revolutionary movement that would come to be known as communism, led by the Soviet Union.

Ultimately, Lenin's and Wilson's creations would collide head-on in the Cold War. Yet this book is about far more than the origins of the Cold War:[1] it is about not only what Wilson and Lenin created that year, but also what was lost in the scramble as both men set out to make the world a better and more perfect place through the power of politics—including lost opportunities for which we still pay a heavy price.

That is why 1917 marks such a watershed. When this book begins, at the very end of 1916, the world is still one that, say, George Washington or Thomas Jefferson from the eighteenth century or even Louis XIV from the seventeenth century would have found familiar, at least in geopolitical terms (though each would probably have been startled by a map showing a unified Germany or Italy). The fortunes of the world were still in the hands of European Great Powers, including Britain, France, Habsburg Austria, and czarist Russia. Also, those powers were fighting a war that was not much different from the ones Europeans were fighting in Washington's or the Sun King's time—bloodier and more destructive, perhaps, but still determined by armies and navies at war, rather than entire societies and economies and ideologies.

Above all, the world on New Year's Day 1917 was one still governed by long-standing traditional concepts of power and policy: balance of power; nation-state interests; colonial dominion; and power through legitimacy, either by consent of the governed or by traditional means of kingship and imperial rule.

These concepts had managed to keep the peace in Europe for almost one hundred years, since 1815. They had also led to the war begun in 1914, one that by 1917 none of the Great Powers of Europe could either win or stop. It was a war that came to symbolize what both Wilson and Lenin saw as a traditional world order mired in corruption and decay beyond redemption. In 1917, they would dedicate themselves as thinkers and political leaders to overturning that corrupt and moribund global order, and to creating a new, more perfect world order in its place.

And the war would be their springboard for changing it.

To most of us today, and to most of those who witnessed it, World War One, or the Great War, stands as one of the great tragedies of history, an apocalyptic struggle unrelieved by any hint of redemption or (like its even bloodier counterpart twenty years later) liberation. Wilson and Lenin saw matters very differently. They saw the Great War as the perfect means to their ends, even though neither man was a soldier or had any military experience. In a profound sense, they were not even politicians, let alone statesmen. They were dreamers, intellectuals who had attained positions of power through the impact of their speeches, writings, and ideas alone—in Wilson's case, by being elected president of the United States; in Lenin's, by thrusting himself into the leadership of a small but ruthless band of revolutionaries. As we will see, both men were also obsessed with their personal missions to change the world, missions mandated (in their minds) by historical necessity.

In Lenin's case, that historical necessity was dictated by the works of his intellectual mentor, Karl Marx. Like Marx, Lenin had spent his life believing that the existing order, capitalism, was doomed by its own internal contradictions; the war that had dragged Russia to the brink of collapse was proof of capitalism's historical as well as moral bankruptcy. Like Marx, Lenin believed that a new order was poised to take capitalism's place: a dictatorship of the proletariat and the working class in which humanity's true destiny would be realized.

Also like Marx, Lenin believed that direct revolutionary action would be required to overthrow capitalism once and for all and to bury its bourgeois class. But Lenin was convinced that the revolution would start not in an advanced capitalist country such as Great Britain or Germany, as Marx had imagined, but in the *least* advanced one, where the apparatus of civil and police control that the bourgeoisie imposed on society would be rudimentary or even breaking down—a "failed state," as we would say today, where a revolutionary elite could run free to realize their Marxist dreams. In Lenin's mind, that failed state was his native Russia. When he returned to Russia from exile in April 1917, he set himself to starting the revolution that he believed would spread around the world.

Wilson's historical mission was more complicated. It, too, sprang from an intellectual mentor—in his case, the German philosopher Georg W. F. Hegel (who, as it happens, was also Karl Marx's)—but it was as well wrapped up in his vision of America as the symbol of and inspiration for the universal value of human freedom. In contrast to Lenin's dream of a sweeping violent working-class revolution, Wilson's dream was a peaceful revolution in which humanity's universal desire for freedom, for people's right to govern themselves, to feel safe and secure, and to live without fear of violence or want, would finally be realized for all peoples everywhere. To Lenin, Wilson's dream seemed hopelessly bourgeois and quasi-religious—which it probably was. To Wilson, Lenin's seemed an invitation to a nightmare of violence and terror—which it certainly was.

Yet, as we will see, Wilson shared Lenin's dogmatic belief in the rightness of his own mission, which brooked no opposition or even criticism. Like Lenin, he saw himself as the one man who could bring redemption to humanity, and make its fondest wishes reality. As he told the World League for Peace in January 1917, "I would fain believe that I am speaking for the silent mass of mankind everywhere who have as yet had no place or opportunity to speak their real hearts out."

Wilson strongly believed that those freedoms were embodied in the American Declaration of Independence and the American Constitution, but in his mind, they were far more than American ideals. "[T]hey are also the principles and policies of forward-looking men and women everywhere, of every modern nation, of every enlightened community. They are the principles of mankind and must prevail."

At first, as readers will learn, Wilson believed he could best achieve that goal by staying out of the Great War then raging in Europe. Three months after his speech to the World League for Peace, he believed he could achieve it only by entering that war.

On April 2, 1917, Wilson called on Congress to declare war on Germany. Seven months later, Lenin struck at the heart of Russia's post-czarist Provisional Government and imposed the world's first one-party state dictatorship. The world would never be the same again, on both counts.

One mission of this book, therefore, is to show how these two intellectuals and dreamers managed to achieve those two ends and, in the process, overthrow traditional standards of geopolitics and alter forever the distribution of world power. Indeed, the world that both sought to bring into being was one that would be dominated not by laws and institutions, but by ideals and ideologies. The great goal of future foreign policy for both the United States and the eventual Soviet Union would be, not to protect their own national interests as narrowly understood, as almost all nations understood foreign policy before 1917, but to make others see the world as they did. As the philosopher Jean-Jacques Rousseau wrote on the eve of the French Revolution, "[S]ometimes men must be forced to be free." That was a challenge the French revolutionaries took on, with disastrous results for Europe. It was one Wilson and Lenin both accepted in 1917, with (one is forced to conclude) disastrous results for the entire world.

That is one part of this book. The other part involves pointing out that Lenin and Wilson were stalked by two other men who are generally seen as their political rivals: Republican leader of the U.S. Senate Henry Cabot Lodge and prime minister of the Russian Provisional Government Alexander Kerensky. By and large, history has not been kind to them. Lodge is often caricatured as a die-hard isolationist for opposing, and then defeating, Wilson's effort to make the United States a charter member of the League of Nations. Historians of the Russian Revolution, even those deeply unsympathetic to Lenin, are usually harsh about Kerensky, whom Lenin overthrew that fateful November and who then fled into exile and historical oblivion.

Keeping Lodge and Kerensky in view in this story, I believe, helps to cast events, and Lenin and Wilson, in a new light. As we will see, Lodge and Kerensky were both refreshingly free of the utopian fantasies of their more famous rivals. Both saw what was happening in the world in 1917 through a lens as urgent as but also more realistic than Wilson's or Lenin's. Unlike the two revolutionary dreamers, Lodge and Kerensky saw the value of more traditional ways of thinking about politics, alliances, and humanity's hopes for the future—and the future of their own countries.

For example, as we will see, the issues swirling around America's membership in the League of Nations were far more complicated than previous historians sometimes acknowledge—and blame for the League's defeat lies far more with Wilson than with Lodge. At the same time, while there is no doubt that Kerensky underestimated the Leninist threat until it was too late, and that his commitment to keep Russia in the war on the side of the Allies opened the door to disaster, he, unlike Lenin, was a believer in the Western and very bourgeois ideals of democracy, representative government, and the rule of law. As readers will learn, his one great desire was to make Russia a full partner with the other liberal democracies that were fighting Germany, including the United States—then and into the future. There can be no doubt that if Kerensky had somehow prevailed over Lenin during those fateful forty-eight hours in Petrograd in November 1917, instead of the other way around, Russia would never have known the Great Purge or the Great Famine—nor would China have undergone the Great Leap Forward.

Likewise, if Wilson had listened to Henry Cabot Lodge regarding the League of Nations, instead of fighting him literally to the brink of death, it can be argued that there would have been no Mussolini or Hitler or Second World War—possibly not even a Great Depression.

In the event, however, it was Lenin and Wilson who prevailed, not Lodge or Kerensky. As a result, America and Russia would never be the same; neither would the world. There is a lot to regret about the world the two men unleashed with their reckless idealism, a world of totalitarian states, of murderous wars of liberation, of national and ideological insurgencies, of terrorism and genocide. The English historian Alan (A. J. P.) Taylor once pointed out in an essay on the German statesman Otto von Bismarck, a figure whom both Lenin and Wilson loathed as a symbol of everything that was corrupt and evil about the old world order they set out to overthrow, that "Bismarck fought 'necessary' wars and killed thousands, the idealists of the twentieth century fight 'just' wars and kill millions."[2] That unhappy contrast is, to a great degree, the legacy of Lenin and Wilson and what they started in 1917.

And yet, it seems unfair to compare the pair too closely by emphasizing their similarities and ignoring or downplaying their differences. At the end of the day, Wilson's utopian dream, impractical and ignorant of reality though it was, summed up a vision of human beings joining together in peace and bringing an end to violence in international and human affairs. "I sometimes think," Wilson once said, "that . . . no people ever went to war with another people"; only governments did.[3] He may have been wrong, but he was wrong for high-minded reasons.

Lenin's dream, by contrast, was of one class of human beings obliterating the other classes, and using violence to perpetuate the power of a ruling revolutionary elite. It sprang not from lofty idealism but from boundless cynicism, summed up in Lenin's famous dictum "The only interesting question in life is 'Who, whom?'" In other words, who exploits whom? In Lenin's worldview, everything that happens in history is the result of one class (or race or gender) taking advantage of another. *Homo homini lupus est.* It's the rationale of the Marxist-Leninist and Islamic terrorists alike—who share more than their respective admirers like to admit.

In any case, the final argument of this book is that this fundamental difference in outlook has left its imprint on Wilson's and Lenin's respective legacies, right down to today. It marked the character of the two world superpowers they spawned and of the influence they both exercised in the two global conflicts to come, World War II and the Cold War.

It was also A. J. P. Taylor who said that the historian's inevitable task is to decide whether something that happened in history was a Good Thing or a Bad Thing. From that perspective, we have to say Woodrow Wilson and the emergence of the United States as a global power represent a good thing; Lenin and the emergence of the Soviet Union, a very bad thing. From a global perspective, the one would emerge as the defender and protector of human freedom (an ideal not so different from what Wilson had hoped), the other as the enslaver of peoples and annihilator of freedom (again, a reality not very different from the one Lenin imposed on his native Russia).

Finally, a personal note. When I was a boy, more than forty years after he was driven from power in Russia, I met Alexander Kerensky. He was a fellow at the Hoover Institution, and my father was studying philosophy at Stanford. From time to time, Kerensky and my father would share lunch on the lawn of the quad, and the day I came along, Kerensky (I am told) pointed to me, age three, and said to my father in his thick Russian accent, "You and I will not live to see the end of communism. But he will."

Kerensky's prediction was a trifle inaccurate. My father is still alive. Yet, in the end, Kerensky was right because Wilson's creation overcame Lenin's—at the price of the new world disorder we still live with today.

If there is any single lesson to be drawn from this book, it is that utopian dreamers in power tend to breed disaster. But not always, and not forever.

THE GERMAN NOTE

*The great questions of the day will be settled not by
speeches or majority decisions but by iron and blood.*
—OTTO VON BISMARCK

BERLIN, DECEMBER 1916

GERMAN CHANCELLOR THEOBALD von Bethmann-Hollweg was
in a better mood than at any time since the world's bloodiest war
began. At last he had a plan he thought could turn the war in his
favor. By taking advantage of Germany's recent good fortune on the
battlefield, in the waning weeks of 1916 he might have a way to get at
least one of its enemies to the peace table. He knew he was making a
gamble, but after two and a half years of unimaginable bloodshed and
destruction, success would shorten the odds of something even less
imaginable: Germany's losing.

After two and a half years of the greatest war the world had ever
witnessed, the conflict had come up with no winners, German or Allied. The swift victory Germany's generals had promised in 1914 had
not panned out. The strategy of driving through neutral Belgium and
into France, a plan devised by the chief (now dead) of the German
General Staff, had failed to deliver on what it had been created to
do: knock France out of the war before the Russians could fully mobilize. Worse, it had drawn an even more formidable opponent into
the conflict on France's side, namely, Great Britain. Britain and its far-
flung empire had been able to put nearly three million men side by

side with France's four million. Germany's army of fewer than three million on the Western Front found itself waging an increasingly desperate titanic struggle along a line running through the heart of eastern France from the Swiss border to the English Channel—not to mention having to fight an entire other war in the east, against Russia, where its ally, Austria-Hungary, had proved more a hindrance than a help.

Those two and a half years of unrelenting bloodshed had cost Germany more than 1.75 million casualties.

The worst had come that past April, when a major German offensive hinged on the French fortress at Verdun. Hundreds of thousands of men from both sides were drawn into a battle of attrition on a scale so immense that neither Germany nor France (nor even its ally Great Britain) could ever look on the war, or even the nature of war itself, the same way again. One hundred fifteen divisions, nearly a million and a half men, had been crammed together in a death embrace along a front scarcely five miles wide.[1] Six weeks into the battle, Bethmann-Hollweg had remarked to a friend, "After such dramatic events history knows no status quo." Two and a half months later, when the battle that produced nearly three hundred thousand German casualties ended in a bitter stalemate, Bethmann-Hollweg was not the only politician in Germany to wonder if Germany would ever be able to recover.

Then had come the British offensive along the Somme River in July, when Germany faced an onslaught of men and steel that dwarfed even the scale of battle at Verdun. Before the last British attack sputtered out on November 13, more than 420,000 British and 450,000 Germans had been killed or wounded—again, with no victory for either side in sight.

The Germans had staved off defeat, just barely. But farther east had come fresh disasters. The first was the Russian offensive in June, through the Carpathian Mountains, as the Russian army at last found a general, Aleksei Brusilov, with the skills to engineer victory after two years of disappointment and failure. The so-called Brusilov Offensive finally shattered Austria-Hungary's will to fight. The Russians took more than a quarter million prisoners: Austrians, Czechs, Hungarians, Poles, and other Slavs who owed loyalty to a Habsburg monarchy that had ruled them for nearly five hundred years but who had finally decided it was better to live than to die for an emperor they had never met in a war they didn't want.

With painful difficulty, the Germans had managed to prevent a complete collapse. With the skill and professionalism that were the hallmarks of the German army, they regained the ground lost to Brusilov, while inflicting a million Russian casualties. Now, however, they would have to hold the line in the east without even the half-hearted help of their Austrian ally. By the fall of 1916, the alliance of so-called Central powers at the start of the war, Germany, Austria-Hungary, and Italy, had been reduced to one Central power alone, Germany. (Italy had allowed itself to be bribed by Britain and France, first, to stay out of the war in 1914 and, then, to come in on the Allied side the following year.) It would now have to conduct all-out war on two fronts at once. While the Russians were hardly as formidable an opponent as the British and French, there was a genuine fear that if one more front opened up, it would be the tipping point.

Then that moment came, at the worst possible time. On August 27, just as the Brusilov Offensive was in full flood and the British were battering away along the Somme, neutral Romania suddenly entered the war on the Entente's side. The crack this opened in Germany's exposed southern flank was so large and unexpected that Bethmann-Hollweg was driven to something close to despair. In the Bundesrat, he called the situation "the most serious yet since the first days of the conflict," and he warned, "Everything now depends on Rumania."[2] Even the Kaiser lost his nerve and began telling everyone that the war was all but lost.[3]

In the event, there was no need for worry. The German general on the spot, Erich von Falkenhayn, quickly rallied German forces and turned the tables on the Romanians. With help from Germany's eastern allies Bulgaria and Turkey, the campaign was run so successfully that on December 6, the German army, with Field Marshal Augest von Mackensen at its head on a white charger, entered Bucharest as the Romanian government fled. Meanwhile, a German counterattack had checkmated the Brusilov Offensive, as the Russians stopped advancing and began retreating. It was at this moment, with Romania crushed, German armies on the move into Russia's Baltic provinces, and an exhausted calm on the Western Front, that the German chancellor decided he would offer to negotiate a peace with the Allies.

There had been whispers before about ending the war with a negotiated settlement, but no leader or head of state of any of the combatants had ever extended any formal offer—that is, until now. Bethmann-Hollweg's strategy sprang from more than a desire to end the bloodshed, however. It was born out of cunning and desperation. It tells us at least as much about those pushing for continuing the war on the German side as it does about those, such as the chancellor, who believed that if the war went on any longer, Germany would not survive.

The cunning part was Bethmann-Hollweg's hope that a peace move could somehow detach one of the Entente powers, France, Britain, or Russia, from the other two in order to arrive at a separate peace. Russia seemed the most likely candidate: in fact, Bethmann-Hollweg had already sent up a trial balloon in St. Petersburg's direction earlier that autumn, offering to pull German forces back to their 1914 borders. The czar's government was on the brink of responding, too, when the German chief of the General Staff, Erich Ludendorff, wrecked the whole plan. He was not ready to give up the territories he had conquered for Germany since the outbreak of war.

He had a different plan for driving Russia out of the war. It was to promise Poles living in the Russian Empire an independent nation of their own: a Polish dream since the Napoleonic Wars. Ludendorff confidently predicted that the gesture would bring hundreds of thousands of Poles rallying to the German banner to win independence for their homeland from Russia. Once again, a skeptical Bethmann-Hollweg yielded to the general, and in November, the German government made the pledge, as a Polish state was carved out by German hands from a map of Russia.

The pledge proved a disaster. Instead of the fifteen Polish divisions Ludendorff confidently predicted, Germany netted only fourteen hundred volunteers. (It turned out Poles didn't trust German promises any more than they believed Russian ones.) Support for Polish independence also killed any hope of a separate peace with the czar, but it did leave two curious legacies. The first was that, at the start of 1917, German soldiers on the Eastern Front found themselves in the position of ostensibly fighting for the independence of Poland, a strange anomaly that would grow a lot stranger from the perspective of events twenty-odd years later.[4]

The second legacy, and one far more significant, was that without realizing it, the Germans had stumbled on the issue that would soon engulf all the combatants, including Germany: the problem of nationalist aspirations for peoples living under the rule of others. No one had coined the term *national self-determination* yet, but by pledging that victory in this war would mean freedom for a people governed by another people, Germany had thrown open the door to a wholesale remaking of the map of Europe, indeed of the world, regardless of which side won or lost.

*   *   *

IN THE LAST days of 1916, these lofty issues were far from the chancellor's mind. He was focused on more immediate matters. As things stood that winter, Germany's options for winning were fading fast. The war (and the demands it made for men and matériel) had been a disaster for what once was Europe's most dynamic economy. Without the iron- and coal-rich French territories Germany had captured in the first months of the war, it was unlikely the country could have survived this long, let alone sustained a two-front war. The reason for the growing desperation was the Allied blockade, imposed in the opening months of the war and maintained by the most powerful oceangoing force in the world, the Royal Navy.

In the Great War, Britain was never able to impose the kind of "close" blockade it had used against opponents since the Napoleonic Wars. Mines, submarines, and advances in coastal artillery made intercepting ships at the mouths of German harbors, as Horatio Nelson would have done, impossible. Besides, neutral nations, particularly the United States, that persisted in trading with both sides in the conflict would not have stood for it. So, Britain's blockade of Germany was maintained at a distance. German ships were at once seized at sea; neutral vessels were treated more gingerly. Royal Navy ships would stop them and then escort them to a British port, where their cargo was checked for war matériel, sometimes with rudimentary X-ray machines. Any matériel found would be confiscated; the neutral vessel was then free to return to sea.

A neutral merchant captain could even get a permit from the nearest British consulate stating that his cargo contained nothing to help the German war effort—in effect, a free pass through the blockade.[5] Even so, neutral nations, especially the Americans, resented the entire process, and without a doubt, a blockade done this way was bound to leak like an old rowboat.

Still, it was enough. Germans didn't anticipate the blockade in time, and failed to stockpile essential goods, especially the raw materials needed to keep an army of five million men fed, clothed, and armed. The result was that, inch by inch, the German economy was slowly strangled by the blockade. By the winter of 1916, German civilians were starving, even starving to death. Unless the war ended very soon, Germany faced catastrophe even if not a single Allied soldier advanced another step.

The blockade had another aspect, one even more disastrous for Germany. The naval forces that were able to keep goods and supplies from reaching Germany were also making sure such goods and supplies reached Great Britain, and then France. And if merchants in the world's biggest economy, America, complained about the blockade when it came to doing business with Germany, they certainly couldn't complain about the booming business they were doing with

Britain, as ships loaded with wheat, cotton, oil, semifinished products, gunpowder, explosives, and, above all, ammunition landed almost around the clock in British ports. Indeed, if any one factor had kept the Entente nations able not only to fight the war but also to mount one massive offensive after another, it was America's contribution to their war effort, even though the United States remained neutral.

Nor were war matériel and other goods America's most crucial contribution to the effort against Germany. A steady flow of loans from the leading banks on Wall Street, led by J.P. Morgan, had enabled the British, French, and Russians to purchase what they needed to sustain the war effort as their gold reserves dwindled from larger and larger war purchases. By the end of 1916, American investors had bet some two billion dollars on an Allied victory. During the Somme offensive, for example, the House of Morgan alone discharged more than one billion dollars in America for the British government, totaling some 45 percent of Britain's entire wartime spending. "The most powerful states of Europe," writes economic historian Adam Tooze, "were now borrowing from private citizens in the United States"— citizens who, when those notes came due, would be able to demand a financial reckoning neither Britain nor France dared contemplate. Indeed, with the fate of the war hovering in the balance, it was a reckoning they had no time or energy to contemplate.[6]

That, however, was not Germany's problem—or so it seemed at the end of 1916. (As we'll see, within three years, it would be, with a vengeance.) Instead, what Bethmann-Hollweg faced was a situation that was increasingly unsustainable for his country, unless something broke the war's impasse. That something, he now hoped, would be peace—if not with all three Entente countries, then at least with one. He hoped others in the German government could see the same reality, especially those in the German High Command. In fact, one reason he had supported removing Erich von Falkenhayn, the man behind the failed Verdun offensive in the west, and replacing him with Paul von Hindenburg and Ludendorff, the two titans who had overthrown Russian power in the east in 1914, was that he was sure they would immediately see the insuperable obstacles Germany faced and would build a consensus within the army that winning the war was impossible and that a compromise peace was the one remaining option.

Ludendorff, however, had other ideas. Bull-necked, supremely self-assured, with a cold, arrogant stare from behind an ever-present monocle, he was the very picture of the brutal aristocratic Prussian officer in the Allies' cartoons. In fact, he came from humble origins; he had negotiated his way through the exclusive military Junker class by a combination of brains, energy, and boundless self-confidence. Ludendorff's confidence in his ability to win the war for Germany was surpassed only by his contempt for Bethmann-Hollweg or any other civilian who dared to try to tell him his job. Ludendorff's formula for ultimate victory was simple and came in two stages. First, pull all Germany's forces on the Western Front back behind the Hindenburg Line, the long line of trenches and fortifications on French soil stretching from Arras, in the north, southward to Laffaux, near Soissons, on the Aisne River. Then Ludendorff would turn loose Germany's ultimate weapon, the one he and the other generals were firmly convinced was the remaining key to victory: its formidable submarine fleet.

The submarine—*Unterseeboot*, or "U-boat," in German—was one of this war's newest technologies and, as it happened, potentially the most decisive. In German hands, it had evolved from a minor naval weapon for protecting home ports or breaking a harbor blockade into one that could bring the Allied war effort to a halt. The fleet had grown from just 20 U-boats in the High Seas Fleet at the start of the war to more than 146 on patrol at any given time two years later. By systematically hunting down and sinking the merchant ships supplying France and Britain with the food and matériel they needed to keep fighting, German U-boats were poised to impose a blockade of the British Isles that threatened that island nation with starvation as well as defeat.

In early 1915, Germany had unleashed its submarines to sink enemy shipping without warning, but that plan had backfired with the sinking of the *Lusitania*. President Wilson's carefully worded but clearly hostile note to the German ambassador had confronted Germany with the possibility that it might be at war with the most powerful economy in the world, the United States, and the world's third-largest naval fleet, the U.S. Navy, at the same time that it was fighting France, Britain, and Russia.

Sobered by Wilson's note, Bethmann-Hollweg had forced the German navy to reimpose restrictions on its use of the U-boat. Those restrictions limited the kind of ships the navy could sink (no neutral vessels) and where it could sink them (attacks were limited to the waters around the English Channel). Germany even offered to halt its U-boat campaign if Britain stopped its naval blockade, but Britain refused. Nonetheless, the shipping slaughter was still impressive, rising to 400,000 tons a month by the end of 1916. The damage to the British and, by extension, the French and Russian war effort was still palpable if not overwhelming.

It was devastating force that Ludendorff now wanted. "Necessity knows no law." Those had been Bethmann-Hollweg's own words when Germany invaded Belgium in August 1914. They were Ludendorff's now in the waning days of 1916. As the number of U-boats swelled, and their captains became more adept at finding and sinking their targets, the chief of the German General Staff was convinced Germany could turn the war around if the restrictions imposed after the *Lusitania* incident were finally irrevocably lifted. If the German submarine fleet was unleashed, the transatlantic lifeline that kept Britain and France in the war would be cut for good. The two powers would have to sue for peace, or starve—because, as Ludendorff knew, the cargo that would be sunk included not just ammunition and spare parts for weapons but also millions of tons of foodstuffs for hungry populations.

Besides, as 1917 neared, the options became bleak. Ludendorff was convinced that Germany no longer had the strength to win the war in the west on the battlefield; the cost in matériel as well as human lives would be too much. As the outgoing general Falkenhayn had told the Kaiser, "You now face the alternative—either Verdun or submarine warfare." The war had come down to a race, to who would be starved out first, the Germans or the Allies.[7]

Bethmann-Hollweg, however, sensed that unrestricted U-boat warfare would spell doom for Germany. It would not only trigger a revulsion at German barbarism that would sustain the Allies' morale, but also almost certainly bring the United States into the war.

However, as Ludendorff and his chief, Paul von Hindenburg, assumed the reins over the army, they presented the Kaiser, and the German people, with a stark choice. If Germany didn't shut off the flow of shipping in the Atlantic, they said, the war would be lost. The risk was that America would enter the war, but this was a risk worth running now that Germany's back was to the wall.

Still, the sudden victories in the east that autumn had given Germany some breathing space in the west—not the first time that events in one theater changed the momentum of war in another. So, Bethmann-Hollweg bought himself time for his peace offensive, a last stab at finding a negotiated settlement before the submarines moved in for the kill, and a last stab at somehow convincing Wilson to rouse himself and intervene—not for war in this case, but for peace.

Either way, for the first time in more than a year, it seemed that Germany not only could survive this war but could even emerge on top—that is, if one or another of its opponents could be convinced to go to the peace table.

So, all in all, it was a cool and confident Bethmann-Hollweg who spoke to the assembled deputies in the Reichstag on December 12, 1916. After summarizing recent events, including the victory over Romania, he proclaimed, "With God's help our troops shaped conditions so as to give us security which not only is complete but still more so than ever before." Germany was standing firm in the west, with more troops and matériel than ever; "great stocks of grain, victuals, oil, and other goods fell into our hands in Rumania," including the rich Romanian oil fields around Ploesti.

The chancellor did not forget about the German submarine fleet, as "the spectre of famine, which our enemies intended to appear before us, now pursues them without mercy." Nonetheless, despite Germany's recent successes, "[d]uring these long and earnest years of the war the Emperor has been moved by a single thought: how peace could be restored to safeguard Germany after the struggle in which she has fought victoriously."

The Kaiser, therefore, "in complete harmony and in common with our allies" Austria-Hungary, Turkey, and Bulgaria, "decided to propose to the hostile powers to enter peace negotiations." The chancellor told the Reichstag that "this morning I transmitted a note to this effect to all the hostile powers," meaning Great Britain, France, and Russia. Bethmann-Hollweg then concluded: "Gentlemen, in August 1914 our enemies challenged the superiority of power in the world war. Today we raise the question of peace, which is a question of humanity . . . God will be the judge. We can proceed upon our way."[8]

Bethmann-Hollweg's note went out that same morning—but not to the British, French, or Russian governments; all diplomatic relations with them had been severed at the start of the war. Instead, it went to German diplomats in neutral Switzerland, Spain, and the United States, to be delivered to the Allied countries on Germany's behalf.

The note was barely six paragraphs long. It read, in part, "The most terrific war experienced in history has been raging for the last two years over a large part of the world—a catastrophe which thousands of years of common civilization was unable to prevent and which injures the most precious achievements of humanity." Germany's aim was never "to shatter or annihilate our adversaries." Therefore, to "make an end to the atrocities of war, the four allied powers [meaning Germany and its allies] propose to enter forthwith into peace negotiations." The note pointed out that "the most recent events" had demonstrated that Germany's will and ability to fight on could not be broken, "and the whole situation with regard to our troops justifies our expectation of further successes."

Nonetheless, "if in spite of this offer of peace and reconciliation, the struggle should go on," Germany and its allies were determined to push on to victory, "but they solemnly disclaim responsibility for this before humanity and history."[9]

This was Bethmann-Hollweg's final roll of the diplomatic dice, for peace this time instead of war. Yet, even as the note fanned out along the diplomatic route to a dozen foreign capitals, including the Vatican, he could not guess that he had just signed his political death warrant.

*   *   *

THE NOTE ARRIVED in a cold, wet, overcast London, where dark clouds had been bringing rain and even snow all that week. It was a city made even colder and grimmer by the situation at the front, where just weeks before, Britain's massive offensive along the Somme River had finally petered out after five months of futile effort—but not before some 420,000 Britons were either dead or wounded. If Germany's chances of winning this war on the ground looked slim to nonexistent, they didn't look much better from the perspective of Britain's new prime minister, David Lloyd George.

Short in stature, with a florid face, a shock of thick white hair, and a white mustache, Lloyd George had been minister of munitions before taking over as prime minister on December 5, 1916. No one knew better Britain's fitness to carry on a war that had already consumed money, lives, and munitions on an unprecedented scale, a war that, without American loans, would have pushed the world's greatest empire—one out of every four persons on the planet in 1914 was a British subject—into bankruptcy. Nor did he have any illusions that the conflict was anywhere close to ending in Britain's favor. He had told his military adviser Sir Maurice Hankey in November, "We're going to lose this war." Now, as prime minister, he saw his top priority as preventing that from occurring.[10]

As it happened, Lloyd George was as dissatisfied with his nation's generals as Bethmann-Hollweg was with his, and for most of the same reasons. All promised that one last big offensive that would finally break the deadlock and bring victory, and none had succeeded. The only one who had had an inkling of what was going to happen was Field Marshal Horatio Herbert Kitchener, or Earl Kitchener, Britain's greatest living war hero and the conflict's first secretary of state for war. Following the bloody battles of the Marne and First Ypres, as the system of trenches along the Western Front was getting established, Kitchener had left a strange and prophetic note for the commander of the British Expeditionary Force in France, Sir John French: "I suppose we must now recognize that the French army cannot make a sufficient break through the German lines of defense to bring about the retreat of the German forces from northern France," he wrote. "If that is so, then the German lines in France may be looked upon as a fortress that cannot be carried by assault, and also cannot be completely invested."[11] It was a prediction of stalemate long before that idea had crossed anyone else's mind on either side. Almost two years later, after two and a half million casualties—one of them Kitchener himself, who drowned when the transport ship he was on was torpedoed and sunk by a German U-boat on June 5, 1916—it was still true.

The Somme was just the latest, and biggest, of the British offensives that had failed to break the deadlock. There had been Loos in 1915, which ended with 50,000 British casualties as opposed to 20,000 Germans. The French had lost even more with their offensive along the Champagne front, 190,000 versus 120,000 Germans. There had been the landings at the Gallipoli peninsula in the Dardanelles that same year, an attempt to drive Turkey out of the war and open a southern flank into Central Europe. That, too, had ended in stalemate and cost more than a quarter of a million casualties. It also ended the political career of the man who had dreamed up the operation, Lloyd George's friend Winston Churchill.

All that sacrifice, yet no resolution. What the combatants were only beginning to understand was that while their generals' strategies committed them to taking the offensive, the new tools of modern warfare gave the overwhelming advantage to the defender. The machine gun; bigger and bigger artillery firing high-explosive shells; the development of more and more elaborate trench networks, with ever-deeper dugouts and bomb shelters; the use of airplanes to monitor an enemy's forces as it organized for the next big push—all these gave defenders a commanding edge over soldiers who, no matter how powerful the advance barrage or how big the clouds of poison gas aimed at disrupting or immobilizing the enemy, still had to attack across open ground in the same way armies had done from the Greeks and Romans to Napoleon. And on those very rare occasions when a breakthrough of a few miles was achieved, another tool of modern warfare, the railway train, would ensure that the defender could move his forces to plug the gap faster than the attacker could move his forces to exploit it.

This was especially true on the Western Front. On the Eastern Front, different rules applied. The systems of railways and modern communications hadn't caught up with the vast distances involved—this was one reason the war in the east had been a seesaw affair from its first months, with first the Russians advancing and the Germans and Austrians retreating, and then the Russians retreating and the Central powers advancing—until now, at the end of December, as the Germans rolled back the Russians once again and pressed on into eastern Poland.

Yet it was on the Western Front that the big decisive victory over Germany would have to be achieved—or so all the French and British generals and politicians except David Lloyd George assumed. Besides, Lloyd George knew there were other problems with Allied strategy in the west. There had been no coordination of men and resources among the Allies; generals such as Douglas Haig and his French counterpart, Joseph Joffre, tended to make their plans almost as if the other ally didn't exist. There had never been any plans for a general offensive; no one had thought, for example, of combining a Franco-British push in the west with a similar Russian one in the east, so that Germany would come under pressure from both sides at once.

Above all, so far, there had been no full mobilization of all Britain's might, including its economic might. Munitions factories had continued to work regular business hours; other factories continued to make civilian goods; hundreds of thousands of draft-age males—conscription had been introduced in January 1916—still held their peacetime jobs. A huge untapped labor reserve, women, remained at home tending to domestic duties. In addition, a whole other resource, Britain's vast empire, had only barely begun to be tapped.

Lloyd George was determined to change all this. His plan was one he shared with his Conservative counterpart, Andrew Bonar Law, and many other members of Parliament: "a more energetic conduct of the war," meaning a national commitment of people and resources to deliver "a knock-out blow" that would defeat Germany and end the bloodiest war in history.

Therefore, Bethmann-Hollweg's note came at the perfect moment for Lloyd George's purposes. By denouncing it, he could make it clear that he and Britain were "all in." In fact, his first speech in the House of Commons that week was a steadfast attack on the note. In it, he promoted the idea that a negotiated peace was tantamount to surrender—and others couldn't criticize him without seeming to endorse Bethmann-Hollweg. Britain had only one goal: victory. "We accepted this for an object, and a worthy object," he told Parliament, quoting Abraham Lincoln during the American Civil War, "and the war will end when that object is attained. Under God, I hope it will never end until that time."[12]

To no one's surprise (not even the German chancellor's), then, the December 12 note fell on fallow ground at Number 10. Over the next several days and weeks, Lloyd George would start to assemble his war coalition. He set up a slimmed-down War Cabinet of only five men: himself, Bonar Law, former viceroy of India George Curzon (Lord Curzon), Alfred Milner (Lord Milner) of South Africa and Boer War fame, and Arthur Henderson of the Labour Party. This was Labour's first appearance in the corridors of power in Whitehall, and highly significant. Lloyd George intended to get the unions and British industry working full tilt to mobilize the nation for war.

By doing so, he would change both the political landscape and Britain itself.

The age of total war was coming. At the start of 1917, it would embrace not only Britain but all the combatant nations—all, that is, that managed to survive the major trials ahead. As we will see, commitment to total war would forever change the nature of war and the relationship between government and society. Lloyd George and Britain would be officially the first to head down that road. Lloyd George knew what maximum effort was about. As minister of munitions at a time when the generals had wanted two or, at most, four machine guns per infantry battalion, he had forced them to take forty-three. When the War Office turned down the Stokes mortar, one of the most effective light artillery weapons of the war, with an eight-hundred-yard range and capable of firing twenty-five shells a minute, Lloyd George convinced an Indian maharaja to finance its production from his own bank account.[13] As prime minister, though, Lloyd George sensed that even if he were able to mobilize all Britain's manpower and resources, including those of the empire, for the war effort, they still wouldn't be enough to defeat Germany unless one other entity joined in to tip the balance.

That entity was the United States. As the New Year dawned, a major priority for the prime minister was emerging: how to get President Wilson to commit his country fully on the side of the Allies. Financial and logistical support for the Allies was one thing; adding the full weight of American manpower as well as industrial power, not to mention the U.S. Navy, the third-largest in the world, would be another entirely.

What Bethmann-Hollweg feared most at the end of 1916 was what Lloyd George and Great Britain wanted more than anything else. The desire to get the United States to take the plunge and join the war in Europe was, if anything, even more prominent in the next Allied capital the German peace note reached—namely, Paris.

* * *

IT ARRIVED AT the Palais Élysée the same day that another momentous event was taking place. This was the removal of the man who had been France's commander in chief since the war began, Gen. Joseph Joffre.

To many, even after almost thirty months of bloody conflict, Joffre was still a national hero. Big, bluff, with a hearty smile and a deceptively Santa Claus twinkle in his eye, "Papa" Joffre had prevented the collapse of the French armies during the initial German onslaught in August 1914, and then had saved Paris (and France) at the Battle of the Marne. His reputation as national savior had sustained him for two more years of bloodshed and stalemate, while Joffre himself had done nothing to change his strategy, which was attack, attack, attack, regardless of the losses or, incredibly, without any substantive sign of success. Instead, Joffre had watched impassively as the French casualties mounted. Fifty-five thousand casualties for five hundred yards' gain on the Champagne front in February 1915; 60,000 lost again that spring at the Battle of Saint-Mihiel; 120,000 in May at Arras. The next year brought the slaughter at Verdun stretching from February to June, with 315,000 total French casualties. Then came the French support for the British offensive along the Somme from July to November, in which another 200,000 were killed or wounded—all for little significant gain.

At that point, the French politicians, including Prime Minister Aristide Briand, had had enough. Criticism of Joffre and his conduct of the war began to build in the Chamber of Deputies. Yet Briand realized that even now he could not dismiss France's supposed savior outright. So, instead, he elevated him into insignificance, by making Joffre a marshal of France, the first since the days of Napoleon III. That took Joffre out of the role of commander in chief and most powerful man in France—even the prime minister had had to ask Joffre's permission before visiting the front—and left him as the symbol, then and later, of Great War leadership at its most callous, brutal, and futile.[14]

Joffre's successor, Gen. Robert Nivelle, cut a very different figure.

Slim, youthful, and vigorous-looking, Nivelle brought with him the smell of success instead of futility. He had been theater commander around Verdun during the Somme offensive, when, taking advantage of momentary German weakness, he swept his divisions forward in September 1916 and with very few casualties recaptured almost all the ground France had lost there since February. Virtually overnight his exploit made him a national hero, a role he assumed with grace and style. Even before he was made commander in chief, he was telling politicians and other generals that he had discovered the secret to winning the war—a secret that, for now, he refused to divulge. But Nivelle's promise, like his brisk, jaunty salute for the cameras, offered new optimism about the war's future—not to mention France's.

France had been devastated by the war, and not just by the loss of human life. Its richest industrial region, northeastern France, had been seized by the Germans at the start of the war, and systematically raked over to supply the German war machine. It was sorely missed by the French economy, and by the French army. In addition, the costs of war on this unprecedented scale had pushed France's financial system to the brink of collapse. In 1914, Paris had been the second-largest center of international finance, after London. As 1916 ended, the only credit it could get to keep itself in the war came from Britain via London's bounteous cornucopia of loans from Wall Street.[15]

For that reason alone, the French were even more eager to get the United States into the war on their side, and no one understood that more than the leader of the Radicals in the Chamber of Deputies, Georges Clemenceau. At age seventy-five, Clemenceau was a white-haired veteran of French politics going back to the very origins of the Third Republic, in the aftermath of the Franco-Prussian War in 1871. Before that, however, he had lived in the United States for several years, working as a journalist; he had even had an American wife when he returned to France. Certainly, no other French politician understood America quite as well or realized how important it would be to play up the theme of Franco-American friendship reaching back to Lafayette and the American Revolution.

In addition to winning the war, nothing would prevent a future war, Clemenceau insisted, "like a close entente among America, Great Britain, and France."[16] Clemenceau's willingness, even eagerness, to cooperate with the Americans would be important, even crucial, later on in his dealings with President Wilson. For now, however, his focus, like that of every other French politician, was on how to defeat Germany and break the German threat to France forever. Moreover, negotiating a treaty with Germany that left any French soil (or Belgian, for that matter) in German hands was not an option.

Prime Minister Briand shared Clemenceau's view. Although, after the war, his name would be linked to pacifism thanks to the Kellogg-Briand Pact to ban war, at the end of 1916 he was firm on continuing the war to the point of defiance. Prime minister since October 1915, he had witnessed the worst of the carnage. Yet it was Briand, not General Joffre, who had made the commitment to stand firm at Verdun in the face of other officers arguing that abandoning the fortress would shorten the line as well as save lives.

"You may not think losing Verdun a defeat," he had thundered, "but everyone else will. If you surrender Verdun you will be cowards, cowards, cowards and I will sack the lot of you." So, it was Briand, the future pacifist, who had pushed France into its ultimate sacrifice that spring, and the French army to its Calvary.[17]

There was, therefore, no chance that Briand would greet Bethmann-Hollweg's note with anything but a firm *non* (although Briand, like Lloyd George, took the precaution of not making the note's contents public). Besides, by appointing Nivelle as France's commander in chief, Briand had committed himself to a fresh offensive whatever the Americans did—even though other French generals were saying the army was in no condition to go on the attack again.

Under all these circumstances, rejection of the peace note by France and Britain might have seemed a foregone conclusion. But if Bethmann-Hollweg hoped for a conciliatory answer from any of the Entente powers, it was going to be from the third capital his note reached, St. Petersburg (or Petrograd, as it was now officially known) in Russia.

RUSSIA AND AMERICA CONFRONT
A WORLD WAR

It may be that peace is nearer than we know.
—WOODROW WILSON,
DECEMBER 18, 1916

PETROGRAD, DECEMBER 1916

BETHMANN-HOLLWEG'S HOPES WERE founded on the fact that the German peace note was reaching a Winter Palace (and a Russia) rapidly nearing the point of collapse.

For France and Britain (and Germany, for that matter), the coming of war and its rigors in August 1914 had meant an abrupt shift from the delights of peace. Not so for Russia. As a then-member of the Russian parliament, or Duma, Alexander Kerensky, noted years later, "On the day when war was declared, Russia was already in a revolutionary turmoil."[1] A series of punishing strikes had racked its largest cities, including St. Petersburg, through the first half of 1914. Almost half of Russia's entire workforce was involved. Some observers, including Kerensky, and some historians (particularly Marxist historians) have highlighted this fact to suggest that the revolution that would descend on Russia three years later was somehow preordained. In short, the old regime in Russia was bound to topple, war or no war, and those politicians who foresaw its doom had simply been clever enough to take advantage of that fact—including Kerensky.

Yet that diagnosis is probably wrong. Labor disputes, even violent ones—and there were many such across Russia after 1905—are just as often triggered by workers' rising expectations with an improving standard of living as by destitution or desperation. In fact, an economist looking from the outside might have seen the strikes as reasons to be *optimistic* about the Russian future, rather than pessimistic.

Russia's industrial production had grown by 3.5 percent per year from 1900 to 1910; after 1910, the rate surged to 5 percent a year. If contemporary Russian observers wrung their hands over their country's labor problems, it took a French economist, Edmond Théry, to predict in 1912 that if Russia were able to sustain the rate of growth it had achieved since 1900, by 1950 the land of the czars would rule Europe economically and financially as well as geopolitically.[2]

Physically, at least, Russia was poised to be the colossus of Europe. It was the largest empire in the world after the British Empire. It stretched over three continents, had a population of 166 million, and had abundant resources of coal, iron ore, gold, and oil, in addition to the rich agricultural lands of Ukraine and Poland—in short, everything a nation needed to sustain modern economic growth on an impressive scale. Yet, for centuries, Russia had always seemed to lag behind the rest of Europe, especially western Europe, in its cultural and economic development. Then, with the dawn of the new century, it began to catch up. Compared with where Russia had been fifty or even twenty years earlier, the numbers by 1914 were impressive.

Two things, however, boded ill for its future. First, the surge in economic growth also meant a rapid surge in Russia's industrial labor force, with tens of thousands leaving their tiny rural villages for the slums and tenements of Russia's already teeming cities. Between January 1910 and July 1914—that is, in the four and a half years before war began—the number of factory workers in Russia grew by one-third. As Russia mobilized for war, more than half the industrial workers living in St. Petersburg came from someplace else. They were largely fresh arrivals from the country, seeking a better life for themselves and their families, but also impatient to see results. They were the human fodder for the strikes in early 1914, and for the events of three years later.[3]

The second problem for Russia was how much of its economic growth depended on the public sector and the government in St. Petersburg. In 1914, the government owned two-thirds of the nation's railways; it owned many of the coal mines, the gold mines, and thousands of factories. The Ministry of Trade had representatives on the boards of nearly all Russia's major industrial corporations; it was also heavily involved in setting prices, regulating profits, and procuring raw materials. Russia's official State Bank was not an independent body like the Bank of England, but a department of the Finance Ministry. It was deeply entangled in the country's financial structure and served as chief regulator of the economy—the Russian equivalent of the U.S. Federal Reserve Board, the Federal Trade Commission, and the Securities and Exchange Commission all rolled into one.

This unprecedented huge public-sector involvement in and supervision of Russia's economic life impressed outside observers. It was one of the chief reasons Edmond Théry could make his confident prediction about Russia's growth curve, and why Bethmann-Hollweg himself had once declared, with not a little foreboding, that "the future belongs to Russia."[4]

But the Russian government was not like that of France or Germany. Administrative law was in its infancy. The government was chronically short of competent civil servants and able administrators; too many used their position as bureaucrats to enrich themselves rather than to make things work better or faster. Despite some cosmetic changes since the 1905 uprising, Russia was still an old-fashioned autocracy—rigid and unwieldy at the top, weak and slow moving at the bottom. If something happened to loosen or break the government's less than firm hold on the helm, if a crisis in the capital suddenly brought paralysis at the top, then the disruption would be felt through every sector of Russian society, even down to the state-owned estates and the "state peasants" who toiled away in the new eastern territories.

As fate would have it, that something would be the war.

Like all the combatants that crucial August 1914, Russia counted on a short conflict, a few months at most. That was not to be. Russia's initial advance into East Prussia was checked by a crushing German victory at Tannenberg in August, and then by the Austrian occupation of Russia's western provinces in 1915. These setbacks guaranteed that the war on the Eastern Front was going to be a long slog. The fighting on the Eastern Front never reached the same level of intensity as that on the Western Front. The trenches were more temporary and lightly manned; cows grazed peacefully, and peasants sowed and harvested their crops, all in no-man's-land. But the vast distances, and the seesaw nature of the fighting, guaranteed that the demand for manpower and resources was, if anything, more overwhelming— especially for an "emerging" economy such as Russia's.

At first glance, Russia seemed well prepared for the long haul. Its standing army was the largest in the world, more than 1.4 million men. Fully mobilized, it could put more than 12 million soldiers in the field—three times Germany's and Austria-Hungary's armies put together. But it was an army chronically short of every modern weapon, from airplanes, heavy artillery, and machine guns to motorized transport and reliable logistical rail support. Its reservists were poorly trained and badly led; its generals viewed technologies such as the machine gun with suspicion, preferring the old-fashioned bayonet charge. When the Russian army went up against a well-led, well-equipped force such as the German army, no one was surprised that it suffered defeat after defeat, accompanied by horrendous casualties. By December 1914, Russia had lost more than 1.2 million men, almost its entire prewar strength; its commander in chief, Grand Duke Nicholas Nikolaevich, warned London and Paris that Russia would not be capable of any further offensive actions. Nor would anyone have been surprised to learn, at the same time, that half of all Russian replacements reaching the front had no rifles.[5]

What was surprising, however, was that Russia was also running out of men. It was a measure of the incompetence of the czar's government that it could not even properly mobilize its huge draft-age male population for war. Despite an elaborate conscription system (borrowed from the Germans, as a matter of fact), far too many men were able to get exemptions, and far too many reservists were being housed for training in barracks near Russia's cities, including the capital, rather than being rushed to the front—a policy that would have disastrous political consequences later on. And in a country stretching thousands of miles with no adequate communication system, not even a telegraph in some areas, many young men simply never got the word to enlist or join up with their reserve units. By the end of 1916, after the rapid but fleeting success of the Brusilov Offensive, Russia's armed forces were starved for manpower. Yet the heaviest demands on its ability to fight were still to come.

By then, also, the wreckage had spread to the other sectors of Russian society. The loss of Poland to the Germans and Austrians meant the loss of Russia's most advanced industries. Getting basic materials for the army became an epic battle by itself; getting such goods to the civilian economy proved impossible. Russian consumers found themselves starved of the basics. By the end of 1915, even food was becoming scarce in the capital city of Petrograd (St. Petersburg's new name since the outbreak of war, when the government decided that "St. Petersburg" sounded Teutonic) and in Moscow. In the countryside, the situation was even worse. Feeding an army as large as Russia's required 16,000 tons of foodstuffs, hauled in 1,095 wagonloads, a day. Feeding the horses to haul that food required another 32,000 tons of barley, oats, and hay a day, or 1,850 wagonloads.[6] The only way to accomplish this Augean task was to seize from the peasants their food, livestock, wagons, tools—everything. Russia's peasants responded by resorting to subterfuge, even violence. The sight of a government official or an army inspector was enough to send an entire village into panic: whatever prestige the czarist regime still had after the series of military disasters that cost Russia millions of men and seventeen provinces soon vanished in a blaze of rural uprisings and bloodshed.

Indeed, "by the end of 1915," writes historian Nicolas Werth, "it was clear that the forces of law and order no longer existed" in Russia.[7] Yet the attention of the government in St. Petersburg was entirely fixed on the war effort and the army. Overseeing that vast ramshackle war machine was a Russian High Command dominated by the minister of war, Vladimir Sukhomlinov, and overshadowed by its commander in chief, the single most powerful political figure in Russia, Czar Nicholas II.

Forty-eight years old in 1916, conscientious but weak, Nicholas was trapped by an autocratic mind-set and by traditions running back more than three centuries, to the founder of the Romanov dynasty, Czar Mikhail Romanov. In 1915, Nicholas had dismissed the commander in chief, Grand Duke Nicholas (who also happened to be his uncle), and assumed command of Russia's armies himself. Russia's military disasters continued nonstop, but his new role gave the czar a personal stake, and it became almost a matter of honor for him somehow to see the war to victory.

In his sixteen years as "czar of all the Russias," he had already overseen two major defeats. The first was a humiliating drubbing at the hands of the Japanese in 1904–5; the second was the revolution of 1905, which had foisted on the supposedly all-powerful czar a representative parliament, or Duma. The Duma's powers were nugatory; the czar and his inner circle, including his beautiful German wife, Czarina Alexandra, continued to run the country as they saw fit. Yet the Duma remained a forum for political debate and discussion, including consideration of the conduct of the war. Nicholas resented the continuing torrent of criticism, especially from those deputies on the liberal and socialist left, who included a young lawyer and son of an elementary school teacher named Alexander Kerensky. But the czar could not shut down the Duma without setting off a political firestorm that would quickly spill out into the streets, just as it did in 1905. Instead, he kept it and its members at a frosty arm's length, thus missing the opportunity to bring Russia's only representative institution (albeit one elected by the tiny minority of Russians who passed the property qualification for voting) into a genuine partnership to sustain the war effort.

Nor were Nicholas, Alexandra, or any of their advisers interested in enlisting the help of Russia's business and industrial leaders. They, too, were kept at arm's length; many government officials even considered the Duma's opposition leaders and Russia's business class as much a threat as the Germans. From the perspective of the Winter Palace, the government faced two enemies, the Germans and the "enemy on the home front," namely the Duma. And from his railway carriage in his private train at Mogilev, the army headquarters set up in Belarus more than 480 miles from the capital, Nicholas saw himself waging two fights at once: one against the Germans, the other against the liberal opposition based in the capital.[8]

During his absence at army headquarters, Nicholas had left his wife, Czarina Alexandra, in charge of the government. This was his second disastrous decision. Alexandra was beautiful, cold, headstrong, deeply superstitious, and profoundly out of touch with reality. Everyone, including Nicholas's ministers, knew she was incompetent and believed she encouraged Nicholas's worst reactionary impulses. The fact that she was also a German princess did not help her credibility: indeed, there were whispers (on the streets of Petrograd, more than whispers) that Russia's series of disasters on the battlefield was no accident, that Alexandra was secretly working hand in glove with the German government.

It was true that she was an aid and comfort to the enemy, but not out of any sympathy with her former homeland. On the contrary, she firmly believed her husband was the spiritual father of Russia, and she had a mystical faith that the Russian people would always follow him (and her) out of a devotion born of tradition and trust, no matter how bad things got. Alexandra's problem, then, was poor judgment joined with an almost paranoid hatred of anyone who criticized her, her husband, or their intimate friend and confidant, the notorious "mad monk" Grigori Rasputin. Alexandra had turned to him more than a decade earlier, in 1905, when the doctors proved incapable of dealing with her son's hemophilia. Rasputin, however, through a combination of hypnosis and positive reinforcement, supposedly could deal with it. He became a hated figure at court, as jealous courtiers spread rumors about his increasingly reckless behavior, including wild sexual escapades, but Alexandra and Nicholas had dismissed the stories as malicious gossip.[9]

Now, with her husband at the front, the czarina turned to the monk for political and personal advice. Most of that advice was worthless, even disastrous. Rasputin inserted himself into decisions regarding food supplies and transport; he handled government loans; at one point, he was even issuing orders regarding military strategy and writing letters to the kings of Serbia and Greece.[10]

Above all, Rasputin convinced the czar and czarina that, in order for the war to continue, or even for the Russian Empire to survive, no compromise with the forces for liberalization and reform was necessary. Blinded by pride, prejudice, and a misplaced faith in the mystique of the Romanov dynasty, the czar and czarina were steadily driving their regime toward extinction. One Duma member, the conservative Vasili Maklakov, even compared Russia to a runaway automobile on a narrow, steep mountain road, where one single mistake by the driver (i.e., the czar) could send the car into the abyss, killing everyone on board.[11]

Perhaps so, but in the last days of 1916, only one thought occupied the mind of that driver: Russia must somehow emerge victorious from this two-and-a-half-year war. It was preordained, then, that his response to Bethmann-Hollweg's note would be negative. "What are the circumstances in which the German proposal was made?" Russian foreign minister Nikolai Pokrovsky told the representatives in the Duma on December 15. "The enemy armies . . . occupy Belgium, Serbia, and Montenegro, and part of France, Russia, and Rumania. Who then, with the exception of Germany, could derive any advantage under such conditions by the opening of peace negotiations?"[12]

The Duma agreed and issued its own resolution opposing the German peace proposal. "It considers that the German proposals are nothing more than a fresh proof of the weakness of the enemy," it read in part, "a hypocritical act from which the enemy expects no real success, but by which he seeks to throw upon others the responsibility for the war and for what has happened during it." It concluded: "The Duma considers that the premature peace would not only be a brief period of calm, but would involve the danger of another bloody war and renewed deplorable sacrifices on the part of the [Russian] people."[13]

Later, some in the Duma would change their tune regarding the possibility of a "premature peace," but now, for once, the Duma and the czar were in perfect agreement. Not that the resolution had any influence on Nicholas; nor did it tone down the fierce criticism the government faced from more radical Duma members such as Alexander Kerensky and Nikolai Chkheidze, who now added "Rasputinism" to the list of abuses they wanted eliminated. But on the issue of the war at least, the members of the Duma's leading parties, the so-called Progressive Bloc, were one with the czar.

Yet Nicholas's determination to fight on was undergirded by a nagging fear of what might happen if Russia accepted Germany's peace terms, and if he emerged with anything less than victory. Among the papers on his desk was an explosive memorandum by a former minister of the interior, Pyotr Durnovo. Dated February 1914, five months before Archduke Francis Ferdinand's assassination, it presciently warned of what might happen if Russia found itself dragged into a general war and lost. In that case, Durnovo wrote, "a social revolution in its most extreme form will be unavoidable for Russia." All sectors of Russian society would blame the government for the defeat. The army's loyalty would slacken, and it would become "too demoralized to act as a bulwark of law and order." The masses would rise up and take to the streets; the government's liberal opposition would be "unable to turn back the waves of uncontrollable popular protest [they had themselves] stirred up." Russia "will be thrown into total anarchy, the consequences of which cannot be foreseen."[14]

Here, Durnovo was wrong. There was one man who could foresee the consequences—indeed, who was counting on them. That week in December, he was sitting in his comfortless apartment in Zurich, his brow furrowed as he contemplated from the remoteness of exile the possibilities of the collapse of his country. Lenin saw Nicholas and Alexandra's headlong rush toward disaster not as a tragedy, but as an opportunity: a chance to trigger a mass revolt by the world's working classes against their aristocratic and bourgeois masters; a chance to change Russia, and humanity, forever. "This then is my destiny," he had written, "of not only fighting but also of winning victory in the forthcoming proletarian revolution," starting with Russia itself.[15]

The revolutionary breadth of Lenin's vision of the future was equaled by that of only one other man in the last days of 1916. He happened to sit in the White House in Washington, DC, where he would match Bethmann-Hollweg's peace note with one of his own.

WASHINGTON, DECEMBER 1916–JANUARY 1917

"THE WORLD ITSELF seems gone mad," Woodrow Wilson wrote to his friend Mary Hulbert, on September 6, 1914, the day German and French armies became locked in the Battle of the Marne, and three days after Russian troops sacked and looted the city of Lemberg (today Lviv), in their drive into Austrian Galicia (today part of Poland).[16]

Not yet two years into office since his election in 1912, Wilson had watched with horrified fascination as the assassination of Archduke Francis Ferdinand led Austria and Serbia into war; which brought Austria into war with Serbia's ally Russia; which then led Russia into war with Austria's ally Germany; which led Germany to declare war on Russia's ally France; which led to the German invasion and Britain's entry into the war as France's ally. By the second week in August, all the Great Powers of Europe were locked in war—a war from which Wilson was determined to keep America free.

There were those Americans who felt otherwise. One was former president Theodore Roosevelt, who saw history's greatest conflict not as a great tragedy but as a great opportunity for the United States to assert its status as a major world power. Roosevelt also had no doubt as to which side the United States should join. "If I had been president," he wrote to the British ambassador in Washington in October 1914, "I should have acted [against Germany] on the thirtieth or thirty-first of July."[17] But Roosevelt was not president. He was somewhat in disgrace with his own Republican Party; his decision in the 1912 election to form a third, breakaway party, the Bull Moose Party, was what had enabled Wilson to defeat GOP president William Howard Taft and gain the White House.

Roosevelt also worried about what would happen if the Allies lost. "Do you not believe," he wrote, "that if Germany won this war, smashed the English fleet and destroyed the British Empire, within a year or two she would insist upon taking the dominant position in South and Central America . . . ?" It infuriated him that Woodrow Wilson seemed unable to see things the same way. "I think this administration is the very worst and most disgraceful we have ever known," he wrote wrathfully to his friend Massachusetts senator Henry Cabot Lodge. Roosevelt was particularly upset at Wilson's tepid response to the sinking of the *Lusitania*.[18]

The former president's view of what was holding America back was clear: "Thanks to the width of the ocean, our people believe that they have nothing to fear from the present contest, and that they have no responsibility concerning it." In the hope of changing minds, he even published a book, *America and the World War*. But in the same letter, TR confessed his impotence to change that view: "If I should advocate all that I myself believe, I would do no good among our people, because they would not follow me." But Roosevelt also knew the American people had a current president who shared their myopic perspective—namely, Woodrow Wilson.[19]

Yet, even if Roosevelt's fears were wrong, there were compelling reasons, economic reasons, for seeing the United States as the natural ally of the Entente powers. Wilson's own treasury secretary, William McAdoo, saw that clearly as early as 1915, when Britain's and France's growing dependence on the United States for essential war materials and foodstuffs was proving a financial bonanza.

"Great Britain is, and always has been, our best customer," McAdoo wrote to Wilson, who happened also to be his father-in-law. "Since the war began, her purchases and those of her allies, France, Russia, and Italy, have enormously increased . . . The high prices for food products have brought great prosperity to our farmers, while the purchases of war munitions have stimulated industry . . . Great prosperity is coming."[20] Think how much greater prosperity would come, it was easy to conclude, if the United States fed and equipped its armies and navies in the conflict as well.

None of these concerns, however, moved President Wilson. He considered himself, and America, above such petty interests. He was not a pacifist, although antiwar feelings ran deep in his own party and his secretary of state, William Jennings Bryan, was an avowed pacifist. (Even more remarkably, his secretary of war when the German peace note arrived, Newton Baker, was a pacifist, too.) Wilson had just finished a brutal little war with Mexico, and had no fear of flexing America's muscle where he believed right reinforced might.

For the war in Europe, however, he had his own plan. From the opening shots, Wilson had looked forward to the day when he would appear on the scene as mediator, an impartial party to resolve the disputes between the combatants. That would be impossible if the United States found itself on one side or the other in the conflict. Therefore, keeping America neutral was a matter of not only America's destiny but Wilson's as well.

It was about America's destiny, however, that he publicly spoke whenever the topic of war came up. His feelings on the subject were made clear in a speech at Independence Hall, in Philadelphia, on the Fourth of July, only weeks before the war broke out, when he spoke of the holiday as a moment of renewal not only for America but for the world, and of its universal meaning.

"My dream," he said, "is that, as the years go on and the world knows more and more of America, it will also drink at these fountains of youth and renewal; that it also will turn to America for those moral inspirations which lie at the basis of freedom . . . and that America will come into the full light of the day when all shall see that her flag is the flag, not only of America, but of humanity."[21]

Going to war would destroy that global providential mission; or so Wilson believed. In short, his desire to stay out of the conflict did not spring from a desire to isolate America from the world; just the opposite. He didn't want the United States to be only one of the world's Great Powers, as Roosevelt and his friends did; he wanted it to be the greatest power of all. To enter the war, to dirty its hands like the European powers, would forever sully America's universal legacy and future.

Instead, Wilson focused his energies and hopes on his role as possible mediator. "God's Providence had given America this opportunity such as has seldom been vouchsafed any nation, the opportunity to counsel and obtain peace in the world."[22] In order to do so, it was necessary, he repeatedly told his countrymen, that they "exhibit the fine poise of undisturbed judgment, the dignity of self-control," in order to remain impartial and "truly serviceable for the peace of the world." America must be "neutral in fact as well as in name . . . impartial in thought as well as action."

In 1915, the year that fighting on the Western Front was bogging down in stalemate and Russia was suffering its first major setbacks, Wilson imagined a conversation among European leaders as they realized they had been wrong, and Wilson right, about the war. "Do you not think it likely that the world will some time turn to America and say, 'You were right, and we were wrong. You kept your heads when we lost ours . . . Now, in your self-possession, in your coolness, in your strength, may we not turn to you for counsel and for assistance?'"[23]

Wilson began offering that counsel in 1915, sending his friend and closest adviser, Col. Edward House, to Europe with offers of mediation that no one accepted, and then again in 1916. In May of the latter year, he told an audience at the Willard Hotel in Washington that he foresaw America's role in the world as leading a "feasible assembly of nations" that would underwrite any future peace, mentioning an idea that would blossom into his vision of a League of Nations. Regardless of what the future held, though, America's role as leader still required staying out of any present war.[24]

But in 1916, two things were steadily upsetting his grand plan. The first was the growing extent of U.S. economic support for the Allied war effort. Wilson and his treasury secretary, McAdoo, were uncomfortably aware of the degree to which the United States, led by Wall Street, was becoming entangled financially in the fate of the Entente. Defeat of France, Britain, and Russia could mean their default on their debts; default by the Entente would almost certainly mean bankruptcy for America's leading investment firms, not to mention the corporations that depended on the growing transatlantic business between the United States, the Allies, and their chief entrepôt, the port of London.

To Wilson, these considerations mattered less than a far more encompassing one, America's place in the crosshairs in the war at sea. As early as 1914, Wilson had the premonition that war in Europe would have a profoundly adverse effect on America's maritime commerce. The negative impact began with the British blockade, which hurt many American companies as well as Germany.

It grew worse with the German submarine threat, and the sinking of the *Lusitania* in May 1915 marked a parting of the ways between Wilson and Berlin, and America and Germany. From his mission in Europe, House wrote to Wilson four days afterward, "America . . . must determine whether she stands for civilized or uncivilized warfare. Think we can no longer remain neutral."[25] Despite his outrage, Wilson, however, refused to be moved. He believed it important not to react emotionally to the atrocity, as millions of Americans were doing, and restricted his response to several arch paragraphs from his typewriter to the German ambassador. He was pleased his words had the desired effect, and for a time the German submarine threat faded.

By the autumn of 1916, however, as his reelection campaign was reaching its climax, Wilson could sense the Germans were leaning toward resuming unrestricted warfare. He feared that news of fresh ship sinkings and American deaths would rouse the public to an unmanageable emotional state, one that would make staying out of the war impossible. Something had to be done, fast, to head off that possibility, before it ruined America's destiny.

So, when, during the 1916 campaign, he described America as "too proud to fight," he was not rationalizing the nation's disengagement from events in Europe, as critics thought. In his mind the phrase summed up why the United States had an absolute moral duty to stay aloof from those conflicts no matter what the provocation.

When the German peace offer landed on his desk at the White House, then, Wilson's reaction was very different from that of leaders in Paris, London, and Petrograd. He saw it dovetailing perfectly with his own plans. Back in November, he had told his most intimate adviser, Colonel House—they often shared a bedroom while on the road—that he wanted to write a note to the belligerents demanding that they cease hostilities. Bethmann-Hollweg's note was therefore the perfect opening for Wilson to begin drafting a peace note of his own, which he finished on December 18, 1916.

President Wilson's peace note was passed along to America's ambassador in London, Walter Hines Page. In introducing it, U.S. secretary of state Robert Lansing pointed out that President Wilson "is somewhat embarrassed to offer it at this particular time because it may now seem to have been prompted by the recent overtures of the Central powers. It is in no way associated with them in its origin," Lansing hastened to add; he also pointed out that the president "can only beg that his suggestion be considered entirely on its own merits and as if it had been made in other circumstances."

This preface by his secretary of state was, in effect, Wilson's putdown of the Germans and their transparently disingenuous peace offer. Everyone, including Wilson, grasped that Bethmann-Hollweg's note had been aimed not at suing for peace, but at breaking up the Entente. Yet, writing in the third person, Wilson then proceeded to administer the same medicine to the Allies: "[The U.S. president] takes the liberty of calling attention to the fact that the objects which the statesmen of the belligerents on both sides have in mind in this war are virtually the same." Whether Germany or France or Britain or Russia, "each side desires to make the rights and privileges of weak people and small States as secure against aggression and denial in the future as the rights and privileges of the great and powerful States now at war." By "small states" he meant Belgium on the Allied side and Bulgaria on the Central powers side.

"Each wishes itself to be made secure in the future . . . ," the president went on. "Each would be jealous of the formation of any more rival leagues to preserve an uncertain balance of power amidst multiplying suspicions; but each is ready to consider the formation of a league of nations to insure peace and justice throughout the world."

So, there it was: a "league of nations," an idea that would have a controversial and bitter history before Wilson was done with it, but one that was injected into the discussion in order to offer the combatants in Europe a way out of the world order that had led to history's bloodiest conflict.

"But," Wilson warned, "the war must first be concluded." It was not up to him or the American people to propose what terms were needed to end it, he hastened to add. However, regarding "the measures to be taken to secure the future peace of the world[,] the people and Government of the United States are as vitally and as directly interested as the Governments now at war." Therefore, "the President feels altogether justified in suggesting an immediate opportunity for a comparison of views as to the terms which must precede those ultimate arrangements for the peace of the world."

On what terms would the various combatants accept a final negotiated peace? "The leaders of the several belligerents have, as has been said, stated those objects in general terms. But, stated in general terms, they seem the same on both sides." Perhaps "peace is nearer than we know; that the terms which the belligerents on the one side and on the other would deem it necessary to insist upon are not so irreconcilable as some have feared." But now had come the time, Wilson insisted, to spell out those terms in more detail: what kinds of concrete guarantees, what kinds of territorial changes or readjustments, "what stage of military success even," would be needed to bring the war to an end.

Wilson finished by saying that he was not proposing peace, or even offering to mediate. "He is merely proposing that soundings be taken in order that we may learn, the neutral nations with the belligerent, how near the haven of peace may be for which all mankind longs . . ." while "he confidently hopes for a response which will bring a new light into the affairs of the world."[26]

The feelings in London, Paris, Berlin, and Petrograd when Wilson's note arrived are not difficult to imagine. It's not often that world leaders get lectured to by one of their own, admonished as if they were errant schoolchildren who needed to be brought to account. But it was a particularly bitter blow to the French and British. The French press declared it the worst blow the country had received in twenty-nine months of war. It is even said that King George V wept when he read it.[27]

What Wilson had done was declare a moral equivalence between the Entente and the Central powers. Both were fighting for the same thing, the American president said, a position London and Paris vehemently denied. From their perspective, the whole justification since August 1914 had been that they were the forces of civilization fighting against their opposite, while the Germans were ruthless and bloodthirsty Huns whose aggression and violations of international law knew no bounds.

However, both Lloyd George and Briand understood that how they answered the American president mattered a great deal more than how they had answered the German chancellor's peace note. Both very much wanted the United States on their side, and both were very much relieved when, on December 27, Arthur Zimmermann, the new German foreign minister, gave Wilson's proposal a vigorous thumbs-down. Lloyd George and Briand had another concern.

They knew Wilson was very close to severing the financial lifeline on which Britain, France, and Russia were entirely dependent.

On December 1, 1916, the bankers at J.P. Morgan had been set to issue a new Anglo-French bond worth at least $1.5 billion—the equivalent of the entire cost of the Somme offensive. On November 27, however, the Federal Reserve Board suddenly sent a letter to all its member banks stating that it was no longer desirable for American investors to increase their holdings in British and French securities. Wall Street immediately flew into a panic. The British pound sterling sank like a stone; J.P. Morgan, after hurriedly deciding to postpone its bond offering, had to use its own considerable reserves to prop up the pound, as did the UK treasury. Also, Britain had to suspend its support of French purchasing.[28]

In a single day, the Allies' entire financial support network hovered on the brink of collapse.

It had all been Wilson's doing, the response to a note he had sent to the Federal Reserve shortly before the election. The president was determined not to let America's financial entanglement with the Allies' cause draw it further into support of their war effort. The Allies were just as determined to use that leverage to get America "all in"—that is, unless Wilson decided to use their dependence on Wall Street to force them to sue for peace.

Everything depended, then, on how they replied to Wilson's December 18 peace note. So, on January 10, 1917, even as the Entente powers were planning to meet in Petrograd to coordinate their strategy for the next phase of the war, they responded with a document carefully worded to elicit Wilson's sympathy.

If they could not draw America into the war, the plan was at least to keep the money and supplies flowing.

For the first time after nearly two and a half years of war, the Allies were forced to state in detail what they were fighting for. The result was a revealing, even revolutionary document. With regard to Germany, their demands were easy: the evacuation of neutral Belgium and territory taken in western Russia; the restoration of the governments of Serbia and Romania; the return to France of Alsace and Lorraine, which Germany had taken in the Franco-Prussian War in 1871. With regard to Germany's allies Turkey and Austria-Hungary, however, the Entente's demands were more complicated. They included "the liberation of the Italians, as also of the Slavs, Romanians, and Czechoslovaks from foreign domination," meaning domination by Austria, and "the freeing of the populations subject to the bloody tyranny," meaning all the peoples living from Armenia and Mesopotamia to Syria, Arabia, and Palestine.

In a single swipe, the Allies were saying that peace would require the breakup of both the Habsburg and the Ottoman Empires, which together represented more than a thousand years of history. It said nothing about other empires, or about the liberation of the Poles, since Czar Nicholas was their ally. Nothing, of course, about Britain's overseas empire, or France's. (In fact, that spring, Britain had ruthlessly suppressed the one attempt at national liberation during the entire war, by the Irish in the Easter Rebellion.) Yet Britain and France were now on record as saying that they were fighting not just to defeat Germany but also to free subject peoples from centuries of imperial rule. In so doing, they put a new term on the diplomatic table for the first time: *national self-determination*. It was a concept deeply embedded in nineteenth-century liberalism, one that had roused up Europe (including Germany) once before, in the revolutions of 1848, and one they assumed (correctly) would connect with a self-declared Progressive such as Wilson.

Sure enough, Wilson was impressed. Just twelve days later, he responded with a speech that would be one of the most important of his career, one that fired the signal pistol for a new era in world affairs.

As such, January 22, 1917, also marked a milestone in American history. Wilson decided to deliver the speech before the Senate, the first time a president had done so since George Washington. Copies would be distributed to every major capital in Europe at the same time. He also did what no president had ever done, not Washington nor Jefferson nor Abraham Lincoln nor even Theodore Roosevelt: he explained why American leadership was essential to the world.

Wilson began by asserting that the Founding Fathers had set up their new nation in the hope that it would "show mankind the way to liberty." It was up to America now not to withhold that solemn service, nor to try to offer the service alone. Instead, if it cooperated with other nations "through a formal and solemn adherence to a League for Peace" to guarantee peace, then Wilson was prepared to take that unprecedented step.

He made it very clear that his goal in the current world war was not to choose sides but to make peace. His term for it was "peace without victory." He said that "victory would mean peace forced upon the loser, a victor's terms imposed upon the vanquished." Such a peace would only breed shame and resentment on the part of the loser, "a bitter memory upon which terms of peace would rest, not permanently, but only as upon quicksand."

But a peace without victory America (or, more precisely, Woodrow Wilson himself) was prepared to help mediate. It would come, however, with certain inviolable principles. One would be, picking up on the phrase the Allies had used, national self-determination ("no right anywhere exists to hand peoples from sovereignty as if they were property"), along with freedom of the seas, a shot at Britain's policy of stop-and-search naval blockades and at Germany's conduct of submarine warfare. Another principle was formal limitations on armaments, which would allow countries to keep their armies and navies "a power for order merely, not an instrument of aggression or of selfish violence." (Just how one decided which was which, especially among the Great Powers, was not explained.)

If these requirements seemed unrealistic, that did not bother Wilson. He was convinced he was "speaking for the silent mass of mankind everywhere who have as yet had no place or opportunity to speak their real hearts out concerning the death and ruin they see to have come already upon the persons and the homes they hold most dear." So, having spoken for mankind, Wilson left the podium.[29]

Some were bowled over by the speech, which made "peace without victory" an international catchphrase just as Wilson's note of December 18 had done with "league of nations." Editor Herbert Croly of the *New Republic*, the house organ of high-grade Progressivism, was quoted as calling it the greatest event of his life. Wilson's secretary of state, William Jennings Bryan, told the president that "the basis of peace you propose is a new philosophy . . . that is, new to governments but as old as the Christian religion." It would put Wilson, Bryan averred, "among the Immortals."[30]

Theodore Roosevelt was less impressed. He wrote that "peace without victory is the natural ideal of the man who is too proud to fight"—a sideways shot at Wilson's manhood and his naïveté. Roosevelt also reminded Americans that in 1776 it was the Tories, the loyalists to Britain, who had preached "peace without victory," and likewise the Copperheads, or sympathizers with the slave-owning South, who preached the same during the Civil War. "Now Mr. Wilson is asking the world to accept a Copperhead peace of dishonor; a peace without victory for the right; a peace designed to let wrong triumph; a peace championed in neutral countries by the apostles of timidity and greed."[31]

Another critic was Roosevelt's friend the senator from Massachusetts Henry Cabot Lodge. Lodge had once been a supporter of the League to Enforce Peace, the organization founded by former U.S. president William Howard Taft, who had applauded Wilson's efforts to end the war without entering the conflict. Now Lodge found the speech to be "collections of double-dealing words under which men can hide and say they mean anything and nothing."[32] His criticism, like Roosevelt's, stung the sensitive president to the quick. Wilson and Lodge were slated to speak together at a centennial celebration at St. John's Church in Washington, DC. When Wilson learned that Lodge was on the program, he declined to appear.[33]

The accusation that Wilson was either a coward or a hypocritical double-dealer was as unfair as it was inaccurate. But just what did he mean by pushing a program of "peace without victory"?

In looking over that remarkable speech, it's clear that Wilson was raising America up as the new global colossus based on its moral authority as a universal nation. The United States already had the world's leading economy; now it was poised to be the world's moral master as well, towering over the course of world civilization. There is no doubt that Wilson was a strong believer in American exceptionalism. But his version of American exceptionalism was one that put other nations at a severe disadvantage, as benighted and ignorant of the true course of history, which Wilson (and Wilson alone of world leaders) understood. The outbreak and course of world war only confirmed that verdict. This was why Wilson was willing to set aside arguments about whether Germany had "caused" the war. The war was a disease that all the Great Powers of Europe had carried in their political DNA, as it were. Now it was up to America, and Woodrow Wilson, to point the way to the cure.

Yet, by making that argument, Wilson had also done something unexpected. He had put America and Germany at the same starting point, as far as peace negotiations went. Bethmann-Hollweg's December 12 offer and Wilson's "Peace Without Victory" note had suddenly converged.

Only one man saw this, and realized what an opportunity for Germany it had opened up. That was the German ambassador in Washington, Johann von Bernstorff. He sent a note to his supervisor, pointing out that if Germany were to accept Wilson's terms for negotiation now, on the basis of his speech, it would be able to keep all its conquests, using the ones it didn't want as bargaining chips in a final peace settlement brokered by Wilson and the United States.

Indeed, right after the speech, Wilson told House, "If Germany really wants peace, she can get it, and get it soon, *if she will but confide in me and let me have a chance* . . . Do they in fact want me to help?" Bernstorff was urging Berlin to say yes before it was too late.[34]

In the end, Berlin said no. It ranks among the great missed opportunities in history, of which there would be several more as 1917 unfolded. That January, Germany had never looked stronger; by accepting peace without victory, it would actually have been the clear winner, while Wilson could have used America's financial leverage to force Britain, France, and Russia to go along.

In fact, Wilson's offer was already too late. On January 9, Ludendorff had overridden the objections of Bethmann-Hollweg and compelled the government to restart unrestricted submarine warfare on the last day of the month, January 31. Even as Wilson was striding to the podium to deliver his "Peace Without Victory" speech, German U-boats were silently headed deep into the Atlantic, to form a wide arc of death along the French and British coastlines.[35] When he learned of the government's decision, Bernstorff made one last stab at stopping the madness of resuming unrestricted attacks on neutral ships, including American ones. "If submarine warfare is now begun without further ado," he wrote in an anguished note on January 27, "the President will take this as a slap in the face and war with the United States cannot be avoided . . . In my view the end of the war will be unforeseeable because—despite all that can be said to the contrary—the power and resources of the United States are very great."[36]

The note was useless. Even if Ludendorff had wanted to accept Wilson's offer, there was no way to halt the U-boats on their deadly mission. But Ludendorff and the other German generals were not so convinced that Wilson would enter the war. Their gamble was that even when American ships began to be sunk in greater numbers, Wilson would still hesitate to choose sides in a conflict that, as he had stated over and over again, was of no concern to the United States—and now with his peace offer on the table, it would be even more imperative that the United States not choose sides, in order to preserve its moral leadership over the planet.

That was, of course, the Allies' worst fear: that Wilson's high-minded message and assumption of world leadership—Wilson "thinks he's president of the world," one disgruntled listener said after the speech[37]—had doomed America to the sidelines for good. In Britain, a young treasury official named John Maynard Keynes was issuing warnings about how the entire Allied war effort now depended on Wilson's keeping the credit flowing from America. Britain's prime minister, Lloyd George, was more convinced than ever that only American intervention could break the stalemate.

The Allies and Wilson were further apart than London or Paris imagined, even in their statement of basic principles. Wilson and the Entente, for example, parted company on the issue of self-determination. The British and French evoked "self-determination" for selfish, even cynical reasons, not altruistic ones. The goal was not setting peoples free but, rather, destroying their antagonists from within. They saw Czechs, Slovaks, Poles, Armenians, and even Palestinian Jews rising up to claim their sovereign inheritance from the empires that held them down, but not Indians, Malays, or the inhabitants of the Cameroons or French Equatorial Africa.

Once they let loose that principle, it was hard to see where it would stop. If it applied to Italians and Czechs and Jews and Armenians, why not to Arabs and Kampucheans and Ibos? In 1917, there were strong racial reasons for believing it did not. When, two years later, the Paris Peace Conference wrapped itself around the principle of self-determination, it was automatically assumed that the principle posed no threat to the existing colonial empires of the victorious powers—the United States included.

And yet, by planting the self-determination flag, the Entente had unwittingly set the table for the transformation of a world war into a global revolution. Before 1917 was done, that revolution would be unleashed, and Woodrow Wilson would not be the only visionary to seize the slogan to overthrow the existing order—one other would be the revolutionary temporarily in deep freeze in Switzerland, Lenin. In fact, even after Wilson's speech, he was the only person in Europe thoroughly convinced that America would enter the war—indeed, would be compelled to enter it by the forces of history, German submarines or no German submarines.

Sitting in his Zurich apartment the previous summer, Lenin had been putting the finishing touches on the manuscript for *Imperialism, The Highest Stage of Capitalism*. It would be one of the seminal and original works in the Communist canon, and also deeply revealing of Lenin's thinking in the midst of the world's bloodiest war—and his thinking about America.

The theme of Lenin's slim volume is that concentration of wealth in capitalist countries must inevitably lead to war. That intense concentration—Britain, France, Germany, and the United States together, Lenin noted, controlled nearly 80 percent of the world's financial capital—had reduced the possibility for fresh profits in capitalist countries themselves, including the United States. With the new century, Western capital required new outlets, and it found them in the proliferation of colonies and imperial possessions around the world. "Capitalism has grown into a world system of colonial oppression and of the financial strangulation of the overwhelming majority of the people of the world by a handful of 'advanced' countries."[38]

Lenin's conclusion: the competition for outlets for capital must lead inevitably to competition for empire itself, which must lead to war. The current conflict was proof that he was right, he believed, and while the United States was a relative latecomer to the imperial feast, with its war against Spain in 1898 and its takeover of the Philippines, Cuba, and Hawaii, the involvement of the world's mightiest capitalist economy in the larger conflict in Europe would be only a matter of time.

From Lenin's perspective, which side the United States chose didn't really matter because, in the end, the war would bring about the end of capitalism itself, and the collapse of all the powers that had participated in its cataclysm. Imperialism, and the "striving to violence and reaction" it unleashed, was not only the highest stage of capitalism but also its *last* stage. The war would send the entire capitalist system and its political offshoots, including bourgeois democracy, crashing to the ground. Out of the rubble would emerge the international working-class movement, ready to take power in the name of the proletariat and to complete the destruction that the world war had started.[39]

By the logic of history, then, America would inevitably declare war on Germany and join the Armageddon that spelled the end of capitalism.

In a strange way, Lenin foresaw "peace without victory" like Wilson, but in very different terms. No one was going to win this war except the working classes; the peace they would bring would be built on the rubble of capitalism. The speech Lenin gave to young socialists in Zurich on January 22 (the same day as Wilson's speech to Congress) predicted as much, with the added proviso that this transformation would certainly take place in their lifetimes, though perhaps not in his.

So, as 1917 began, both men saw the world as a stage set for a massive upheaval, with each imagining himself at the center of it.

Who were these two extraordinary men, so different, so far apart, yet so much alike? And how had their very different lives led them to this point, when they would both transform world history forever?

┌─────┐
│ 3 │
└─────┘

TOMMY AND VOLODYA

The most powerful weapon on earth is the human
soul on fire.
—GENERAL FERDINAND FOCH

T HOMAS WOODROW WILSON—"TOMMY" to his family—did not
learn to read until he was ten years old. This seems shocking
for a man who would spend his life at his desk and typewriter
writing important books and memorable speeches, for a man who
personified the Progressive American intellectual for his generation.
Biographer H. W. Brands speculates that Wilson's reading problems
may have been a form of dyslexia. Certainly, the problems Tommy
had in school were pronounced enough that his father had to find him
a special tutor.[1]

Eventually, Wilson conquered his dyslexia, but the long struggle
with reading may have given him an excessive awe for the power
of words and language, a belief that they could shape reality and
even formed their own reality. If so, it's a conviction he shared with
Lenin—Vladimir Ilyich Ulyanov, "Volodya" to his family.

Both men were unlikely world leaders in a time of action, as both
made their lives about words and ideas. This commitment was combined with a compelling physical presence that moved and at times
frightened friends and contemporaries. In Lenin's case, "there was
above all his enormous capacity to see to the root of things," one of
his fellow revolutionaries, Mikhail Pokrovsky, later wrote, "a capacity
which finally awakened in me a sort of superstitious feeling . . . He

understood things better and was master of the power denied to me, of seeing about ten feet down into the earth."[2] In Wilson's case, there was his acceptance speech as Democratic nominee for governor of New Jersey, a speech that so moved his audience that they refused to let him stop and sit down, shouting, "Go on! Go on!"[3]

If the overused word *charisma* has any meaning, it applies to both Lenin and Wilson. But their almost magical effect on those who saw or worked with them didn't spring from larger-than-life warmth or a passionate personality. It sprang from the opposite: a chilly, almost icy intensity reinforced by a sense of the utter rightness of their vision and ideas. That sense of rightness made opposition virtually an immoral act of betrayal. Someone once said of Lenin that he insisted on imposing his will on others "not because power is sweet to him, but because he is certain he is right and cannot tolerate anyone spoiling his work."[4] The same was true of Wilson, who was willing to hurl hundreds of thousands of Americans into the carnage of the First World War in order to fulfill the vision he spelled out for the first time to those enraptured New Jersey delegates six years before the war began: "America is not distinguished so much by its wealth and material power as by the fact that it was born with an ideal, a purpose to serve mankind."

He went on: "When I look upon the American flag before me, I think sometimes it is made of parchment and blood. The white in it stands for parchment, the red in it signifies blood—and blood that was spilled to make those rights real."

Just how much blood both men, Wilson and Lenin, were willing to spill in order to move the world on their respective revolutionary courses would be the overriding narrative of 1917.

* * *

THOMAS WOODROW WILSON was the son of a Presbyterian minister, Joseph Wilson, who gave his son a respect for the power of the greatest words of all, the Word of God. All Woodrow Wilson's life, the Presbyterian faith, and its belief that God and Providence watched over every aspect of American life as well as his own, never wavered. Even when Wilson was president, his God was a demanding taskmaster, one who insisted that man's highest duties in life, and highest destinies, had to be fulfilled without question. His father's faith gave Wilson a sense of moral rectitude that, to others, bordered (or more than bordered) on self-righteousness. Watching the American president during the Paris Peace Conference in 1919, John Maynard Keynes would remark that "he would do nothing that was not honorable; he would do nothing that was not just and right"—that is, Keynes cynically concluded, unless Wilson could justify an action as a way to serve some higher moral purpose.[5]

Likewise, Wilson's friend and biographer Ray Stannard Baker wrote that Wilson's greatest ideal, "the League of Nations[,] was a matter of *faith*, and the President is first of all a man of faith. He believes in the L. of N. as an organization that will save the world." While others strongly supported the League, the president *"sees it, grasps it, feels it,* with the mighty tenacity of faith."

Baker added, "He is willing even to compromise desperately for it, suffer the charge of inconsistency for it," a charge that would haunt Wilson all through his political life, the charge of hypocrisy.[6]

If the Word and continuous presence of a Presbyterian God were one decisive influence on Wilson's life, the other was the American Civil War.

Born in 1856, Wilson was nine when the War Between the States ended. His father served briefly in a Confederate regiment before returning to his life as a man of the cloth. Tommy Wilson experienced the 1861–65 conflict not as an epic struggle to reaffirm the principle that "government by the people, of the people, and for the people shall not perish from the earth" or to free an enslaved people, as Northerners did and as most Americans do today. To Wilson, it was a war of unwarranted destruction, of occupation and degradation of his beloved South. When he was fourteen, the Wilson family moved to a devastated Columbia, South Carolina, which Yankee soldiers had all but burned to the ground five years earlier.

The sense that the Civil War and Reconstruction were undiluted tragedies for the South and the nation—perhaps, even, that the wrong side had won—had a profound effect on Wilson's views of domestic policies. That included his support for segregation, then justified under the rubric of separate but equal, including segregating the U.S. armed forces. It also included endorsing the idea that the civilization he and America needed to protect was above all a white one, led by the "progressive" Caucasian race. As we'll see, this view affected his policy toward China and Japan both before and after the Paris Peace Conference in ways that would sow the seeds of trouble long after.

But the Civil War also left him with a deep, abiding horror of war itself. Wilson worried that if America were dragged into war for the wrong reasons, it would ignite an enthusiasm for war and violence like the emotion that had swept the North during the Civil War. This was why it was important in the days following the *Lusitania*'s sinking to keep America cool and levelheaded.[7]

There was also a deeper, racialist component to his fear of war. That fateful January of 1917, Wilson met with his Cabinet to discuss the war raging in Europe. One listener wrote that Wilson was "more and more impressed with the idea that 'white civilization' and its domination in the world rested largely on our ability to keep this country [i.e., America] intact . . . He had come to the feeling that he was willing to go to any lengths rather than to have the nation actually involved in the conflict."

If America slipped over the edge and into war, Wilson felt, the result would be "a crime against civilization," meaning white civilization.[8] The young Woodrow Wilson matriculated at Princeton in 1875, and was soon in the thick of organizing the Liberal Debating Club and competing in public speaking contests. It was his fascination with oratory, particularly political oratory, that led to his discovery of his first heroes, the great British statesmen of the eighteenth and early nineteenth centuries, men such as William Pitt, Edmund Burke, and John Bright. His enthusiasm for all things British led him to compose his first serious essay, published in the *International Review* in 1879, arguing that it was time to make the American Cabinet responsible to Congress in the same way British Cabinets were responsible to Parliament. The article made a minor splash; by an irony of ironies, the editor at *International Review* who accepted Wilson's piece would be his future antagonist Henry Cabot Lodge.[9]

Thanks to the article, Wilson was launched on his career as a scholar and intellectual, and as a leading expert on the American political system and the role of Congress. After an unhappy year and a half at law school at the University of Virginia, and an equally unhappy stint hanging out his shingle in Atlanta, Woodrow Wilson decided to embrace his scholarly side by heading off to Baltimore and the graduate school at Johns Hopkins University.

Published in 1885, his Hopkins dissertation was *Congressional Government*, a penetrating analysis of the central role of the legislative branch in American government—an ironic choice of subject for the man who would come to symbolize the executive branch at its most self-assertive, even dictatorial.

Yet there is important conceptual overlap between Wilson the dedicated student of the importance of Congress in 1885 and the later Progressive author of works such as *The State* and *Constitutional Government*. First of all, both the early and the later Wilson thought it a mistake to see the U.S. Constitution as a rigid set of rules or mechanisms that set limits on future expressions of the will of the American people. What the men of 1787 saw as the role of government was not the role of government in the twentieth century; nor should it be, Wilson concluded. Today, he would be an enthusiastic supporter of the idea of the "living Constitution." He was also a biting critic of the doctrine of separation of powers—indeed, his early 1879 essay on Cabinet government was an implicit rejection of the idea of a wall of separation between the executive and legislative branches. Instead, he insisted that this outdated notion was the trace of an "older liberalism," as Wilson termed it, one that worried about the possibility of government tyrannizing the individual, and so it used separation of powers as a way to limit that possibility. Wilson's view was that this worry no longer applied to the modern age. Instead, the threat now was that separation of powers would be a permanent brake on the ability of government to address the most pressing issues of the age. In fact, Wilson expressed amazement that American democracy had survived at all, given the self-mutilations imposed by the separation of powers.[10] Even more, the separation of powers prevented the sovereign will of the people from being expressed through the system originally devised by the Constitution.

The bespectacled son of the Presbyterian preacher was now an academic star. One reviewer called *Congressional Government* the best study of the American Constitution since *The Federalist Papers*.[11] Teaching jobs came quickly, first at Bryn Mawr College and then at Wesleyan. His next book, *The State*, appeared in print in 1889 and became an instant classic in comparative government studies and then a standard textbook in the field. In 1890, his alma mater Princeton beckoned him back to teach. By now, the thirty-four-year-old Wilson had dropped his first name, "Thomas," and signed his name and his books simply as "Woodrow Wilson." At Princeton, students flocked to his classes; colleges and universities around the country asked him to speak. In just twelve years he would be Princeton's highest-paid professor, and Princeton's board of trustees would unanimously vote to make him president of the college.

It was 1890, the same year Bismarck was dismissed as German chancellor and Wyoming and Idaho became states. That same year, on the other side of the world, a twenty-year-old Lenin was busy translating the works of Karl Marx into Russian.

* * *

ALTHOUGH LENIN WOULD see himself as a lifelong champion of the proletariat and an enemy of the bourgeoisie, his background was solid Russian middle class: his father, Ilya Ulyanov, was a school inspector, and his mother, Maria Alexandrovna Blank, the daughter of a successful lawyer and landowner.

His hometown also was in many ways illustrative of the "other"

Russia, the one far away from Europeanized urban centers such as Moscow and St. Petersburg. When he was born, for example, more than one-third of Simbirsk's population were not ethnic Russians. These inhabitants included Jews, one of whom was Lenin's maternal grandfather, Alexander Blank (a convert to Russian Orthodoxy); Germans; Tatars; and Kalmucks, a Mongol people whose number included Lenin's paternal grandmother. A distance of about two hundred miles north of Simbirsk lay Kazan, once the capital of the Muslim Tatars; this was where Lenin would attend university. Throughout his life, people noted that there was something "Asian" about Lenin, with his slanting eyes and broad, high cheekbones. That un-Russian something went beyond genetics, however. It was rooted in the world in which he grew up, where the mark of galloping Cossacks and rampaging Mongols was still real; where Russian rule, like Russian Orthodoxy, had been imposed by force; where civilization was a thin veneer—and where a young man growing up could well conclude that all power came from the barrel of a gun or the swing of a scimitar.

Lenin's parents, it must be said, were entirely untouched by these turbulent cultural crosscurrents. They saw themselves first and foremost as good Russians. They raised their six children (three girls and three boys, including Vladimir, one of the two middle children) in the Russian Orthodox faith and sent the boys to Russian schools. Ilya Ulyanov was also a loyal civil servant under the czar, becoming a state inspector of schools after building a successful career as a teacher of physics and mathematics. As such, he held a rank in the Russian civil service equal to that of major general in the army.[12]

By any measure, Lenin's father was an educated, cultivated man. For all his traditional religiosity, he was in many ways liberal in his broader outlook. He admired Russia's liberalizing czar Alexander II, who had emancipated Russia's serfs, laid the foundation for local self-government, and would have carried out more reforms if an assassin's bomb, on March 1, 1881, had not stopped the reforming czar in his tracks.

The assassination of Alexander II was a harsh blow to Lenin's father, and a tragedy for Russia. If the American Civil War was the one great formative event shaping Woodrow Wilson's life, the apparent failure of Russian liberalism forms the backdrop for understanding Lenin.

For centuries, Russians had felt themselves far behind the West in terms of economic, political, and social development. (Some would argue that they still are.) The big question was how to close the gap. At first, it was left to autocratic rulers such as Peter the Great and Catherine the Great to use their virtually unlimited power to push Russia forward on the path to becoming respected as an equal by the Western powers. Then, following the French Revolution, Czar Alexander I opened the way to thinking about a different route to Russian greatness. It was not through building bigger armies or navies (although the drive for military power continued nonstop), or through acquiring territories that would give Russia sea routes to the West. Alexander's approach was to introduce some of the ideas and concepts flowing into Russia from the European Enlightenment, ideas that paralleled trends in France and Britain that we usually identify with classical liberalism: individual rights, free trade and social mobility, freedom of thought and expression, representative government, and the rule of law.

This intellectual "window to the West" didn't stay open very long. By the time of Alexander's death in December 1825, it had been firmly shut. Yet enough of this Westernizing liberalism had made its way into Russian thought and culture to lay the foundation for a series of programs pushing important social and political reforms, including freeing Russia's vast population of serfs. It also spawned a class of educated individuals ready to advocate for this Western-style reform through books, articles, and seemingly endless discussions in coffeehouses and university classrooms.

In an autocratic empire that was still largely feudal in nature and overwhelmingly illiterate, the Russian intelligentsia's ineffectiveness was matched only by its frustration with failure. Every proposal for reform (including any in fictional works) was met with scrutiny from the czar's censors and secret police. What they judged as going too far could lead to exile in Siberia or imprisonment. The failure over several decades to advance changes in a liberal, Western direction spurred those who believed change in Russia was more necessary than ever to look at a more drastic solution—namely, revolution.

The Russian revolutionary tradition found its roots in the days after Alexander I's death, when a handful of young Russian army officers led a coup in St. Petersburg to prevent the late czar's conservative successor, Nicholas I, from assuming power. The so-called Decembrist Revolt ended in arrests and executions, including that of the poet Kondraty Ryleyev. Still, it had blazed a trail for other radicals to follow, and over the years those radicals would agree with Ryleyev's testimonial before the revolt: "An upheaval is essential. The tactics of revolution may be summed up in two words, to dare. If we come to grief, our failure will serve as a lesson to those who come after us."[13]

And so it did, as one group of revolutionaries and conspirators was succeeded by the next. There were the Russian anarchists, led by a renegade aristocrat, Prince Kropotkin, in the 1840s and '50s; the Narodniks, or agrarian socialists, in the 1860s and '70s; a violent breakaway faction of the Narodniks, who dubbed themselves the People's Will, in the late 1870s and early '80s—it was one of their number who planted the bomb that killed Alexander II.

That act embodied the revolutionary paradox: choosing to kill a liberal czar because reforms were no longer considered enough. Only revolution, the People's Will assassins were saying, could bring about the drastic changes Russia needed to become a modern nation. Liberals like Alexander II were bound to be trampled in the violent tracks.

But how would revolution happen in a backward country such as Russia? Some, the Narodniks, for example, saw Russia's peasantry as the potentially decisive force to bring about a violent overthrow of the existing system; others saw terrorist attacks as the way to propel Russia's ramshackle empire into chaos, from which a new order would somehow emerge. Theorist P. N. Tkachev speculated in the 1870s about what it would take to bring about a total collapse of his country. His conclusion? "Not much . . . Two or three military defeats . . . some peasant uprisings . . . open revolt in the capital."

He might have been describing events in Russia in 1917, some forty years later.

Needless to say, these terrorist conspirators (vividly captured on paper in Fyodor Dostoevsky's novel *The Devils*) did not bring about actual revolution. The only change they managed to achieve, especially after the failure of an attempt to assassinate Czar Alexander III in 1887, was to make the government more reactionary and repressive. The rigid autocracy of Alexander's son Nicholas II, with its inflexible rejection of any notion of reform, froze Russia in time politically. By 1900, Lenin's country was in many ways more isolated from the main currents of Europe than at any time since Peter the Great.

In literary terms, the clarion call to revolution had reached its climax earlier, in 1863, with the publication of Narodnik spokesman Nikolai Chernyshevsky's novel *What Is to Be Done?* (Even though it was a novel, it earned its author a lengthy spell of exile in Siberia.) Chernyshevsky called on his fellow intellectuals to lead Russia's toiling masses on a path to socialist revolution, bypassing the capitalist phase of social development that Karl Marx had said was necessary to prepare the way for the working class to seize power and overthrow capitalism's class-based society.

In the novel, Chernyshevsky's two principal enemies are the czarist reactionaries, who are incapable of accepting progressive change; and Russian liberals, who are too slow and cowardly to impose it. Lenin was perhaps seventeen when he first read *What Is to Be Done?* It coincided with some traumatic experiences in his own young life, and became a decisive influence. "It completely transformed my outlook," Lenin wrote later. The book, he said, "taught me how to be a revolutionary." He even stole the title for his own programmatic work on revolution.[14]

Chernyshevsky's work contained one arresting line that Lenin could have adopted as his own motto: "A man with an ardent love of virtue can only be a monster."

* * *

IN A FAMILY of remarkably obedient and orderly children, including the eldest, Alexander, Volodya was a regular discipline problem, often spending hours in the "black chair," the stool in the corner where misbehaving children in the Ulyanov family were sent to sit. At school, his native ability was such that, as Lenin's sister Anna recalled, the *Gymnazia's* headmaster "forgave him certain acts of mischief that he would not so easily have forgiven in respect of others." The headmaster wrote one glowing report after another. Vladimir Ilyich's success in the wider world seemed guaranteed, like that of his equally brilliant brother Alexander.

By 1886, when Vladimir Ilyich turned sixteen, Ilya Ulyanov could look proudly on no fewer than six children on the threshold of rewarding middle-class lives and careers. Then came the watershed event that changed the Ulyanov family, and Vladimir's life, forever.

It's not clear exactly when his brother Alexander, who had entered St. Petersburg University in mathematics and physics, fell under the spell of a cell of revolutionaries headed by Orest Govorukhin and Pyotr Shevyrev.[15] The assassination of the czar five years earlier had precipitated an extensive crackdown by his reactionary son Alexander III, and the radical revolutionary impulse among groups such as the Narodniks had all but died away. Then Alexander Ilyich and his friends hatched their own amateurish plot to revive the revolution by killing the czar. Instead, the czar's secret police, the Okhrana, easily caught on to the threads of the plot and arrested the would-be assassins one by one, including Alexander Ilyich. On May 8, 1887, he was hanged in Shlisselburg Prison in St. Petersburg—but not before he was permitted to kneel before his mother and beg her forgiveness.

It was a family tragedy. Vladimir's father was not alive to see it unfold; he had died of a sudden stroke the January before last, in 1886. Perhaps the death of that traditional but warm and understanding

father figure had something to do with Alexander's turn toward revolution and violence. It is certainly true that Vladimir Ilyich's turn
against religion came shortly after his father's death.

Yet the death of his beloved older brother was more traumatic for
Vladimir, and the impact greater. It is very likely that he was already
exposed to radical revolutionary ideas before Alexander went to the
gallows. The official story told years later was that he turned to his
sister afterward and said stoically, "No, we must not take that road,"
meaning solo assassination.

There's no reason to believe that version, though. More likely is
the one given by his tutor Vera Kashkadamova, in which, in the same
stoical vein and showing the same political sympathies as his brother,
Vladimir Ilyich exclaimed, "It must mean he had to act like this; he
couldn't act in any other way."[16]

So, how would Vladimir Ilyich act, in the shadow of his brother's
death? He was barely seventeen. He had been admitted to Kazan Imperial University; he seemed likely to study law. A career leading to
steady government service lay open to him if he kept his nose clean
and avoided political controversy. Yet, for the brother of a convicted
and executed would-be regicide, that would not be easy. Indeed, the
entire family found themselves ostracized in Simbirsk. Virtually the
only person who would speak to the Ulyanovs was Vladimir Ilyich's
former schoolmaster from the *Gymnazia*, who remained supportive
of young Vladimir through thick and thin, even in the darkest days
leading up to and following Alexander Ilyich's execution.

The schoolmaster's name? Fyodor Kerensky. His own son, Alexander, grew up almost side by side with Vladimir Ilyich—the same
Alexander Kerensky who would become Lenin's most dangerous
opponent.

After his brother's death (or, rather, his martyrdom, in Vladimir's
eyes), Lenin's turn to revolutionary radicalism was probably inevitable. So was his turn to Marxism. Leading the way was former Narodnik Georgi Plekhanov, now in exile in Switzerland, who organized
the first Marxist political circle and who proclaimed that Marx's the-

ory of proletarian revolution was the best path to revolution in Russia. By the mid-1890s, Marxism would be the dominant ideology among the Russian intelligentsia.

In some ways, this was a strange development. Marx had spent a lifetime despising Russia and all its works. He saw the country as a cesspool of ignorance and reaction, rather than a possible centrifuge for socialist revolution. Marx had scornfully dismissed peasants everywhere as a "sack of potatoes; all different shapes but all the same." In his view, revolution was possible only in a country with a fully developed capitalist economy and a widespread working class; Russia flunked on both counts. For Marx, it might take at least another forty or fifty years of struggle before the working class in western Europe was even ready for socialism. The idea of Russia getting there first appeared ridiculous.

Yet Plekhanov and his colleagues were saying: take another look. Marx had been wrong. Russia was indeed well advanced on the capitalist path, with growing numbers of factories and railroads crisscrossing the country, and a revolutionary vanguard indeed taking shape. This was Russia's tiny but steadily growing urban working class. Plekhanov urged his fellow Russian revolutionaries to put their faith in the embryonic proletariat in cities such as Moscow and St. Petersburg.

With the right leadership, Russia's industrial workers would be poised to strike. There would be no need to wait for the long-drawn-out process of capitalist development, as had happened in the West. And forget about the peasants, the Marxists were telling their Narodnik rivals. Revolution would come to Russia's cities first, and would then spread steadily as the working class took over the reins of power.

Marx had been right about revolution but wrong about Russia. That was the position of Russian Marxists by the time Lenin first read *The Communist Manifesto* in 1890–91 and took his first steps toward becoming an orthodox Marxist. Proving his intellectual master wrong about his home country became Lenin's self-appointed task, in the one scholarly work he wrote in his life (his one book that is comparable to Woodrow Wilson's output): *Development of Capitalism in Russia*. The book was a long time in gestation; it appeared in print only in 1899, by which time Lenin's life had gone through many drastic changes.

The first had come with his expulsion from the Kazan Imperial University for participating in an antigovernment demonstration only months after matriculating, in 1887. He withdrew to his mother's large estate at Kokushkino, a comfortable country residence she had inherited from her wealthy father, Alexander Blank, ostensibly to continue his plans to study law but also, increasingly, to immerse himself in the radical literature of the era. It was at Kokushkino that he first read *The Communist Manifesto* and began translating it into Russian; it was at Kokushkino that he learned to read English and also read the works of Georgi Plekhanov, which, paradoxically, were rather easier to find in Russian than the works of the Marxists' Narodnik rivals.[17]

By January 1892, Lenin emerged from this period of enforced study with enough knowledge of Russian ecclesiastical and police law to receive a first-class certificate from St. Petersburg University and to join a local law firm in the Ulyanovs' new hometown, Samara, with the title of assistant barrister. On the surface, he was a promising young white-collar professional. Beneath the surface, however, he was a budding Marxist revolutionary, waiting to join whatever conspiratorial circle seemed most committed to overthrowing the empire of the czars.

He did not wait long. In 1893, he moved to St. Petersburg, where he worked as a barrister and continued his Marxist studies. There he met Julius Martov, later leader of the Marxist Menshevik Party, and in 1895 he obtained permission from the government to travel abroad to Switzerland, where he finally met Georgi Plekhanov and his circle.

The two would later be bitter rivals—but in Lenin's life, virtually everyone who did not become his unquestioning acolyte and disciple would become a bitter rival. For now, though, Lenin followed in the ideological path the older man had laid out. Russia was ripe for revolution, they both believed; the only question was how to find the right levers to bring it about. When Lenin returned to Russia, he founded his first political organization, the St. Petersburg League of Struggle for the Emancipation of the Working Class. It had a short shelf life. In a few months, the czar's police rounded up and arrested Lenin and the group's other members. Lenin was sentenced to the dismal fate that he and virtually every other Russian rebel against the czar had to face sooner or later—namely, exile to Siberia.

We have to note: exile, not imprisonment or execution. By contrast with the way Lenin himself dealt with dissidents or opponents when he came to power, the czarist government was remarkably lax and quaintly old-fashioned in the way it chose to punish those who plotted its overthrow. From this perspective, the hanging of Alexander Ulyanov and his colleagues was exceptional. Declared enemies of the regime usually got herded out to the desolate wastelands of Siberia for a specified time, even as the Marxist tracts that inspired them were allowed to circulate more or less freely in Russia. (The czarist police focused more on conventional antigovernment pamphlets by Narodnik or anarchist writers.) Hence, a strange irony: by 1900, Siberia had become as much an incubator of revolution inside Russia as the radical Russian circles in Western cities such as Geneva and London where Plekhanov and his friends talked and wrote and talked and talked.

That irony certainly applied to Lenin. His "exile" sent him to the town of Shushenskoye, near the confluence of the Yenisei and Big Shush Rivers, and known to other exiles as the Siberian Italy because of its relatively mild climate. A lighthearted Lenin even wrote a poem that began, "Shu-shu-shu, the place where I will eventually find peace," when he learned this would be his home for the next three years, although he never finished his first and last effort at verse.[18]

Nor did the authorities disappoint him in another matter. Lenin was allowed to have his fiancée, Nadezhda Krupskaya, join him in Shushenskoye. "Nadya" Krupskaya was herself a budding revolutionary and a member of the St. Petersburg League. She had been given her own sentence of exile, to the more remote town of Ufa, but the czarist authorities gave her permission to join Vladimir Ilyich. They would also be joined by her mother, who voluntarily moved to Shushenskoye to be with her daughter, something unimaginable in the later days of Lenin's own gulag, or Stalin's.

In July 1898, Nadya and the twenty-eight-year-old Volodya were married by a Russian Orthodox priest. From that point on she would be an inseparable part of his life: his housekeeper and cook, his secretary, his all-around workhorse, even when Lenin turned to other women as mistresses. Nadya Krupskaya would follow him unfailingly down the revolutionary path, until the very end.

The three years of enforced sabbatical from political organizing allowed Lenin to finish his latest work, *The Development of Capitalism in Russia*. When his sentence ended in January 1900 and he returned to St. Petersburg, he was something of a minor intellectual celebrity. An *Encyclopedic Dictionary* published that year gave him a brief entry, listing him as an economist.[19]

Yet Lenin's real desire was to be known as a revolutionary, not as an academic: a professional revolutionary whose career would be to create the conditions—ideological, organizational, and political—in which the existing order in his country could be destroyed and a new, Marxist order could take its place, as prelude to the larger, worldwide workers' revolution Marx and Friedrich Engels had confidently predicted. To this task Lenin brought a sense of fierce urgency that the other Russian Marxists, accustomed to talking revolution while surrounded by vodka bottles and tea samovars until late in the night, never felt. During his exile, he had read *Evolutionary Socialism*, by the German Marxist Eduard Bernstein, which presented the argument that current trends in bourgeois Europe—the development of trade unions, the rise in workers' wages, the creation of government social welfare, such as Germany's workers' compensation program—indicated that capitalism itself would inevitably lead to a peaceful transition to socialism, without the need for violent revolution.

Upon reading Bernstein's book, socialists across Europe breathed a sigh of relief. Now they could feel free to push the socialist agenda from within the existing system as organized political parties, instead of trying to impose it by force from outside. Lenin, however, reacted to Bernstein's optimistic message with hostility bordering on fury. His deepest worry was not that Bernstein was wrong about the future of capitalism, including capitalism in Russia, but that he was right. With the dawn of the new century, czarist Russia was feeling the first stirrings of the economic "takeoff" that had swept parts of western Europe, including Germany, during the previous century. A growing economy that expanded Russia's tiny bourgeois class and made its working class feel comfortable and well fed would do more to derail the hopes for a Marxist-led revolution in Russia than anything the czarist government could do.

In a short article entitled "Urgent Tasks of Our Movement," Lenin penned his response to Bernstein's thesis. His essay warned that Russia's labor movement would slide into passivity and "become petty and inevitably bourgeois" unless a strong revolutionary vanguard seized control of that movement, a vanguard of full-time professionals "who shall devote to the revolution not only their spare evenings but the whole of their lives."[20]

Stealing the title from his favorite novel, Lenin turned his short article into the core argument of his first important revolutionary tract, *What Is to Be Done?* The book is a fierce blast against those of his Russian Marxist colleagues who were hinting that it might be best to wait to allow the Russian labor movement to develop its own momentum, like the labor movements in western European countries, in order to advance the socialist agenda. That would be a catastrophe, Lenin averred, at least as far as bringing on a truly Marxist, or "social-democratic," revolution was concerned. The wait-and-see approach would result in mere trade unionism, a movement that restricted itself to getting higher wages and better working conditions, and nothing else.

There cannot "yet be Social-Democratic consciousness among the workers" unless it comes from outside, from an elite leadership dedicated to provoking revolution and keeping the Russian working class on course through constant political activism and agitation. *"In no other way,"* Lenin wrote emphatically, "can the masses be trained in political consciousness and revolutionary activity"—which means, in turn, that "to conduct such activity is one of the most important functions of international Social-Democracy as a whole."

Why hadn't this happened already? "We must blame ourselves," Lenin wrote to his fellow Russian Marxists, and "our remoteness from the mass movement." From now on, he proclaimed, they must put themselves at the head of that movement and never falter from the revolutionary course.[21]

What Is to Be Done? marks the birth of Marxism-Leninism, and the idea that revolution comes not through waiting for the right historical conditions. It comes from a dedicated elite bending history to their will, rather than the other way around. It is also the first work Vladimir Ilyich Ulyanov signed with his new revolutionary nom de plume, "N. Lenin." (Later, he changed it to "V. I. Lenin.")

The stage was now set for the rest of Lenin's career. With the exception of two years in 1905–6, he would spend the next fifteen years, until 1917, outside Russia while he implemented his program—not against the czarist government but against his fellow Marxists. When he often spoke of being surrounded on all sides by enemies, he was referring to them in addition to the czarist police. His first goal as a leader of revolution was to bring his colleagues into his line of thinking or to crush them out of political existence. Starting in 1902, that was exactly what he set out to do, even as he drew around him a small band of dedicated followers who would form the core of his Bolshevik Party, including a fiery middle-class Jewish intellectual named Lev Davidovich Bronstein who would be better known by the revolutionary pseudonym he adopted soon after meeting Lenin, Leon Trotsky; and a Georgian dropout from a theological seminary named Iosif Vissarionovich Dzhugashvili, also better known by his revolutionary pseudonym, Joseph Stalin.

*   *   *

AS COPIES OF *What Is to Be Done?* were rolling off the presses of the publisher Lenin had found in Stuttgart, Germany, Woodrow Wilson was assuming the mantle of president of Princeton University. Over the next half decade, Wilson would be catapulted into national fame not only as a distinguished scholar but also as a spokesman for a new forward-looking approach to American education. He would also be propelled into a controversy that would split Princeton and its alumni down the middle for decades to come—a controversy that would reveal Wilson at his self-righteous and vindictive worst.

Attending his installation as president of Princeton proved to be the hottest ticket on the East Coast. Mark Twain, J. P. Morgan, and Booker T. Washington were all there. President Theodore Roosevelt himself was supposed to attend, but a trolley car accident delayed his arrival at the campus until it was too late.[22]

Even critics admitted that Wilson's early years at Princeton were an impressive success. He recruited top young talent for the faculty; he transformed and modernized the undergraduate curriculum. He also assumed "unprecedented control over faculty affairs," as one historian has put it. "During his eight-year tenure, Wilson was not reluctant to exercise any of his new powers."[23]

Most important, he reinforced his own Progressive idea that the four years of college were to be preparation for assuming life's responsibilities as well as training for the mind. He wanted his Princeton graduates to be ready to be "actors on the stage and stand in the midst of life," with the "largeness of view, of judgment, and easy knowledge of men" that went beyond old-fashioned book learning.[24]

Yet that largeness of view and judgment, that knowledge of men, was precisely what Princeton's own president lacked, and this failing was in full display in the battle royal that developed over the location of a new graduate college for the university.

The dean of the graduate faculty was Andrew West, whose chief credential consisted of having very wealthy friends who gave generously to Princeton. In 1907, he conceived a plan for a new building to house the graduate college off campus. The plan included a lavish budget and a distinguished architect to design the building. Wilson opposed the plan at once. He had his own plan for completely redesigning the campus, one that incorporated the graduate facilities with the new quadrangles for the undergraduates. The resulting quarrel was one of those tedious squabbles that develop in academic institutions and that are soon forgotten a few years later—but Wilson refused to allow this one to be forgotten. His fight with Dean West and his fight over the quads that both students and alumni opposed became more than power struggles. They became a crusade pitting right (President Wilson) against wrong (everyone else, including the board of trustees, who rejected his quads plan).

By 1909, the former star of Princeton was the most hated man on campus, someone who had polarized the university and its board into two irreconcilable factions. In April 1910, Wilson gave a speech that compared his battle with the board to the cause of democracy in America. "What we cry out against is that a handful of conspicuous men have thrust a cruel hand among the heartstrings of the masses of men upon whose blood and energy they are subsisting." This is what was happening at Princeton and other universities, he proclaimed to his audience. The same "handful of conspicuous men" (including President William Howard Taft, who strongly supported Dean West) were corrupting the very institutions of learning, "to forget their common origins, forget their universal sympathies, and join a class— and no class can ever serve America."[25]

Later, even Wilson admitted that the speech had been "a stupid blunder." It gave plenty of ammunition to his enemies. It was also a foretaste of the later Wilson: the man who stubbornly dug in on a position he believed to be right, to the point where those who opposed him were not just wrong but evil. "The most conspicuously contemptible names in history . . . If I did not despise them, I would feel sorry for them" is the way he would later refer to political opponents.[26] This disturbing blend of self-righteousness and paranoia is one others would get to know all too well at the Paris Peace Conference and on the floor of the U.S. Senate in a vote on the League of Nations.

In the ensuing uproar after his speech, it was apparent to Wilson and his wife that his days at Princeton were numbered. It was time to "look for a new career," he informed her, and the one that beckoned most was in politics.

It was clear he had the physical and mental gifts for it. He was a dynamic speaker, a writer with a flair for phrasing. On issues that mattered, he could display irresistible drive and energy combined with the power to charm when necessary. (Unfortunately, he didn't find it necessary often enough.) Even more, Wilson felt his scholarly work at Princeton had given him the background he needed for a political career. He had finally finished his magnum opus, the groundbreaking *Constitutional Government in the United States*.

More than any other work by a prominent American political scientist, the book embodied an approach to understanding American governance derived from the early nineteenth-century German philosopher Georg Wilhelm Friedrich Hegel. Wilson had been exposed to Hegel during his years at Johns Hopkins, where his teachers had been steeped in the German theory of government and the philosophy of history. Wilson wrote to his then-fiancée, "Hegel used to search for—and in most cases found it seems to me—the fundamental psychological facts of society." This was reflected in Wilson's 1890 work, *The State*, which became a standard textbook until the 1920s, and in *Constitutional Government*, which is largely an iteration of Hegel's theory of the state, in an American guise.[27]

What was Hegel saying that appealed so powerfully to Wilson? Above all, Hegel saw government, or the state, as the direct reflection of a society's historical evolution. The higher the level of that evolution, the more active and interventionist that government must necessarily become. In that sense, government, including American government, can have no legitimate limits placed on its power, since that power is actually the expression of the objective will of the people. Otherwise, it would not exist at all.

Indeed, the state is itself the embodiment of human progress. "The State is the Divine Idea as it exists on earth," Hegel wrote. Even in a democratic society such as the United States, those who exercise its functions have the responsibility to wield its influence in keeping with that faith in progress.

Hegel's vision of the power of government to shape society for a better future, and of the need to reform or strip away those institutions that stand in the way of the forward march of history, would be the foundation for Wilson's presidential ideal. It underpinned his lifelong belief that, in the end, the federal government could do no objective harm, and in the fundamental rightness of America's role in world history. "Here is a great people," he once said, "great with every force that has ever beaten in the lifeblood of mankind . . . The United States has the distinction of carrying certain lights for the world that the world has never so distinctly seen before . . . of liberty, principle, and justice."[28]

It was a heady worldview—at least as potent as Lenin's at about the same time: the power of government to do only good, a power that had no legitimate limits, a power that would lead a great people to their irresistible historical destiny. These principles made Wilson one of the outstanding exponents of American Progressivism, and united him with men such as Herbert Croly, Edward Bellamy, and even Wilson's longtime adversary Theodore Roosevelt.

These were also, it has to be said, a far cry from the ideals that had animated America's Founding Fathers: the necessity of limited government and strict formal limits on its powers as the fundamental foundation of freedom. Wilson never went as far as Croly and other Progressives in denouncing those founding ideals as hopelessly out of date, even socially debilitating, in the modern world. But he did see them as reflecting the narrow historical circumstances of the thirteen colonies in the late eighteenth century, and not some larger insight into human nature and the permanent character of the relation between the individual and government—let alone relevant to America as it had developed by 1908. As Hegel had taught him, there was no fixed human nature, anyway, and no fixed set of political principles that applied in all places and at all times.

Wilson's Progressive views had been clearly and concisely set forth in his books. All that was needed next was an opportunity to apply those theories in practice—even though certainly no one could have expected a college professor and university president, no matter how distinguished or dynamic, to have that chance.

Yet, ironically, that's exactly what one national party, the Democratic Party, was looking for.

In 1908, the Democrats had suffered their fourth straight defeat in a presidential election and the third defeat for the man who had come to embody the party for more than twelve years, William Jennings Bryan. Many Democrats now realized that Bryan was part of the problem: once the youthful voice of American Populism and rural small-town virtues, he now seemed anachronistic in a growing, industrializing America. They were looking for a new kind of candidate, one who could assume the mantle of Progressivism that Republicans had adopted since Theodore Roosevelt but that might be a useful way to rally big-city voters to the next Democratic ticket.

The eloquent and vigorous president of Princeton University seemed to be just what the party needed. In fact, Wilson was being considered presidential timber even before he accepted the offer of New Jersey's Democratic bosses to run for the state's governorship in 1908. His lack of political experience made him even more attractive: such a man, they reasoned, would be all the more willing to listen to the wisdom of his party superiors—that is, if he could get his foot in the door of the White House.

The race for governor was the dry run. Starting with his acceptance speech, Wilson used it to outline a political program that not only was Progressive in its policy details, by relying on government to address and solve the many problems society faced, but also raised American politics to a higher, even spiritual level. "We are witnessing a renaissance of public spirit," he proclaimed, "a reawakening of sober public opinion, a revival of the power of the people . . . that makes our thought hark back to the great age in which Democracy was set up in America."

He spoke of government as a matter of "common counsel" rather than competing interests, where "everyone must come into the consultation with the purpose to yield to the general view," that is, the one that most closely adheres to the common interest. American democracy, in short, was about not a multiplicity of views but a single vision embraced by all, with the Democratic Party acting as its political vehicle: as "the instrument of righteousness for the state and for the nation."[29]

In other times or places, this would have been seen as long-winded, overheated rhetoric and nothing more. But in 1908, it struck a chord with New Jersey voters; the state's local bosses delivered the rest. Wilson won the election, beating his Republican rival by more than two to one.

And this was only a prelude to what was to come. Wilson had barely entered the governor's mansion when the Democratic Party leadership began grooming him for the next big contest, the U.S. presidency in 1912. It proved to be an epic struggle. As a virtual political novice, Wilson was running against a sitting president, William Howard Taft, a man with long experience in government and strong support from the monied interests of Wall Street and America's leading industrialists. Indeed, it's doubtful Wilson would have stood a chance if Theodore Roosevelt had not taken a hand in giving him the election.

Furious with Taft's reversal of several of the Progressive reforms Theodore Roosevelt himself had carried out while he was president, Roosevelt turned against his handpicked heir and successor and launched his own, third-party campaign for president, as the candidate of the Bull Moose Party. The resulting split virtually guaranteed Wilson the election, even though he took barely 41 percent of the popular vote. He was the first Democrat elected president in twenty years, and the first southerner since Zachary Taylor, in 1848.

Now he would have the opportunity to carry out the reforms he had advocated and written about for more than two decades. His head was filled with plans and programs, ways to transform America for the better, using the power of the federal government, and to lead the country to that destiny he believed all other nations looked to America to fulfill.

That didn't leave much room for ordinary politicians. When the chairman of the Democratic National Committee came to see him after the election to ask for some political favors, and reminded Wilson that he owed his election to that party and its leadership committee, Wilson coldly cut him down to size.

"Remember that God ordained that I should be the next president of the United States," he told the astonished chairman. "Neither you nor any other mortal could have chosen another president."[30]

In his inauguration speech, he made clear just whom he considered his real constituency: "This is not a day of triumph," he told the crowd gathered on the steps of the Capitol. "It is a day of dedication. Here muster, not the forces of party, but the forces of humanity. Men's hearts wait upon us, men's lives hang in the balance . . . Who shall live up to the great trust? Who dares to fail to try?"[31]

With God, history, and humanity on his side, what chance did his enemies or detractors have? Wilson figured, none.

There was only one possible stumbling block, one he shared with a friend just before his inauguration.

"It would be the irony of fate if my administration had to deal chiefly with foreign affairs," he said with a wry smile, thinking perhaps that of all the spheres of presidential action, that was one about which he knew the least: he had no interest in foreign countries and no travel or other experience overseas.

In fact, that irony of fate would ruthlessly seek him out and make a shambles of his presidency.

*   *   *

THE YEAR OF Wilson's election also saw the first issue of *Pravda*, the newspaper that would become the principal mouthpiece of Lenin and of the regime he would eventually create.

The launching of *Pravda* came after Lenin had experienced a decade of bruising ideological battles with his fellow Russian revolutionaries, battles in which he wound up being the loser more often than the winner. The result was a grim, battle-scarred Lenin, a harder and more ruthless Lenin than the one who had penned *What Is to Be Done?* The previous Lenin had been primarily an intellectual and polemicist, albeit a peculiarly intense one. Ten years later, he had been transformed into the ringleader for a disciplined band of revolutionaries, terrorists, and underworld criminals akin to Dostoevsky's *The Devils*, all waiting for their opportunity to seize power by any means necessary.

Lenin's first Station of the Cross, as it were, had come in July 1903, with the Social Democratic Labour Party Congress, the gathering of exiled Russian activists from across Europe, who met in Brussels and then in London. Lenin was living in London at the time. Although he and Nadya hated English food, and he could barely speak or read a word of English, Lenin had made their flat in Holford Square a safe haven where he could read and write, and meet with like-minded colleagues, much as Marx had done during his years in London when he was writing *Das Kapital*. Neither man ever noted the strange irony: although both despised bourgeois capitalism and considered its characteristic constitutional democracy a total sham, it was only in despised capitalist countries such as Britain, Germany, and the United States that they were allowed to live in freedom and to speak, write, and even publish what they wished—London was the home of the editorial offices for *Iskra*, the official organ of the Russian Social Democratic Labour Party—even when they preached the destruction of the very society that protected them.

Lenin did not feel much comradeship with socialists of the British variety. Although he struggled to read the writings of their current leading intellectual lights, the economists Sidney and Beatrice Webb, he considered them revolutionary wimps and far too accustomed to the comforts of bourgeois life to be of much use in fomenting the workers' revolution. One incident particularly disgusted him. On a visit to a church near Holford Square, he and Nadya found a congregation of socialists all praying to God. In Lenin's mind, true socialism excluded any possibility of belief in a divine being. As he wrote later, "Every religious idea, every idea of God, even flirting with the idea of God, is unutterable vileness . . . Millions of sins, filthy deeds, acts of violence and physical contagions . . . are far less dangerous than the subtle, spiritual idea of God."[32] In Lenin's view, wherever the idea of God took root, there was the danger of counterrevolutionary reaction and, even more important, of competition with socialism for human beings seeking redemption and ultimate freedom. In short, there can be no "heaven on earth" when there's still the possibility of a heaven outside it. For Lenin, therefore, one of the most important tasks of his revolutionary regime would be to wipe out any trace of organized religion or religious belief, before it distracted people with a different kind of salvation, the salvation of God.

At the gathering of the Congress of the Socialist International in 1903, however, Lenin's task was far simpler. First, it was to lead the Russian delegates to reject the incrementalistic views of Eduard Bernstein and his followers, and second, to get them to embrace his declared view that the Social Democratic Labour Party needed to restrict membership to full-time dedicated revolutionaries, and revolutionaries only. The first resolution passed easily; the second proved more difficult. Opposing him was Julius Martov, the former Plekhanov disciple who pushed for a broader-based party with more popular participation. Lenin's proposal lost 28 to 22; even the fiery young revolutionary Leon Trotsky—who had met Lenin in London the previous year and deeply admired the author of *What Is to Be Done?*—voted against his revolutionary hero.

Lenin did score one victory, however. By 22 votes to 20, with 2 abstentions, he and his followers secured control over the party's main political media organ, *Iskra*. From that point on, Lenin and his followers would dub themselves the party's Bolsheviks, or "Majority"; Martov and those who had voted against giving Lenin control of *Iskra* would be known as the Mensheviks, or "Minority." It was a clever ploy, making Lenin's faction look like the dominant faction within the party when it had had fewer votes all along.[33]

In fact, Lenin's views were not finding much support among Marxists in other countries, either. Poland's Rosa Luxemburg penned a furious, and prescient, attack on Lenin's approach to revolution early the following year, in 1904, warning that his belief in entrusting leadership to a dedicated but small revolutionary elite, later known as "democratic centralism," would inevitably lead to tyranny, or worse. "Nothing will more surely enslave a young labor movement to an intellectual elite hungry for power than this bureaucratic strait-jacket," she wrote.[34] The implication of her essay—entitled "Leninism or Marxism?"—was that true socialists had to choose either one or the other ideology. The two were ultimately incompatible. Lenin, of course, disagreed. He saw that entrusting all power over the party to a small elite was the only way to bring revolution to a backward country such as Russia. In any case, he was about to get the chance to test his theory. Less than a year after Luxemburg's article appeared, the streets of St. Petersburg exploded in the 1905 Revolution.

After the massacre of Bloody Sunday on January 22, 1905, strikes spread across Russia's cities with the spontaneous appearance of work-ers' committees, or soviets (the first time that word entered the po-litical vocabulary). By early November, the czar reluctantly granted a constitution and the establishment of a parliamentary Duma. The crescendo of general strikes finally forced the government into mil-itary action: it suppressed all demonstrations and arrested former Narodnik agitators, now dubbed Socialist Revolutionaries, and their Marxist Social Democrat counterparts around the country. The year 1905 proved to be an exercise in frustration and disappointment: it was a year when Lenin saw his opportunity to lead the revolutionary struggle in his home country come and go, and when even his return to Russia to mobilize his followers wasn't sufficient to prevent failure.

Oddly enough, it was the Mensheviks who wound up with their reputation enhanced by the events of 1905. Martov and his followers had rallied around the strikers and demonstrators in the early days of the revolution, while Lenin and the Bolsheviks had hung back, thinking that the revolution was still too much in the bourgeois stage and that the opportunity to mobilize Russia's working class had not yet come. Too late, Lenin realized his mistake; he did not manage to get back to Russia until November, when the popular uprisings were winding down and the forces of czarist reaction were beginning to gather momentum. The Bolsheviks became involved in full-scale violence in the streets of Moscow, with Lenin urging his followers to kill policemen and set off bombs. (Lenin himself avoided any street fighting, staying safely in his apartment.)

By the year's end, it was all over. Lenin remained in Russia, as part of a general amnesty that had been passed by the government, but there was nothing for him to do; Russia seemed set on a very different course. In May 1906, elections were held for the first Duma. Although its franchise was suffocatingly narrow, and although Czar Nicholas and his advisers had made sure that its powers would be almost nil and largely symbolic, it was still a significant step toward a new, more open, and even democratic Russia. The Mensheviks, too, cashed in on their new reputation in the next Congress, in Stockholm in April, forcing through a resolution reunifying the Menshevik and Bolshevik factions. Lenin and his would-be revolutionary elite, now permanently reduced to a powerless minority, had no choice but to submit.[35]

By now, Lenin had also lost *Iskra*. His old mentor Plekhanov had reversed his previous support, and editorship of the periodical passed from Lenin's and the Bolsheviks' hands to those of their Menshevik opponents. The Mensheviks also reversed the previous position of the party, advocated by Lenin, of boycotting the Duma elections. Lenin belatedly came around to the same view, but now his fellow Bolsheviks, led by A. A. Bogdanov, turned against *him*. At the next party Congress, in August 1907, they voted against Lenin, upholding the boycott by a vote of 14 to 1. They even threw him out as their leader at the Congress and put Bogdanov in his place. The irony was that Lenin now had to join forces with the despised Mensheviks to defeat his own Bolsheviks in the final vote to lift the boycott.

By then, though, Lenin had been thoroughly humiliated, and the opportunity for the Social Democratic Labour Party to gain a strong foothold in the present and future Dumas had passed. From now until 1917, socialist-minded leadership in Russia passed to the Socialist Revolutionaries, led by their chief theoretician, Viktor Chernov; and the fiery young lawyer Alexander Kerensky. Those Social Democrats who would take key seats in the Duma were Mensheviks. The Bolsheviks would be nowhere, out of influence and out of favor—Lenin most of all.

After a year and a half of living in fruitless hiding in his home country, at the end of 1907 Lenin headed back into exile, this time in Finland. He now faced a serious rival for Bolshevik leadership in Alexander Bogdanov, and much of the discussion among the frustrated revolutionaries who gathered at Vladimir and Nadya's dacha outside Helsinki centered on Bogdanov's ideas and initiatives, not Lenin's. As 1908 waned, Lenin learned that the czar's police were again on his trail. He and Nadya fled to safety in Sweden; from there, he wound up returning to Switzerland, to Geneva, where a hostile Plekhanov and his circle still reigned supreme. For Lenin, it seemed the end of the revolutionary road. "I've got the feeling that I've come here to lie in my grave," he confessed to Nadya. To a friend, he added, "I know Russia so little. Simbirsk, Kazan, St. Petersburg and that's about it."[36]

Worse was to come. As part of the general easing of government policy from extreme reaction, the czar had appointed a new liberal-minded prime minister, P. A. Stolypin. Stolypin began pushing for serious reforms of Russia's economy, especially in rural areas, with plans for land reform that would let the peasants own more of the land they worked and tilled, and for the formation of rudimentary institutions of local self-government. Nothing threatened to derail the hopes for violent revolution in Russia more than concrete reforms of its civic, economic, and social institutions along Western lines, and Lenin saw this at once. "If Stolypin's policy is continued," he wrote in 1908, "then the agrarian structure of Russia will become completely bourgeois."[37] Such a change would spell the end of Russian feudalism and its autocratic ruling class—and therefore doom any attempt to replace Russia's czarist autocracy with a Marxist autocracy.

Until Stolypin's tragic death in September 1911, his agrarian reforms had a profound effect. By 1917, Russian peasants owned nearly 90 percent of the arable land in European Russia.[38] If any sector of Russian society was bound to oppose efforts to socialize and collectivize all means of production, it was going to be Russia's peasants. It was in these years, 1908–12, that one particular follower of Lenin would rise to prominence, Iosif Vissarionovich Dzhugashvili, better known by his revolutionary name Joseph Stalin. While Trotsky was Lenin's chief spokesman and intellectual conscience, the former seminary student from Georgia would become his chief muscle—and bank robber.

In these lean years, the Bolsheviks turned to crime to raise the funds they needed to stay alive as a movement, and the man who emerged as the John Dillinger of the Leninist faction was Stalin. "Sometimes a scoundrel is useful to our party," Lenin wrote, "precisely because he is a scoundrel." Stalin and a henchman of his, named Koma, led a series of raids on local banks. With the booty, Lenin was able to build his own secret stash of funds separate from that controlled by the Social Democratic Labour Party. Even when the party found out and ordered Lenin to stop, he ignored them. In those years, Lenin's Bolsheviks became a truly criminal organization, not only in the eyes of the czarist police, the Okhrana, but for real: a Marxist mafia with Lenin as its don and godfather, and with the kind of ruthless figures, such as Stalin, who would come in handy in establishing Bolshevik rule by force.

They would need all the help they could get. By 1909, there were only five or six Bolshevik committees operating anywhere in Russia.[39] By 1912—the same year Woodrow Wilson was moving steadily toward being elected president of the United States—Lenin was on the verge of being expelled from the Marxist party he had helped to found. The Bolsheviks were, in the words of Robert Conquest, "a small, defeated sect" in a Social Democratic Labour Party whose entire membership in Russia (according to Leon Trotsky's estimate) numbered perhaps ten thousand. As one of Lenin's closest associates in those years, Vyacheslav M. Molotov (later Soviet foreign minister), confessed many years later, "The First World War found our [Bolshevik] Party in a very weak state, its organization not connected but scattered, and with a very small membership."[40]

The only thing that could save the revolution, Lenin wrote in 1913, would be a war between Austria and Russia. "But it's scarcely likely that Franz Josef and Nikolasha [Lenin's nickname for the czar he despised] would grant us this pleasure."[41]

Then that was exactly what happened.

All the same, the war that began in 1914 came as a dismaying shock to Lenin, and not just because he was nearly arrested as an enemy alien and then had to flee from Austrian Poland. Nor was it because the Great Powers of Europe were now at one another's throats. That such a conflict was inevitable would be the thesis he would develop into *Imperialism: The Highest Stage of Capitalism* as armies and navies clashed by night and day.

What shocked Lenin was how quickly socialist parties of every nation—supposedly his brothers in arms in fomenting a workers' revolution—embraced their countries' cause as their cause and that of the workers they claimed to speak for. In Germany, Britain, Austria, and France, leftist deputies joined forces with their conservative and right-wing deputies to mobilize for war. When Lenin learned that Germany's Social Democrats had approved war credits, he refused to believe it, and assumed it was a government lie—until he discovered his mistake.[42]

For Lenin the Marxist, it was a disillusioning blow. For Lenin the revolutionary and terrorist, however, it confirmed his belief that his was the only possible path to overthrowing the capitalist order, not just in Russia but around the world. As armies, including Russia's, mobilized in July and August 1914, Lenin still believed that the revolutionary project he had devoted his life to fulfilling was possible.

But how was he going to play the leading role that he believed he was destined to play in bringing about the revolution from his exile fastness in Switzerland? This was the problem that would consume his every waking hour for nearly all of the next three years.

*   *   *

THE COMING OF war in 1914 had dismayed Woodrow Wilson, too, but for very different reasons. The sight of the supposedly civilized world consuming itself in a conflict that threatened "an injury [to] civilization itself which can never be atoned for or repaired," as he would put it in his December 18, 1916, peace note, was a shocking betrayal of the principles in which he had invested himself. It also came as a shock to see the rash prediction he had made to a friend shortly before his inauguration, about fate forcing him to deal with a crisis in foreign affairs, suddenly come true.

The year and a half since his inauguration had been focused entirely on domestic policy and reforms such as the Revenue Act of 1913, the Federal Reserve Act, and the creation of the Federal Trade Commission. The latter came into being in September 1914, even as French and British armies clashed with the Germans along the Marne. From that point on, the war and, above all, keeping America out of war became the top priority of Wilson's presidency.

Yet Wilson also faced the same personal, almost existential, problem as Lenin. Like the Russian revolutionary, the American president was convinced that this global conflict had thrust upon him a world-historical role, had given him a personal destiny to fulfill. His reading of Hegel had shown him the inevitable direction of history and his own place in it, just as Marx had shown that direction to Lenin.*

But how were the two men to influence events directly, shape them in the right direction, when both of them were, though for very

---

* This was no mere coincidence. Hegel had had an enormous influence on Marx and Marx's theory of history. In addition, during the early days of the war, Lenin began reading Hegel with fresh eyes, and became convinced that it was impossible to understand Marx's logic of revolution without understanding Hegel first.

different reasons, removed from the center of the action? That was the frustrating puzzle that would consume each man for more than two and a half years as Europe consumed itself in war.

Then, in 1917, very unexpectedly, the German General Staff gave both of them their chance.

NEUTRALITY AT BAY

The submarines will pursue me to the grave.
—THEOBALD VON BETHMANN-HOLLWEG

BERLIN, JANUARY 1917

THE TYPICAL GERMAN submarine at the start of 1917 was a crude instrument for transforming world history. Just over two hundred feet long and barely twelve feet wide, it slept between twenty-five and thirty-five crewmen in a space not much larger than a double-decker city bus. Aft were two diesel-electric motors, which charged batteries that allowed the subs to run silently on the surface at fourteen or fifteen knots, or at less than ten knots when submerged. The charging produced clouds of explosive hydrogen gas, but that was just one of the hazards a U-boat captain had to worry about. If any seawater touched the primitive batteries the boat used to run underwater, it produced deadly chlorine gas that could overwhelm the entire crew in that cramped space.

If that wasn't enough to make the U-boat a death trap, there was no diving gear and no way to escape if something went wrong. That made serving on a U-boat one of the deadliest posts of the First World War. Throughout that war, 10 percent of British soldiers and 17 percent of German soldiers wound up being killed in action. By contrast, the death rate for U-boat crews was 30 percent.

At the U-boat's prow sat its torpedo tubes, and twelve torpedoes. Even though its electric batteries could barely keep the craft submerged for more than two hours at a time, that was long enough to turn this seagoing death trap into a potentially decisive weapon of war. Its ability to sink a ship without warning while leaving that ship's crew to die on the high seas could, if repeated often enough, strike a mortal blow to the Allied war effort.

The German High Command knew this. That was why, on January 9, 1917, Ludendorff shoved through the decision to restart unrestricted submarine warfare, commencing on the last day of the month.

On December 22, 1916, the chief of the German Admiralty staff, Adm. Henning von Holtzendorff, had composed a memorandum that became the pivotal document for justifying Germany's resumption of unrestricted U-boat warfare. Holtzendorff had concluded that breaking Britain's back would require sinking six hundred thousand tons of shipping per month, a figure based on a February 1916 study by Dr. Richard Fuss. Fuss had hypothesized that if Germany sent Allied and neutral merchant shipping to the bottom of the ocean at that rate, Britain would run out of ships and be forced to sue for peace within six months—well before the Americans could intervene decisively in the war. Even if the "disorganized and undisciplined" Americans did intervene, Holtzendorff assured the Kaiser, "I give your Majesty my word as an officer, that not one American will land on the Continent."

The submarines were ready and waiting for the final order. As 1917 dawned, Germany had a fleet of 105 submarines ready for action: 46 with the High Seas Fleet; 23 based in Flanders; another 23 based in the Mediterranean, along with 10 in the Baltic; and 3 based with Germany's ally Turkey, in Constantinople. Fresh construction in the shipyards at Kiel, on the North Sea, ensured that, even with moderate to heavy losses, at least 200 submarines would be available for the entirety of 1917.[1]

All that was needed was the will to give the order—and on January 9, 1917, the Kaiser was ready.

When Bethmann-Hollweg arrived at the imperial headquarters at Pless on that dark and dreary day, he found that the Kaiser had already made up his mind. On Wednesday evening, the Kaiser, "with unexpected suddenness, convinced himself that unrestricted submarine warfare was imperative and declared himself decisively in its favor, even should the chancellor refuse." Bethmann-Hollweg, ill with a cold and deeply depressed because he would have no chance to get his boss to change his mind, bowed to the inevitable. He didn't have the heart to point out that, even with the current restrictions, German U-boats were still sinking four hundred thousand tons of shipping a month; nor did he try to cast doubt on Admiral Holtzendorff's latest memorandum, of January 6, which said that, thanks to poor harvests in both Britain and France, Germany could force England to the peace table in just five months, provided that "all ships are free to be sunk."[2]

After two and a half years of struggling to prevent what now seemed inevitable, Bethmann-Hollweg bowed his head and said only, "Given the chiefs of general and admirals' staffs' analysis of the situation, I cannot oppose unrestricted submarine warfare. That means not endorsement but acquiescence in a fait accompli," he added weakly.

Kaiser Wilhelm tossed his head and laughed. "By God, the man still has scruples." Then, with a flourish, the Kaiser signed the order—not realizing that he was about to change the course of the war and the balance of power in world history forever.[3]

The Kaiser has "done great damage to the dynasty," Bethmann-Hollweg later told friends, but he also said that he would not resign. "If I resign now, the emperor will say, 'The chancellor is deserting me in this critical hour.'" Besides, there was the off chance that the generals and admirals were right, that the campaign would "produce a decisive success. Therefore I ultimately consider it preferable, despite all its great danger." His friend Rudolf von Valentini was more pessimistic—and more prescient. He wrote in his diary that the decision, and Bethmann-Hollweg's acquiescence, meant "the end of Germany."[4]

WASHINGTON, JANUARY 31–FEBRUARY 1, 1917

MAKING THE DECISION was one thing; implementing it was another. It would take a few weeks to get all the U-boats out to their appointed stations and for the campaign to commence. It was agreed that Germany would inform the U.S. president of the decision to resume unrestricted warfare the day before the campaign began, a chivalrous if meaningless gesture. By then, it would be too late to recall any American ships at sea or to halt the slaughter that was poised to begin.

So, all through those crucial days in January, as President Wilson was talking peace and offering to mediate a negotiated settlement—one that, as the German ambassador urgently assured Berlin, could only work to Germany's advantage—the Kaiser and his advisers were silently readying themselves for what they hoped would be the final decisive stroke of the war. At 5:00 p.m. on January 31, a nervous Ambassador Bernstorff presented U.S. secretary of state Robert Lansing with the official declaration of unrestricted U-boat warfare against all shipping, both Allied and neutral, in the Atlantic and eastern Mediterranean. Starting on February 1, "all ships met within the zone will be sunk." To be brutally precise, they would be sunk without warning.

The announcement hit Wilson like a bombshell. Bernstorff tried to mitigate the message by passing along his government's claim that if the campaign was successful, it would mean "a speedy end of the horrible and useless bloodshed" that had occurred since 1914. He also said that his government had "complete confidence in the President" and would continue to work with him on developing a formula for a negotiated peace—although Berlin was not prepared to say what terms it would accept. But once the Allies accepted Germany's December 12 offer, the ambassador would be happy to inform Wilson of Germany's terms personally.[5]

Wilson was not fooled by these flimsy fictions, or by the claim that this resumption of submarine attacks was somehow in retaliation for Britain's naval blockade of Germany. He knew that the Germans' decision was a rebuke to his hopes for peace, and a direct challenge to the United States and its declared stance of neutrality. That evening, Lansing recommended an immediate severing of relations with Germany. Yet, even now, Wilson still hesitated. He told his secretary of state that "he was willing to go to any lengths rather than to have the nation actually involved in the conflict." He had other, racialist reasons for trying to steer clear of the cataclysm sweeping Europe. White civilization's ability to dominate the world "rested largely on our ability to keep this country intact," he told Lansing. How would the defeat of Germany, which would be the result if America entered the war on the Entente's side, affect that racial balance of power? "What effect would the depletion of German power have upon the relations of the white and yellow races," he wondered aloud in a Cabinet meeting two days later. "Would the yellow races take advantage of it and attempt to subjugate the white races?"[6]

It was a strange twist of mind even for a man as fascinated by race as Wilson and other Progressives of the era. It also suggests a man struggling to come to grips with a reality very different from the one he had imagined his January 22 speech would bring into being. The next day, February 1, he sat in his office "sad and depressed," his aide Colonel House related. "I feel as if the world had suddenly reversed itself, and after going from east to west, it has begun to go from west to east and I can't get my balance."[7]

Yet, in the end, there was only one decision to be made. When Lansing showed up that afternoon, the three men agreed: it was time to sever relations with Germany, starting immediately.

Wilson assembled Congress for an uncharacteristically brief statement. He read aloud the German declaration, and then told Congress, "I have directed the Secretary of State to announce to His Excellency the German ambassador that all diplomatic relations between the United States and Germany are severed . . ."

He added, "I refuse to believe that it is the intention of the German authorities to do in fact what they have warned us they feel at liberty to do . . . Only overt acts on their part can make me believe it even now."

However, if American ships and American lives were lost "in heedless contravention of the just and reasonable understandings of international law and obvious dictates of humanity," then Wilson promised he would return to ask Congress to take all necessary steps to protect Americans on the high seas. "I can do nothing less."

He added at the end that "we do not desire any hostile conflict with the Imperial German Government." Indeed, "we wish to serve no selfish ends. We seek merely to stand true alike in thought and in action to the immemorial principles" that made America outstanding among nations, with the "right to liberty and justice and unmolested life.

"These are the bases of peace, not war," Wilson concluded. "God grant that we may not be challenged to defend them by acts of willful injustice on the part of the Government of Germany."[8]

With that, he left the Capitol and returned to the White House. A few hours later, Ambassador Bernstorff was asked to hand over his passport, and a few hours after that, he was headed back to Berlin.

There it was. America had taken the first important step toward choosing sides in the Great War that was devastating Europe. How the Allies themselves chose to react would go a long way toward determining how many more steps America (and Woodrow Wilson) would be willing to take before it became the ally that could finally tip the war on the Allied side.

Certainly, the reaction among the Allies' friends in America, including Theodore Roosevelt, was one of delight. Roosevelt gave his full public support to the president, and even offered to raise a full division of volunteers for military service. Yet the former Rough Rider's pleasure was mingled with apprehension. He convinced himself German barbarism was moving Wilson, entirely against his will, more and more into Roosevelt's camp. But if American ships were sunk, and American lives lost, would Wilson have the guts to take the plunge and declare war on Germany? Henry Cabot Lodge, for one, didn't think so. "His one desire is to avoid war at any cost," he wrote to Roosevelt, "simply because he is afraid. He can bully Congressmen"—he

was thinking of Wilson's relentless pushing of his domestic agenda—
"but he flinches in the face of danger, physical, and moral."

Roosevelt's view was even blunter. "I do not believe Wilson will
go to war unless Germany kicks him into it."[9]

The view in Berlin was not much different. That same evening,
the U.S. ambassador to Germany, James Gerard, and his wife dined
with Germany's newly installed foreign minister, Arthur Zimmermann.

A strongly built, handsome man with a magnificent brush mustache, Zimmermann had studied law at the University of Leipzig before entering the German Foreign Service and knew America well,
or believed he did. In 1900, he was recalled from his post in China
(where he had witnessed the Boxer Rebellion firsthand) and returned
to Germany after a cross-country train trip from San Francisco to
New York. That trip sixteen years earlier was his claim to expertise
on all things American, and the one thing he was most certain and
expert about was that America would never go to war, especially under Woodrow Wilson.

"You will see," Zimmermann reassured the American ambassador Gerard, "everything will be all right. America will do nothing
because Wilson is for peace and nothing else. Everything will go on
as before."

Even the news two days later that Wilson had cut off diplomatic
relations with Germany did not faze the confident Zimmermann. "At
last we have gotten rid of this person as peace mediator" was the way
he put it to the German media. Ever since the *Sussex* affair of the previous spring, when the German government, on the heels of sinking
a French liner, signed a pledge agreeing to give adequate warning
before sinking merchant or passenger ships, Zimmermann was quite
convinced he knew Wilson inside out. He saw the American president as a lying hypocrite who "feels and thinks English" and was
steeped in "shamelessness and impudence," but lacked the guts to do
anything but talk.

Besides, Americans *couldn't* go to war: with 1.3 million German immigrants living in the United States, Zimmermann was fond of pointing out, plus another 10 million Americans of German descent, any military move against Germany would trigger a national uprising.

"In case of trouble," he had once warned Gerard half seriously, "there are half a million trained Germans in America who will join the Irish and start a revolution." Gerard retorted, "In that case there are half a million lamp posts to hang them on"—words that would have horrific resonance in less than a year.[10]

In any case, Zimmermann was not worried. His confidence remained unshaken even as he said good-bye to Ambassador Gerard, now recalled to Washington, and it remained unshaken even as, two weeks before their final meeting, Zimmermann took specific steps that ensured America would indeed enter the war with a fury and a finality that would change the course of the conflict—and Germany's fate.

There was one man on the Allied side who knew all too well what Zimmermann had done, and what it could mean. He was Adm. William "Blinker" Hall, head of British Naval Intelligence and custodian of Room 40. He was the man to whom Nigel de Grey, the beloved Door Mouse, had first brought the decoded telegram Zimmermann sent on January 17. He was also the first to hear, from the British naval attaché in Washington, Capt. Guy Gaunt, the news of Wilson's severing relations with Germany. When he did, Hall rushed at once to the residence of the American ambassador to Great Britain, Walter Hines Page, and threw Gaunt's telegram onto Page's desk.

"Bernstorff goes home," it read; "I get drunk."

Hall smiled at Page. "Thank God!" he exclaimed. Hall knew Page sympathized with Britain and wanted the United States to be its ally. But Hall had other reasons to smile. What he was about to reveal to Page in a few days would put the final touches on Germany's blunder over submarine warfare, and would inaugurate an alliance between Britain and America that would change everything.[11]

PETROGRAD, JANUARY 31–FEBRUARY 21

THE SAME DAY that Ambassador Bernstorff delivered Germany's note to President Wilson, British, French, and Italian delegates were meeting at the imperial palace at Tsarskoye Selo, outside a snowy, frozen Petrograd. They were there to work out a common Allied strategy for the coming year. The discussion over the next two weeks would turn out to be rather one-sided. The other Allies soon realized that the Russians were sadly out of touch with events, including those along their own front with the Germans, and that they were more preoccupied with problems closer to home: particularly the imminent threat of revolution in the streets.

As the French ambassador to Russia, Maurice Paléologue, wrote in his diary, the opening meeting was not propitious. Czar Nicholas was friendly and sincere, but uncomfortable and clearly unsure of what to say; he seemed more at ease with the guests of lower rank than with the more distinguished visitors. With Gen. Édouard de Curières de Castelnau, he proved a disaster. Of Castelnau, one of France's heroes from the early weeks of the war, who had sacrificed no fewer than three sons in the fighting, Paléologue would write, "[T]he nobility of his character and his greatness of soul cast a kind of halo round his brows." The czar, however, seemed unaware of his guest's brilliant record; he asked vaguely whether this was Castelnau's first visit to Russia, and he made no mention of the loss of his sons. Paléologue was fond of the czar, but reflected afterward, "I could not help thinking to myself to what good use a monarch who really knew his business . . . would have put such an event."[12]

The next day, the discussion among the delegates "was animated and candid," but the British, French, and Italian attendees soon realized that the Russians were there largely to make excuses about why they couldn't do more for a coordinated war effort. They astonished their allies by asking, "Are the campaigns of 1917 to have a decisive character? Or must we now abandon the hope of obtaining definitive results this year?"

The British and French replied at once that it was essential that strong coordinated offensives be launched on both fronts "at the earliest possible moment."

That was when the Russians began ticking off their list of excuses. Russia's former prime minister Alexander Trepov "spoke very frankly of the dangers of the internal crisis through which Russia was passing," which in many ways the death of Rasputin had made worse. Russian general Joseph Gourko informed the other delegates that another sixty divisions would be needed before Russia could launch any serious new offensive; that would require months, possibly a year, of preparation. In the meantime, "the Russian army can only undertake minor operations," although General Gourko did promise they would try to pin down as many German divisions as they could during the course of the year.

This was not what the other Allies had expected. They were forced to sit stone-faced while the Russian delegation raised a number of other minor issues, including Greece, Serbia, the Scandinavian countries, and even Japan—the Russians wondered if the Japanese couldn't be convinced to do more for the overall war effort, to take pressure off Russia. From time to time, Lord Milner would turn to the French foreign minister, Gaston Doumergue, and hiss, "This is wasting time!" Doumergue had to agree.[13]

America came up several times, but particularly on February 5, after the news hit of Wilson's severing relations with Germany. "The Russian public has favorably received this important piece of news," Doumergue told his diary, "but the impression it conveys is but vague and superficial. For Russia knows nothing of America; she does not even suspect what a great drama has been taking place in the conscience of the American people during the last twenty months"—or at least in President Wilson's conscience.

The delegates were, however, learning about the great drama now playing out in Russia. Civic disorder was spreading. On February 13, eleven members of the Central Committee of War Industries were arrested on charges of "plotting a revolutionary movement with the object of proclaiming a republic." Paléologue arranged a luncheon for Foreign Minister Doumergue with leading liberals, including Pavel Miliukov, a key figure in the Diet's coalition of liberal parties known as the Progressive Bloc and prominent member of the Constitutional Democrats, known (from their party's initials) as the Kadets. When Doumergue counseled patience, Miliukov and the others exploded with rage. "We've had quite enough of patience," they said. "Our patience is utterly exhausted! Besides, if we don't act soon, the masses won't listen to us any longer!"

Doumergue replied that he was talking about patience, not resignation. "But whatever you do, put the war first!"[14]

Yet that was exactly what the Russian leadership, liberals or reactionary monarchists, seemed unable to do. There had been some hope that the death of the hated monk Rasputin (murdered by a cabal of Russian aristocrats on December 30, 1916) would break the ice that had frozen the czar and czarina in their manifestly self-destructive course. According to Paléologue, "the Rasputin party has survived Rasputin, but it is a body without a head." Even worse, the murder had backfired. While city folk celebrated, to the average Russian peasant, "Rasputin has become a martyr," a well-respected prince with deep connections in the countryside and in industry, explained a leading and well-informed nobleman to the French ambassador. "He was a man of the people; he let the Czar hear the voice of the people; he defended the people against the Court folk, the *pridvorny*. So the *pridvorny* killed him!" Paléologue's informant warned that the split between urban and rural Russia now loomed wider than ever, with forbidding prospects for the future.[15]

Finally, after weeks of fruitless discussion, the Allies seemed no closer to a common coordinated strategy than when they began. "The work of this conference is dragging on to no purpose," Ambassador Paléologue wrote in his diary. "No practical result has emerged from all the diplomatic verbiage."

One thing did emerge, however: the sense that Russia was on the brink of some great internal upheaval that, if anything, the murder of

Rasputin had only made worse. As the conference broke up on February 21, the French ambassador gave Doumergue and General Castelnau a note to pass to French prime minister Aristide Briand.

"A revolutionary crisis is at hand in Russia," it read. "It nearly broke out five weeks ago and is only postponed. Every day the Russian nation is getting more indifferent towards the war and the spirit of anarchy is spreading among all classes and even in the army . . . In case of a rising the authorities cannot count on the army. My conclusion is that time is no longer working for us, at any rate in Russia, and that we must henceforth take the defection of our ally into our calculations and draw all the inferences involved."

Doumergue read the note and said he agreed. "I am just as pessimistic as yourself," the foreign minister said. But even with this growing pessimism about Russia's future, neither man could have guessed that the czarist regime had less than a month to live.[16]

WASHINGTON, FEBRUARY 21–MARCH 1

THAT SAME DAY, February 21, officials in the German Admiralty could look at one another with grim satisfaction. In just three weeks of unrestricted submarine warfare, German U-boats had sunk 134 Allied and nonbelligerent ships—a new record. The submarine campaign was proving as much a success as Ludendorff and the generals had hoped. For the entire month of February, half a million tons of shipping would be sent to the bottom of the sea. The critical number of six hundred thousand tons seemed just over the horizon.

The count of sunken ships now regularly included American ones, even as President Wilson remained on the sidelines and refused to act.

On February 3, a German submarine sank the U.S. cargo ship *Housatonic* off the coast of Sicily. There were twenty-five Americans on board, although none was killed. Back in Washington, President Wilson did nothing.

On February 7, the British steamer *California* went down to a German torpedo off Ireland's coast. Again, there were American passengers on board; again, there were no American casualties, although forty-three people died in the attack. And again, President Wilson chose to do nothing.

On February 14, an Austrian warship sank the *Lyman M. Law*, an American-owned schooner with a crew of ten and a cargo of wooden staves for making lemon-packing boxes. The Austrians ordered the crew off the schooner before they sank it; if it had been a German and not an Austrian vessel, the outcome could have been very different. Once again, Wilson did nothing.

Two days earlier, Roosevelt disparaged Wilson as "yellow all through," and repeated his claim that "I don't believe Wilson will go to war unless Germany literally kicks him into it."

In London, U.S. ambassador Walter Hines Page was even more discouraged. On February 19, he wrote in his diary, "I am now ready to record my conviction that we shall not get into the war at all." Wilson, he wrote, "is constitutionally unable to come to the point of action. That much seems certain to me."[17]

Wilson, however, was not entirely inactive. He was considering a major step and was on the verge of asking Congress for the authority to arm U.S. merchant ships. If that measure passed, it would mean that an armed confrontation with Germany on the high seas would be only a matter of time.

And so it was, in these tense, dark days at the end of February 1917, that the Zimmermann telegram landed on President Wilson's desk.

That telegram had been in the possession of British Naval Intelligence since January 17 (see the prologue). It had come in two coded parts, one long and one relatively short. The long part had been the easiest to crack. It contained the information regarding the German government's decision to renew unrestricted submarine warfare on January 31, news that was no longer news by the end of February.

It was the second part of the message, consisting of 155 coded groups and beginning, "Berlin to Washington, W158, 16 January 1917, Most Secret," that proved the most interesting to the British decoders, but it was also the toughest to crack. Its subtitle, however, kept drawing the decoders on: "For Your Excellency's [meaning, Ambassador Bernstorff's] personal information and to be handed on to the Imperial [German] Minister in Mexico by a safe route."

Mention of Mexico had certainly been intriguing to Hall and his code breakers as they sat in their cramped, damp room at the Admiralty, as far from sunny Mexico as one could get. Their sense of intrigue grew as they decoded the first section of this second message; it was an offer of an alliance between Mexico and Germany, in the event that resumption of unrestricted submarine warfare forced the United States into war, something that the German ambassador was to tell the Mexican president was a distinct possibility.

The next group of coded numbers, thirty groups in all, stumped the code breakers completely. It had taken another two weeks of painstaking, backbreaking labor to force the enigmatic numbers to disclose their secrets, and when they did, Hall and his team realized they were sitting on a detonator that could blow the war wide open.

The telegram offered the promise that if Mexico allied itself with Germany, then Germany would help Mexico "regain by conquest her lost territory in Texas, Arizona, and New Mexico." It went even further, suggesting that Germany and Mexico also reach out to Japan, and encourage that country's defection from the Allied camp by "mediating a peace," while offering to let the Japanese join in the spoils taken from the breakup of America's presence along the Pacific.

At one level, the offer made sense. Mexico's president, Gen. José Venustiano Carranza, was still smarting from Wilson's decision to declare war on Mexico three years earlier and to send one American expeditionary force to Veracruz and another across the Mexican border to pursue the bandit Pancho Villa, an expedition commanded by one Gen. John J. Pershing. The American troops were now gone, but the shame and humiliation remained. Carranza had reached out more than once to Berlin, professing undying friendship and asking for Germany's help in strengthening the Mexican navy. He had even made noises about providing logistical support for German submarines operating in the South Atlantic, and promised to "eventually provide them a permanent base on the Mexican coast." If there was any neutral country poised for an alliance with Germany, and an alliance against the United States, it was the Republic of Mexico.[18]

Approaching Japan in an anti-American alliance also had some reasoning behind it. Japan had taken a dim view of the United States ever since President Roosevelt intervened and negotiated an end to the Russo-Japanese War in 1905, just when Russia was staggering from defeats on land and sea and Japan seemed on the verge of a historic and decisive victory. Anti-American demonstrations broke out across Japan; dozens of Japanese committed hara-kiri out of shame and humiliation. Japan's rapidly growing navy considered the U.S. Navy its single most important future rival—more than the German navy or even Britain's Royal Navy. Zimmermann hoped that by offering Mexico as a jumping-off point for a possible Japanese attack on the American West Coast, and offering American possessions in the Pacific such as the Philippines, Guam, and Hawaii as the spoils of war, Germany could turn Japan from foe to friend—and create enough of a distraction that even if the United States joined the Allies, it would be unable to intervene in Europe until it was too late to save Britain from starvation or surrender.

It was a well-thought-out and clever plan. It was also geopolitical lunacy. Zimmermann's plan involved nothing less than trying to engineer the breakup of the United States. If anything could tempt the world's biggest industrial power to commit itself to total war, and also tempt President Wilson, it would be a scheme like this one. Even if Zimmermann believed that the chief value of the Mexican alliance (and likewise that with Japan) would largely be to distract America's attention at a critical juncture, the plan would instantly boomerang if it were somehow to fall into the wrong hands ahead of time.

This is precisely what did happen, when Zimmermann's telegram arrived at Room 40 that January. The decoding of the last stubborn set of coded groups was finished on February 19. The British government now knew the full extent of the diplomatic bombshell the telegram contained, and when, on February 23, the secretary of state for foreign affairs, Arthur Balfour, walked over to Grosvenor Square to deliver the text of the telegram personally to the American ambassador, it was, he admitted later, "the most dramatic moment of my life."

Walter Hines Page's reaction can be imagined. If any document could propel Wilson out of the passivity Page had been deploring in his diary just four days earlier, this had to be it. He took until 2:00 a.m. to compose a covering message, prefaced by the warning that "in about three hours I shall send a telegram of great importance to the President and the Secretary of State."[19]

After sending Wilson the full text of the Zimmermann telegram and his covering message explaining how the British had obtained it, Page went to bed elated but apprehensive. "This would precipitate a war between any two nations," he wrote in his diary before turning in. "Heaven knows what effect it will have in Washington."[20]

Wilson's reaction after reading the telegram was one of "much indignation," according to an eyewitness. Declaring it "astounding," he sent it along to Colonel House. But the president's immediate thought was not of declaring war on Germany or opening a new line of negotiations with Britain, as Ambassador Page and others had hoped. Instead, he decided he could make political use of it to push his Armed Ship Bill through Congress. Even this half measure, of arming American ships going to sea to allow them to defend themselves against attack, had aroused enormous controversy and opposition from pacifist groups, and from his own former secretary of state William Jennings Bryan. A National Pacifist Congress meeting in New York City, with more than five hundred delegates, condemned the measure. The pressure on Congress to block the bill was intense. Perhaps the release of the Zimmermann telegram, the president reasoned, would be enough to break the logjam.

He had some additional help from the Germans. On February 26, Wilson went before another joint session of Congress, this time to ask the members to authorize providing arms to American ships against attack "in their legitimate and peaceful pursuits on the seas."

As he spoke, a crescendo of whispers began to fill the chamber, as a piece of sensational news spread from one congressman and senator to another. The media were reporting that the Cunard liner RMS *Laconia* had just been sunk by a German submarine off the coast of Ireland. Twenty-five passengers were dead, including two American citizens.[21]

Yet even this could not move the die-hard opponents of the Armed Ship Bill, opponents such as Sen. Gilbert Hitchcock of Nebraska, William Jennings Bryan's home state. They argued that American ships shouldn't be sailing into waters the Germans had designated as sink-on-sight zones, anyway; arming them would only tempt fate and provoke a confrontation. Opposition to the bill therefore was, if anything, only stiffened by the *Laconia* incident.

So, on February 28, Wilson ordered the text of the Zimmermann telegram to be made public. Before he did, he had one last humiliation to endure from the German foreign minister. He learned that the copy of the telegram sent to Ambassador Bernstorff had been transmitted on the U.S. diplomatic cable, which Wilson, as a gesture of goodwill, had allowed the German embassy to use after the British had severed Germany's own transatlantic cables at the outbreak of the war. It was akin to a kidnapper writing a ransom note using a pen his victim's parents had given him as a Christmas present.

"Good Lord! Good Lord!" Wilson exclaimed over and over—the closest he ever came to swearing. The damage that the release of the telegram did now to Germany's reputation as a respectable member of the community of nations no longer mattered to him. All that mattered was turning around his opponents on the Armed Ship Bill.

Certainly, the immediate reactions were gratifying. Shown the text of the telegram, Senator Hitchcock immediately switched sides, calling the Germans' communication with Mexico a "dastardly plot" and promising to help shepherd through the Senate the bill he had previously opposed. Release of the telegram to the media triggered a feeling of outrage and revulsion, both on Capitol Hill and around the country. Congress "is stirred to its depths today," the *New York Sun* reported. On March 1, the House of Representatives passed the Armed Ship Bill by a lopsided 401 to 13.[22]

Yet, even after this, Wilson was still not moved to consider a declaration of war against Germany or to ask Berlin for a retraction of, or even an explanation for, Zimmermann's extraordinary message. (Wilson couldn't, of course, ask the German ambassador; he had been expelled from Washington more than three weeks earlier.) If anything, the telegram only reinforced his position on American neutrality. Given Germany's perfidy and that of other nations, including Mexico, it was all the more important that America remain above the fray and avoid the contaminating touch of alliances and wars of conquest and territorial gain. America's restraint and "self-control," Wilson's obsession since the Great War began, were needed now more than ever, when those wishing to see America join forces with the Entente were using the telegram to push for war.

One of those was Sen. Henry Cabot Lodge: "It is no longer a contest between England and France and their allies on the one side" and Germany and its allies on the other. "It is now a struggle for the existence of freedom and democracy against a military autocracy which reverts to barbarism."[23] Still, Lodge also knew Wilson, or thought he did. He had no faith that the president would elect to go to war if he could help it, no matter the provocation. The Zimmermann telegram, however, might give Lodge his opening to force Wilson's hand at last.

Lodge worked all weekend on what he considered the right plan to do it, and the right place and time. Others were planning something more robust. On March 1, the Senate would meet to debate the Armed Ship Bill, and Sen. Robert "Fighting Bob" La Follette was there to defeat it. Clearly, he was prepared for anything: as he closed the door of his residence on his way to Capitol Hill, in his pocket was a loaded pistol. He checked once more to make sure it was there. Then he descended the steps and was gone.

BREAK POINT

Amidst the chaos and the darkness of the collapse of
Czarism, there arose the bright sun of liberty.
—ALEXANDER KERENSKY

PETROGRAD, MARCH 5–MARCH 12

R ussia's curse as 1917 began was as much meteorological as social or political. A colder-than-usual winter was followed by a warmer-than-usual early thaw. Both would sweep over the government of Nicholas II in ways that doomed the Romanov dynasty.

For instance, the average temperature in Petrograd for the first three months of 1917 was a dismal ten degrees Fahrenheit, compared with an average of forty degrees in 1916.[1] The cold was so severe that food from the countryside could not reach the city; snow closed down the railroad tracks leading into Petrograd, while nearly sixty thousand railroad cars piled high with food, fodder for horses, and coal for fuel were stuck, unable to relieve a capital starved for food or to feed hungry Russian armies in the field.[2]

On March 5, rumors circulated that the government would be forced to ration bread and that every adult would be limited to one pound of bread per day. Despite the bitter cold, people fought for their places in the long lines that appeared in front of stores. Even policemen complained that they couldn't get food for their families. The shortage of coal also forced local factories to close their doors.

By March 6, more than ten thousand unemployed workers filled the streets—tinder for a firestorm to come.

At that moment, Nicholas made a momentous, and another disastrous, decision. He decided to leave the capital and go to his headquarters at Mogilev, to resume command. He would leave the capital in highly incapable hands: those of his minister of war, Gen. M. A. Beliaev, a career bureaucrat of limited skills and intelligence; and city military commander Gen. Sergey Khabalov, who likewise had no experience dealing with urban insurrections. Nicholas's decision to leave Petrograd would decapitate the government at a critical moment. Only his wife, Czarina Alexandra, someone with absolutely no credibility with members of the Cabinet or the Russian people, was left in charge.

Indeed, the day after the czar left, demonstrations broke out across the city. Once again, the weather conspired to make the government's job difficult, this time by going in the opposite direction from the way it had gone all winter. That day, temperatures soared up into the forties. People who had been cooped up in their homes and offices all winter poured out into the streets, many of them joining the mass demonstrations demanding bread and other foodstuffs. French ambassador to Russia Maurice Paléologue was "struck by the sinister expression on the faces of the poor folk" lined up in front of a local bakery.[3]

The real turning point, however, came on March 8. It was International Women's Day, and a parade of Petrograd women, joined by a crowd of workers numbering somewhere between 78,000 and 128,000, went on strike to protest the food shortages. There was no violence, and by 10:00 p.m. the streets were clear. But observers noted that the Cossacks and troops who had kept their eye on the swarming crowds had been reluctant to intervene—a sharp contrast with 1905, and a bad sign of things to come.

Meanwhile, in the Duma, the leaders of the antigovernment socialist opposition were beginning to speak out. One was Alexander

Kerensky, lawyer, member of the Diet since 1912, and Socialist Revolutionary firebrand, who gave a speech demanding that the czar step down at long last. "To prevent a catastrophe," he said, "the Czar himself must be removed—by terrorist methods, if there is no other way . . . If you will not listen to the voice of warning now, you will find yourself face to face with facts—not warnings. Look up at the distant flashes that are lighting the skies of Russia!"[4]

Incendiary stuff—and when the czarina read the speech, she demanded that Kerensky be hanged. A writ came from the Department of Justice requiring that he lose his parliamentary privilege as a member of the Duma. Mikhail Rodzianko, the chairman of the Duma and one of the few members who had influence at court despite being part of the Progressive Bloc, who had already advised the czar that it was time to change government, reassured the young lawyer: "Be sure, we will never give you up to *them*." That night, Kerensky's career was made. As events spun out of control, he would be the politician everyone increasingly turned to.

Still, there were other, more pressing matters at hand, such as feeding the inhabitants of Petrograd. At dinner that same night, French ambassador Paléologue asked former prime minister Trepov what the government was doing to get food into the capital. Trepov's stumbling answer seemed "anything but reassuring." The fact was the czar's ministers had lost all control where it counted most.

On March 9, the situation turned ugly. Some one hundred thousand to two hundred thousand workers began marching out of Petrograd's industrial quarter and into the heart of the city. Officials tried to cut them off by closing the bridges across the Neva, but the workers simply walked across the frozen river to the other side.

The march saw the first appearance of Marxist Social Democratic agitators, a faction known as Mezhraiontsy, even though their titular leader, Leon Trotsky, was in exile in New York.[5] But they were as much helpless spectators at what was happening as the government was. As for Lenin and his rivals Martov and Bogdanov, the news of the events in Petrograd came as a complete surprise, catching them off guard. Far from having a hand in what was unfolding, they were as removed from the action as the czar's ambassadors in capitals such as London, Paris, and Washington, DC.

No one was in charge; no one was directing events. What was happening in Petrograd that week was as spontaneous as any incipient revolution could be. The slogans heard in the March 9 demonstrations included "Down with the autocracy!" and "Down with the war!" Meanwhile windows were broken, stores were looted, and rioters clashed with police. Once again, the military authorities seemed hesitant, and reluctant to get involved. The Russian army, the final firewall between civic disorder and urban insurrection, was looking shaky and unreliable—and the real troubles had yet to begin.

On March 10, the crowds were, if anything, even larger. Gendarmes, Cossacks, and troops roamed the city menacingly, but lacking orders, they did nothing to interfere with the growing crowds. The first red banners, the color of revolution, began to appear among the throngs of workers, students, housewives, and mothers, along with banners reading, "Down with the German Woman!" meaning Czarina Alexandra. Other banners read, "Down with the War!" but also "Down with Germany!" Russian patriotism was by no means absent among the demonstrators who filled the streets. Still, there was a growing feeling, witnesses later said, that the residents of the capital now had the fate of the government in their hands.

Students and workers gathered in Kazan Square, in the center of Nevsky Prospekt, the main street in Petrograd. Under a forest of red flags, they began singing "La Marseillaise."[6] And even as the first deaths occurred—police killed three workers in the shopping district of Gostinyy Dvor, while elsewhere, a crowd beat a policeman to death—people were emboldened by the failure of the government to make any effort to regain control of the capital.

Members of the Duma were emboldened, too, including Menshevik deputies who proposed organizing a "workers' soviet," or deliberative committee drawn from the various factories on strike. As for the Bolsheviks, they were largely nowhere. When one of them was asked if there was a genuine revolution taking place, he replied offhandedly, "What revolution? Give the workers a pound of bread and the movement will die away."[7]

Others had a better grasp of what was happening. That very evening, Saturday, March 10, a worried acquaintance of the French ambassador, Madame du Halgouët, asked Paléologue, "Are we witnessing the last night of the regime?" The French ambassador said nothing, but he knew the country's troubles were just starting.[8]

If the Bolshevik deputies were clueless about what was really happening, so was the czar in his military headquarters at Mogilev. Eight hours' train ride from Petrograd, Nicholas II could not have been farther removed from events if he had been living on the moon—or sharing a bowl of oatmeal with Lenin in Zurich. The vague reports he was getting all suggested that the situation was entirely manageable, when the exact opposite was the case. It was not until March 11 that the czar was finally informed that something had to be done to restore order in the capital, before it was too late.

Nicholas II's first instinct was the same as in 1905: order his troops to shoot. But the soldiers he could give such orders to were not the dedicated, disciplined professionals who, in massacres such as 1905's Bloody Sunday, had mowed down strikers and demonstrators without blinking an eye. The Russian troops garrisoning Petrograd were conscripts, most with barely a few weeks of rudimentary training, and with their minds and hearts still in the villages and factories from which they had been pulled to serve in the army.

This was a crucial problem, one the government ignored until it was too late. When push came to shove, as it did in the second week of March 1917, the average Russian conscript had to choose between supporting people like himself, those parading in the streets demanding bread, or obeying his aristocratic officers and a czar who was nearly five hundred miles away. It was an easy choice. The Petrograd garrison, instead of providing the firewall between order and chaos, was prepared to join the forces of chaos, almost to the last man.

It's not clear if Nicholas, even had he been informed of the reality on the street, would have acted any differently. In any case, he ordered General Khabalov to clear the streets and restore order by the next day.

Khabalov was flummoxed. He had a garrison of one hundred sixty thousand men at his disposal but knew that barely a small fraction would be reliable in a full-scale crisis—perhaps only one thousand to two thousand men.[9] He did issue two proclamations, one banning all large demonstrations and warning that the army would open fire on anyone who disobeyed; the other ordering all workers to return to their jobs by March 13 or risk losing their draft deferments.

Neither proclamation had the least effect on the crowds, which were turning increasingly violent. At one point, troops opened fire on a large crowd in Znamenskaya Square that refused to disperse. Forty demonstrators were killed, and at least that number were wounded. Workers sacked a police station in the working-class district, burning it to the ground. Vasili Maklakov of the Kadet Party in the Duma warned the French ambassador, "We're in the presence of a great movement now . . . There is only [one] step between riot and revolution."[10]

Yet by midnight on March 11, the streets were quiet again. The use of force had worked—or so it seemed. Nicholas II felt confident enough to order the Duma dissolved, and that evening, Petrograd's elite attended a magnificent party at Princess Radziwill's palace, with no sense of fear or foreboding.

They, and the government, got a rude shock the next morning. Soldiers disturbed by the Znamenskaya Square massacre had sat up all night debating what to do if ordered to fire on civilians again. On the morning of March 12, they voted to disobey such an order. One regiment after another joined the vote; soon, soldiers were pouring out into the streets to join the demonstrators. It was the largest military mutiny in history.[11]

Whatever law and order still existed in Petrograd vanished as the day went on.

Mutinous soldiers hijacked armored cars and began driving

around the city brandishing their rifles and shouting revolutionary slogans. Others broke into government arsenals and passed out guns and ammunition to the demonstrators; still others opened fire on the Petrograd police, as gun battles erupted across the capital. At one point a mob sacked the Ministry of the Interior; another rushed the headquarters of the Okhrana, the czar's secret police, and destroyed papers and files.

Soon, the red flag of revolution appeared atop the apple-green walls of the Winter Palace. Meanwhile, the looting of stores, restaurants, and the homes of the wealthy continued without stop.

A stunned eyewitness, French ambassador Maurice Paléologue, could report that, by afternoon, the Law Courts, the Arsenal, the Ministry of the Interior, the Okhrana headquarters, the offices of the minister of the courts, and "scores of police stations" were in flames. The Peter and Paul Fortress was under siege, and the rioters, now full-fledged revolutionaries, had occupied the Winter Palace.

"Fighting is in progress in every part of the city." On the way back to the embassy, Paléologue's own car was halted and surrounded by mutinous soldiers. The situation was about to turn ugly when a noncom recognized the ambassador and yelled out in a commanding voice, "A cheer for France and England!"

At once, the soldiers responded with an enthusiastic shout to Russia's allies, proof that support for the war had hardly died away, and the ambassador drove on amid a storm of cheering from soldiers who had been ready to lynch him and his aides a few minutes before.[12]

That same day, March 12, a desperate telegram reached Nicholas II at Mogilev, from the chairman of the Duma the czar had just dissolved. "Situation deteriorating," it read. "Imperative to take immediate steps for tomorrow will be [too] late. The last hour has struck, decisive [for] the fate of the fatherland and dynasty."

Nicholas read it and tossed it aside with a snort. "That fat fellow Rodzianko has again written me all kinds of nonsense," he remarked to his aide Count Frederiks, "which I won't even bother to answer."

But as evening came, even Nicholas realized that this was a situation he could no longer afford to ignore. At 2:00 p.m., a note came from Prime Minister Nikolai Golitsyn saying that the Cabinet wanted to resign and hand power over to a ministry chosen by the Duma. A stunned Nicholas ordered the Cabinet members to stay where they were; he was now going to take steps to restore order in his capital. That night during dinner, he informed Gen. N. I. Ivanov that, the next day, he was to proceed to Petrograd as military dictator. He also ordered no fewer than eight combat regiments, supplemented by several machine-gun battalions, to leave the front to join with Ivanov. In Nicholas's mind, this was going to be a serious military operation from start to finish.

The final showdown between the czar and his opponents, brewing since 1905, was at hand. The czar's position was actually stronger now than in 1905. Only Petrograd was in revolt. Except for some sympathy strikes in factories in Moscow, the rest of the country was quiet. Nonetheless, what happened in the next forty-eight hours could determine the fate of the Romanov dynasty and possibly the entire course of the Great War.[13]

And thus far, Lenin had played absolutely no role in what was happening.

WASHINGTON, MARCH 1–MARCH 20

WHILE DEMONSTRATORS WERE rioting in the streets of Petrograd, on the other side of the world, Washington was locked in an epic battle over the meaning and significance of the Zimmermann telegram.

The man who had triggered the fight was Sen. Henry Cabot Lodge. He intended to use it to force Woodrow Wilson into doing what the president was still adamantly saying would be a "crime"—namely, declaring war on Germany. To do so would reverse Wilson's policy and transform not only the course of the war but also America's role from disinterested spectator into Great Power, with the means and opportunity to impose its will on world events. Lodge knew this, as did his friend and mentor Theodore Roosevelt, which was why they were set to pursue this policy to the hilt—and to use the Zimmermann telegram to get there.

"The moment I saw it," Lodge wrote to Theodore Roosevelt, "I felt it would arouse the country more than anything else that has happened." Applied properly, it could be "of almost unlimited use in forcing the situation."[14]

On March 1, a Thursday, Lodge took his seat in the U.S. Senate. The other senators streamed in one by one, thinking they were going to debate the Armed Ship Bill. But Lodge had other ideas. He immediately entered a resolution demanding a statement from the president regarding the authenticity of the German foreign minister's telegram of January 17. Lodge then sat down and watched with satisfaction as the drama he had anticipated played out.[15] Every senator in the chamber knew the telegram was an affront to American pride and prestige, perhaps even a *casus belli*. All the newspapers, and much of the public, had said so. For those senators who were still opposed to anything but strict American neutrality, there was therefore only one possible course of action: to assert that the telegram was in fact a forgery.

Indeed, a great deal about the document was still shrouded in mystery, including how it had been obtained. President Wilson himself had said nothing about its authenticity, even when he was having it leaked to the press. Rumor had it that it had come from the British, but no one had said a word about how they had gotten their hands on it. (For good reason: Wilson, Ambassador Page, and other American officials had been sworn to absolute secrecy regarding Room 40 and its code-breaking efforts.) Later the story circulated that it had been picked up by the Americans themselves.[16] Everyone also knew the British were eager to get America on their side in the war, and that many Americans were willing to use any excuse to get their country to join the Allies. What if the document was a British forgery designed to force the issue?

"Did this information come from London?" Sen. William J. Stone from Missouri asked as the debate began. "Was it given to us by that government . . . That is all I am asking at this time." Stone's case was helped by a piece of misinformation that had crept into Associated Press coverage of the story, namely, that the president had been given the telegram not on February 25 but on January 19, two days after it was supposed to have been sent. Why withhold the document for more than four weeks? Was its release now, even as American ships were being sunk by German U-boats, timed as a deliberate propaganda ploy, critics wanted to know, perhaps one engineered by those with a vested interest in committing America to world war?

There were those who took a different tack. Senator Oscar W. Underwood of Alabama, for example, was willing to accept the document's authenticity but said that it was still not reason enough for war. What Zimmermann was doing, Underwood argued, was simply informing the ambassador to Mexico of what Germany *might* do if it found itself at war with the United States, a prudent move with no "unfriendly intention" toward America.[17]

Few in the Senate were willing to bend over that far backward to let Zimmermann, and Germany, off the hook. Instead, most of those who rejected the telegram as sufficient reason to go to war simply refused to believe it could be genuine. As Sen. Ellison Smith of South Carolina brutally framed it, it was a "forgery and a sham born in the brain of a scoundrel and a tool." Smith didn't say who the scoundrel was, but the implication was that he was sitting in an office somewhere in London. He didn't name the tool, either, but there was no doubt in the Senate chamber that he meant the American president.

This was exactly what Lodge had hoped for. He had no doubt the telegram was the real thing. If he could get Wilson to attest publicly to its authenticity, if only to protect his own honor, then the chief point for those arguing against going to war would be blasted to bits. The key was getting Wilson to commit, and that was what today's resolution was intended to do.

The debate raged from midmorning until six that evening. Emotions ran red hot, as they would in the debate over the Armed Ship Bill, which was put off until March 4, the last day of the congressional session. At stake for many were existential questions: What kind of country was America going to be? What would be its place in the world, and how would it be received by other nations once it committed itself to a war far beyond its shores? Lodge knew the battle would be intense; it was one reason Senator La Follette carried a gun with him in those tense days (his fear that he would have to defend himself physically against the bill's proponents proved unfounded: the gun went home unused). Either way, America was headed with great rapidity toward a dark and indefinite shore, and there were some in its highest deliberative body who feared others might not stop at violence to prevent its ever reaching that distant landing.

At six o'clock, the debate finally ebbed. A redrafted resolution, merely asking the president to provide whatever information he safely could regarding the telegram, passed unanimously in the Senate. Lodge was satisfied. The ball was now in Wilson's court.

Wilson, for once, did not hold back or retreat into the recesses of his mind and conscience before responding to the resolution. By eight o'clock, the senators (those who were still in session) had their answer. Wilson could indeed vouch for the authenticity of the Zimmermann telegram, although he could not disclose exactly how he knew it was genuine. He also made it clear that he had received it "during the present week," blowing away speculation that he had been sitting on the telegram for a month, waiting for the right moment to expose it. Other than that, President Woodrow Wilson had nothing to say about the telegram, its contents, or their implications.[18]

As the president's note was read, Lodge was ecstatic. "We have tied the note to Wilson," he wrote to Theodore Roosevelt. "We have got Wilson in a position where he cannot deny it." As the significance of what Germany had proposed—nothing less than the reannexation of Texas, Arizona, and New Mexico by Mexico, and a possible Japanese invasion of the West Coast—sank in, the public would demand war, and Wilson would be helpless to stand in their way. "[Wilson] does not mean to go to war," Lodge concluded, "but I think he is in the grip of events." And Lodge, Roosevelt, and their Republican allies would do everything in their power to keep him there.[19]

Still, Lodge did not count on the resilience of the antiwar party. Even after the president's testimony that the telegram was genuine, newspaper editors and some senators simply refused to believe it. Publisher William Randolph Hearst told his editors to continue branding the Zimmermann telegram as "in all probability a fake and forgery."[20] It wasn't just antiwar ideologues or isolationists who doubted the telegram's bona fides. Captain Guy Gaunt, British Naval Intelligence's man in Washington, was at a swank dinner at the Knickerbocker Club in New York City when the guests, almost all of whom were Anglophiles but resolutely anti-interventionist, "went after me," as he recalled later. They were unanimous in their conviction that the whole thing was a forgery and a setup, and they demanded from him proof that the telegram was real, even though Gaunt warned them that to provide proof would put many lives at risk.

Finally, he told them he was surprised they were willing to interrogate him "instead of accepting the word of your President." That halted the cross-examination, but Gaunt was forced to finish his meal surrounded by a table of skeptics who included a former U.S. ambassador to Britain, a former U.S. secretary of state, and the president of Columbia University.[21]

Even when Wilson met with his Cabinet the next day, March 2, there were several skeptics sitting around the table. What chiefly worried the Cabinet, however, was what would happen if Zimmermann himself called a press conference and denounced the document as a fake. (So far, the German government had maintained a stony silence regarding the entire affair, while the Mexicans and the Japanese had delivered steadfast denials.) Then it would be the president's word against that of a minister of a foreign country that was busy sinking American ships, and there was some concern about which one the American public would believe.

The opponents of the Armed Ship Bill were not put off by the president's avowal. On March 4, hopes for passing the bill died, as the senators Bob La Follette of Wisconsin and George Norris of Nebraska led a filibuster against it until time ran out. Wilson received the news as he was putting on his formal dress pants and cutaway coat. March 4, as it happened, was the day of his second inauguration. Wilson's ringing words on receiving the news—"a little band of wilful men representing no opinion but their own, have rendered the great Government of the United States helpless and contemptible"—would become famous. But there was no denying it was a bad way to start a second term.

As was the second inaugural ceremony, one of the strangest, an observer said, that anyone could remember. It was a miserable, wet day. Armed guards watched from rooftops all along the parade route, the heaviest security for an inauguration since the Civil War. Wilson's speech was perfunctory, hastily written, and read in such a driving wind that only those closest to the rostrum could hear it. Wilson repeated the theme of the need for the United States to remain neutral, but also warned that the day might come when it would be drawn into "a more immediate association with the great struggle itself."

Wilson concluded on an almost plaintive note: "I beg your tolerance, your countenance and your continued aid. The shadows that now lie dark upon our path will soon be dispelled and we shall walk with the light all about us if we be but true to ourselves."[22] Then the weather cleared somewhat, and he and Mrs. Wilson held hands as they sat on the porch of the White House to watch the inaugural fireworks.

One of those shadows he had mentioned was the lingering doubt over the authorship of the Zimmermann telegram and Wilson's motive for releasing it. In fact, as the week progressed, skepticism regarding the telegram refused to fade. It was becoming clear that there was only one way the skeptics would be persuaded that the Zimmermann telegram was the real thing. (Even if the British government had made a clean breast of the whole thing, including Room 40, the announcement would probably have fallen on deaf ears.) That would be for someone in the German or Mexican or Japanese government, or even Zimmermann himself, to confirm that it was true—although no one could imagine anyone involved making such a bald-faced blunder.

Then, almost unbelievably, that's exactly what Arthur Zimmermann did.

On March 3, Zimmermann had called a press conference, almost certainly to comment on the story raging in the United States regarding the telegram he had allegedly sent and what proof President Wilson had that it was genuine. One of the American reporters, a pro-German journalist named William Bayard Hale, who, it later turned out, was secretly in the pay of the German government, buttonholed Zimmermann before the conference began.

"Of course Your Excellency will deny this story," Hale blurted out. Zimmermann turned to him. "I cannot deny it," he replied glumly; "it is true."[23]

"Zimmermann's admission," writes historian Barbara Tuchman, "shattered the indifference with which three-quarters of the United States had regarded the war until that moment." It was a far greater national shock than the sinking of the *Lusitania* two years earlier. That disaster had involved a catastrophic but, still, accidental loss of life, however barbaric the deed. This was a deliberate plot against America, a proposed alliance of Teutonic, Latin, and Oriental despotism to tear the country apart. Almost overnight, opinion in newspapers around the country experienced a seismic shift. The Prussian Invasion Plot, as it was now called, rallied patriotic sentiment like nothing since the British set fire to the White House during the War of 1812. It also changed the perception of the war raging in Europe, and about which side was right and which wrong. "The issue shifts," wrote the *Omaha World-Herald*, "from Germany against Great Britain to Germany against the United States."[24]

Under the circumstances, Congress probably would have demanded Wilson come to a joint session and declare war on Germany— would have dragged him there, if need be. But Congress was out of session, and would be until April 16. Until then, Wilson was on his own, and he still was not willing to commit himself or the country to an act that would irrevocably change its destiny, and his, to light the future of the world.

On March 12, even as Czar Nicholas was ordering General Ivanov to take command of Petrograd and declare martial law, a German submarine, U-62, sank the American steamship *Algonquin* near the Isles of Scilly off Great Britain. No lives were lost, but it was a warning that "armed neutrality" might no longer be enough.

On March 18 came even worse news. Three ships, the steamship *Vigilancia*, the *City of Memphis*, and the oil tanker *Illinois*, had all gone down to German U-boats in the waters surrounding the British Isles. Fifteen Americans were dead. The possibility of heading off the pressure for war was fast diminishing even for a man as determined as Woodrow Wilson.

Two days later, the Cabinet met. Every member recommended a declaration of war against Germany.[25] It is doubtful that, even then, Wilson would have moved to accept their verdict if other news had not broken a few days before.

Russia's czar, Nicholas II, had abdicated his throne, and a new Provisional Government composed of members of the Duma had taken over. After nearly three hundred years, the Romanov dynasty of Peter the Great and Catherine the Great was at an end, and Russia was poised to become a parliamentary democracy for the first time in its history.

PETROGRAD, MARCH 13

WHAT HAD HAPPENED? The what-ifs surrounding the Russian Revolution, including the so-called February Revolution (so called because events took place according to a Russian calendar that was thirteen days behind the calendar used in the United States and the rest of the West), are many, but one in particular stands out. When Czar Nicholas left Mogilev to return to the capital in the early morning hours of March 13, in order to avoid slowing up Ivanov's advance on Petrograd, his train did not take the direct route to his residence at Tsarskoye. Instead, the czar took a roundabout route by rail, traveling first in the direction of Moscow and then turning back northwestward, toward

Tsarskoye. Had he taken the more direct route, he would have been back with the czarina on March 14, and she might have saved him from the series of blunders he would make in the next forty-eight hours.[26]

Instead, he would not reach Tsarskoye until March 17. By the time his wife finally saw him, he was no longer czar.

The extraordinary breakdown of law and order in Petrograd that began in the first week of March had created an authority vacuum in the capital. Two other institutions *were* ready to step forward and assume control of the city, and therefore of Russia. One was the workers' soviet that sprang up in the early days of the Petrograd revolution and that became the object of discussion of two Mensheviks, K. A. Gvozdev and B. Bogdanov (no relation to Lenin's adversary A. A. Bogdanov), who had been freed from prison by the revolutionary mob on March 12. Their idea was to turn the Petrograd Soviet into a democratic governing body, with soldiers, workers, and other citizens of Petrograd coming to the Tauride Palace to elect their representatives. In short, the Petrograd Soviet was a Menshevik project from the start; the formation of its Provisional Executive Committee of the Soviet of Workers' and Soldiers' Deputies, or Ispolkom, was done on the spur of the moment that night, with fewer than two hundred fifty people present, of whom only forty were actually considered eligible to vote.[27]

The entire membership of the Ispolkom at the time consisted of eight or nine men, including some Mensheviks and two self-styled Socialist Revolutionaries, Nikolai Chkheidze, who became chairman, and Alexander Kerensky. The committee resolved to publish a newspaper, *Izvestia*, to spread its revolutionary message, and to ask the Provisional Government that the Duma was putting together to withhold funds from the State Bank and other institutions. It was a modest request from an institution that soon would become crucial to the future of Russia, but in the tumultuous days of March 1917, no one anticipated how potentially powerful the Ispolkom would become or how whoever was a member and whoever had the dominant voice would determine the future of Russia.

The Petrograd Soviet's Ispolkom was one institution trying to fill the authority vacuum; the other was the Duma. At first, its chairman, Mikhail Rodzianko, had refused other members' requests that he disobey the czar's order to dissolve the parliamentary body. But he did ask Nicholas for permission to form a new Cabinet. When he heard no reply, he consented to a meeting of the entire Duma to decide what to do next. It met on March 12, even as General Ivanov was receiving his marching orders. As one eyewitness described it, the members were "frightened, excited, somehow spiritually clinging to one another" for support. What scared them wasn't the prospect of loyal czarist troops descending on Petrograd; it was the hundreds of thousands of armed rioters swarming in and around the Duma building. "One could feel its hot breath" as the Duma members agreed to form an executive committee of twelve members, a "Provisional Committee of Duma Members for the Restoration of Order in the Capital."[28] Chaired by Rodzianko, it included other members of the so-called Progressive Bloc, along with Chkheidze and Alexander Kerensky. Since these two also happened to be members of the new workers' soviet executive committee, the Ispolkom, and since they would emerge as the dominant players on the Duma's own committee, both men are worth a closer look.

Chkheidze was born to a Georgian aristocratic family and in 1907 was elected to the Duma, where he soon became chief spokesman for the Menshevik group. From the perspective of a Czar Nicholas, he was a wild-eyed radical. From the perspective of a Lenin, however, he was a contemptible moderate representing the Eduard Bernstein faction of European Marxism, with its belief in gradualism and in working through representative institutions. In the next several months, some of Lenin's most vicious verbal attacks would be aimed not at the czar or even at "counterrevolutionaries," but at Chkheidze and his ilk.

Three years younger than Lenin, and thirty-five years old in March 1917, Alexander Kerensky came from the same hometown, where his father had been Lenin's teacher, headmaster, and almost mentor. Like Lenin, Kerensky had earned himself a law degree, and for the next decade he built a reputation as a fearless advocate for political dissidents, a kind of William Kunstler for Russian radicals. Winning a seat in the Duma in 1912, Kerensky had been one of the first to call for the czar to abdicate; his speech on February 27 had fired the first verbal shot of the revolution, as it were, and he had been one of those most insistent that the Duma disobey the czar's order to dissolve and instead choose its own government to lead Russia. Now, over the next three days, he would be one of the pivotal figures in Russia's transition, as he put it later, "from pure absolutism to absolute democracy."[29]

Czar Nicholas and the imperial train never reached Tsarskoye. Instead, warnings about rebellious or "unfriendly" troops occupying parts of the tracks leading to Petrograd led to a series of diversions by rail until, on March 14, the train came to a halt at Pskov, less than two hundred miles from the capital. There the czar found himself confronted by the commander of the Northern Front, Gen. Nikolai Ruzskii, "his face pale and sickly, an unfriendly gleam from under his eyeglasses," who urged him to accept a Duma Cabinet. From acting commander in chief Gen. Mikhail Alekseev came more dire warnings. Sending General Ivanov to Petrograd to restore order was a hopeless mission. There were so few loyal troops left in the capital, Alekseev averred, that Ivanov's men would be unable to halt the revolution. Indeed, Mikhail Rodzianko also cabled that "the troops [here] are completely demoralized, they not only disobey but kill their officers." The same might happen with Ivanov's troops, was the implication, if they reached the city and became infected with the revolutionary contagion.

This barrage of resigned pessimism convinced Czar Nicholas. On March 14, he sent a note to Ivanov: "Until my arrival and receipt of your report, please undertake no action."[30] He had surrendered his last chance to restore law and order in his name.

Nicholas also heeded the advice that he accept the ministry formed by the Duma as his new government, and allow it to form a Cabinet. After some discussion, at a single stroke, Russia had taken a major step toward becoming a constitutional monarchy. The former autocrat agreed to welcome as heads of his government men he had despised and scorned less than two days before.

It was a startling turnaround. In the early morning hours of March 15, however, his advisers, including Rodzianko, convinced themselves that this was still not enough to quell the unrest. The only possible solution was for Nicholas himself to step down from his throne and to pass it to someone less hated by the revolutionary mobs. The issue was not just the czar: "Hatred of Her Majesty [i.e., Czarina Alexandra] has reached extreme limits," Rodzianko wired in response to General Ruzskii's telegram informing him that Nicholas would accept a Cabinet chosen by the Duma. "I must inform you what you propose is no longer adequate, and the dynastic question has been raised point-blank."

This telegram reached Nicholas in the predawn hours of March 15, after he had spent a sleepless night haunted by the realization that his authority, which had seemed so ironclad and secure just days before, was steadily slipping away.

It was 10:45 a.m. In the czar's carriage, Nicholas read the exchange of telegrams between Rodzianko and Ruzskii, and then stood motionless, gazing out across the snowy fields. Then he turned around and said it was clear he had brought great misfortune to his nation. Although he believed the people would not understand his giving up his throne, "If it is necessary, for Russia's welfare, that I step aside, I am prepared to do so."[31]

Then came a cable from General Alekseev, Nicholas's stand-in as commander in chief. The general had read Rodzianko's telegram to the czar and had sent his own cable to Nicholas. Alekseev's view coincided with that of the others weighing in on the issue of abdication. The czar would have to abdicate; there was, the general added, no other way in which Russia would remain in the war. Alekseev knew that this argument (that by sacrificing his throne, the czar would spare Russia a humiliating defeat and save the army from complete collapse) would overcome any lingering objections the czar had, and it did.

Alekseev's telegram was the final blow. If any adviser carried weight with Nicholas, it was Alekseev (who was also privy to the doom and gloom Ruzskii and Rodzianko had exchanged in a series of private telegraph conversations that military intelligence had forwarded on to their acting commander in chief). It was as if a bomb had hit the railway carriage, as men rushed to the czar's·side in a state of near hysteria. Grand Duke Nicholas fell to his knees and begged his cousin to step down. Aleksei Brusilov and the other generals had to agree. Cables were arriving from other fronts urging the same—Alekseev had sent his bleak message calling for the czar to step down to the other Russian brass, including commanders of the Russian fleet.

There was a brief pause. Then Nicholas crossed himself and said he was ready to abdicate. He disappeared into his dressing room and, fifteen minutes later, emerged with the text of a telegram to both Alekseev and Rodzianko, stating that "there is no sacrifice that I would not make for the sake of the true well-being and salvation of our Mother Russia," and that therefore he was renouncing the throne in favor of his son the czarevich, with his brother Grand Duke Michael as regent.

It was clear to everyone present that, in the words of historian Richard Pipes, Nicholas "chose to give up the crown to save the front." But in a few hours, he decided that even this was not enough. After another round of tense discussions, he said that his son's health was too precarious to risk putting him on the throne, and that he would abdicate in favor of his brother instead.

Many then and later thought this a mistake. Around the country, Czarevich Alexei enjoyed a popularity born in part from sympathy over his tragic illness, hemophilia. Also, everyone knew he was too young to have any connection with recent political events. "A beautiful myth could have been created around this innocent and pure child," one of the czar's supporters later wrote; "his charm would have helped to calm the anger of the masses"—and perhaps served to rally those Russians who, whatever their feelings about Nicholas and Alexandra, were not yet prepared to plunge the country into full-scale revolution.[32]

Be that as it may, the fact remained that the czar had renounced his throne. A three-hundred-year-old political system had come to an end. Moreover, Russia now had no legal national government except the Duma, which, in the formal telegram he sent at 3:05 p.m. on March 15, Nicholas had specifically named as a partner in shaping Russia's future constitutional order. No one, though, least of all Nicholas, had any clear idea of what that constitution might be. Yet never in history, past or present, had an autocratic regime handed over power with so little upheaval or bloodshed. The old order was dead; the new order had yet to be born.

It was after midnight when the imperial train finally pulled out of Pskov and made the sad, dismal journey back to Mogilev and then to Tsarskoye Selo, which Nicholas had last left as czar of all the Russias and would now return to as Nicholas Romanov, private citizen. In his diary, he wrote, "Left Pskov at 1 a.m. with oppressive feeling about events. All around treason and cowardice and deception." A feeling of regret, bitterness, and betrayal had followed the sense of having to accept necessity the day before—perhaps naturally in a person as insecure and weak as Nicholas Romanov. On the train the next morning, he said, he read "a great deal about Julius Caesar." The question "Et tu, Brute?" was clearly much on his mind.[33] But it was too late to reverse course.

Back in the capital, the members of the Provisional Committee received the czar's telegram with a sense of shock. No one had anticipated a move like this. Their first instinct, in fact, was to keep the news secret, in order to prevent fresh rioting. Their second was to send a delegation to Grand Duke Michael so that he might begin to take steps to form a new government.

The grand duke was Nicholas's brother, the youngest son and fifth child of Alexander III. He had stirred court circles by taking a married woman, Natalia Wulfert, as his lover. This led to a major court scandal that forced him and Natalia to live in virtual exile abroad, first in France, then in England, and—ironically, given the similarity of this fate to Lenin's—finally in Switzerland.

The declaration of war in 1914, however, had brought Michael back to Russia to take command of a cavalry regiment and then a division. His bravery during fighting in 1915 in the Carpathian Mountains won him Russia's highest military honor, the Order of St George. Conscientious, unconventional, intelligent, and popular with the military, Grand Duke Michael was a natural choice to take over the future of the Romanov dynasty—and unite a divided Russia in time of war.

It was Alexander Kerensky who cut this plan short. He agreed they should send a delegation to Michael, but only to persuade him to renounce the imperial throne altogether. The time had come for no more czars. Russia was on the verge of violent revolution; only a complete break from the past, Kerensky insisted, would persuade the masses that a new, more just future was dawning, and that the forces of despotism were now yielding to the forces of freedom.

Kerensky won the argument. The next morning, at the residence of Prince Putianin, where Grand Duke Michael was staying, a tense debate broke out in the grand duke's presence between the leader of the conservative Kadet Party, Miliukov, who argued that "without a monarch, the Provisional Government [is] liable to sink in the ocean of mass unrest," and Kerensky as spokesman for that Provisional Government.

"Miliukov is wrong," he exclaimed. "By accepting the throne you will not save Russia! Quite the contrary. I know the mood of the masses . . . [T]he monarchy now is deeply resented . . . I beg of you, in the name of Russia, to make this sacrifice."[34]

Michael was convinced. He had been caught off guard by his older brother's move anyway, and resented being put on the spot with no prior warning or consultation. He therefore agreed to abide by the will of the Provisional Government and step aside. Kerensky was ecstatic. "Your Highness!" he cried. "You are a most noble person. From now on, I shall say this everywhere!"

Kerensky had won. Russia's future course was set: no more czars. A new government elected by the people (albeit by a tiny sliver of the people), for the people, and of the people was taking shape. "That which only the day before appeared as a distant dream came true so suddenly and so very completely," Kerensky would write later. Russia was poised to enter the modern era at last, like its counterparts in the West, and Kerensky had no doubt that he would be the man to lead it toward those bright new democratic headlands.[35]

In retrospect, it would be a mistake to underestimate Kerensky's talent for emerging as the George Washington of the new Russia—or at least its key Founding Father. A brilliant and passionate orator; a handsome, charismatic presence on the speaker's rostrum or in a committee room; a politician who combined a lawyer's attention to detail with a would-be revolutionary's instinct for seizing the moment— Kerensky was only thirty-six years old but was already the dominant personality of the new Provisional Government. He also had considerable physical courage. During the tumultuous days of March 12–14, he had personally saved members of the czar's government, including the hated interior minister Alexander Protopopov, from being lynched by angry mobs. "The Duma sheds no blood," Kerensky had sternly proclaimed—and he meant it, as he stared the rioters down.[36]

He also had a unique advantage over the other members of the new Provisional Government. He was deputy chairman of the Petrograd Soviet as well, and although he soon stepped down from that official position, he remained a powerful and influential figure in the Ispolkom. When the other members, for example, tried to remove him altogether on the grounds that he had accepted the portfolio as minister of justice in the Provisional Government, soldiers and sailors had rushed the building and, carrying Kerensky on their shoulders up the stairs to the Ispolkom conference table, insisted that their hero be immediately reinstated.

Certainly, if any one person was poised to lead the Duma in its new constitutional role while also handling the revolutionary crowds milling in Petrograd's streets and squares, it was Kerensky. He was deeply committed to Russia's continuing the war—one reason the other Entente powers should have been eager to support him. But Kerensky did have one weakness that would ultimately prove fatal.

As Russia was headed on its revolutionary course from autocracy to constitutional democracy, Kerensky fully expected there would be those who would try to derail its new destiny—but he assumed they would come from Russia's pro-czarist right, not from his supposed allies on the left. All his reading of history, especially the history of the French Revolution, had led him to this conclusion: what revolutions had to fear most was counterrevolution by those trying to reverse direction.

In the coming months, this would keep him from realizing two things: First, those who seemed to be trying to stop further revolution might actually be allies in preserving it. Second, the real threat would come from someone who until now had been entirely removed from events, and who had the smallest political following of anyone in Russia, namely Lenin.

ZURICH, MARCH 16

"DON'T YOU KNOW anything? Revolution has broken out in Russia."

These were the words an astonished friend of Lenin's, M. G. Bronski, spoke when he arrived breathlessly at Spiegelgasse 14. Lenin had just finished lunch and was preparing to go as usual to the Zurich public library, where he always had a seat by 2:00 p.m. Bronski told him briefly what had happened back home, and Lenin and Nadya both sprinted down to the lake, where newspaper headlines were regularly posted on public display.

Sure enough, there it was, in black and white, in French and German: revolution had come to Russia. The czar had abdicated; the government was now in the hands of the Duma and a Provisional Committee. Russia's future was up for grabs, as was the course of the revolution that had started without Lenin but that he now desperately wanted to put himself at the head of, by any means necessary.

He and Nadya spent the rest of the day, March 16, meeting with their fellow émigrés, all of whom were in a state of almost uncontrollable excitement. Yet, even as they embraced, shook hands, and sang

revolutionary songs—Lenin was a powerful and sonorous baritone—
the leader of the Bolshevik Party, however tiny and fragmented, never
lost sight of his larger goal. That same day, he fired off a telegram to
the Central Committee in Petrograd via his mistress, Alexandra Kol-
lontai, who was then living in Oslo.

In no way should they allow these amazing events to distract them
from their policy on Russia and the war, Lenin told them. The Bolsheviks should in no way approve of "the defense of the motherland" in
the name of the new government, however tempting it might be to
become part of the current action. Any effort to form an alliance with
the Mensheviks, even a temporary one—that, too, should be avoided
at all costs. The goals should still be "international proletarian revolution and the seizure of power by Soviets of workers' deputies," not
by the bourgeois members of the Duma.[37]

Then there was the question of what Lenin himself could do. He
was determined not to repeat the mistake he had made in 1905, when
he arrived in Russia too late. But how was he going to get there? Every
route passed through enemy or hostile territory. The Germans and
Austrians would arrest him the minute he tried to cross their borders.
Heading south through the Mediterranean to reach the Black Sea
meant crossing territory held by Turkey, also Russia's enemy. Trying
to go to France and finding a freighter to take him to Petrograd via
the North Sea would require the cooperation of the French and British, which would never happen.

In every direction Lenin looked, he was blocked. In his frustration, he even came up with a scheme to disguise himself as a deaf-
mute Swede and chance taking a train across Germany to Denmark,
in the hope of finding his way from there to Finland and then Petrograd. Nadya had to persuade him to give up the idea.

"You'll fall asleep," she warned him, "and see Mensheviks in your
dreams, and you'll start swearing and shouting, 'Scoundrels, scoundrels,' and give the whole game away."[38]

In those heady days of mid-March 1917, when Russians were cele-
brating and dancing in the streets across their country and the rest of

the world was agog at what was happening in the former Romanov Empire, Lenin was a desperately unhappy man. A man frozen in time and place by events, while the historical destiny he had planned for himself and his country sped further and further away from his grasp.

That is, until another man took up Lenin's cause with enthusiasm, for his own very special reasons—a man sitting at a desk in Berlin, at the Foreign Ministry. He was Arthur Zimmermann. Just as he had taken one action that was changing the course of the war, not to mention world history, he was about to take another that would have the same momentous effect, this time on Russia—one that would enable Lenin's great vision to forge ahead just as Wilson's was doing that same week.

PRESIDENT WILSON GOES TO WAR;
LENIN GOES TO THE FINLAND STATION

*The law of history imposes our leadership, because it
is through us that the proletariat speaks.*
—LENIN, APRIL 7, 1917

WASHINGTON, MARCH 20–APRIL 2

THE NEWS FROM Russia had filled Woodrow Wilson with a sense of buoyancy he hadn't felt for weeks. He told the Cabinet that the new Russian government must be a good one; it was headed by a professor—this was Miliukov, who had once been invited to lecture at the University of Chicago. On March 20, Wilson ordered the American embassy to recognize the new Provisional Government as the official government of Russia.[1]

The events in Petrograd, however, could not distract him from the more immediate issue at hand: what to do about Germany. That same day, March 20, he had his fateful meeting with his Cabinet to decide on a course of action. After the news on March 18 about the sinking of the *Vigilancia*, the *City of Memphis*, and the *Illinois*, none of them had any hesitation about the necessity of war. Every member, without exception, recommended declaring war. "Well, gentlemen," Wilson said in a strangely distinct, unemotional voice, "I think there is no doubt as to what your advice is. I thank you." The meeting was over. Yet, as the Cabinet members, including Secretary of State Lansing and Secretary of War Newton Baker, left, none had any idea what Wilson would do.[2]

Nor did anyone else, not even Mrs. Wilson or his aide Colonel House. Wilson did release a statement the next morning, calling Congress into extraordinary session on April 2, to receive "a communication concerning grave matters of national policy." The president's desk piled up with neglected letters and other documents, a sure sign that Wilson was focused on a major decision. Still, it was not until March 28 that he told his staff he was going to lock himself in his study and should not be disturbed by anyone.[3]

No one knows what thoughts were going through Wilson's mind as he sat clacking away at his typewriter two days later—the White House staff, meanwhile, were walking on tiptoe and speaking in whispers—but the big change in Russia had to be one of the paramount issues. Until now, the struggle unfolding in Europe had involved the clash of two Great Power alliances whose war aims, so it seemed to Wilson, were mirror images of each other. Now the conflict had taken on a new dimension. On one side were Germany, Austria, and Turkey, all autocracies under one-man rule. On the other, however, were three democracies: two more mature, Britain and France; and the third, Russia, just beginning to bud. A new way of thinking about the war, and America's possible involvement in it, was taking shape in Wilson's mind. As he wrote and wrote on into the evening and until the next day, Saturday, a speech of truly historic proportions was forming on the page.

In a strange way, he was doing exactly what another man, Lenin, was doing on the other side of the Atlantic at exactly the same time. Both men were struggling to transform events (the world war for Wilson, the Russian Revolution for Lenin) in ways that would make those events consistent with their larger vision, instead of contradicting or correcting that vision. Both men were obsessed with the power of mind over matter, and held the belief that by sheer force of will, one could send physical events in a certain direction simply by insisting that history dictated such a course of action. This belief would become one of the moral diseases that would afflict the twentieth century until its end. Here, in April 1917, was where it would start with Lenin and Wilson. And whereas Lenin had Marx to encourage him in this conviction, Wilson had Hegel and his own belief in an omniscient providential God.

Both were now ready to put their visions into action. The only person who knew the contents of Wilson's coming address was Colonel House; even Cabinet members remained in the dark.[4]

On the evening of April 2, President Wilson left the White House in a driving rain to head for the Capitol, carrying in his pocket a speech that would transform the war and the United States—while Lenin was about to be launched on the enterprise that would transform events in Russia into an earth-shattering cataclysm almost as destructive as the world war itself.

COPENHAGEN, APRIL 2

THAT SAME DAY, even as Wilson was mounting the steps of the Capitol Building, the German ambassador in Copenhagen had a bright idea. He suggested to the Foreign Ministry that the best way to use the Russian Revolution to take Russia completely out of the war was to encourage its political extremists, especially those in exile, to return and spread chaos in their home country.

The man at the head of everyone's list was Lenin.

In fact, the German ambassador to Switzerland, Gisbert von Romberg, had been aware of Lenin's activities for some time, especially his desire to see Russia taken out of the war. Romberg had been made aware of Lenin's presence and activities through Alexander Helphand-Parvus, a German businessman who was also a Marxist (a not uncommon phenomenon, then or later), who kept the embassy informed of the goings-on among Russian exiles in Switzerland. According to Lenin's biographer Robert Service, there is strong circumstantial evidence that Romberg had even taken the extraordinary step of providing secret financial assistance to Lenin and the Bolsheviks in exile in Zurich, through Helphand-Parvus and a series of financial intermediaries.[5] If true, that bit of information might have ruined Lenin with his fellow revolutionaries—although, in Lenin's mind, taking secret subventions from German businessmen and imperialists was just a variation on Marx's well-worn dictum that the capitalist will sell you the rope you use to hang him with.

Nor would Lenin be averse to getting safe passage to Russia from the German government, if the Germans were willing. And in the last days of March and the first days of April, there was every indication they would be.

It was the German chancellor himself, Bethmann-Hollweg, who now advised Romberg to get into contact with the Russian exiles in Switzerland to give them permission to go to Russia. It was the German foreign minister, the same Arthur Zimmermann, who asked the German Supreme Command to approve the decision to invite those exiles, including Lenin, to cross German territory on their way to their home country. The generals were as enthusiastic about the idea as Zimmermann at the Foreign Ministry.[6] Ludendorff understood that Berlin's goal was "to improve peace possibilities through the internal weakening of Russia." He and they had always seen Russia as the weakest link in the Allied chain, and the one most likely to fall out of the war. The revolution unfolding in Petrograd, and now spreading elsewhere, only made it more so. Sending Lenin there seemed the best way to finish the job.

This was an important point. Everyone involved in the subterfuge maneuver from the German side assumed that Lenin would fail. The goal was to sow chaos and more chaos, not to see a Marxist-Bolshevik government come to power—indeed, nothing seemed less likely. The only person who was convinced Lenin could succeed was Lenin himself. If the Germans were willing to use him as a tool for their ends, he was more than willing to use them for his.

Other exiles had more scruples. They thought it would be best to get permission from the Provisional Government to make the trip under German auspices. There was even talk of a prisoner swap, with German detainees being released from Russia in exchange for the exiles' returning home. Lenin, however, brushed these objections aside. (Besides, Foreign Minister Miliukov in Petrograd had turned them down flat.) Instead, he had a far-left German friend, Fritz Platten, approach Ambassador Romberg with a plan hatched by Lenin and his closest ally in exile, Grigory Zinoviev.

The idea was for Germany to provide a train for their travel to Russia, regardless of the Provisional Government's wishes. Lenin's conditions were that the train have extraterritorial status during the journey, and that the exiles pay their own fares, so that there was no appearance of their acting as paid German agents. Although Romberg thought it odd that an "individual," as he put it, should set conditions for a "government," he passed Lenin's request along, and on April 4, Zimmermann and the Foreign Ministry approved the plan.[7]

Lenin was delighted. He plunged into making plans with Zinoviev. A total of thirty-two exiles would make the trip. They were to assemble at the Zähringer Hof hotel in Zurich on April 9. The next day, Lenin made a kind of farewell address to the revolutionaries who were staying behind, many of whom were furious with him for what they saw as an act of betrayal. Lenin told them he was perfectly aware that "the German Government allows the passage of the Russian Internationalists only in order to thus strengthen the antiwar movement in Russia." What the Germans wanted didn't matter. The worldwide workers' revolt would soon topple them, too—but that revolt would start first in Russia.

This was also part of Lenin's new thinking, ideas he would lay out on paper during his journey across Germany, the so-called *April Theses*. The fact that Russia was still far behind the rest of Europe in its economic development, and that its government was in a condition of monstrous turmoil, would make establishing a Marxist-led workers' revolution easier, not harder. In Lenin's mind, Russia was now what we today would call a failing state, and like other radical fanatics (including Mao Zedong, Fidel Castro, and, nearly a century later, Osama bin Laden), he sensed that a failing state offered a huge opportunity for even a tiny revolutionary minority, provided it was dedicated and ruthless enough to seize it.

No one would prove more dedicated, or more ruthless, than Lenin.

The date set for his departure was April 7. When that day came, America had been at war for exactly twenty-four hours.

WASHINGTON, APRIL 2–APRIL 6

WOODROW WILSON STRODE to the rostrum at eight o'clock on the evening of April 2 with a calmness and resolve that stirred observers. He was about to give the speech of his life, yet his physical presence—he leaned one arm nonchalantly on the lectern—suggested a man who habitually dealt with world-changing events with ease.

He began with a grim recitation of German aggressions against the neutral nations of the world, including the United States. "Vessels of every kind, whatever their flag, their character, their cargo, their destination . . . have been ruthlessly sent to the bottom without warning and without thought of help or mercy," he said. "Property can be paid for; the lives of peaceful and innocent people cannot. The present German submarine warfare against commerce is a warfare against mankind . . . The wrongs against which we now array ourselves are no common wrongs; they cut to the very roots of human life."

At this point the entire chamber was standing, applauding as one. Wilson's next words rang out like the tolling of a bell: "With a profound sense of the solemn and even tragical character of the step I am taking . . . in unhesitating obedience to what I deem my constitutional duty, I advise that the Congress declare the recent course of the Imperial German Government to be in fact nothing less than war against the government and people of the United States."

It was an extraordinary moment. Instead of Wilson and Congress declaring war on Germany, the speech implied it was Germany who had declared war on the United States. Wilson added, perhaps with an eye to the large and very active German American minority inside the United States, that "we have no quarrel with the German people." This was a war, Wilson averred, "determined upon as wars used to be determined upon in the old, unhappy days when people were no-where consulted by their rulers and wars were provoked and waged in the interests of dynasties and little groups of ambitious men"—an echo of his accusation against the senators who had blocked his Armed Ship Bill.

Now Wilson closed on the heart of the matter, at least as far as he was concerned. This was his ever-present hope for a future "league of nations," especially democratic nations, as the guarantors of world peace.

"A steadfast concert for peace can never be maintained except by a partnership of democratic nations," he explained. "No autocratic government could be trusted to keep faith within it or observe its covenants. It must be a league of honor, a partnership of opinion . . . Only free peoples can hold their purpose and their honor steady to a common end and prefer the interests of mankind to any narrow interest of their own."

That lofty sentiment then led him to speak of Lenin's homeland: "Does not every American feel that assurance has been added to our hope for the future peace of the world by the wonderful and heart-ening things that have been happening within the last few weeks in Russia? Russia was known by those who knew it best to have been always in fact democratic at heart . . . The autocracy that crowned the summit of her political structure, long as it had stood and terrible as was the reality of its power, was not in fact Russian in origin, charac-ter, or purpose . . ."

So much for three hundred or more years of Russian history, go-ing back at least to the master builder of the Russian Empire, Ivan the Terrible. Wilson plunged on: "Now it has been shaken and the great, generous Russian people have been added in their naïve majesty and might to the forces that are fighting for freedom in the world, for jus-tice, and for peace. Here is a fit partner for a League of Honor."

Germany, however, was clearly not. It embodied all the faults and brutalities that characterized despotism—brutalities so blatant, Wilson noted, that even Germany's ally Austria-Hungary had disavowed its campaign of unrestricted submarine warfare. And it was to eliminate those brutalities and the regimes that perpetrated them that Wilson and America were now prepared to take this next momentous step.

"The world must be made safe for democracy," he declared. The events in Russia had demonstrated that the democratic principle was on the rise around the world. America's direct involvement in this war would provide a way to secure it, both for Russia and for the other Allied powers.

"We have no selfish ends to serve. We desire no conquest, no dominion. We seek no indemnities for ourselves, no material compensation for the sacrifices we shall freely make. We are but one of the champions of the rights of mankind."

If that wasn't enough to bring his audience to its feet again, Wilson finished with these thoughts: "It is a fearful thing to lead this great peaceful people into war . . . But the right is more precious than peace, and we shall fight for the things which we have always carried nearest our hearts—for democracy, for the right of those who submit to authority to have a voice in their own government, for the rights and liberties of small nations, for a universal dominion of right by which a concert of free peoples shall bring peace and safety to all nations and make the world itself at last free."

In short, by going to war, America was pledging to do nothing less than set the rest of the world free.

Then Wilson added this: "To such a task we can dedicate our lives and our fortunes, everything we are and everything we have . . . America is privileged to spend her blood and her might for the principles that gave her birth and happiness and the peace she has treasured. God helping her, she can do no other."[8]

Never had there been a declaration of war quite like this one—one that ended, as anyone with a modicum of knowledge of history had to notice, like Martin Luther's famous declaration at the Diet of Worms:

"Here I stand; I can do no other." It was a commitment not just of a nation but of its entire heritage to the enterprise of war—and all in exactly thirty-two minutes.

Admirers of the speech virtually swooned with admiration. Walter Lippmann, editor of the *New Republic*, wrote, "Only a statesman who will be called great could have made America's intervention [in the world war] mean so much to the generous forces of the world, could have lifted the inevitable horror of war into a deed so full of meaning." From London, Ambassador Page wrote, "Your speech cheers the whole enlightened world and marks the beginning of a new international era."[9]

The references to Russia also drew admiration and attention. In Paris, Georges Clemenceau not only welcomed Wilson's declaration of war but was pleased with his mention of the revolution enveloping France's ally. "The Russian Revolution and the American Revolution complement each other in a miraculous way," the French Radical leader wrote effusively, "in defining once and for all the moral stakes in the conflict. All the great peoples of democracy . . . have taken that place in the battle that was destined for them. They work for the triumph not of one alone, but of all."[10]

Wilson would have agreed wholeheartedly with Clemenceau's sentiment, just as he would agree with Ambassador Page, that the speech marked the beginning of a new international era. That was what he had planned, but this would be an era very unlike the one before. It would rest not on concepts such as balance of power or spheres of influence, but on higher moral ideals—with the United States sitting at the center of the new world order.

On the one hand, Wilson seemed to be acquiescing in the arguments of Roosevelt, Lodge, and his own secretary of state, Robert Lansing, regarding whether America should go to war and which side it should be on. On the other, he had carefully distanced himself from the geopolitical assumptions that had led them to the conclusion that the United States was a Great Power and, as such, it needed to exert its influence in the world.

For example, he did not include Germany's allies, Turkey and Austria-Hungary, in his declaration of war; he had even spoken in praise of Austria. Nor did he highlight France and Britain as examples of "the league of honor" or the "partnership of democratic nations" he believed would be the foundation of a future concert of peace. Nor did he refer to them as allies at all. In fact, Wilson avoided entering any formal alliance with the Entente powers; instead, he insisted on the United States' being an "Associated Power."[11]

Wilson's eye was still on the goal he had set out in his "Peace Without Victory" speech of January 22: establishing America as the arbiter of a new kind of global power, one based on ideals and ideology, not physical force or material interest. In January, he had tried to do it by avoiding war. Now he was prepared to do it by *entering* the war. Either way, his idealistic, even utopian, vision of America and the world remained undimmed. It was only the means of achieving it that had drastically changed.

Still, he had some lingering doubts about the new course he had chosen.

For one thing, he doubted his own abilities as a war leader. He even told House on March 27 that "he did not believe he was fitted for the presidency under such conditions." House had to agree. "It needed a man of coarser fiber and one less a philosopher than the President to conduct a brutal, vigorous, and successful war"—although, as we will see, when it came to the real thing, Wilson could be as vigorous and even as brutal as any Prussian general.[12]

For another, he worried about the effects of war on the American people themselves. He confided his fears to a newspaper editor friend, Frank Cobb, even earlier in March, shortly after the sinking of the *Illinois* and the *City of Memphis* had been announced and when the clamor for war against Germany was growing.

"Once lead this people into war," Wilson ruminated, "and they'll forget there ever was such a thing as tolerance . . . The spirit of ruthless brutality will enter into the very fibre of our national life, infecting Congress, the courts, the policeman on the beat, the man in the street." Wilson worried that the Constitution itself would not survive: "a nation can't put its strength into a war and keep its head level; it has never been done."[13]

Again, Wilson was haunted by those childhood memories of the Civil War: of a nation waging war to the hilt, of a president suspending habeas corpus, of Sherman's March to the Sea, and of a peace and Reconstruction ruthlessly imposed on a defeated South, with (in Wilson's mind) black men taking the rightful place of whites in statehouses and at the polls.

Nor was Wilson the only one worried about whether this was indeed the right course for America. Emotions were running high on all sides. That same morning of April 2, Henry Cabot Lodge had been visited by a delegation of pacifists from his home state, Massachusetts. One of them, a former ball player named Alexander Bannwart, had become verbally abusive when Lodge told the delegation that he fully intended to support the president if he asked for a declaration of war. "Anyone who wants to go to war is a coward," Bannwart blurted out. "You're a damned coward."

Lodge replied, "And you're a damned liar!" He then reared back and smacked Bannwart in the jaw. Bannwart answered with a punch of his own, hurling Lodge back against the closed half of the double doors to his office. The other pacifists sprang forward to continue pummeling the stunned senator, but his staff now moved in and broke up the fracas, and a bruised and battered Bannwart was hauled off to jail.[14]

"At my age there is a certain aspect of folly about the whole thing and yet I am glad that I hit him," Lodge wrote to Theodore Roosevelt. When Lodge arrived at the Senate two days later for the vote on the declaration of war, he found that many of his fellow senators were glad, too. They congratulated him on his fisticuffs with the pacifists. Some said there were rumors that Lodge had actually killed Bannwart, which had made the senator very popular in their home states.

The vote in the Senate on April 6 was overwhelmingly for declaring war, 82 to 6. The vote in the House of Representatives was less lopsided. One of the votes against war came from the very first woman ever to sit in the House of Representatives, Jeannette Rankin of Montana, who had assumed her seat that January. Hers was one of fifty votes against war with Germany; 373 other congressmen had agreed with the president, however, and so the resolution easily passed.

For the fourth time in its history, America was officially at war. This would be unlike any other war it had ever fought: it would demand of the United States resources and manpower that would dwarf all its previous efforts combined, including the Civil War. The Great War was the bloodiest war that history had ever seen. American troops would be entering a slaughterhouse that had already claimed more than two million lives. Now it was American boys who would be scythed down by blazing machine guns, blown to bits by massive artillery shells, coughing their lungs out from clouds of poison gas, tumbling from their machines flying in the sky, or sinking into the sea in vessels turned into iron coffins.

To Wilson, however, it would be worth the sacrifice. By entering the war, America was also transforming the conflict from a competition for empire and national interests into a crusade to make the world safe for democracy and to secure mankind's hopes for future peace. He believed it would transform America as well, making it fully worthy to be the arbiter of a new world order.

ZURICH, APRIL 8

THE SCENE IN Bern on April 8 was a moment for expectant dreams and high ideals as well.

Bern was where Lenin and his fellow exiles would board their train for Russia, and where Lenin was due to arrive from Zurich. Lenin was almost beside himself with excitement and impatience to begin the long journey home to Russia and his revolutionary future. Nadya had other ideas. She suggested he go on ahead without her; there was so much to do before they left, including collecting the nine or so years' accumulation of papers and correspondence with other

Bolsheviks; paying their landlords, the Kammerers; and returning books to the library—or perhaps she simply needed a break from her increasingly frenetic and hyperactive husband. She was also unhappy about having to leave behind her mother's ashes, which were in Bern, where Yelizaveta Krupskaya had died two years earlier.

Lenin impatiently refused. They would go together or not at all. The revolution was calling. So, she relented, saying good-bye to Frau Kammerer, whom she had always liked. The Swiss landlady expressed concern about Nadya's going off to Russia, "that insecure country at such an uncertain time." Nadya shrugged. "You see, Frau Kammerer, that's where I have work to do." Lenin's parting words to his landlord were: "So, Herr Kammerer, now there will be peace."[15] The words were not meant to be reassuring. What he meant was that the current war would end so that the war of the working class against the rest could begin.

The news of Lenin's departure exploded across the expatriate community, and not just the Russians. "Pandemonium broke out" at the Pfauen Café, a favorite haunt of writers, journalists, and hangers-on, when they learned he would be traveling under the protection of the German government. The reaction was close to fury at what they saw as Lenin's betrayal of the socialist movement. Lenin had invited the French writer Romain Rolland to join him on the journey to Russia; Rolland contemptuously refused, and showed the telegram Lenin had sent him around the café. One of the writers there, a tall Irishman with thick spectacles, shrugged when he saw it. The Germans "must be pretty desperate," he remarked sourly; "sounds like a Trojan Horse to me." That, at least, was James Joyce's view on Lenin's mission.[16]

Lenin did not care. He was going regardless of what other socialists, even his fellow Bolsheviks, thought. The night before he left, he spoke to a gathering of Russian exiles in Bern. "We have before us a struggle of exceptional gravity and harshness," he said. "Let us go into the battle fully conscious of the responsibility we are taking. We know what we want to do. The law of history imposes our leadership, because it is through us that the proletariat speaks." They were words that brooked no dissenting voices.[17]

That morning, Lenin and his followers gathered at the Volkshaus in Bern. Then, suitcases packed and blankets and pillows ready for sleeping on the train, the procession of thirty-two would-be revolutionaries walked from the Zähringer Hof hotel to the Zurich rail station. A gaggle of socialists and other exiles met them at the station and berated Lenin and the others for resorting to help from the hated German government.

Lenin ignored them. He was standing on the platform, a knapsack full of books and papers on his back; he nervously checked his watch from time to time. At last the group boarded the train. There was a brief fracas when Lenin threw off one of the passengers, German socialist Oscar Blum, fearing he might be a police spy. Then Lenin stood at the window for a few minutes, answering questions in German from the crowd gathered on the platform. As the doors closed and the train began moving, he shook hands with one last onlooker. "Either we'll be swinging from the gallows in three months," he said sardonically, "or we shall be in power." Then the train pulled out of the station.[18]

Their first train ride was also the shortest, to Schaffhausen, on the edge of the German frontier. There the train that Romberg and Ludendorff had arranged for them was waiting. Later, it would be described, wrongly, as a sealed train. It was true that two German officers would stay in the rear of their carriage, behind a line drawn in chalk, to separate the Russian passengers from the rest of the train, and that three of the four doors to the carriage were affixed with special seals; but the fourth was left unlocked. Also, far from being isolated, the Russian passengers met and spoke to other passengers during their journey. The Polish socialist Karl Radek even tried to talk to some railway workers who got on the train, encouraging them to start a revolution of their own in Germany.[19] He was met only with stony stares.

What most struck Lenin and the other passengers, however, as they sped across the German countryside was the absence of adult men. At every station, and in the fields and streets they passed, they saw women, children, and elderly men, but no young or middle-aged men; they were all at the front. It was Lenin's first exposure to what the war meant to the world outside Switzerland and his tiny circle of exiles and revolutionaries. It was perhaps his first inkling, too, that if he indeed brought Russia out of the war, desperate people in the other countries, including Germany, might be inclined to follow.

As the train rumbled on, however, the Bolshevik leader's nerves grew tauter. What if he and his group were spotted and shadowed by police agents, who would have them arrested the minute they set foot in Russia? At the last minute, Lenin had arranged for his Swedish contact to get Nikolai Chkheidze, the Menshevik leader and now president of the Petrograd Soviet, to agree to admit the exiles into Russia, since their number included several Mensheviks—a good example of Lenin's willingness to beg favors from someone he despised personally and ideologically. Yet there was no guarantee that Chkheidze would keep his word, or that others would keep it for him. There was always the possibility, especially as they were technically in enemy country, that the Germans would renege on *their* word and have them all arrested.

All these worries and others plagued Lenin's mind, making him irritable as the journey wore on—as did the lack of sleep, since none of the passengers had sleeping berths, and rest was limited to catnaps in the overcrowded and stuffy compartments. When the neighboring compartment, where Radek; Grigory Safarov; Safarov's wife, Olga Ravich; and Lenin's French admirer and on-and-off-again mistress, Inessa Armand (whom Nadya warily tolerated), traveled together, got too boisterous one night—its occupants were singing and laughing at Radek's incessant jokes—Lenin completely lost his temper. He rushed to the compartment and grabbed Olga Ravich's arm with a painful wrench, in an effort to throw her out into the corridor. The other passengers, however, stood up to him and forced him to back down. He returned to his compartment to sulk.[20]

Then there was the matter of the toilet paper. Smoking in the compartments was strictly forbidden, out of consideration for the other passengers, so the regular smokers, including Radek, took their puffs in the toilet. This meant the toilet was often locked when others needed to get in there for more urgent reasons. As a result, long lines of resentful fellow passengers formed outside a toilet marked "Engaged" while someone in it was finishing a cigarette or cigar.

So, Lenin finally put his foot down and instituted a system of toilet rationing. He cut up some paper strips and issued them to the other exiles as tickets. One type of ticket was for using the toilet for normal purposes; the other was for having a smoke. Since there were fewer tickets for smoking than for handling bodily functions, the long lines soon disappeared. And so, it was official: the first act of Lenin's revolutionary justice (based, after all, on Marx's dictum "From each according to his ability; to each according to his need") was the rationing of toilet use.[21]

It wasn't until the train reached Stockholm on April 13 that the party encountered its first friendly reception. The city's mayor, Carl Lindhagen, threw a celebratory breakfast, while a local socialist paper, *Politiken*, published a piece on the returning émigrés, with a photograph of Lenin. He was for the first time emerging as an international celebrity.[22]

But Lenin refused to stop and rest in Stockholm. The next day, the group crossed the Swedish-Finnish frontier on horse-drawn sleighs. Russian authorities in Finland stopped Radek and Fritz Platten, who had been with them all the way, from going any farther. Nowhere before had there been any sign of soldiers; now, suddenly, they were everywhere. There were soldiers on the railway platforms, soldiers on the train, soldiers squeezing into their train compartments. Lenin had no time to panic; he was reading copies of *Pravda* he'd picked up in Helsinki, and he was deeply unhappy with what he read. A comrade leaned out the window and yelled, "Long live the revolution!" The soldiers on the platform, their rifles slung, bayonets fixed, stared in puzzlement. Then the train and the exiles were gone.

The train stopped at Beloostrov, twenty-four miles north of Petro-grad and the entrepôt at the Russo-Finnish border. There, time was spent sorting out passports and doing customs checks. A delegation was there to meet Lenin: Joseph Stalin, Lev Kamenev, and Lenin's sister Maria. All Lenin's attention was focused on Kamenev and Stalin, then editors of *Pravda*, and he poured his vial of accumulated wrath on both of them as the train sped along for the Finland Station, in Petrograd. "What have you been writing in *Pravda*?" he kept shouting at them. "We've seen a few copies and have called you all kinds of names!" Both Kamenev and Stalin had been calling for support for the new Provisional Government. Lenin intended to nip that in the bud the minute they reached Russia. Glumly Kamenev and Stalin took their verbal punishment in silence.

Then, as the train eased toward the Finland Station, Lenin became nervous again. At any moment, he was thinking, he would be arrested. A chastened Kamenev assured him he was wrong, and Kamenev turned out to be right.

The train pulled into a shabby stucco station, colored putty gray and flamingo pink, where a strange delegation had gathered to receive the Bolshevik leader. It was 11:10 at night on April 16, yet standing on the platform was Chkheidze himself, next to a man carrying a large bouquet of flowers: Nikolai Sukhanov, a nonparty socialist who had decided that Lenin's return to Russia represented a turning point he could not miss. What kind of turning point, he could not say as yet—nor could anyone else.

Chkheidze, meanwhile, was launching into a standard speech of welcome. Lenin completely ignored him and instead addressed the assembled crowd of Bolshevik adherents and general curiosity seekers with the words: "Dear comrades, soldiers, sailors, and workers, I am happy to greet you in the victorious Russian revolution, to greet you as the advance guard of the international proletarian army."

He went on: "The war of imperialist brigandage is the beginning of civil war in Europe. The hour is not far when the people will turn their weapons against their capitalist exploiters . . . Not today, but tomorrow, any day, may see the collapse of European capitalism. The Russian revolution you have accomplished has dealt it the first blow and has opened a new epoch . . . Long live the International Socialist Revolution!"[23]

He left the station. On the platform, a single Russian army officer raised his arm in salute. Lenin, almost against his instinct, saluted back. Then the officer signaled to a detachment of sailors, who presented their arms in salute, while a band started playing "La Marseillaise." Lenin said some words of support for the revolution, and the soldiers and sailors carried him out of the station on their shoulders while searchlights scanned the sky. He boarded an armored car that the Provisional Government had forbidden to appear directly at the station; the searchlights were from the Peter and Paul Fortress, which was Petrograd's "Bastille" and the city's main military citadel.

The next day, the German government's agent in Stockholm sent a jubilant telegram to Berlin: "Lenin's entry into Russia successful. He is working exactly as we wish."[24]

PETROGRAD, APRIL 17

TO THE OTHER exiles arriving with him, it must have seemed as if Lenin were poised to take a commanding position, if not *the* commanding position, in the new Provisional Government or the Petrograd Soviet. But he had no interest in either. His first remark to the sailors who had greeted him was that they had been betrayed by the Provisional Government.[25] That would become his chief message: no one should cooperate with the new revolutionary government or its chief organs. A workers' revolution led by the Bolshevik Party, and no one else, was Russia's and the world's only future.

It was a stunning letdown for those who had been in Russia during the war years and the tumult that followed, which Lenin had completely missed. The doubters included Kamenev and Stalin, who had written that as long as Germany waged war on Russian soil, the Russian soldier "must stand at his post, and answer bullet with bullet and shell with shell." Even Nadya wondered if her husband was on the wrong track and was preaching a revolution that could never happen or, if it did, would totally destroy all the progress that Russia had made in the weeks since the revolution began.[26]

Still, Lenin was adamant. Later, he would write, "I did not arrive in Petrograd until the night of April 3 [Old Style; April 16 New Style], and therefore at the meeting on April 4[,] I could, of course, deliver a report on the tasks of the revolutionary proletariat only on my own behalf . . . The only thing I could do to make things easier for myself—and for honest opponents—was to prepare the theses in writing." These were the theses he had written during the long train trip from Switzerland. They contained his political strategy for the next several months, which he revealed, first, at a meeting with his Bolshevik supporters and, then, at a larger meeting of both Mensheviks and Bolsheviks—Lenin's first step in driving a permanent wedge between his minority faction and the Social Democratic majority who still claimed to speak for Marxism in Russia.

The key to what happened next, in Lenin's mind, was, first, to give up on the war. It had nothing to do with Russian patriotism and was "a predatory imperialist war owing to the capitalist nature of the government," which stood as an obstacle to a truly revolutionary war launched by a "class-conscious proletariat."

The second was to abandon all support for the Provisional Government. "The utter falsity of all its promises should be made clear . . . This government, a government of capitalists, should cease to be an imperialist government."

Third, even though "in most of the Soviets of Workers' Deputies our Party is in the minority . . . the masses must be made to see that the Soviets of Workers' Deputies are the only possible form of revolutionary government." In the meantime, "as long as we are in the minority we carry on the work of criticizing and exposing errors" and preaching "the necessity of transferring the entire state power to the Soviets of Workers' Deputies, so that the people may overcome their mistakes by experience."

These lessons, as inculcated by the Bolshevik deputies, included the abolition of the police, army, and bureaucracy; confiscation of all estates; nationalization of all lands in the hands of "the local Soviets of Agricultural Laborers' and Peasants' Deputies"; and the collectivization of all banks in the country into a single national bank.

Above all, there could be no parliamentary republic. To embrace the existing Provisional Government as the real government of Russia would be, in Lenin's words, "a retrograde step." Instead, the Bolshevik Party must now embrace *his* agenda, which was to collapse the two revolutions into one while overthrowing the Provisional Government.[27]

All this Lenin laid out in a speech on April 17 in Room 13 at the Tauride Palace, now home to both the Petrograd Soviet and the Provisional Government following the collapse of the czarist regime. Those who heard Lenin's words and then read his article "The Tasks of the Proletariat in the Present Revolution" in *Pravda* a few days later were aghast. Lev Kamenev was convinced that Lenin had finally lost his mind.[28] Other Bolsheviks just hoped that their leader would eventually come around and recognize reality. The Russian Revolution was off and leaving the station. The best they could do as a political party was what Chkheidze and the Mensheviks were doing: hitch a ride and hang on while hoping that an opportunity would arise when they could press their Marxist agenda on a fully formed democratic-socialist government.

Lenin wasn't listening. He had his own vision of how a Marxist revolution would happen in Russia, and where it would lead. He also had no doubt that it *would* happen. He was willing to wait for the February Revolution to collapse. And in the next few months, he would have a powerful if unwitting partner in undermining what Miliukov, Kerensky, and the others were trying to create.

That partner would be Woodrow Wilson.

RUPTURES, MUTINIES, AND CONVOYS

Firepower kills.
—GENERAL PHILIPPE PÉTAIN

PARIS AND CHEMIN DES DAMES, APRIL 9–MAY 2

THE FIRST WORLD WAR presents a strange paradox. In most wars, prolonged stalemate on the battlefield encourages the participants to look for a compromise to end the fight. In the Great War, however, stalemate produced the exact opposite. With the exception of Austria-Hungary, all the major combatants in 1917, Germany, Britain, France, and even Russia, felt a profound desire for a fight to the finish, *à outrance*—no matter the cost, especially if it was before the Americans appeared on the scene.

At the start of the year, the Germans had fastened on unrestricted submarine warfare as the way to achieve decisive victory. In much the same mood, Britain's prime minister, David Lloyd George, was gearing up his country for total war. This included plans for one final big push along the front that had been the scene of virtual stalemate since the end of 1914—the front along the Ypres Salient near the Belgian border, the graveyard of hundreds of thousands of dead on both sides.

But it was the French who sprang their plan on the ground first, in mid-April—after Wilson's declaration of war but well before the Americans could make their full presence felt on the battlefield. The so-called Nivelle Offensive was the last time the French High Command would insist that the British act as their subordinates in supporting a major French operation. It was also the last time the French government was able to act as a Great Power as it had under Napoleon or even Louis XIV. In so doing, it would also destroy France as a Great Power once and for all.

If some of the tragedies of the coming century were the result of French politicians and others acting as if France were still a first-rate power when it was in fact a second-rate one, from the outbreak of World War II and Vichy to Algeria and Vietnam, the 1917 Nivelle Offensive was where it all started.

The Nivelle Offensive took its name from Gen. Robert Nivelle, the commander along the Verdun front after the German offensive had died out. In a series of sudden, swift moves, backed by massive artillery bombardments, he managed to recapture nearly all the ground France had lost in that sector since April 1916, including the storied Fort Douaumont, with minimal casualties. His success shot him to the forefront of French generals. When General Joffre lost his job as supreme commander in December, Nivelle was the obvious replacement. His style seemed the perfect antidote to the slow, plodding victory-by-attrition strategy Joffre had followed since the start of the war, a strategy that had nearly bled the French army dry and left the Germans still in possession of much of northwest France.

Nivelle was a star. Intellectually alert and energetic, he combined a sense of personal style with the gift of gab. Observers remarked on how "he explained his methods in the most enchanting way" so that listeners would leave "enthralled and enraptured."[1] It's not surprising, therefore, that he soon convinced the government that the operational strategy he had used so successfully at Verdun could be adopted at the strategic level. He liked to call it his secret plan to end the deadlock on the Western Front, but it was really not so secret. The key was concentrating all his forces on a single narrow front, and then saturating the enemy with an intense artillery barrage. Trained as an artillery officer, Nivelle knew that the artillery was probably France's strongest arm. Its primary weapon, the 75-mm howitzer, had a relatively short range but could lay down a devastating volume of fire.[2]

Nivelle's idea was to use a vast mass of artillery to bombard a limited area to achieve what he called a *rupture*, punching a hole "across the whole depth of the enemy position." Also, there would not be the usual waves of attacking troops advancing shoulder to shoulder through no-man's-land to the enemy trenches after the bombardment. Instead, small groups of infantry would lead the assault even as the barrage rolled over the enemy positions. The French infantry would sweep over the stunned defenders, bypass any remaining pockets of resistance, and then push out into the open country beyond. Since 1915, what every general, Allied or German, had been dreaming of, breakout, would be achieved with a minimum of casualties and a maximum of damage to the enemy.

That was Nivelle's promise: a "hard" and "brutal" offensive lasting less than forty-eight hours, during which the entire German position would be overrun in successive two- to three-thousand-yard advances. All he needed, he informed the government, was a suitable front on which to practice his magic. The front along the Somme River, in the center of the Allied line, was too chewed up by the previous year's fighting to be a good place for launching a breakout. Instead, he aimed to pinch out the German salient straddling either side of the Somme. From the southern edge of the German position, French armies would strike up into the Champagne region of the southern Aisne River, known as the Chemin des Dames; in the northern sector, the British would advance eastward toward Arras, with an eye to capturing Vimy Ridge, the one piece of high ground overlooking the Douai Plain—and what Nivelle hoped would be the entry point into the German rear.[3]

At a summit meeting in Calais in December 1916, the British had agreed to some kind of combined offensive, so they were obliged to go along with Nivelle's plan. Starting in January, both armies began assembling their troops and artillery for what looked like the one-two knockout punch that would force the broken Germans to stream back toward the Rhine.

Then the Germans ruined everything.

Even as Nivelle's staff was putting the final touches on his plan, the Germans began pulling back along the entire sector between Arras and the Aisne. They had no inkling of Nivelle's impending attack; they had simply decided that with German forces more or less on permanent defense for the rest of the year, they needed to shorten their line by abandoning the Somme Salient. Instead, their forces drew back into the great maze of entrenched fortifications known as the Hindenburg Line. Shortening the German line in this way freed up no fewer than fifteen divisions for action.

The Allies realized what was happening as early as March 15, and by March 18, the German withdrawal to the Hindenburg Line was complete. Instead of administering an irresistible hammer blow to an enemy just across no-man's-land, Nivelle's men would be drifting across a wide, empty plain almost fifty miles deep.[4] It made nonsense of the idea of *rupture*. Generals and politicians on both sides of the Channel urged Nivelle to reconsider his plan. Yet he insisted on pressing ahead. He threatened to quit; the French public would be outraged, he said, when they learned that he had been overruled and that the government had given up this one chance to have British forces do the bidding of the French High Command rather than (as during the Somme offensive) the other way around. Whatever Nivelle lacked in flexibility or insight, he more than made up for in self-confidence and nerve. With deep misgivings, then, Lloyd George and the new French government gave their assent.

The British struck first, on April 9. For the assault, the commander, Gen. Edmund Allenby, had assembled sixteen divisions, including four divisions of Canadians, and 2,817 pieces of artillery and heavy mortars—one gun for every twelve yards of enemy front.[5] The key objective was the crest of Vimy Ridge, which the Canadians were supposed to storm and take, opening the way into the unprotected

German rear, where the British and Canadians would eventually link up with Nivelle's French divisions coming up from the south. The weather the morning of April 9 was atrocious, with rain coming down in sheets mixed with snow and sleet. The Canadians were going to have to advance on Vimy Ridge through fields of icy, glutinous mud. Even after an artillery bombardment that would be double that used in the first day of the Somme offensive, the prospect of reaching the summit looked bleak.

The Germans, however, were caught flat-footed. Their commander, the master of strategy at Verdun and the conqueror of Romania, General Falkenhayn, had made a fatal error. He had thinned the German front line down to just seven regiments while holding the rest fifteen miles back, in reserve for counterattacks. Also, four of those seven regiments were out-of-shape, overage reservists.[6] When the British bombardment started, every communication line between the front and German headquarters was blown up and severed, as was communication with German artillery. When the British and Canadians finally reached the German line, either the defenders were killed or wounded, or they fled for their lives.

The attack had been a stunning success. The British and Canadians had cut a hole one to three miles deep in the German line; they had taken nine thousand prisoners. Canadian troops standing on Vimy Ridge could see across the entire Douai Plain beyond, and watched German gunners desperately limbering up their guns and heading for the rear. "There appeared to be nothing at all to prevent our breaking through, except the weather," one of the lieutenants on the ridge later remembered.[7] Then the predictable happened—as it always did following every successful initial advance in this war, at least on the Western Front. While attackers moved at foot speed, defenders could move at rail speed. Modern railway networks allowed even a badly shaken defender to move his reinforcements to a threatened sector faster than an attacker could get his troops in position on foot. In the next world war, airpower could be used to sever those railway lines and isolate an enemy position; in 1917, no such option existed. Besides, exploiting a breakthrough required moving hundreds of artillery pieces and hundreds of thousands of artillery shells. That meant more lost time while the defender was shoring up his fortifications, digging fresh trenches, and pouring in fresh troops to close the gap.

This is exactly what happened over the next several days. On April 10, German reserves arrived to pull together the German line. In desperation, Allenby tried a cavalry charge to widen the gap; German artillery and a fierce counterattack held off the attackers.[8] By the eleventh, the British and Canadians had suffered thirteen thousand casualties, still a small fraction of those suffered by comparable forces during the opening days of the Somme offensive. But hopes for a significant breakthrough were fading, as more and more German reinforcements came up. Fighting dragged on for another month, by which time the British First and Third Armies had lost more than one hundred thirty thousand men for no real gain. The Germans had taken similar losses, but their line was reorganized and stronger than ever. There would be no breakthrough at Arras.

There would be none in the Chemin des Dames, either.

For one thing, the Germans learned of Nivelle's plans even as his headquarters was handing them out to divisional, brigade, and regimental commanders. A French sergeant-major was captured by the Germans with his pockets full of Nivelle's orders. Also, Nivelle had boasted of his "secret" plan during a series of recent dinner parties in London, so advance warning could have leaked out to German agents in that way. In any case, by the day the assault in the Chemin des Dames was supposed to start, April 16, the Germans had as many divisions in place as Nivelle did.

In addition, the distance between the French and German lines now stretched so far that the tight timetable Nivelle had laid down was no longer feasible. By the time the French reached their initial objectives in the opening hours of their attack, they would still be two thousand yards short of the real German defenses.[9]

Still, the soldiers under Nivelle's command were filled with confidence and expectation. A British liaison officer remembered their grinning faces and shining eyes. "The Germans won't stand there," they kept saying to him, "any more than they did before you at Arras. They fairly ran away there, didn't they?"

Then the French artillery began its work, while the German return barrage seemed ragged and uncoordinated. "Almost at once, or so it seemed, the immense mass of troops within sight began to move. Long, thin columns were swarming toward the Aisne" as the artillery barrage intensified. "Then it began to rain and it became impossible to tell how the assault was progressing."[10]

Another barrage; another assault on another line of trenches—this had been the story of the world war for almost three years, and each time, it had ended in heartbreaking slaughter and stalemate, for both attacker and defender. This time, however, it seemed to the thousands of men in horizon-blue uniforms, with their blue steel helmets glistening with rain, it would be different.

Except it wasn't. The rain and mist hid the scene so that the artillery and infantry lost touch with each other. The lines of French troops began to slow as German machine guns popped out of shell holes and the mouths of dugout caves and began taking the same terrible toll on the French attackers in the same old way.

The conditions, in fact, were the other problem that beleaguered commanders in the First World War, and made being on the attack so difficult. The fog of war became virtually impenetrable, and not just because of the miserable weather that was typical of northwestern Europe. While the distances over which battles were fought had vastly increased compared with distances in previous wars, the lack of radio or other wireless communication equipment meant that commanders at headquarters had to rely on telegraph or primitive telephone lines, which were constantly being blown up by artillery or cut by the enemy, or which simply couldn't be laid down in time to keep up with the pace of the action.

Throughout the Great War, from first to last, by the time a commanding general or one of his staff was able to get an inkling of how an assault was going or what was happening to troops up at the front, either from a stray telephone call or a physical message carried by a runner, the news was usually already out of date. On average, it took eight to ten hours for a message from divisional headquarters to reach the front—by which time the momentum of battle could have changed dramatically, or even been reversed.[11]

Defenders had a much better time of it. Even if communication lines were cut, officers and soldiers knew that they just had to hold on, and sooner or later the attack would slow down and peter out. This was what now happened along the Aisne.

"Everywhere the story was the same," the British liaison officer, Gen. Edward Spears, reported. "[T]he attack gained [ground] at most points, then slowed down, unable to follow the barrage which, progressing at the rate of a hundred yards [every] three minutes, was in many cases soon out of sight. As soon as the infantry and the barrage became disassociated, German machine guns . . . opened fire, in many cases from the front and flanks, and sometimes from the rear as well."[12]

After an agonizing morning and afternoon, the attack on April 16 halted as night fell. The French had advanced just six hundred yards instead of the six miles Nivelle had promised. On the third day, April 19, troops finally reached the Chemin des Dames road. On the fifth day, April 21, the Nivelle Offensive ground to a halt. The French army had suffered one hundred thirty thousand casualties to gain four miles and take twenty-eight thousand prisoners. But the old pattern had reasserted itself, despite Nivelle's reassurances. His tenure as commander in chief lasted only eight days after his offensive ended, as he was summarily dismissed. His jaunty, ebullient presence was seen no more at headquarters. But he had left a more somber legacy than just another failed offensive. He had been unable to produce any break in the German line, but he had managed to create one between the average French poilu and his officers.

The first sign of trouble came on April 21, when a convoy of trucks carrying troops from the elite First Colonial Infantry Division was headed from the front to the rear. As it moved along, weary soldiers leaned out of the trucks and shouted at passersby, "We're through with killing! Long live peace!" while their officers stared in mute embarrassment. Little more than a week later, survivors from a battalion of the Eighteenth Infantry Regiment, which the fight for the Chemin des Dames had reduced from six hundred to just two hundred men, was ordered back into the line. The men point-blank refused.[13]

Their officers immediately blamed their disobedience on drunkenness, and ordered their men to get back in the line once they had sobered up. Eventually the battalion did—although four of their number were arrested and later shot. Still, their behavior turned out to be more than an isolated case. More "acts of collective indiscipline," as their officers euphemistically termed it, began to sprout up in the French lines in the days after the offensive stopped. The severity grew to the point where, on May 3, when troops of the Second Colonial Division went to the front, they told their officers they would stay and defend their trenches but would not participate in any further attacks. Other units on other fronts told their commanders the same thing. By the end of the first week of May, the entire French army was on the brink of mutiny.

The reasons for the revolt were many, but they had a good deal to do with what was happening in Russia. Officers searching the belongings of arrested mutineers often found pamphlets preaching socialism and the downfall of the bourgeoisie; some suspected the discontent was being sown by German agents. Most of the revolutionary sentiment among the mutineers, however, was sincere, and much of it was inspired by the news stories from Petrograd of soldiers leaving the misery of the front and joining demonstrators in the streets, to demand change—in the spring of 1917, high prices and dwindling hopes for peace had provoked a wave of strikes across France as well as in Russia—even to the point of overthrowing the existing government. It was a cause that the average French soldier, especially after downing a bottle of cheap red wine and reflecting on all the *copains* he had seen killed around him, could identify with.

In the French case, however, soldiers did not leave their units to head for the capital—although at one point a band of soldiers armed with red banners did try to hijack a train for Paris (whether to lead a revolution or to get some much-needed rest and relaxation is not entirely clear), and the number of straight desertions did shoot up alarmingly. In most cases, men simply refused to fight anymore. Usually they didn't blame their officers for their plight. They knew officers suffered an even higher rate of mortality than enlisted men.[14] But they did blame the army and the government for the shabby way they were being treated, with bad food, little or no leave, and poor pay, not to mention their throwaway use as cannon fodder in tactics that had failed for almost three years running. In France, unlike Russia, there were almost no cases of violence against officers, or any violence at all. By and large, the soldiers' chief demands at organized mass meetings were for better treatment for their families, better food for themselves, the need for "peace," and an end to "the butchery." These were demands their officers, if they were honest enough, couldn't disagree with.

In any case, the French army mutinies soon became a strategic liability. As May passed into June, nearly half the French troops (some fifty-four divisions) were officially in a state of "collective indiscipline."[15] The army mutiny had become a national crisis that, if the Germans had been aware of what was happening and seized the moment, could have delivered victory to Berlin.

But the Germans did not seize the moment, and the one man who could save the French army from collapse was already in command. He was Gen. Henri-Philippe Pétain, and what he accomplished that spring and summer of 1917 may well have saved his country.

Known as the Lion of Verdun, Pétain replaced Nivelle as commander in chief on April 29, five days after his sixty-first birthday. The son of a farmer from the Pas-de-Calais region, Pétain had no aristocratic or political connections, and his army career therefore developed slowly after his graduation from Saint Cyr Academy, with service in various remote colonial posts. A bachelor until his midsixties, Pétain was best known in the army for his womanizing and his motto "Firepower kills." The coming of war in 1914 had proved him right, and soon catapulted him into senior posts, until he took over the Second Army on the eve of the German attack on Verdun in February 1916.

In holding Verdun during those harrowing, horrific months, Pétain raised defense to a military art form—whereas almost all his fellow generals had been entirely focused on the offensive, with pre-dictably horrible results. He understood, as few others did, that the new military technologies favored the defender over the attacker. At Verdun, he succeeded in inflicting unacceptable losses on a German army that had thought it could bleed the French defenders to death; instead, it wound up being bled nearly to death itself. Pétain's promise "They shall not pass" became a national catchphrase. When someone was needed to replace Nivelle, there was simply no other choice.

Pétain took command at a time of profound crisis in his beloved army, one that was crippling its effectiveness as a fighting force, pos-sibly permanently. All military plans had to be laid aside so that the state of the army itself could be dealt with. Urgently but quietly, Pétain got to work. He relied on two tried-and-true methods of reviving an army's spirit: the carrot and the stick. The stick in this case was mass arrests and trials for mutiny of soldiers from the most rebellious units. Literally hundreds of thousands of soldiers were court-martialed; 23,000 were found guilty, and a total of 432 were sentenced to death.

Movies such as Stanley Kubrick's *Paths of Glory* paint a particularly gruesome and misleading picture of the punishments handed out un-der Pétain. In the end, only 49 soldiers in the entire army were actually shot—although, in some units, officers took matters into their own hands and executed notorious mutineers without formal trial. Those men put on trial were selected by their officers and NCOs, with the knowledge and implicit consent of the rest of the men in their units. Therefore, it can be assumed that most of, if not all, the men tried and convicted were in some way seriously guilty of violating the military code. Several hundred mutineers were deported, but of the hundreds sentenced to life imprisonment, many were later reprieved.[16]

That was the stick, or hard edge of Pétain's restoration of discipline. The carrot, or softer side of his approach, included his reforming how French soldiers were treated, specifically at last making them feel that their commanders saw them as more than mere cannon fodder. In this task, Pétain had the advantage of knowing and liking the average soldiers, and they in turn liked and respected him. They knew, for instance, that during the Siege of Verdun, he had taken care to ensure that units were rotated out of the trenches every two weeks, instead of leaving them to fight until they died, as the Germans and many other French generals did.

Now, as commander in chief, Pétain set out on a "listening tour" of his units in the field, visiting ninety divisions in thirty days. He met informally with soldiers to hear their complaints and gave impromptu speeches standing on the hood of his touring car, promising soldiers that he would not send them into battle again until they were properly rested and trained, and that he would fire incompetent and dishonest officers. He met with junior officers, too, listening to their ideas and urging them to give recommendations on restoring a sense of pride in an army whose morale had been shattered.

Pétain instituted more generous leave for his men, too, and pressured the government to raise their pay. There were important changes in how the troops were fed; rest camps were introduced; and socialist tracts were replaced with his own "trench pamphlets," which stressed the importance of duty, honor, and country—and of obeying one's officers.

By July, the incidents of "collective indiscipline" were steadily falling; by August, the crisis had passed. Pétain had saved the French army—one could argue that he had saved France—but it had come at a price. He had promised his men he would not send them against the Germans again until they were ready, and for an entire year, from June 1917 to June 1918, they were deemed not ready. France had lost the ability to mount large-scale offensive operations on its own; its reputation as a premier military power was at end. This spelled the end of France's position as a Great Power as well.

The implications for the future were huge. In 1914, France and Germany were more or less equal rivals for power and influence. In 1918, Germany would be a broken nation, while a triumphant France led the other Allies to victory. But two decades later the once-defeated Germany would emerge as the most powerful country in Europe, while France was reduced to a distant second or even third place, behind Great Britain and the Soviet Union. All this was the direct result of the Nivelle Offensive and the mutinies of May and June 1917. Together they spelled the end of glory, and the end of greatness.

Pétain had managed to save the French army by a combination of his firmness and reforms. There was, however, one other thing he needed: for the Americans to get to France. On April 27, three weeks after America's declaration of war, Marshal Joffre visited Washington to urge the dispatch of an American division as soon as possible, and as many divisions as the United States could put in the field, as an independent command. At the time, Joffre knew nothing about the mutinies; neither, of course, did the Americans. But Joffre's plea worked. On May 2, he met with President Wilson, who agreed to the request.[17]

From that point on, whenever anyone asked Pétain what his plans were for the rest of 1917, he would answer, "I'm waiting for the tanks"—that is, the new armored vehicles being produced at the Renault autoworks outside Paris—"and the Americans."

LONDON, MAY–JULY

BY JUNE, THE possibility that the Allies could lose the war through the collapse of France had faded. But the even greater threat to the war effort still had to be faced: the impact of Germany's all-out submarine warfare.

In April, sinkings increased to more than 516 ships, or 880,000 tons of merchant shipping—well beyond the minimum of 600,000 tons Germany believed it needed to force Britain out of the war. A crisis was looming, and the two men who came to confront it would forge a new strategic relationship between the United States and Great Britain, one that would extend beyond this war into the next—and right down to today.

The first was David Lloyd George. He had been made Britain's prime minister in December 1916, not because he commanded the confidence of Parliament, the essential requirement for becoming prime minister going back to the days of Queen Anne, but because he commanded the loyalty of the British public. His party, the Radical Free Churchers, did not have a majority in Parliament. But the majority of those of other parties, Liberal, Unionist, and above all Labour, believed he was the only man for the job of getting Great Britain, and the British Empire, fully committed to the war effort.

That included both industrialists and labor unions. At a time when many crusty conservatives still thought of unions as illegal "combinations" and the British workingman as essentially a different species of humanity, Lloyd George was able to get the men who dug the coal mines and worked the factory floors, and their leaders and shop stewards, fully behind a maximum effort for the war. His close partnership with Arthur Henderson (nominally president of the Board of Education but in fact the fledgling Labour Party's "man" in the coalition government) included putting Henderson into his War Cabinet. Together, in person or on the phone, they would tackle incidents of strikes and labor unrest, persuading recalcitrant workers to go back to work or an employer to give way on some minor pay issue. Together they never quite got rid of labor problems during the war, but Henderson and Lloyd George did more than anyone else to make sure these problems were not a drag on mobilization for war.[18]

Meanwhile, it was the First World War and Lloyd George's premiership that put Britain's labor unions on the political and social landscape for the first time, and gave them some power over the economic life of Britain, power they have never completely lost.

The same was true of women. The suffragette movement in the prewar years had mobilized an activist minority in pursuit of the right to vote, though without result. When war came, its leader, Christabel Pankhurst, and thousands of other suffragettes marched on Whitehall with a new slogan: "We demand the right to work." As minister of munitions and then prime minister, Lloyd George gladly took them up on their offer. By 1917, 20 percent of Britain's labor force was female, from bus conductors and clerk typists to truck drivers and restaurant staffs. The army and navy had started up auxiliary services for women, providing them with their own khaki uniforms. As historian A. J. P. Taylor once remarked, "by the end of the war the woman's place was no longer in the home," thanks to Lloyd George's willingness to defy ordinary sexual convention.[19]

In the effort to mobilize, Lloyd George did not hesitate to challenge another of Britain's most cherished traditions. This was the workingman's habit, some would argue his right, to have a pint or a wee dram in the mid-afternoon or even on the way to work in the morning. Lloyd George decided that the consumption of alcohol at this rate and on this scale (nearly 200 gallons of alcohol per capita per year) represented a serious drag on the war mobilization effort. Even before becoming minister of munitions, he had declared in February 1915, "Drink is doing more damage than all the German submarines put together." His one-man wartime temperance campaign—Lloyd George himself was not a teetotaler, but many of the voters in his party were—convinced no less a personage than King George V himself to take the pledge of "no spirits, wine, or beer" for the duration of the war.

Millions enthusiastically followed their sovereign's example, but in Lloyd George's mind, voluntary compliance was not enough. Therefore, in May 1915, he oversaw creation of the Central Control Board to regulate the sale and distribution of alcohol in Britain. For a time in 1917, as prime minister, he even contemplated nationalizing the country's entire beer and liquor industry, but then decided that this was a draft too large to swallow.[20] He did, however, impose strict regulation of the hours during which establishments, particularly local bars or public houses, could serve alcohol. The regulations (letting pubs open only shortly before lunch and then closing them after lunch, until late in the afternoon) survived the war; indeed, they survived in Britain until the 1980s. They were Lloyd George's most lasting gift (if that is the word) to the nation whose fate had fallen into his hands, and his hands alone, when 1917 began.

Of all the issues that confronted him in the first months of that year, the most important was what to do about loosening the noose around Britain's neck: the German U-boat campaign.

The first step Lloyd George had to take was to get the nation's merchant shipping under control. Incredibly, after two and a half years of war, the requisitioning of ships for carrying wartime supplies had not essentially changed since the days of Nelson. The task was largely in the hands of the Admiralty, which sent its requisition orders to private shipping companies as the need arose. There was no central coordination, no centralized planning, no clear sense of what ships might be available to carry vital supplies, or when, let alone from where.

All that changed under Lloyd George. His most important decision was to create a Ministry of Shipping under a hardworking Scot, Glaswegian shipping magnate Sir Joseph Maclay. A private businessman, Maclay opposed nationalizing the entire merchant marine fleet, which was Lloyd George's first instinct. But he did see the good sense in bringing all the fleet's resources under public control, with a regular system for sending ships where they could get the cargo that would do the most good for the war effort.

Very shortly, 90 percent of Britain's merchant fleet was subject to control by the Ministry of Shipping.[21] At the same time, Lloyd George put another Scot, Admiralty official Sir Eric Geddes, in charge of all shipbuilding, both naval and merchant marine. Although Geddes was separate from the Ministry of Shipping, he and Maclay worked together to build vessels as fast as, or even faster than, the Germans could sink them. In the end, Geddes and Maclay set up a shipbuilding program that made more than three million tons of merchant shipping available every year.[22]

Maclay's other achievement was to figure out where the nation's shipping trade needed to be concentrated in order to have the maximum result. Before April 1917, much of Britain's overseas trade still rested on the long, long voyage to Australia and back.[23] Maclay quickly decided that the Atlantic trade with North America alone could meet almost all Britain's wartime needs. That decision early on prevented Britain's merchant fleet from being spread out all over the globe, even as the German submarine campaign was reaching full flood. Yet it also meant that securing the North Atlantic lifeline from Canada and the United States was now crucial to the course of the war—and even to the survival of Britain.[24]

To do that, Britain had to adopt one strategy from the Napoleonic Wars that would work in this war, namely, a convoy system. Unfortunately, the Admiralty was unalterably opposed to this idea. Its reasons were many, and superficially sound. Ships traveling in a convoy would present too large a target for U-boat captains, Britain's top admirals had told Lloyd George when he raised the issue back in November 1916; convoys would also require more escorting warships than the Royal Navy could possibly spare from its other vital missions. Besides, the admirals doubted that the average merchant captain had the skill to "keep station," in other words, to stay in orderly formation on a long voyage across the Atlantic. Really, First Sea Lord John Jellicoe told Lloyd George as late as January 1917, sailing in convoys would only make merchant ships more vulnerable to attack, not less.[25]

Maclay, who knew his merchant sea captains, thought these arguments absurd. Still, neither he nor Lloyd George could get the Admiralty to reconsider its opposition to convoys—even after Germany unleashed its unrestricted attacks on the high seas and the number of ships sunk surged.

Fortunately, the prime minister was about to get a persuasive ally in his campaign to shift to convoys: an American who was the new naval attaché at the American embassy in London, Vice Adm. William Sims.

Sims was an experienced hand in naval warfare, having served as an observer during the Russo-Japanese War. He also understood the danger Britain was facing in the war at sea: on his way into Liverpool Harbor, the ship he was on struck a German mine. Yet when Sims met the prime minister and asked what Britain needed most from the United States, Lloyd George said nothing about convoys, but he did say over and over again, "Ships, ships, ships," meaning naval vessels that could deal with the U-boat threat.

At the time, this meant destroyers, of which the United States had more than fifty. Using primitive hydrophones (a British naval invention) to track its submerged prey, a destroyer would then either drive the U-boat off or sink it, with pressure-detonated depth charges, another new naval technology. Now it was the Americans' turn to lend a hand. By May 4, 1917, the first six U.S. destroyers arrived at Queenstown, Ireland, the terminus of the typical transatlantic voyage from New York or Boston to Britain. By July, there would be thirty-four.[26] But there was also a need for smaller, faster, and more agile craft that could hunt down U-boats in coastal waters and approaches.

Here, again, the Americans stepped up. In the spring of 1916, the U.S. Navy Department had approved a new "sub chaser" design, 110 feet long, made entirely of wood, and armed with one or two 3-inch guns on the prow and a Y-shaped depth charge gun on the stern. Here at last was a design that could supplement the war against the submarine in home waters while letting the larger vessels concentrate on escorting convoys across the ocean.

The first of the sub chasers, designated SC-boats, came out of American shipyards in early 1917. In the end, more than four hundred of them would be stationed to guard Allied shipping from Ireland and the Mediterranean to Archangel, in Russia. Their success would be the making of the career of the young assistant secretary of the navy who first approved the design: Franklin Delano Roosevelt, a cousin of former president Theodore Roosevelt. Franklin Roosevelt's first steps to national prominence, and toward the White House his cousin had once occupied, began that spring of 1917 in the war against the U-boat.

Yet, even with the right ships, and the right number of ships, there was no winning the war for the Atlantic without convoys. Here Sims turned out to be a willing and persuasive ally in Lloyd George's campaign to overcome the Admiralty's obstinate resistance.

Fortunately, both found help from a study done by a junior officer inside the Admiralty, Cdr. R. G. H. Henderson. His study took on the argument that protecting the large number of merchant vessels entering British waters every week—more than 2,500, statistics showed—would require far more warships than the Royal Navy could possibly provide. Looking more closely at the numbers, Henderson was able to show that the vast majority of those 2,500 vessels were actually engaged in coastal trade. The real number of merchant ships completing a transoceanic voyage, the ones most vital to the war effort, was closer to 120 to 140, a far more feasible mission even for a heavily stretched and stressed Royal Navy.[27]

Besides, with America now in the war and U.S. Navy vessels available to provide additional escorts, the argument that convoy duty would overtax Royal Navy resources fell apart. A closer look at the numbers also dispelled the Admiralty's other argument against convoys: that so many ships traveling grouped together would be too easy a target. Instead, a quick lesson in statistics showed that the large number of individual ships not traveling in convoy actually *increased* the odds of a U-boat captain's finding ships to sink. In other words, a single large convoy (replacing multiple widely dispersed targets) would be harder to find in the vast reaches of the North Atlantic.

Sims had one final argument for the convoy system. "The thing to do," he wrote, "[is] to make the submarines come to the anti-submarine craft and fight in order to get merchantmen." In short, when the convoy was used as bait, the U-boat became the prey rather than the predator. So, if the Admiralty wanted to take the offensive against the German submarine fleet, the convoy system was the way to do it.

Slowly, in meeting after meeting, the Admiralty began to relent in its opposition. A personal visit by Lloyd George to the Admiralty offices on April 30 marked the tipping point. Sims cabled Washington joyfully: "The Admiralty has decided to give trial to convoy scheme."

On May 10, 1917, the first organized convoy sailed from Gibraltar. Not a single ship was lost.[28]

On May 25, Sims cabled again: "The principle of convoying merchant ships is approved by the Admiralty." Yet he still faced resistance to convoys from his own navy, including objections from navy secretary Josephus Daniels. In June, as plans were made for sending the first troopships from America to France, Sims warned that it would be "suicidal" not to organize them in escorted convoys, as the British were now doing.[29]

His arguments were backed by solid results by the British. Shipping losses had dropped off significantly in May, owing at least in part to the first convoys, from 516 ships to 413. The numbers took a slight jump to 433 in June, but then dropped to 311 in July and fell steadily after that, as the use of the convoy became standard practice—with the Admiralty's Convoy Room coordinating merchant sailings in convoy formation from all across the globe. In August, the number of sinkings stood at 242, less than half of what it had been in April, with only 511,000 tons lost—well below the 600,000 threshold. It never reached that existential danger level again.

As A. J. P. Taylor has written, the margin of survival remained narrow. "At one time there was less than one month's supply of grain in Britain." The sinking of a single ship carrying sugar from the United States meant that jam factories in Britain had to close their doors.[30] On the whole, though, the ships got through. Average losses for vessels traveling in convoys were less than 1 percent. And thanks to the Scottish duo of Maclay and Geddes, British and American shipyards were building ships far faster than the U-boats could send them to the bottom.

By July 1917, the German bid to win the war by sea alone had failed. Lloyd George's admirers, including historian Taylor, would like to claim that the adoption of convoys was due almost entirely to the prime minister's efforts—an impression not contradicted by Lloyd George's own account.

As Lloyd George's most recent biographer, John Grigg, admits, the prime minister never pressed the issue on the admirals as frequently or consistently as he might have. The fact that his famous in-person visit to the Admiralty coincided with the navy brass's change of mind seems to have been exactly that: coincidence. Yet Lloyd George's championing of the convoys that saved Britain deserves great credit, a credit shared with Admiral Sims.

Sims's cooperation with the prime minister on convoys extended to all matters naval. At one point, he even advocated integrating American naval forces directly with Britain's, although this proved too much for either side to accept. Nonetheless, William Sims's dedicated work on coordinating America's plans for the war at sea with London's efforts, including combined convoy escorts, was the first step in developing what would come to be called the "special relationship" between the United States and Great Britain, a relationship that went far beyond simply a strategic alliance. Lloyd George, for one, was all for it. As he told Secretary Lansing, he looked forward to building a world around "the active sympathy of the two great English-speaking countries"—words that anticipate Winston Churchill's Iron Curtain speech of nearly thirty years later, in March 1946, in Fulton, Missouri, in which he first coined the phrase "special relationship." Lloyd George told Colonel House that "if the United States would stand by Britain the entire world could not shake the combined mastery we would hold over the seas."[31]

The events of spring and summer 1917 proved him right. Still, he knew there was also a risk. With America fully engaged and committing all its industrial resources to the war, Britain's dependence on its former colony could become more than financial. It would eventually be strategic, with America pulling Britain along on whatever great enterprises President Wilson had in mind—whether Britain wanted to go or not. Lloyd George believed the brake that would prevent this from happening would be America's realization that its interests and Britain's were closely interconnected—that and President Wilson's personal horror of Great Power realpolitik.

But this was all. By taking America to war, Wilson had irreversibly

redefined its relationship with other nations, including soon-to-be allies such as Britain. As it became an active military player, the United
States would find its role to be not that of partner but increasingly that
of master. If Wilson's goal of making America the arbiter of a new
world order couldn't be achieved by staying out of the war, it would
surely be realized by plunging in headlong. It would take a long time
for Lloyd George's worries to come true, and for British power to be
eclipsed by the colossus of the Western Hemisphere. But the first
steps down that road, the road somewhat misleadingly marked "special relationship," were made in those spring days of 1917.

July saw the war at sea turn away from Germany and toward Britain and the Allies. That month, Lloyd George made another decision,
one that would have long-term consequences for both Britain and the
world.

In June, his successor at the Ministry of Munitions, Christopher
Addison, had stepped down. Lloyd George sensed he needed someone
as energetic and creative as he himself had been at the post, someone
who could combine administrative drive with a keen understanding
of what Britain's armed forces would need to fight, and how to get it
to them.

There was one person in his orbit who fitted the bill: Winston
Churchill. As first lord of the admiralty, Churchill had seen his political reputation destroyed when he championed the Gallipoli invasion,
the joint Franco-British expedition to Turkey that was supposed to
knock Germany's ally out of the war but that, instead, turned into a
fiasco, with more than 154,000 Allied lives lost for no gain. Churchill
had taken responsibility for Gallipoli's failure (not entirely justly) and
left the government in disgrace. He had even taken a commission in
the trenches in France, serving as a major in the Royal Fusiliers. In the
months following his political eclipse, perhaps he hoped a stray bullet
might end the humiliation and disappointment of seeing a promising,
even predestined, future die along with thousands of British, Australian, and New Zealand soldiers on the rocky slopes of Souda Bay.[32]

But in 1917, a year after the debacle of the Somme, memories of Gallipoli had faded. When generals such as Douglas Haig continued to keep their jobs despite failure after failure, for someone such as Churchill to lose his after just one seemed slightly unfair. Lloyd George certainly thought so. He had hoped to bring Winston back when he first assumed the premiership in December 1916, but the extreme hatred of Churchill still felt by the Tories in his coalition government had held him back.[33] Now, in July 1917, he tried again. A parliamentary commission study on the Gallipoli disaster in March had partially vindicated Churchill; in May, the former first lord of the admiralty paid a visit to Douglas Haig and the other generals in France; it went well. Those steps had cleared the way for Churchill's rehabilitation, although, when he and Lloyd George sat down to discuss Winston's possible portfolios in the Cabinet, Churchill made it clear that, grateful though he was for a second chance, he would accept a position only if it had a direct bearing on the war.

The War Office and Admiralty were clearly out. So was the brand-new Air Board, which would have suited Churchill perfectly, with his interest in airplanes and airpower. But the Tories, led by George Curzon and Alfred Milner, would never have stood for it. The appointment, a young Conservative MP said gravely, "would strain to breaking point the Unionist Party's loyalty [to Lloyd George]."[34]

The Ministry of Munitions was really the only choice. In the end, it proved to be a brilliant choice, and one that restored Winston Churchill's political career. He proved as energetic and innovative a minister as Lloyd George could have hoped, and for the rest of that year and the next, he would oversee key developments of the new weapon that would transform the World War I battlefield and the history of warfare: the armored vehicle code-named "the tank."

Eventually, Churchill came to epitomize the "special relationship" he first defined in his Iron Curtain speech after his own premiership had ended. By 1946 it was widely recognized that Churchill had saved Britain in World War II. It was much less clear until later that Lloyd George had done the same during World War I. Both men had done it by turning to the United States for help. In Lloyd George's case, it had involved Admiral Sims's support for the concept of convoys, and what happened next. In Churchill's case, it was getting the fifty World War I–era destroyers America sent to Britain's rescue in September 1940, Lend-Lease in March 1941, when Britain's fortunes in the war against Hitler seemed at their bleakest.[35]

Yet both episodes were merely stages in a process that began unfolding in 1917 and gathered momentum only as time passed. That process was the eclipse of Britain as global hegemon and the rise of the United States as its increasingly self-conscious heir.

MR. WILSON'S WAR

We are mobilizing the nation as well as creating an Army.
—WOODROW WILSON TO SEN. CARTER
GLASS, APRIL 9, 1917

WASHINGTON

D ECLARING WAR WAS one thing. Getting ready to fight a war, specifically one that was supposed to make the world safe for democracy, was going to be quite another.

This would be a war on a scale no American government had ever confronted before—a war demanding a transatlantic strategy as well as coordination with the Allies on land, at sea, and in the air—and there was no doubt on anyone's part that Wilson was not up to the task. Having never served in the military himself; having little knowledge of how the war in Europe was actually being fought and what resources would have to be mobilized to meet the challenge (much larger than the small-scale expeditions he had sent into Mexico in 1914 and 1916); having personal questions himself as to whether he was the right man to be a war leader; and still plagued by lingering uncertainty that joining forces with the Entente was the right course of action, President Woodrow Wilson looked woefully unprepared for what lay ahead.

As did the rest of the government, and the country. Even after the sinking of the *Lusitania* alerted Americans to the fact that what was happening in Europe might inevitably draw them into war, the steps that had been taken to get ready for that possibility remained minimal. On July 21, 1916, for example, Congress passed and Wilson signed the Naval Appropriations Act, which authorized five hundred million dollars to build ten new battleships, six battle cruisers, thirty submarines, and fifty destroyers over the next three years. The act's immediate target, however, was not Germany's maritime challenge, ironically enough, but Britain's. Wilson was still smarting from Britain's imposition of its naval blockade. "Let us build a navy bigger than [the United Kingdom's]," Wilson remarked, "and do what we please."[1]

Earlier, on June 3, Wilson had signed a National Defense Act, calling for the creation of the largest U.S. Army since the Civil War, with 175,000 regular troops and 450,000 National Guardsmen—still a tiny fraction of the size of the armies then fighting in Europe. Wilson's theme was "national readiness" in case the war in Europe did spill over onto American shores. Eight months later, national *unreadiness* was more like it. Even as late as February 1917, Gen. Hugh Scott, army chief of staff, complained that "the President does not want to do anything which will give the Germans an idea that we are getting ready for war, so we are not allowed to ask for any money or get ready in any serious way."[2]

Indeed, when Wilson learned that the Army General Staff was drawing up contingency plans for a war with Germany, his first instinct was to have the staff fired.[3]

Now, with war officially here, Wilson would have to scramble to make up for lost time. His task included figuring out how to add the half million new men for the armed services he had mentioned in his April 2 speech. A military draft seemed the only possible answer, but even as late as January, Wilson had dragged his feet about imposing the country's first draft since the Civil War, when the draft had provoked bloody riots in New York City and nearly split the North in two.

Now, however, in the face of modern war's demand for manpower, there was no choice. On May 18, 1917, six weeks after war had been declared, the Selective Service Act came into effect.

It could have been a logistical as well as a political disaster. There were many people alive who could still remember how unfair and arbitrary the draft had been during the Civil War, when the wealthy (among them John D. Rockefeller) were able to buy their way out by paying a substitute. But the trio who drew up the plan for Selective Service in 1917—army judge advocate Gen. Enoch Crowder; Lt. Col. Hugh Johnson; and a thirty-six-year-old major who had been running the War Department's Bureau of Information (in effect, its propaganda and censorship wing), Douglas MacArthur—managed to craft a system that turned out to be as fair as it was efficient. By handing control of the selection process over to local boards of ordinary citizens from the same towns, even the same neighborhoods, as the young men they were drafting, Crowder, Johnson, and MacArthur turned what could have been a public relations and administrative nightmare into a crowning success—it was so successful that it would serve as the model for an even bigger military draft effort during World War II.[4]

In the end, more than two million young Americans would get the call for the army, the navy, or the marines. Across the ocean, in Europe, America's allies were eager to have these fresh troops breathe new life into the war effort. But in what capacity? That was the question Wilson had to take up when the former French commander in chief Joffre and British foreign secretary Arthur Balfour arrived in Washington during the third week in April.

Wilson had not wanted these visits. He was afraid of any summit meetings or public gestures that seemed to imply that the United States was joining the Entente as a formal ally rather than an "Associated Power," as he had insisted. Also, he worried that Joffre and Balfour would try to pressure him to embrace the entire Entente war agenda, which he saw as just another extension of typical Great Power geopolitics.

His fears were unfounded. Somewhat to his surprise, and certainly to his relief, Joffre and Balfour respected Wilson's desire to stay at arm's length from the Allies as an Associated Power. They were willing to take U.S. support any way they could get it. Their meeting was also a chance for the two spokesmen for their countries to take stock of the American president. Balfour and Wilson did not hit it off at first, but later, the foreign minister had to aver that the president was "at that moment by far the most important man in the world."[5]

The French delegation was even more intrigued by this "lay Pope," as Joffre's interpreter, Émil Hovelacque, sardonically described Wilson. To the Frenchmen, Wilson seemed wooden and impassive at first. When he spoke, though, "the subtle inflections of his musical voice" revealed "a sudden intensity of life" that his icy, buttoned-down appearance belied. "I watched this austere, wise face of a Scottish dialectician," Hovelacque remembered, and "the Celt appeared to me in the rapid flash of a smile, in the sudden humanity of [his] clear eyes."[6]

While Joffre went on a rapid cross-country tour extolling French-U.S. ties going back to the American Revolution, Balfour stayed in the States for five weeks, giving a rousing address to a joint session of Congress before he left. By then, the awkwardness with which the two scholars (one a political scientist turned politician, the other a politician turned philosopher) had started their relationship with each other had thawed to a mutual respect. Before he left the United States, Balfour met privately with the French ambassador to the United States, Jean Jules Jusserand. Balfour was now convinced that Wilson was fully committed to the war "until the security of the liberal nations is assured." He was also sure that victory was near. "You will no doubt come then to Europe," he told the ambassador gleefully, "and we shall celebrate together."

Only one incident in his meeting with Wilson still bothered Balfour. After a private dinner at the White House, Balfour took the bold step of revealing to Wilson some of the secret treaties that had been drawn up among the Allies, such as the 1915 Treaty of London, which had brought Italy into the war on the Allied side in exchange for future territorial gains at the expense of Austria; and the 1916 Sykes-Picot Agreement, which in effect would divide up Turkey's empire in the Middle East between Britain and France once the war was won.

Wilson seemed unfazed by this news, which was passed to him confidentially, "man to man," as Balfour later put it. Balfour realized that "when Wilson had made up his mind about coming into the war, it was the *present* and the future that mattered to him, not the past . . . those Treaties had no importance to him."[7]

Here Balfour was wrong. In fact, the treaties mattered very much to Wilson, not at the time perhaps, but later, at the very end of the year, after a series of devastating revelations would force him to reassess his commitment to the Allies and their war aims and lead him to push the entire agenda regarding the war in a sharply different and radical direction.

Those revelations would come from the Russian Foreign Ministry, and would be an unexpected gift to the American president from Lenin.

* * *

SECRET TREATIES OR no, Wilson now had to get into the serious business of drawing together the resources, both material and human, of the United States into the means of achieving victory. In doing this, he made a serious mistake at the very start—one with fateful consequences later on.

The minute he heard of Wilson's speech calling for war against Germany, Theodore Roosevelt had thrown himself in the effort with all his usual energy and enthusiasm. He became overnight the president's biggest supporter, and followed up on a project he had first broached with the secretary of war, Newton Baker, back on March 19: that of raising, at his own expense, a division of volunteers to be trained at Fort Sill, Oklahoma. Baker had given the former Rough Rider the cold shoulder, but on April 10, four days after Congress declared war, Roosevelt followed up with a visit to the White House and buttonholed the president himself.

At first Wilson was cold and uncommunicative with the man who for more than a year had publicly branded him a coward. But Roosevelt's enthusiasm was not to be resisted. "First he commended in the warmest terms the President's message to Congress and gave his entire approval to the administration's program."

Roosevelt went further. All the animosity of the past, he said, "would be dust in a windy street, if we can make your message good . . . If we can translate it into fact, then it will rank as a great state paper, with the very great state papers of Washington and Lincoln." High praise, indeed—and Wilson was not immune to flattery, especially from a charismatic personality such as Theodore Roosevelt. "There is a sweetness about him that is very compelling," Wilson told his aide Joe Tumulty afterward. "You can't resist the man."[8]

Soon, the two men were laughing and talking like old friends, and after twenty-five minutes, Roosevelt left. But if he thought the thawing of relations would bring him closer to his goal of raising and commanding a division of volunteer troops as he had done with the Rough Riders, he was to be bitterly disappointed. On April 13, a formal letter came from Secretary of War Newton Baker turning Roosevelt's offer down flat. Baker said command in this war would go to men who had "devoted their lives exclusively" to military service—a slighting dismissal of Roosevelt's own experience leading men in combat in Cuba less than twenty years earlier.[9]

For Roosevelt, it was a disappointment and a gratuitous put-down—and for Wilson, a missed opportunity. The visit had been Roosevelt's offer to bury the political hatchet, to throw aside personal and ideological bitterness now that he and Wilson had found themselves on the same side. But Wilson could not bring himself to agree or to respond in any way except, unforgivably, through a letter from a third party. The good reasons for turning Roosevelt down were few, and the good reasons for accepting his offer many. Even giving TR a token military command, or redirecting his offer of combat duty by making him a special military adviser, if only in an honorific role, would have given Wilson regular access to a former president and commander in chief who understood the vagaries of modern warfare far better than he himself did, both from the viewpoint of geopolitics and from having served on the battlefield.

But such an idea, or such a generous gesture, was beyond Wilson. As historian Richard Striner has said, "Wilson missed a priceless opportunity to turn an enemy into a friend"—and instead, he turned a possible friend into a dedicated enemy.[10]

Roosevelt never forgot the slight, and to the end of his life he believed it had been made out of personal spite. He communicated that feeling to his friends, including Henry Cabot Lodge. Acceding to Roosevelt's request would have cemented Wilson's standing with pro-war Republicans; turning him down alienated them permanently. If people sometimes wonder why the Massachusetts senator's opposition to Wilson and the League of Nations was so bitter and personal, it wasn't just because Lodge thought Wilson's utopian global vision dangerous and his version of the League a direct threat to the United States. He also remembered Wilson's humiliation of his friend Roosevelt, whose only wish had been to serve his country alongside his three sons, who would go on to fight in France—one of them, the eldest, Quentin, would die there in the last months of the war—and to command men under fire one last time.

It was still up to Wilson to choose a general to command American troops going to France. There were two possible choices for commander in chief of the American Expeditionary Force: Gen. Leonard Wood, hero of the war in the Philippines; and Gen. John J. Pershing, whom Wilson had sent on the punitive expedition against Mexican bandit Pancho Villa in 1916. Wood, however, was close to Republicans and had been a vocal critic of Wilson's failure to prepare the country for war. So, even though Pershing and the president rarely saw eye to eye on anything, Wilson opted for him, the man known as "Black Jack."

Fifty-six years old, strong-minded, and at the peak of physical fitness, Pershing had seen his army career take him from president and first captain of his West Point class of 1886 to three tours of duty in the Philippines and then to commander of the American expedition to Mexico. When he returned to West Point in 1897 as a tactical officer, cadets nicknamed him "Nigger Jack" (or, more politely, "Black

Jack") because he had commanded the African American Tenth Cavalry, or Buffalo Soldiers, on the frontier, and he liked and respected his black soldiers. In 1898 he had led them up San Juan Hill, where the Buffalo Soldiers fought with desperate bravery and 50 percent of the regiment's officers were killed or wounded.

Pershing's racial views were bound to clash with Wilson's. The Progressive president was also a keen white supremacist and insisted on segregating the U.S. Army in the same way he had most of the federal government. Even though the army was desperate for men, the number of blacks being drafted was kept artificially low. By the war's end, more than 350,000 African Americans were serving in the American Expeditionary Force on the Western Front. Pershing made sure they earned pay equal to that of white soldiers, but Wilson had approved the policy that assigned them only to segregated units commanded by white officers. Most units were also supply or logistical units, which meant that the vast majority of black soldiers saw no combat and were left out of any chance for medals or promotion.

Wilson's support for segregation led to trouble and violence. When the all-black Twenty-Fourth U.S. Infantry Regiment was transferred from Columbus, New Mexico, to Houston, the soldiers were confronted with segregated streetcars and white workers at their camp who demanded separate water fountains. This led to clashes with local authorities, and the beating of a black soldier by a white policeman. On August 23, 1917, that set off a full-scale riot, which ended with the shooting deaths of two soldiers, four police officers, and nine civilians (a fifth police officer and another soldier died later from wounds sustained in the riot, while a fourth soldier died from injuries he received during his capture the next day). The army deemed the riot a mutiny, and nineteen black soldiers were executed, while another forty-one received life sentences.

Wilson had told a group of black soldiers who came to protest his policy that "segregation is not a humiliation but a benefit, and ought to be so regarded by you gentlemen." His commitment to white supremacy left a stain on America's armed forces, especially the army, that would remain long after they were desegregated after World War II.

If Wilson lacked the gift of handling the human factor in leading the country to war, he was more than eager to deal with the bureaucratic, institutional side. From his Progressive perspective, however undesirable war was, it did offer a sterling opportunity to extend into the arena of military and industrial relations, and into the larger economy, the principles of the strong administrative state he had developed in his writings and deployed in domestic reforms in his first term as president.

Starting that April, he seized on this opportunity like a man possessed. When he told Sen. Carter Glass on April 9 that his goal was to mobilize a nation as well as create an army, he foresaw that "we must keep every instrumentality in it [i.e., the nation] at its highest pitch of efficiency and guided by thoughtful intelligence"—and the way to do this was by flexing the fullest powers of the federal government.[11]

At the start of 1917, there wasn't much bureaucratic machinery to accomplish all this. But Wilson did have something to build on, thanks to Thomas Alva Edison.

After the *Lusitania*'s sinking, it wasn't surprising that, as America's most famous inventor and robust media personality, Edison was asked what he thought America should do to protect itself. "If any foreign power should seriously consider an attack upon this country, a hundred men of [scientific] training quickly would be at work here upon new means of repelling the invaders," Edison told reporters. "I would be at it myself."

In the summer of 1915, navy secretary Josephus Daniels met with Edison, and together they set up the Naval Consulting Board, or NCB, which would solicit suggestions from scientists and other private citizens on how to help the U.S. Navy better defend America in case of war.[12]

The NCB included members of the country's leading technical and engineering associations. One of them, Howard Coffin, president of the Society of Automotive Engineers, declared, "Twentieth-century war demands that the blood of the soldier must be mingled with three to five parts of the sweat of the men in the factories, mills, mines, and fields of the nation in arms"—a sentiment David Lloyd George or even Erich Ludendorff could have endorsed.

Coffin also opined that the war was "the greatest business proposition since time began"—an opening for American entrepreneurial instincts if ever there was one.[13]

The idea of American business joining, even taking the lead, in making the country well armed as well as prosperous would be realized during the making of FDR's "Arsenal of Democracy" in World War II.[14] For Woodrow Wilson in 1917, however, it was enough to encourage direct Washington intervention into which businesses were producing which military resources, and which economic resources could be deployed to make war matériel. By an act of Congress in June 1916, the NCB spawned the Council of National Defense, or CND, which was charged with building a detailed inventory of the scientific and industrial resources that could be put to use for the military in case of war.

Remarkably, the army was largely uninterested in getting a handle on how it would obtain the guns, artillery, uniforms, and bullets it would need if pushed into the kind of modern warfare under way on the battlefields of Europe—let alone how it was going to feed the hundreds of thousands of draftees it would be taking on in a matter of weeks. "If we really have a great war," one high-ranking officer remarked sourly in June 1917, after the army had been officially committed to hostilities for two months, "our War Department will quickly break down."[15] The Navy Department did somewhat better, but it, too, was largely unprepared for the demands in terms of the industrial and technological base it would need to fight a modern war at sea, particularly a war against the world's biggest and most modern submarine fleet.

In the end, it was up to civilian Washington and private industry to figure out how to arm, clothe, and feed a nation at war. After several false starts and hesitations, in July 1917 the CND gave way to the

War Industries Board, or WIB, under the chairmanship of Wall Street wizard and Wilsonite Progressive Bernard Baruch. The choice was significant: Baruch's experience as a financier provided him with an overview of American business and industry that no one else in the country could match at the time. Even then, the WIB struggled to achieve the kind of meshing of government, business, and military resources needed for a smooth-running industrial machine.

Yet, in the growing alphabet soup that was Wilson's Washington at war, the WIB represented a turning point. The one great continuity of the American economy since its founding, the transformation of resources into wealth through private initiative and capital, was now superseded by a new transformative force, that of the federal government. America's "empire of wealth," as historian John Steele Gordon has dubbed it, would now be matched by an empire of government.

Legislative as well as executive action emanating from Wilson's desk made this a reality. At Wilson's request, the Food and Fuel Control Act—called the Lever Act after its chief congressional sponsor, Rep. Asbury Lever of South Carolina—passed in Congress in August 1917. It authorized the government to set prices for wheat, cotton, pork, coal, and petroleum (the last two were now vital to both the army and the navy and to the nation's railroads that supplied them) and to license all large-scale food producers and distributors. One newspaper pronounced the Lever Act "the most revolutionary measure ever enacted by an American Congress"; another branded it state socialism. Both were right.[16]

Nonetheless, since it seemed justified by wartime necessity, the measure stuck. Out of it would sprout two new federal agencies. Wilson would appoint to head the Federal Fuel Administration Harry Garfield, president of Williams College and son of former president James Garfield. Garfield and his colleagues were now empowered to set the prices and supply of coal and oil for the entire country, using local boards at the state and county level to enforce their regulations and rules. Out of the effort to cut back on civilian use of fuel, it was the Federal Fuel Administration that first introduced daylight saving time a year later, in 1918. Anyone who gets confused today about how to set his clock when the official time change rolls around, or who has to recite "Spring forward, fall back" before he does, can thank Harry Garfield and Wilson's Fuel Administration.

The head of the Federal Food Administration had even more sweeping powers. The man Wilson selected to head it up was an Iowa-born engineer named Herbert Clark Hoover. Hoover had led the administration's one major intervention in the war in Europe before 1917, albeit a humanitarian instead of a military one: the Commission for Relief in Belgium, which fed millions of starving refugees with American wheat and corn. (In a few years, Hoover would have the opportunity to do so again, this time in Russia.)

Hoover's spectacular success with the war relief program made him an obvious pick to lead the Federal Food Administration. He never had occasion to issue the kind of sweeping directives his counterpart Garfield did when, for example, Garfield mandated "gasless Sundays" and at one point ordered the closing of thousands of factories across the country to end a coal shortage. "Although Americans can be led to make great sacrifices," Hoover said at one point, "they do not like to be driven."[17] Yet Hoover did regulate prices for nearly every agricultural commodity and controlled an elaborate licensing system that prevented the export of foodstuffs by private businesses. He forced wheat farmers to sell their product at a set price to a government-controlled corporation and worked with farm organizations and financial institutions to rein in speculation on food-related futures in America's commodity markets.

Hoover liked to think of his efforts and initiatives as "voluntary," but in fact, as historian Robert Zieger points out, each relied on compulsory requirements and sanctions: "The de facto suspension of market forces placed the government in every wheat field, grain silo, and kitchen."[18] That suspension generally benefited the biggest and most established agricultural interests and distributors, and shoved smaller businesses into the background—and marked the emergence of an American version of corporatism, of big business and big government forming a permanent alliance. Progressive writers such as Herbert Croly and Charles Van Hise had argued for something along these lines; it underpinned aspects of Theodore Roosevelt's "New Nationalism."[19] Now it became a tool for President Wilson, not only to get America prepared for war and then to fight it, but also to realize his Progressive dream of a nation that responded to the agenda and needs of government—as opposed to the other way around.

As 1917 rolled along, the arms of the federal octopus would extend into other areas of American life. American shipbuilding had long fallen into the purview of the Shipping Board; the need to pay for the war meant a sharp increase in corporate and personal taxes (although not as much as some Progressives, such as Sen. Bob La Follette, wanted). The big breakthrough, however, came when the federal government became the nation's biggest bond salesman, with the first "Liberty Loans," or Liberty Bonds, authorized by Congress on April 27.

Treasury secretary McAdoo saw the issue of Liberty Bonds as a way not only to help pay for the war but also to reduce unnecessary consumption (and therefore fend off inflation) by encouraging people to invest in these government-issued war bonds instead. McAdoo used every trick in the book to get Americans to buy the bonds. Boy Scouts fanned out across the country to urge people to devote some of their paychecks to the Liberty Loan drive; actors such as Charlie Chaplin and singers such as Enrico Caruso lent their prestige to the drives. McAdoo also didn't hesitate to use more coercive ways of persuading people that they had to buy, or else.

"A man who can't lend his government $1 per week at the rate of four percent interest is not entitled to be an American citizen," he declared. In fact, the five successive Liberty Loan drives during the war were outstanding successes. All together, they raised some $20 billion—almost a third of that from people who earned less than $2,000 a year.[20] But the Liberty Loans were only the tip of the financial iceberg.

Of the initial authorization of $5 billion, more than $3 billion was set aside for the Entente powers. "Unlike American troops," writes historian Adam Tooze, "American money flowed quickly." By July, McAdoo had advanced $485 million to Britain alone. Most of that money, in turn, was used to purchase goods in the United States: Congress had imposed the condition on the loans that they be used to buy American. "After April 1917, the US Federal government was operating a gigantic, publicly funded export scheme." To keep the scheme going, the Inter-Allied Supply Council, set up to speed the placing and filling of orders for the matériel the Allies needed, was overseen by a U.S. assistant treasury secretary. The council also worked directly with the War Industries Board—just to complete the corporatist circle.[21]

How much of this transatlantic arrangement driven by American financial/industrial synergy led from Washington would survive the war was anyone's guess. Most observers, including McAdoo, probably assumed very little. And it was very little—but it would shape the postwar world decisively. One result, for example, was that the dollar came to replace the pound sterling as the world's reserve currency (one of McAdoo's declared goals in the spring of 1917).[22] The U.S. loans were made on the condition that they could not be used to support either the pound or the franc, or to repay the loans that J.P. Morgan had made before America entered the war. The consequence was that while Britain's debt (and France's) only continued to mount out of sight, so did America's financial leverage over its Allies once the war ended. They would be reduced to junior partners, even if they won the war—as now they must, with America on their side.

In this way Wilson's desire to see America emerge as the world's leading power was now ensured. The hegemony he desired on the moral plane would be undergirded and reinforced by the fact that the world's Great Powers owed America more than they could ever repay—while only the United States would come out of the war with a currency still founded on gold.

Only one of the Allies managed to avoid the debt trap Wilson and

McAdoo had set for them: Russia. It would do this not just by dropping out of the war before everyone else did, but also by, in effect,
dropping out of the community of nations. The revolution that had
come to that unhappy country would, as we'll soon see, have many
unexpected twists and turns. In the end, Lenin would lead Russia into
the abyss, but arguably, Woodrow Wilson helped lead it to the preci-
pice, and doomed its democratic revolution to frustration and failure
while that revolution was still less than eight weeks old.

This is not what Wilson had intended, of course. Robert Lansing
had written to Wilson that it was not enough just to recognize the
new government in Petrograd. Some words of encouragement from
the American president would send the right message: Stay the democratic course, stay the course of war with Germany. Help is on the
way.[23]

Yet that was exactly the problem.

PETROGRAD

ON THE SAME day that Wilson's Cabinet recommended war against
Germany, March 20, the president had issued his official recognition
of the new Duma-based government that had replaced Czar Nicholas.
In his April 2 address, he embraced the Russian Revolution as America's revolution as well, part of the "wonderful and heartening things
that have been happening within the last few weeks."

But fear haunted London, Paris, Rome, and eventually Washington. If, for whatever reasons, a confused and disrupted Russia decided
to cut its losses on the international scene and opt out of the war, the
result could be disastrous: the release of dozens of German divisions
from the war on the Eastern Front to weigh in on the Western Front.

The men who had risen to the surface in both the Duma and the
Petrograd Soviet in the early phase of the revolution—Pavel Miliukov; Alexander Kerensky; Nikolai Chkheidze; and Chkheidze's fellow Menshevik Irakli Tsereteli, a Georgian who was the party's main
foreign policy spokesman—were still committed to keeping Russia in

the war, but not for the reasons that had animated Czar Nicholas II. "The time has come to take the decision on war and peace into one's own hands," members of the Ispolkom had declared on March 28, in a document loftily entitled "An Appeal to the Peoples of the World."[24] Their goal was not taking control of Constantinople and the Black Sea, or acting as the protector of Serbia and other Slavic nations and peoples. It was simply to secure what another generation would call peace with honor: not to surrender to Germany, but to stand tall until Berlin was willing to say, "Let's talk."

In a strange way, Russia's new government faced a problem that was the obverse of Wilson's. The U.S. president wanted to figure out how to reshape the world for the better by entering the war he had hitherto tried to avoid. Kerensky and his colleagues needed to decide how to reshape Russia for the better by staying in a war when every political instinct said they should leave it—and when staying the course might mean a huge foreign relations bonus, including financial and material aid from America.

Yet how to stay the course when the nation was in chaos and when public support for the war was ebbing away, among civilians and in the Russian army? And how to do so while also reopening the door to the negotiated peace proposed by Germany in December (and to Wilson's peace note of December)—a door that the czarist regime had firmly shut in order to prevent Russia's collapse? That was the delicate balancing act that the new government in Petrograd was now forced to carry out in the tense weeks following the abdication of the czar, thanks to Wilson's hesitations. The alternative was catastrophe, although no one quite grasped it entirely at the time.

No one, that is, except Lenin, who could sense weakness and disaster as a barracuda senses blood in the water.

The Provisional Government had made two fatal blunders that would weaken its ability to control events in Russia, or to sustain the war effort. The first was its so-called Order No. 1, which it promulgated on March 14 without consulting the Duma. Its aim was to address the grievances that soldiers in the Petrograd garrison had about their treatment by their officers—grievances, they told the Provisional Government and Ispolkom, that had driven them into mutiny. The order was addressed to the "Garrison of the Petrograd Military District," but everyone who read it immediately assumed it applied to all army units, even those at the front.[25]

The first article called for the creation of representative soldiers' committees (or soviets) in every military unit, down to the company level. The second allowed every company in the Russian army to send a representative to the Petrograd Soviet. The other articles ordered officers not to use their honorific titles and not to address soldiers in an offensive manner; took control over all military equipment, including artillery pieces and machine guns, away from officers and gave it to the soldiers' soviets; and gave off-duty soldiers the same rights as Russian civilians, which meant they didn't have to salute their officers or even (by implication) obey them.

If anything was designed to overthrow all discipline in the Russian army and deprive it of the means of maintaining order in the country, this was it. As one sailor said when a debate ensued over what Order No. 1 actually meant, "We understood it straight: disarm the officers."[26] Even worse, it also gave the Petrograd Soviet the power to overrule the Provisional Government on military matters. The goal of Order No. 1 was to appease mutinous soldiers and sailors, to make them feel that they were now part of the political process. The actual result was to turn the Russian army into an armed mob that the Provisional Government could neither depend upon nor control.

The second blunder was adopted soon after Order No. 1. It was the Provisional Government's decision to abolish the czarist provincial bureaucracy and, even more critically, the Russian gendarmerie and the Department of Police. At one stroke, it eliminated the organs of government that represented and enforced law and order across the country. Again, the goal was to overthrow the law enforcement agencies, including the hated Okhrana, that had come to represent tyranny and oppression to millions of Russians. But it also meant that only two weeks after the revolution, Russia had no police force—and no way to enforce laws made by the government in the rest of the country. No wonder that, on March 22, Duma member Alexander Guchkov could telegraph General Alekseev:

> The Provisional Government has no real power of any kind and its orders are carried out only to the extent that this is permitted by the Soviet of Workers' and Soldiers' Deputies, which controls the most essential strands of actual power . . . One can assert bluntly that the Provisional Government exists only as long as it is permitted to do so by the Soviet.[27]

In other words, the Provisional Government had allowed a major shift of power to the Petrograd Soviet, which was itself a chaotic nonstop debating society that had thousands of members and followed no agenda. This in turn meant that the real power was in the hands of the Soviet's political committee, Ispolkom, whose members were becoming more and more at odds with the men in the Provisional Government and the Duma. By the beginning of April, it had become clear: whoever controlled Ispolkom controlled the fate of Russia, starting with the capital.

All the same, none of this worried the man who was emerging as the leading figure in the Provisional Government, Alexander Kerensky. His prestige in the Ispolkom remained undimmed. He was convinced that, despite some mistakes, the revolution had been a success. For all the turmoil and chaos, it had been relatively bloodless. Total casualties were fewer than 1,500, with only 169 deaths. Many of these were of army and navy officers lynched by their soldiers and sailors; the mass shootings of protesters that many had feared (or hoped for) had never happened.[28]

Kerensky also saw the transition of power from Nicholas II to the Provisional Government as more than an unqualified success. "What happened I can only describe as a miracle," he wrote later. "Amidst the chaos and darkness of the collapse of Czarism, there rose the bright sun of liberty to shine on a country broken with suffering."[29]

Nor did he feel any bitterness toward the former autocrat. In the first week in April, he had an unexpected encounter with the deposed czar and his family at Tsarskoye. He saw a "small man in uniform" and recognized him at once. "I quickly went up to Nicholas II, held out my hand with a smile, and said abruptly, 'Kerensky' . . . He shook my hand firmly, smiled, seemed encouraged and led me at once to his family." Kerensky then realized he was not "the outcast, the inhuman monster, the deliberate murderer I used to imagine. I began to realize that there was a human side to him."

Yet "authority, like everything else, [the czar] held too cheap," Kerensky mused. "He was altogether weary of it."[30] But that authority was now in the hands of men who were not weary, who were ready to use it to make a better, more progressive Russia—and to revive Russia's standing in the world, and with its Allies. "Those who have lived through" the revolution, Kerensky wrote, "as I did, feeling the sudden load of responsibility for the destinies of the State descend on their shoulders, will never forget it to their dying day."[31]

Everything depended now on what America, and its president, Woodrow Wilson, decided to do next.

In April, representatives from Britain and France had come to Petrograd to meet with the new government. Their goal was to convince Russia to stay in the war. They found the government firmly set against any separate peace with Germany, but it did urge the British and French representatives, both leading socialists, to reassess the Entente's war aims. A negotiated peace would allow the new government to avoid having to fight a war to the finish: a war that many Russians no longer had faith in and, to put it bluntly, the Provisional Government was not sure it had the means to sustain. Both representatives, Arthur Henderson and Albert Thomas, went home deeply worried about the future of Russia's democratic revolution, and its ability to stay in the war.[32] By the same token, Kerensky and the Provisional Government were left deeply worried that London and Paris didn't care whether the new Russian government survived, as long as it didn't open separate negotiations with Germany.

This left America and Wilson as their last hope. Wilson knew the democrats in Petrograd faced almost insuperable challenges. He also knew that the Russians, "in setting up their new government and working out domestic reforms," might reach a point where they found "the war an intolerable evil and would desire to get out of it on any reasonable terms."

Yet Wilson was now also inalterably convinced that Germany's imperialist ambitions could be broken only through force. And as long as Germany's record of militarism went unpunished, so would France's and Britain's.[33] Therefore, when the Provisional Government adopted on April 4 what came to be called the Petrograd formula for ending the war—"self-determination, no annexations, no indemnities" (a formula that bore an eerie resemblance to Wilson's earlier "peace without victory")—it was Wilson who now spoke for the Entente as well as the United States in a warning message to the Russian people on May 22. His message had fateful consequences for the future of the Russian Revolution.

In it, Wilson highlighted the continuing German menace to civilization. Berlin sat at the center of "a net of intrigue directed against nothing less than the peace and liberty of the world," he declared. "The meshes of that intrigue must be broken, but cannot unless wrongs already done are undone," meaning the freeing of Belgium and withdrawal from France.

"The day has come to conquer or submit," Wilson declared. "If we stand together, victory is certain and the liberty which victory will secure. We can afford then to be generous, but we cannot afford then or now to be weak."[34]

When Wilson's address was released, its impact in London and Paris was very different from that in Petrograd. The American president's recent visitor, British foreign minister Balfour, was pleased that Wilson's words "counteract effects which some of his earlier pronouncements have apparently had in Russia," particularly his now troublesome January 22 "Peace Without Victory" speech.[35] Lloyd George likewise breathed a sigh of relief.

By contrast, in Petrograd, the effect was stunned disappointment. Still, there was no going back now. Pro-Entente foreign minister Miliukov had just been forced to step down, and Alexander Kerensky had taken his place. Kerensky himself had doubts about how long the Russian army could stand to remain active and in the field. In a heart-wrenching address on May 14, he had told his audience he was sorry he had not died two months earlier, when it seemed Russia had a bright new future to look forward to. As affairs are going now, he said gloomily, "it will be impossible to save the country. Perhaps the time is near when we will have to tell you that we can no longer give you the amount of bread you expect or other supplies on which you have a right to count. The process of the change from slavery to freedom is not going on properly. We have tasted freedom and are slightly intoxicated. What we need is sobriety and discipline."

For that reason, Kerensky made an anguished plea to Russia's soldiery: "There is no such thing as a 'Russian front,' there is only one general allied front. We are marching toward peace and I should not be in the ranks of the Provisional Government if the ending of the war were not the aim of the whole Provisional Government; but if we are going to propose new war aims we must see we are respected by friend as well as by foe . . . The fate of the country is in your hands, and it is in most extreme danger. History must be able to say of us, 'They died, but they were never slaves.'"[36]

Fine words, but there was another man now in Petrograd who had a very different idea of how to go forward, and how to bring the war to an end. He was Lenin, and even as his closest advisers thought that his plans for having the Bolshevik Party seize the government were delusional at best and potentially suicidal at worst, Lenin himself had no doubt he was on the right path to power.

* * *

THE NIGHT THEY arrived in Petrograd, Lenin and Nadya had no idea where they were going to stay. One of Lenin's sisters, however, was living with her husband in a small apartment at 48 Broad Street, northeast of the city center. The couple made their way there, and for the next three months this would be their home: in a crowded apartment—another sister, Maria, also lived in the flat—in a shabby tenement, where Lenin would write speeches and articles (more than fifty for *Pravda* in May alone) and plan the revolution, the *real* Russian Revolution, that he sensed was coming.

Lenin believed with all his powerful emotional and intellectual convictions that what had taken place in March in Petrograd was no revolution at all, merely the substitution of one faction of the ruling class for another. What was needed now was a revolution like the one he had pointed out in his *April Theses*: a "proletarian class revolution" that would sweep Russia's elites and bourgeoisie into the gutter of history and then ignite a similar upheaval around the world. Like Wilson, Lenin in the spring of 1917 was thinking in global, not national, terms. That was one of the limitations of Socialist Revolutionaries such as Kerensky and Mensheviks such as Chkheidze, he felt: they were still thinking about how to change Russia, how to use the war to bolster Russia's standing. Lenin was thinking about how to change the *world*, and how to use *ending* the war to trigger a world revolution.

As for those, including those in his own party, who argued that Russia's working classes were simply too few and too isolated to set off the sweeping changes he envisaged, Lenin scoffed at their ignorance. There was another, much simpler tool at hand for achieving the same thing—the government's own peace formula had even mentioned it. This was "self-determination." That, Lenin declared confidently, was where the Bolshevik Party should plant its revolutionary hopes and stake its insurrectionary plans.

That term again, *self-determination*—but in Lenin's hands it took on a sense very different from, and much darker than, its meaning in Wilson's or even in the hands of the Allies who had first brought it up and put it on the geopolitical table. For Wilson, "self-determination" was the fulcrum of progressive change, the means of achieving democracy and freedom for dozens of nationalities and millions of people.

For the French and British, "self-determination" had been a rhetorical device to grab Wilson's attention and convince him that they were on his side—but also a possible crowbar for pulling apart the empires of their opponents, the Turks and the Austro-Hungarians.

For Lenin, "self-determination" was a clarion call not for democracy and freedom but for revolt and bloodshed that would rock the capitalist imperialist order down to its foundations. While other Marxists looked at the Easter Rebellion in Ireland the previous year (which had cost who knew how many lives and destroyed the heart of Dublin) as an exercise in atavistic futility, Lenin saw it as exactly the sort of revolt he and the Bolsheviks should be looking to achieve. "To imagine that social revolution is *conceivable* without revolts by small nations in the colonies and in Europe . . . with all their prejudices . . . is to *repudiate social revolution.*"

The Bolsheviks "would be very poor revolutionaries if, in the proletariat's great war of Liberation for socialism, we did not know how to utilize *every* popular movement," whether it was outside Russia, as in Ireland, or inside Russia, where the Poles, Georgians, Ukrainians, Latvians, and other subject nationalities were champing at the bit to achieve their independence, now that the Russian Empire seemed teetering on the brink of chaos.[37]

A war of all against all—that was what Lenin ultimately wanted to emerge after the end of the war Russia was currently waging. "He wanted this peace only because he hoped that it would unleash an even more encompassing international class war," as historian Adam Tooze has written—a class war that would eventually sweep the globe.[38]

Lenin's apocalyptic revolutionary vision, however, was too much even for committed Bolsheviks. One of them wrote, "Lenin's program is sheer insurrectionism, which will lead us into the pit of anarchy. These are the tactics of the universal apostle of destruction." Menshevik leader Chkheidze, when he learned of Lenin's agenda and realized there was no ground for a reconciliation of Mensheviks and Bolsheviks as some had hoped, simply said with a shrug, "Lenin will remain a solitary figure outside the revolution."[39]

For Lenin, of course, that didn't matter because, in his mind, there still hadn't been a revolution. That spring, however, he did learn to temper his message slightly, and focused on the immediate goal of ending the war for Russia: "Peace, land, and bread" would become the Bolshevik slogan, with peace first and foremost, and Lenin would use it to gain control first of his party and then, he hoped, not of Russia itself—that was pointless at this juncture—but of the real center of power, the Ispolkom, which led the Petrograd Soviet.

The turning point in the first case came on April 24, when the Bolshevik Party met at the Kschessinska Mansion in Petrograd, where Lenin made sure his allies were elected to key positions and where skeptics about his *April Theses* were voted out. Most doubters about Lenin's views had deserted the party by then, anyway. On the desirability of a socialist dictatorship, on the "agrarian question" (i.e., confiscating all land in Russia and giving it to the peasants), on the "national question," and on ignoring the usual Marxist stages of historical evolution and going straight to a proletarian dictatorship, Lenin won by large majorities. The party was his personal property once again.

Over the next month and a half, Lenin became a man on fire. He spoke at every meeting that would have him; he wrote articles for *Pravda* on every conceivable topic; he harangued every crowd of soldiers, sailors, or passersby who would stop to listen. Everywhere, he preached the same message: Ruin is imminent. Catastrophe is on the way. Capitalism is bringing every country, including Russia, to the brink of destruction. The only possible salvation is revolution and the transition of all state power into the hands of the revolutionary class. As Lenin's biographer Service notes, "ruin, catastrophe, and destruction ran like a red thread through his vocabulary."[40] By his constant hammering, day after day, Lenin began to make an impression on those milling through the streets of Petrograd who wondered whether the revolution they had carried out in March was going to make their world better or worse. So far, with bread still in short supply, with law and order collapsing because there was no police force, and with the same dismal, dreary news from the front, of soldiers with no rifles, no ammunition, and no hope—*Pravda* and other Bolshevik media liked to heighten the bad news coming from the fighting—it looked as though worse was winning.

That suited Lenin. He was finally in his element. As he confided to Nadya one day in the apartment at 48 Broad, he had found himself at last. He and Nadya had also reached a decision, made the very night they first arrived. This would be the end of the years of exile, the end of the wandering. At last they were in Russia to stay, to make a revolution. As it happened, they were wrong, but their determination lingered far beyond anyone else's ability to cast them a different fortune.

For, despite Lenin's success at regaining control of the Bolshevik movement, and in building on the budding popular following, revolution seemed as far away as ever.

And despite Woodrow Wilson's May 22 pronouncement, America and the Allies were far from abandoning Russia. On May 16, the U.S. Treasury gave the Provisional Government an immediate loan of one hundred million dollars, an almost unimaginable windfall. When Wilson learned that tons of foodstuffs were waiting at the port of Vladivostok to be shipped to Russia's starving cities, he at once sent a mission of American engineers and railroad technicians to figure out how to get those supplies moving across Russia's crumbling Trans-Siberian Railway. In July, the U.S. Railroad Administration, in charge of all America's railroads during wartime, even authorized the sending of no fewer than 2,500 locomotives and 40,000 freight cars to Russia.[41]

Meanwhile, Kerensky and his colleagues were throwing themselves into one last effort to rebuild the Russian army. To a sensible man, time might have seemed to be running out for staging a major revolution. But Lenin was not a sensible man; he was a single-minded, dedicated man, ever fiercer and more fanatical in his conviction that time and history were on his side.

Besides, by now he had a man who, at critical moments in the coming months, would provide the means of moving events to the revolutionary tipping point.

His name was Leon Trotsky.

SUMMER OF DISCONTENT

I tell you heads must roll, blood must flow.
—LEON TROTSKY, JULY 1917

LONDON

IF ANYTHING DEMONSTRATED that Europe's Great Powers no longer controlled their own world war, and that the war was now controlled by two outsiders, Wilson and Lenin, it was the unprecedented events of June through August 1917. It was then that the global balance of power began to shift away from Europe and toward other, farther shores.

The wave of disruption and discontent that swept across that summer struck London and Paris first. Ironically, it coincided with an event that seemed to promise hope that the war was finally taking a positive turn. This was the arrival of General Pershing in Paris in June 1917, to a tumultuous reception. He was embraced with enthusiasm that offered a foretaste of what would overtake Wilson when he reached Paris a year and a half later. As Pershing passed by, it was not unusual to see people kneeling in the street weeping. Then, on July 4, Independence Day, people shouted their approval, American and French flags waving, as elements of the American First Division paraded down the Champs-Élysées. Pershing's promise, "Lafayette, we are here"—actually said by an aide, not Pershing himself—seemed a harbinger of a fresh new start.

But that was it. As July progressed, it became clear the Americans weren't coming—at least not for a long stretch. London and Paris had expected 175,000 American troops to arrive by the end of July. Instead, there were not even 17,000.[1] In declaring war, Wilson had not paid enough attention to how he was going to raise the men to fight overseas, let alone get them there. Now his inattention was putting enormous pressure on his new allies. The French army was virtually comatose after its wave of mutinies; it was incapable of returning to the offensive, perhaps even of defending its own lines. That meant Britain and its commander in chief, Sir Douglas Haig, would have to step up.

In Whitehall circles, especially with Prime Minister Lloyd George, Haig's reputation was at a low ebb. Along with Joffre, he was the general who seemed most to embody a military mind-set that combined strategic failure with needless slaughter. That certainly was Lloyd George's view in the early summer of 1917. Haig had led the British army to two colossal failures in two years, at the Somme and then in the Nivelle Offensive, with heavy losses. The prime minister would have preferred to remove Haig altogether, but that was politically impossible. Haig still had the confidence of others in the War Cabinet, including Lord Curzon and Gen. Jan Smuts, the extraordinary South African philosopher and statesman who always seemed ready to defer to the wisdom of British generals even though he himself had decisively beaten them a few years earlier, in the Boer War.[2]

Besides, Haig had announced that he now had a new plan, one that would succeed where the Nivelle Offensive had failed, and that would decisively shift the balance of the war in the Allies' favor before the Americans came. In addition to the diminishing but still potent threat of German submarines, Lloyd George and the Cabinet had another distraction to deal with. In the summer of 1917, London was under regular attack from the air by German bombers—the first sustained strategic bombing campaign from airplanes in history—and unless the bombers could be stopped or contained, the prime minister worried that the attacks would spread panic and disorder throughout the capital like nothing else in the war.

It was true that, since 1915, London had seen sporadic German attacks by zeppelin airships, as had Paris. Even St. Petersburg had been threatened in December 1916—although the weather proved too cold, and the zeppelins never left the ground. Yet the damage, and casualties, from the great, slow-moving dirigibles had been negligible. The Germans also paid a heavy price, as their hydrogen-filled zeppelins made relatively easy targets for British pursuit planes armed with incendiary ammunition, and heavy weather or unfavorable winds forced them to miss their targets altogether and even to crash and burn without dropping a single bomb.

The Gotha IV biplane bomber, which first went into service in February 1917, was an entirely different order of war machine. Forty feet long, with a seventy-eight-foot wingspan and a crew of three, and powered by two 260-hp Mercedes DIV engines, the Gotha resembled an enormous bird of prey, a black-green pterodactyl of the skies that, at eighty-three miles per hour, traveled at almost twice the speed of the zeppelins. Each Gotha was armed with eleven hundred pounds of bombs—far less than the great zeppelins could carry, but the Gotha could also deliver that payload with deadly accuracy, as its very first raids on England showed.

The first came on May 25, when a flight of Gotha IV bombers dropped sixty bombs on a Canadian military camp and on Folkestone, a port town on the English Channel. Ninety-five people were killed and 195 wounded, while all the attackers got away.

Then, on June 13, came the first Gotha attack on London, which caused more casualties than all the zeppelin raids put together. It began at 11:30 a.m., and within two minutes the German planes had dropped seventy bombs on a one-mile radius around Liverpool Street Station. The Royal Albert Dock and Southwark were also hit, as were other parts of the city. The raid killed 162 and left 432 injured. The dead included 18 children, who died when a bomb hit a school in Poplar, in the Docklands. The modern age of strategic bombing, which would pass through London to Guernica and Rotterdam down to Dresden and Hiroshima, began that day in June 1917.

There was another devastating attack on July 7, which was also the last daylight raid on London, as British air defenses began to gear up to protect the city. The Germans then shifted to nighttime raids, an eerie (though smaller-scale) forerunner of the Blitz that Londoners would experience in 1940.

All through the following September and October, residents could hear the bombers roar overhead in the night, scattering bombs throughout the city while people scrambled into the Underground and their basements for shelter. "At the slightest rumor of approaching aeroplanes," Lloyd George would write in his memoirs, "tubes and tunnels were packed with panic-stricken men, women, and children. Every clear night the commons around London were black with refugees from the threatened metropolis."[3]

The panic was fed by the worst wave of labor unrest Britain had seen since the beginning of the war—much of it fueled, as it happened, by events in Russia. Thirty-two Liberal and Labour MPs voted on a resolution calling for peace negotiations based on the Petrograd formula. Lloyd George warned his Cabinet about the looming threat of a British soviet unless something were done to contain the unrest. Even the king himself worried about the growing threat with "too much democracy in the air," and in June, he made a drastic decision that would seal the fate of the Russian czar and his family (see chapter 13).

In short, the pressure was mounting for that swift "knockout blow" against the Germans that Lloyd George had been promising since becoming prime minister; patiently waiting for the Americans was no longer an option. That meant reining in his impatience with Haig and listening to the commander in chief's plan.

From where Haig was sitting, the best place for that knockout blow was in the north, up along the Ypres Salient, where British troops had halted the initial German advance in 1914 but which still stuck out into the Allied lines like a malignant blister west of Lille and into northern France. Haig's idea was to push through the salient and move up into Belgium, where he could capture Ostend, just thirty miles from his planned breakthrough point. Taking Ostend would

shut down German submarine operations there. It would also allow
Haig to sever the enemy's main railway links with Germany and roll
up his flank from the north.

There were several problems with this plan. The first was that the
Belgians had broken the dikes and let in the sea north of the German
lines, so this flank was protected by impassable sheets of seawater.
The second was that Ostend and neighboring Zeebrugge were not
the main bases for German U-boats; Germany's own ports were. A
major ground offensive would do far less to halt the existing German
submarine threat than the convoys were already doing, and might
even consume valuable resources better spent shoring up the Western
Front until the Americans finally arrived.

That, at least, was the Frenchmen's argument when they learned
of Haig's plan. Commander in chief Pétain did want the British to
distract German attention away from his vulnerable army, but with
small-scale diversionary operations, not a massive Somme-like attack
that might leave British forces as demoralized as his own. The rising
star of the French command, Gen. Ferdinand Foch, also warned that
the muddy terrain along the Ypres Salient would require a plodding
"duck's march," and Pétain added that one could not fight both the
Germans and the mud—*Boche et boue* in French.[4]

Yet Lloyd George felt himself not in a strong enough position to
say no. Haig had been planning such an offensive since January 1916;
the other British generals, including the chief of the Imperial General Staff, Sir William Robertson, refused to come up with any better
ideas. On June 19–21 came the showdown at Whitehall, with Haig
on one side of the table and Lloyd George on the other. One by one,
Haig shot down Lloyd George's doubts, objections, and alternative
suggestions, including sending the troops who would be used in the
attack at Ypres to Italy to reinforce Italian plans for a new offensive.
In the end, Haig said that "it is necessary for us to go on engaging
the enemy" and that he was confident he could at least secure his
first objective (the town of Ypres, now shattered beyond recognition
by three years of constant war) in the first attack and then "achieve

great results" before the year was out. Besides, Haig had just scored an unexpected success on the battlefield, which gave his plan both credibility and increased urgency.[5]

The place was the Messines Ridge, a one-hundred-fifty-foot-high promontory south of the Ypres Salient from which the Germans were able to watch everything going on behind British lines. For two years the British commander in the sector, Gen. Sir Herbert Plumer, had dug a series of deep mines under the ridge and filled them with explosives—hundreds of thousands of tons' worth. On June 7 at 3:10 in the morning, the British turned the detonator. The explosion was so large that Lloyd George heard it from his bedroom at Number 10. In an instant, the entire geographic feature known as the Messines Ridge vanished. British troops moved up and occupied the sector with almost no losses. It was an amazing success. Still, two years' preparation to move two miles made Berlin look farther away than ever.[6]

Besides, Haig could now argue that with the loss of Messines, the Germans would not be able to observe his preparations in front of the Ypres Salient as they had before. So, Lloyd George gave way, as politicians generally did on both sides when met by the arguments of confident generals. Along the Ypres Salient—where the regular British army had met its death in 1914, and where the Germans first used poison gas in 1915—preparations began for the mightiest British offensive of all, and it was the last time the fate of the war, and of the world, was in the hands of western European powers alone.

BERLIN

AT ALMOST THE same time, the summer's discontent was seeping into Germany's leading cities and into the Reichstag. Germany's chancellor, Bethmann-Hollweg, found himself besieged from both the left and the right. Before the summer was out, he would be shoved from office and Germany would be headed in a direction that would culminate sixteen years later in the ascent to power of another German chancellor, Adolf Hitler.

The winter of 1916–17 had been the most brutal of the war for Germany, and not only because of the cold weather. The German people had stoically endured war and blockade, and sacrificed more than two million of their sons since the first German soldier stepped across the Belgian border, in a hope for victory that had gone unfulfilled. Now they were running out of patience as well as food.

Food rationing had gone into effect across Germany in 1915. As 1917 began, rations were now cut to less than one thousand calories a day, less than a third of what the average German ate in 1914.[7] Families were living almost entirely on potatoes, bread, and milk—infants and children under the age of two were limited to one quarter liter of milk a day. The government had paid for the war largely by printing money, which meant that the price of everything, including food, soared on the wings of inflation. Eggs—only two were allowed per week—cost thirty pfennig apiece, compared with eight pfennig in 1914. The black market soared. Those who couldn't, or wouldn't, participate in it suffered constant deprivation, even as they waited for the telegram informing them that a husband or another brother or son had been killed at the front.

The president of police of Greater Berlin warned the minister of the interior that the public was mired in a sense of "despondency as well as fear for the future." In 1917, even the potatoes began to run out. From New Year's Day until the end of March, Kiel, a port city with 220,000 residents and a major naval and industrial center, had to go without a single potato.[8] The food question, the police official warned, had come to dominate every other aspect of life. "One fears the fourth winter of the war."

Over the spring, the despondency had reached the factories. On March 27, the workers in two major shipyards in potato-less Kiel went on strike; they were soon joined by striking workers from other facilities in Kiel. When authorities tried to send one hundred of the striking workers to the front as punishment, the Ministry of the Interior vetoed the plan—it worried that the punitive action would only spread the unrest. Nonetheless, more strikes followed in other

German factories and cities, while food riots struck in cities such as Cologne, Dortmund, and even Berlin. At the beginning of July, the Reichstag met to vote on the next round of war credits. The government's critics were ready and waiting.

The criticism came from an unexpected source. Matthias Erzberger, a Center Party stalwart, was one of the most enthusiastic "hawks" when the war broke out, and a keen supporter of unrestricted submarine warfare. On July 6, however, he rose to his feet and gave a speech that sank a dagger deep into the heart of the government. He declared that hopes for "a submarine victory" were an illusion. Instead of Britain's being starved into submission in six months, as the generals had promised, it was Germany that was starving.

It was time to face reality, Erzberger declared. "We must prepare a platform which will make peace possible this year." He sat down amid applause and shouts of support.[9]

The effect of Erzberger's speech was to shatter the political coalition that had stayed the course since the war began. Words like his might have been expected from a Social Democratic deputy, but coming from a center-right figure such as Erzberger, they carried weight and even urgency that they would have lacked if they came from someone on the left side of the political aisle.[10] Twenty-four hours after he spoke, a coalition committee of Center Party, Progressive, and Social Democratic deputies launched a joint resolution calling for peace and an end to the war "without annexations or indemnities"—in effect, and with no sense of irony, the Petrograd formula.

Erzberger's "ambush," as Bethmann-Hollweg put it, sighted the chancellor in the political crosshairs. He scrambled to correct the damage by trying to get the Kaiser to agree to a fresh round of democratization after the war. However, the Kaiser and Generals Hindenburg and Ludendorff knew right away who was really to blame for the crisis: Bethmann-Hollweg. It was he who had sent the Allies the original peace note that got all this started; it was he who had halfheartedly endorsed the resumption of unrestricted submarine warfare. (Ironically, it was his approval of this same measure that had made him persona non grata among the Reichstag's doves.)

On July 12, Hindenburg told the Kaiser he considered Bethmann-Hollweg no longer fit for office. Both he and Ludendorff, he said, felt that the chancellor's "gloomy views" regarding his appeasement of the German left would eventually turn Germany into a "republic," just like the one taking root in Russia. Hindenburg added, "We [meaning he and Ludendorff] will not go along with that"—and so they handed the Kaiser their resignations.[11]

In the end, there was only one resignation Kaiser Wilhelm was going to accept, and that was his chancellor's. Bethmann-Hollweg was thoroughly hated and despised by his Kaiser and the military command; he also had no credibility left among their opponents. On July 9, he rose in the Reichstag to announce, "My position does not matter . . . I myself am convinced of my own limitations . . . I am considered weak because I seek to end the war. A leading statesman can receive support neither from the Left nor the Right in Germany." He quit on July 13, a day celebrated equally by those on the left and the right. On July 19, even as British guns were being wheeled out to begin the bombardment of the Ypres Salient, the Reichstag voted by a large margin to approve a peace note calling for a "permanent reconciliation of all peoples" and a new, more equitable international order based on free trade, freedom of the seas, and the creation of an "international judicial organization." No one mentioned a "league of nations," but the echoes of Wilson's "Peace Without Victory" speech of January were unmistakable. His goal six months earlier, peace without victory, was now the goal of the German Reichstag as well.[12]

But it was too late. A future German chancellor, Gustav Strese-mann, had risen on July 9 to call for Bethmann-Hollweg to quit, be-cause "no one is more poorly equipped to conduct peace negotiations, both with America and Russia."[13] In fact, Wilson had already moved on; his high-minded call for war on April 2 had rendered his equally high-minded earlier position totally irrelevant. Just as his commitment to war, total war, had doomed the original Petrograd formula and, with it, the future of Russian democracy, so now it doomed any chance of a peace with Germany before the final hammer blow fell.

Besides, the resolution went nowhere. If German doves imagined this was a victory, they were mistaken. The Kaiser quickly passed the chancellorship over to a political nonentity, Georg Michaelis, who had been commissioner of food supply since 1917. All that Wilhelm II knew about him was that "he's supposed to be short, a midget."[14] Michaelis swiftly buried the Reichstag's peace resolution; he knew his job now was to listen to and obey the real master of Germany: not the Kaiser but Erich Ludendorff.

Ludendorff's main effort now was to fully implement the "commitment to total war" made the previous year as part of the Hindenburg Program. That meant complete mobilization of all the resources of the German economy for the war effort, and victory. Even disabled and maimed veterans returning from the front, he reasoned, should learn to hold down jobs in munitions factories and shipyards. The goal had been to double Germany's wartime output by August 1917. Germany's iron, steel, and coal industries were already firmly under the control of the German army. As 1917 wore on, the clamps grew even tighter.

Later claims that the Hindenburg Program, when implemented, doubled or even tripled war production of certain critical items such as gunpowder and artillery pieces were largely propaganda.[15] Still, it created the illusion (useful later to rulers in both Nazi Germany and the Soviet Union) that large-scale coercive centralization could achieve powerful economies of scale, that a command economy could dramatically increase output without any loss of efficiency or opportunity costs, and with enough public benefits in terms of output to more than compensate for the inconvenient "collateral damage" that such a system does to human beings.

That damage was palpable, and not just to German citizens caught in total war's industrial meshes. The Auxiliary Service Law of December 1916 was supposed to put to work in Germany's war economy all males between the ages of seventeen and sixty not serving in the armed forces and not employed in agriculture, and to sharply curtail the ability of Germans to change or leave jobs.[16] But with no fewer than thirteen million German men now in uniform, there simply weren't enough hands to tend to all the machines or to work on all the assembly lines. The workforce had to be supplemented with a large rise (of more than 75 percent) in women's labor participation, not all of it voluntary, and a sharp rise in child labor.

More than a quarter million children age fourteen and fifteen were put to work in the factories, while the remaining deficit had to be made up with foreign workers, most of them dragged in from Germany's occupied territories. Tens of thousands of Belgians, Poles, Frenchmen, and Balts were deported to work in German industry, while more than four hundred thousand POWs were put to work in the agricultural fields of the Reich. It was a chilling prelude to what would happen in the next war, when Germany's insatiable demand for war production would turn nearly all Central Europe into a vast slave labor camp.

It was also not good for the situation at the front. That July, at a time when they were most sorely needed, almost two million men had to be released from military duty to return to factories, mines, and farms. In the end, concludes historian Holger Herwig, "the attempted mobilization of the nation for 'total war' was well beyond the means of the Wilhelmian state."[17]

But the administrative and ideological legacy of what Ludendorff had attempted to do remained. On September 2, the anniversary of Germany's great victory in the Franco-Prussian War, retired grand admiral Alfred von Tirpitz, the original architect of all-out submarine warfare, announced the creation of the German Fatherland Party, which took a strong stand against the Reichstag's peace resolution and against any alternative to total victory. *"Deutschland Erwache!* [Germany, awake!]" Tirpitz proclaimed. "Your hour of destiny has arrived!" The result was an explosion of patriotic sentiment on the German right. Within six months, the German Fatherland Party had more than 1.25 million enrolled members, and its legacy would extend far beyond the war. Tirpitz's "Deutschland Erwache!" would go on to become the slogan on Nazi Party banners. Likewise, General Hindenburg's maxim, "The entire German people should live only in the service of the Fatherland," would be the motto, and epitaph, of a Germany that sprang into being over the summer of 1917 and only finally died in 1945 in a graveyard of ashes.

At the time, of course, it could have been argued that if Germany had any remaining chance of winning this war, there was not a moment to lose. On August 2, mutiny broke out among the sailors on four navy battleships in a harbor near Wilhelmshaven. Although the mutiny was quickly suppressed—two of the mutineers were immediately executed, and three others were given lengthy prison sentences[18]—it was a warning of what might happen if victory, or peace, did not come soon. In addition, a month earlier, Germany had had to face another unexpected threat.

Almost out of nowhere, the Russians were on the move again, with Alexander Kerensky at their head.

PETROGRAD

KERENSKY WAS LEADING not as a general in the field but as the Provisional Government's new minister of war. Earlier that summer, he had emerged as the revolution's political powerhouse, and the last hope for the war in the east. Kerensky sensed that the survival of what he called "the freest democratic republic in Europe"—which had embraced equal rights for women, including the right to vote; abolished capital punishment and punishment by exile; and established full liberty of conscience and separation of church and state—now depended entirely on a strong and unified army.[19] That in turn meant resuming the initiative on the battlefield once more, to galvanize the troops and nation but also to demonstrate to the other Allies, including America, that Russia could still be counted on—even though many in and outside the government worried that Russia might not be able to count on the Allies.

That May and June, Kerensky threw himself into the job with the same energy and emotional dedication that he applied to everything. He replaced his top general and toured the front tirelessly, meeting common soldiers and giving one rousing patriotic speech after another. His appearance had the desired effect. "Crowds gathered for hours to catch a glimpse of him," an eyewitness recorded. "His path was everywhere strewn with flowers. Soldiers ran for miles after his motor car, trying to shake his hand or kiss the hem of his garment."[20] When he returned to Petrograd, the crowds were equally large, and audiences shouted themselves hoarse.

Another eyewitness said of him, "[W]hen he stretches his hands out to you . . . you feel that he touches you, grasps you with those hands, and irresistibly draws you to himself."[21] The Russian Revolution had at last found its Garibaldi, almost its Napoleon—someone on whom the fate of the entire nation now seemed to rest.

Kerensky's preparations weren't limited to the cult of personality, however. He also reinforced military discipline, trying to counter much of the laxness and insubordination that the earlier Order No. 1 had unleashed inside the ranks. He even reimposed the death penalty for military offenses, a step for which he would be much blamed later on. He fought hard to counteract defeatist propaganda from German and Bolshevik sources—he was just beginning to get the sense that they were in fact one and the same[22]—but his main achievement was to restore some belief that the Russian army could once again be an effective instrument of war, and now also the spearhead of Russian democracy.

By June 29, everything was ready. There was a two-day preliminary bombardment, and then Russian troops, led by one of the ablest commanders in the army, pushed toward Lemberg, which had been the principal target of the Brusilov Offensive in 1916.[23] For two days, everything went well, and as patriotic emotion surged in the Congress of Soviets, even Lenin did not dare oppose motions in support of what history has come to call the Kerensky Offensive.

Then things fell apart. After their initial successes, the soldiers decided they had done enough; their officers could not get them to resume the advance. On July 19, the Germans came to the rescue of their Austro-Hungarian allies, as they had so many times before, and counterattacked. In no time, discipline in the Russian ranks collapsed. Thousands of soldiers began streaming for the rear; others stayed behind to loot and rape. Thousands of others simply laid down their rifles and quit. Even the otherwise demoralized Austrians were able to take the offensive, and pushed the crumbling Russian front as far as the River Zbruch, on the Romanian border—while the advancing Germans shifted their attention north, toward the Baltic coast and the port of Riga, Latvia's capital, only three hundred fifty miles from Petrograd.

It was not just that the Kerensky Offensive collapsed, and with it, Kerensky's reputation as savior of Russia. The death knell of the Russian army, and even Russia itself, had been sounded—unless some way could be found to halt the advancing Germans in their tracks.

It was at this moment that Lenin decided to overthrow the Provisional Government.

Or did he? A hundred years later, the historical record remains murky. If Lenin did order the insurrection that would become known as the July Days, he carefully airbrushed away that fact later. Certainly, everyone involved, including Lenin, would later deny that he had anything to do with it. Yet it seems incredible that a party as centralized and disciplined as the Bolshevik Party could have taken such bold, decisive action—that is, seizing upon a major governmental crisis to stage a coup d'état—without the knowledge and approval, not to mention the direct orders, of its iron-willed leader. In any case, if it's not entirely certain that Lenin was directly behind the move, it is clear who was its chief instigator: Lenin's newest close associate, Leon Trotsky.

Born in 1879 to a Jewish farming family in southern Ukraine, Leon

Trotsky (originally Lev or Leiba Bronstein) first met Lenin in 1902 and had always been largely sympathetic to his radical views on how to bring about revolution in Russia. Yet it would be a mistake to think of Trotsky as Lenin's disciple, let alone his heir apparent. In July 1917, Trotsky was not even officially a Bolshevik. Before the war, the two had seriously split over Lenin's doctrine of democratic centralism, which Trotsky believed (prophetically, as it turned out) would end up handing over too much control to one man, a dictator who could act in the name of the proletariat with no checks on his power.

He also differed from Lenin in having had firsthand experience of the one country that most symbolized capitalism at its highest pitch—namely, America. Trotsky's fierce opposition to the war had driven him from his safe haven in France to Spain, from which he had then escaped to New York, where he could write, speak, and organize more or less freely without being stalked by the Russian secret police. For three months, from January through March 1917, he and his wife, Alexandra, lived in "the monster known as New York," as Trotsky later described it, in an apartment at 1522 Vyse Avenue, just off 175th Street in the Bronx.

While Trotsky spoke almost no English, he edited the Russian-language socialist paper *Novy Mir* and wrote for the Yiddish-language *Forverts*. Although he traveled to Philadelphia and other cities on the East Coast, giving speeches that helped to pay for the apartment, and though the country intrigued him, his ignorance of America remained abysmal. It is probably not true that he once opened a public meeting with the words "Workers and peasants of Brooklyn!" but he did firmly believe that the only reason revolution had not come to America was that the American Socialists (who, at the time, had two members in Congress and controlled one hundred fifty newspapers, and whose presidential candidate, Eugene V. Debs, scored 6 percent of the national vote in the 1912 election) were too weak and infected by bourgeois values.

Trotsky was particularly adamant in saying that it would be a mistake for America to join the Allies in the war. When, after the release of the Zimmermann telegram, some Socialist Party politicians came out in support of going to war against Germany, Trotsky's contempt and rage were palpable. He insisted that socialists and workers should engage in "mass action" to prevent this—a forlorn hope. So, when the news of the czar's fall reached him, surprising him as much as it had surprised Lenin, he made feverish plans to head back home.

His brief glimpse of America continued to intrigue, and trouble, him. The night he left, he told an audience at the Harlem River Park Casino, "Keep on organizing until you are able to overthrow this damned, rotten, capitalistic government of this country."[24] Yet, even after he set sail from New York on March 27, he left "with the feeling of a man who has had only a glimpse into the foundry in which the fate of man is to be forged." Even more than Lenin, Trotsky saw that the United States represented the future that most threatened their own Marxist vision of the future.[25]

When he arrived back in Russia on May 4, he still resisted formally joining the Bolshevik ranks.[26] Once he had acquainted himself with the centers of power in revolutionary Petrograd, however, he realized that joining forces with Lenin's Bolshevik Party would give him two advantages. The first was a press organ, the newspaper *Pravda*, where he could publish a seemingly endless stream of revolutionary articles and op-eds. Trotsky was a far better writer and speaker than Lenin, and felt a compulsive need to write down every thought he had, in language as vivid and vituperative as possible. The second advantage of partnership with the Bolsheviks was at last being in a band of fellow revolutionaries who were willing to take direct, decisive action to bring down the existing order, something that Lenin, for all his inflammatory rhetoric and violent apocalyptic vision, was largely unable to do (how unable, we will soon find out).

Now, with the collapse of the last Russian offensive, Trotsky saw a chance for the Bolsheviks, and him, to seize control of events.

It started on July 15, when the Bolsheviks organized a concert for the men of the First Machine Gun Regiment at Petrograd's Narodni

Dom (or "House of the People"). The soldiers had just learned that they were about to be dispatched to the front. Trotsky and his fellow Bolsheviks Zinoviev and Kamenev figured this was a good moment to spread their propaganda to the troops, and encourage disaffection. Trotsky was scheduled to speak, as were Zinoviev, Kamenev, and Lenin. None but Trotsky showed up, the others probably fearing arrest.

Lenin was not even in Petrograd. On July 2, he had taken the train across the border; his friend Vladimir D. Bonch-Bruevich was astonished when the now notorious Bolshevik suddenly appeared outside the door of his villa near the Finnish town of Vyborg. Why had Lenin left town? According to historian Richard Pipes, it is "virtually certain" that he had been tipped off that the Provisional Government had found evidence of his covert dealings with German agents and was about to have him arrested. The issue of the German connection would rear its ugly head in just a few days, and Lenin was careful to be out of town and out of reach as the events Trotsky was setting in motion took place.[27]

That evening, Trotsky gave a blistering speech to an audience of at least five thousand soldiers and civilians, ripping into the government and demanding the transfer of all power to the Petrograd Soviet. That would be the battle cry—"All power to the Soviets!"—over the next several days. It was actually Lenin's, but Trotsky made it his own, a rallying slogan for revolution but also a bludgeon against the government.

What drove Trotsky was not just Marxist revolutionary fervor but also a deeply romantic fascination with the purging power of violence and bloodshed. In June, he had told a crowd from the Kronstadt naval garrison (another highly disaffected, pro-Bolshevik military unit), "I tell you heads must roll, blood must flow. The strength of the French Revolution was in the machine that made the enemies of the people shorter by a head. This is a fine device. We must have one in every city."[28] What another Bolshevik orator might have meant as a metaphor, Trotsky meant literally. Of all Lenin's associates, it was Leon

Trotsky who, if they really were going to start a full-scale revolution, was most eager to fire the first shot.*

As it happened, a willingness to unleash the forces of violence was about the only political asset the Bolsheviks possessed. They were incredibly underpowered in their political support and at the polls; in elections in May and June, they ran a dismal third to the Socialist Revolutionary Party and the Mensheviks, with only 105 delegates, compared with 285 for Kerensky's party and 248 for Chkheidze's.[29] What sustained them was, first, Lenin's tireless energy and fervor; second, support from provincial labor union groups susceptible to Bolshevik propaganda and promises of "Down with the War" and "All Power to the Soviets"; and, finally, the continuing flow of money from Germany.

The records from the German Foreign Office Archives leave no room for doubt. The money assigned to support Lenin and the Bolsheviks in 1917–18 came to between six million and ten million dollars. Most of that was sent as cash via neutral Sweden, and most was spent on party organization and propaganda in Russia. But some was deposited for Lenin at the Disconto-Gesellschaft in Berlin; the bank then forwarded the sums on to the Nye Bank in Stockholm. That money would be regularly withdrawn by a confidant of Lenin's living in Stockholm, Jacob Ganetskii (aka Fürstenberg), and deposited in the bank account of Lenin's relative Eugenia Sumenson, who co-owned a pharmaceutical business that served as a cover for passing money on to Lenin.

Nor is there any doubt that Lenin knew that the money he was receiving was from the Germans. In fact, in a letter of April 12, he complained to Fürstenberg-Ganetskii that he was not getting it. At least one other document shows him acknowledging receiving subventions from Sumenson's partner, a Pole named M. Iu. Kozlovskii.[30] Certainly, the leading members of his inner circle, including Kamenev and Radek, knew their political fortunes depended on German

---

* In fact, Trotsky, an avid hunter, was a crack shot.

gold—and by the end of June, the Provisional Government was start-ing to learn this, too. That is certainly why Lenin felt it necessary to run to Finland, to avoid arrest as a German agent. That is also why the events of July 16 and 17 seemed the best shot at toppling the gov-ernment before all of them were rounded up and arrested.

After Trotsky's rousing speech on July 15, the men of the First Machine Gun Regiment were too agitated to sleep. An all-night dis-cussion (or bull session), reinforced by plenty of vodka and shouts of "Beat the bourgeoisie!" ended the next morning with a vote on the resolution to take to the streets, fully armed, and march on the Tau-ride. That evening, some of them boarded machine-gun-equipped automobiles and headed for the Troitskii Bridge, followed by several thousand soldiers marching and shooting off their rifles.

The shooting, plus some looting, continued all night and into the morning. Nonetheless, it was not until midday on July 16 that Trotsky, Kamenev, and Zinoviev decided they needed to catch up with the Ma-chine Gun Regiment and put the Bolshevik banner at its head. They decided they would convince the Workers' Section of the Petrograd Soviet to proclaim full governmental power in the name of the entire Soviet—a pre-coup, as it were, to prepare the way for the real thing.

Two days later, July 18, *Pravda* ran an article by Lenin, "All Power to the Soviets," which was supposed to be the signal for a general up-rising in support of Bolsheviks in the Workers' Section of the Soviet and the soldiers of the Machine Gun Regiment.[31]

The government had no way of stopping them. It had figured out as early as July 15 what was in fact happening,[32] but there were very few loyal troops left to suppress a serious armed revolt. In the absence of any force to maintain law and order, power belonged to whoever was strong enough to seize it. On the morning of July 17, that looked like Lenin, Trotsky, and their armed supporters. Those consisted of the Machine Gun Regiment and the five thousand to six thousand armed sailors from the Kronstadt naval base who had landed in the city and were marching down to the Kschessinska Mansion. There Lenin, freshly back from his brief diversion to Finland, was waiting for them.

"I am delighted to see what is happening!" he shouted to the cheering sailors. "The transfer of all power to the Soviet of Workers' and Soldiers' Deputies is finally becoming a reality!"

From there, the sailors started their march toward the Tauride, where Lenin now headed. His plan was to have the Bolsheviks in the Workers' Section proclaim him, Trotsky, and a colleague, Anatoly V. Lunacharsky, heads of the new government. By 4:00 p.m., after opening fire on some members of the crowd and killing several, the sailors and contingents of workers, whom the Bolsheviks had arranged to be released from their jobs in order to join the march, reached the Tauride. Sailors and soldiers were soon swarming in and around the building, demanding action and shouting, "All power to the soviets!" They nearly lynched Socialist Revolutionary minister of agriculture Viktor Chernov—he was saved by Trotsky, who had just arrived and pulled the minister bodily back into the hall.[33] Kamenev, Trotsky, and the others turned to one another in triumph. The Soviet was theirs; the city was theirs; rule over Russia was theirs. All they needed was for their fearless leader to give the order, and they could proclaim that the Soviet was now the official government of Russia and assume formal power—but Lenin did not. Sitting nervously next to Zinoviev in the Ispolkom conference room, with the entire building in a state of pandemonium, he turned to his fellow exile from Zurich and muttered, "I wonder if this is the time to try, but I don't think it is."[34]

The rest of the evening, the Bolsheviks and supporters milled around the Tauride, waiting for orders that never came from a leader who seemed to have lost his nerve. That was all the breathing space the government needed. That same evening, Kerensky, who was at the front, urged his colleagues to release whatever information they had on Lenin's German connections. They did so the next day, in the mass-circulation daily *Zhivoe slovo*, whose July 18 issue carried the splashy headline "LENIN, GANETSKII & CO SPIES." The effect on the soldiers who had supported the would-be Bolshevik coup the previous day was, according to historian Richard Pipes, electric.[35]

The average Russian soldier may have despised the sitting government; he certainly hated the war and the deprivations it had caused for himself and his family. He was therefore inclined to listen to anyone such as Lenin, whose slogan had become "Peace, Land, Bread"—one that resonated with every average Russian, not just the men in the army. Yet cold, deliberate treason was another matter. News of Lenin's possible complicity with the German government aroused suspicions many had always had, but had buried, about Lenin's unexplained safe passage through enemy territory to Russia. Now soldiers and sailors who twenty-four hours earlier were prepared to carry Lenin on their shoulders into power were so hostile that Lenin had to ask for bodyguards in order to leave the Ispolkom. "Now they are going to shoot us," a flustered Lenin told Trotsky; "it is the most advantageous time for them." That night, he slipped out the back of the building. It would be more than four months before anyone saw him again in public.[36]

After the headline hit, the rioters began to melt away, confused and embarrassed at the revelation that the man they were supposed to be supporting might be a German agent. At the same time, over the course of the day, one loyal regiment after another marched into Palace Square to show its support for the government—and its opposition to the would-be Bolshevik coup.

By July 19, the government had regained its nerve and was ready to take decisive action. It ordered the arrests of Lenin and eleven colleagues on charges of "high treason and organizing a mass uprising." That same day, loyal soldiers from the front took over the garrisoning of the city, and Alexander Kerensky was made prime minister. A new minister of justice began collecting evidence on the Bolshevik-German collaboration for a possible future trial. And over the next several days, the coup conspirators, including Trotsky, were rounded up one by one—all, that is, except Lenin.

Lenin and Zinoviev had managed to elude the dragnet around the city (which, given the fact that the gendarmerie and police had been abolished, was not terribly difficult) and slip into the countryside. There Zinoviev decided he would take his chances with the police and turn himself in; Lenin prepared to flee to Finland. (He had to shave his beard.) He and his companions were nearly nabbed twice before they finally found refuge across the border, where friends and ideological comrades once again provided shelter for the man who was now the defeated and humiliated leader, branded a traitor from one end of Russia to the other.[37]

As he began, once again, the dreary process of trying to start a revolution from exile, Lenin published a couple of short articles denying the story that had appeared in *Zhivoe slovo*, and denouncing as "lies" the stories of his links to Ganetskii and other German agents. This denunciation was actually his biggest lie.

He also began working on a new book, one that would (as he told anyone willing to listen) prove once and for all that his interpretation of Marx was right and the others were wrong. The truth, however, was that even he sensed he was finished. In his mind, the book, later published as *State and Revolution*, was his intellectual last will and testament. He even issued instructions for its posthumous publication, in case he was killed or assassinated.

In August, still hiding from the police, Lenin started planning to move the entire Bolshevik base to Finland, or possibly Sweden. This episode in the sorry history of Marxist revolution in Russia was done; all that was left, it seemed, was to turn out the lights as the door closed behind him.[38]

As for the government, with the July Days, it had survived the most serious crisis since the fall of the czar, and had emerged looking stronger and more popular than it had been in months. It was true that the front was still in turmoil, and the Germans were advancing on Riga, but now the revolution's brightest hope, Kerensky, was fully in charge, serving as prime minister and as minister of war and of the navy. Kerensky swiftly ordered the rebellious army and navy units disbanded and the troops sent to the front. Some semblance of order returned to the capital.

Pravda was shut down. The Bolshevik movement now silenced

and broken, with its leaders arrested and Lenin in hiding. After a very near escape, Russia seemed at last safe for democracy.

YPRES, JULY 17–AUGUST 4

THE SAME DAY Lenin made his abortive bid for power, July 17, British forces began their first attack along the Passchendaele front. More than three thousand guns were pouring four million artillery shells on German lines. It was a one-hundred-million-dollar offensive, all paid for by Wilson and his son-in-law Secretary of the Treasury William McAdoo—proof that the transatlantic alliance was more formidable than ever, and that Britain was shutting the door on any negotiated peace.[39]

The real battle got under way two weeks later, on July 31. As the bombardment reached its climax, just before four o'clock in the morning, nine British infantry divisions backed by 136 tanks started creeping their way toward the German lines. Very soon, they were swept over by mist and driving rain. Once again, bad weather, the wettest summer in seventy-five years, would make it difficult for the offensive's officers to figure out what was happening as the battle unfolded.[40]

Then, at two in the afternoon, the British lines were also inundated—by waves of German shells, as the Germans counter-attacked. The battlefield soon turned into a great lake of mud and rain-filled shell holes, as one tank after another became bogged down and the British advance slowed to a crawl. Communication with command in the rear had all but broken down. "Some pigeons got through," wrote one observer, "but the only news from the assault was by runners, who sometimes took hours to get back, if indeed they ever did."[41]

The rain poured down for three days straight as the British attack sputtered out and died. "The ground is churned up to a depth of ten feet and is the consistency of porridge," a British brigadier reported.

"[T]he middle[s] of the shell craters are so soft that one might sink out of sight." Some men did, as others struggled through mud up to their waists—and all the while, the artillery shells continued to rain down, taking a frightening toll on British attacker and German defender alike.

On August 4, Haig finally had to call a halt to the attack. The farthest gain was less than half a mile—not even half of what Haig had promised in the opening days. The British and French had suffered more than 23,000 casualties, while some of the units commanded by British general Sir Hubert Gough had lost 30 to 60 percent of their effectives.[42]

Nonetheless, Haig persisted in renewing the attack all through the rest of the month. Twenty-eight of all forty-two available Allied divisions were committed in one way or another to the offensive, as the rain continued to pour and pour. Each day brought the same dismal news: limited progress in some areas, none at all in others. And the names on the casualty lists kept mounting. The British army suffered 68,000 killed and wounded for an advance that, at its farthest, extended less than four thousand yards.

On August 25, even Haig realized the attacks weren't working, and he called a halt to the proceedings. On September 4, he was summoned to London to explain what had gone wrong.[43] Like France's Nivelle Offensive, Haig's Passchendaele offensive had proved a bloody failure.

It really was up to the Americans now.

AMERICAN LEVIATHAN

War is the health of the state.
—AMERICAN SOCIALIST RANDOLPH
BOURNE, 1917

WASHINGTON

O N JULY 7, 1914, three weeks before Germany began to mobilize, Bethmann-Hollweg told an aide that "a war, whatever its outcome, will result in the uprooting of everything that exists." In fact, the German chancellor was wrong. By 1917, much had indeed been uprooted. The global balance of power that had kept Europe at general peace since 1815 lay in permanent ruins. Three great empires, Austria-Hungary, Turkey, and Russia, were teetering on the brink of collapse. Millions of lives had been lost, billions of dollars in property destroyed, and assumptions about the nature of war and humanity overturned forever.

Moreover, the European Great Powers no longer played the central role; they had been upstaged with America's entry into the Great War.

One thing that had not been destroyed—on the contrary, it was being immeasurably strengthened—was the power of government. Among the Great Powers before 1914, government's share of GNP had averaged between 5 and 10 percent. In America, the share of total income accounted for by federal and local government came to just 9 percent.[1] Three years later, those numbers had been transformed.

In many ways, the intrusion of national governments into their nations' economies was necessary; there was no way private initiative or industry, no matter how large or organized, could have built the mighty land, sea, and now air forces needed to fight a war on this mammoth scale. At the same time, government's ability to intervene in, and even run, the lives of private citizens had expanded beyond anyone's imagining. This, too, marked the start of something new then but all too familiar now. Emerging from the forge of war in 1917 was the active role of government in every aspect of daily life, and the rising expectation that government can fix every problem and deal with every crisis from economic depression to childcare and climate change.

Certainly, no world leader was more eager for the chance to fulfill the promise of government at war than Woodrow Wilson. The idea that "war is the health of the state," although uttered with bitter sarcasm by his countryman, the pacifist Randolph Bourne, fitted perfectly with Wilson's Progressive agenda and his vision of an America transformed for the better by the power of federal government, even in wartime. Yet six months after dragging the country into the world conflict, Wilson was finding the job a lot harder than he had thought.

It's true he had set his expectations high. For him, the arsenal of new wartime bureaus and agencies he had created since April was not going to be enough. In his mind, an America at war demanded a unity of hearts and minds as well as material resources. "Variety of opinion among ourselves there may be—discussion, free counsel as to what we ought to do—but, so far as every other nation is concerned, we must be absolutely a unit." Those words were spoken at a luncheon in Buffalo, New York, in November 1916, well before Wilson even contemplated entering the war.[2] He returned to the same theme in his second inaugural address the following March, still before he was thinking of intervention.

"We are being forged into a new unity amidst the fires that now blaze throughout the world," he proclaimed. "In their ardent heat we shall, in God's providence, let us hope, be purged of faction and division." By "faction and division," Wilson now meant dissent from his vision of what America was fighting for, and why it was fighting. How far he was willing to go to purge that dissent would become clear in the following months.

His first step in doing so came with his creation of the Committee on Public Information, or CPI, on April 13, 1917, and his appointment as its first head the editor of the *Rocky Mountain News*, George Creel.

Forty-one years old and with something of a reputation as a muck-raking journalist, Creel had been a Wilson enthusiast as far back as 1905, when Wilson was still president of Princeton University. During the 1916 election, Creel had published a book, *Wilson and the Issues*, which proclaimed, "It is the capacity of a people for self-government that is on trial. It is the honesty, intelligence, and faith of the mass that are up for judgment. There is not a lie that has been told that lacks its answer; there is not a slander for which refutation cannot be found; there is not an ugly charge that does not come clean in the light of truth. It remains to be seen whether the people of the United States prefer facts to clamor, fairness to betrayal, and democracy to oligarchy; in a word, whether they are able to think for themselves."[3]

It was precisely to ensure that the American people *didn't* think for themselves that Creel would throw himself into his job at the Committee on Public Information. "To Creel there are only two classes of men," a friend once said. "There are skunks and the greatest man in the world."[4] That greatest man in 1917 was Woodrow Wilson. The skunks were Wilson's opponents, who, after April 6, included Germany and anyone sympathizing with it.

Shortly after the declaration of war, Creel was one of Wilson's first visitors at the White House. Into his hands the president would entrust mobilizing the nation's public opinion.

That was not going to be easy. Despite widespread stories of German atrocities in Belgium and the release of the Zimmermann telegram, the American public was still not entirely convinced that going to war was a good idea. Pacifists such as leftist journalist Randolph Bourne and socialists such as Eugene Debs were voicing opposition to participating. Large numbers of descendants of Irish immigrants opposed becoming allies of Britain, especially in the wake of the bloody suppression of the 1916 Easter Rebellion.

In addition, many American Jews were opposed to joining with Russia, given its legacy of pogroms and anti-Semitism. "If American Jews could be said to have sympathy for any side in World War I," an article in the Jewish newspaper the *Forward* noted in 2014, "it would have been for the armies of Germany and Austria-Hungary."[5] And for millions of Americans of German descent, their ties to their homeland were still real. They may not have been fans of the Kaiser, but they failed to see why Germany's use of submarines to starve the enemy's civilian population into submission was considered inhumane while Britain's use of a naval blockade to achieve the same end was not.

Getting a disparate and divided American public to rally around the war would require a two-pronged effort. The first part was to craft a positive message that would appeal to the American majority; the second was to limit access to negative messages that undercut or contradicted this positive narrative. The usual term for the first is *propaganda*; the term for the second is *censorship*. Creel recoiled from both. As he assumed the helm of the CPI, he was convinced he could generate a wave of enthusiasm for the war by propagating a message that was as truthful as it was upbeat.

He scorned the idea of being Wilson's propaganda minister. "That word, in German hands, had come to be associated with deceit and corruption," he wrote later. "Our effort was educational and informative throughout, for we had such confidence in our case as to feel that no other argument was needed than the simple, straightforward presentation of facts."[6]

That "straightforward presentation" involved coordination with all the other federal agencies, as well as with many private businesses, ranging from newspapers and advertising agencies to movie studios. The Committee on Public Information, comprising seven separate divisions, created a panoply of initiatives and efforts that would not only generate public support for the war but also reshape American culture.

The Division of Pictorial Publicity, for example, as led by Charles Dana Gibson, creator of the famed Gibson Girl, recruited America's most celebrated artists and illustrators to the mobilization cause. Meanwhile, America's media became the obedient conduit for the CPI's Division of News, which bombarded the public with six thousand press releases a week. According to Creel's memoirs, on any given week, more than twenty thousand newspaper columns carried material that the Division of News deemed fit to print—and all of it was free.

The CPI's Division of Civic and Educational Cooperation recruited respectable scholars to compose pamphlets urging support for the war; leading Progressives John Dewey and Walter Lippmann happily chimed in. A host of syndicated newspaper columnists were encouraged to spread the pro-war message to their readers, a total of twelve million Americans every day.

Creel didn't stop at the written word or the graphic image. The Division of Films also turned to the motion picture industry, still in its infancy, to mobilize pro-war, anti-German sentiment. Hollywood jumped in with both feet. As a 1917 editorial in *Motion Picture News* put it, "every individual at work in this industry wants to do his share," so studios large and small got involved in churning out movies with titles such as *The Kaiser: The Beast of Berlin* and *Wolves of Kultur.* They proved popular; a screening of *To Hell with the Kaiser!* triggered a riot when crowds couldn't get tickets for admission.

Recruiting moviemakers was a farsighted policy, not unlike recruiting social media or Instagram to carry government propaganda today. It also helped burnish the image of an industry that had seemed cheap and sleazy but that very much wanted to be seen as patriotic and respectable. Indeed, if any year marked the emergence of the American cinema as a positive conveyor of moral and civic values as well as entertainment, it was 1917.

And the propaganda didn't stop when the picture was over. As the last reel ended and the image faded from the screen, a message would regularly pop up: "Please remain seated. A representative of the government is to deliver an important message." Then, one of the so-called "Four-Minute Men," usually a government official or a prominent local businessman, would step onstage to deliver a rousing speech on America's war aims, registering for the draft, buying Liberty Bonds, going meatless, or not driving your car one day a week—whatever was the latest campaign or narrative Creel and his team were working on.

Nor was the style of delivery left to chance. Official instructions were passed along to the Four-Minute Men to "use short sentences . . . avoid fine phrases . . . Be natural and direct . . . Finish strong and sharp . . . Stick to the four minute limit."[7] There was even an effort to recruit African American speakers, especially clergy, to carry the messages to their communities, and a Women's Division to promote the same thing at women's clubs, luncheons, and church gatherings. Four-Minute Men worked with teachers to get their pupils to buy Liberty Bonds, or to urge their parents to do so. McAdoo's use of Boy Scouts to promote the bonds overlapped with Creel's message at CPI: the children of America expect their parents to do their patriotic duty.

The result was a media storm that was coordinated, comprehensive, and virtually around-the-clock. In every newspaper an American citizen opened (except socialist papers, which were soon under pressure from Washington to shut down); at every street corner where he stopped at; in every trolley, ferry, train, or subway car he traveled on; at every school he visited and in every classroom his child attended, he was exhorted by word and image to buy Liberty Bonds, save gas or food, watch out for spies, hate the Kaiser, or join the U.S. Navy, Army, Marines, or Coast Guard—or kiss those who did. The famous poster of Uncle Sam, "I Want You," may have been inspired by British artist Alfred Leete's 1914 poster of General Kitchener making the same commanding gesture at the viewer, but it also summed up a powerful message: acceptance of the United States' role as arbiter of the new global order was going to require effort and sacrifice by every American.

Later, Creel called the war "a vast enterprise in salesmanship, the world's greatest adventure in advertising."[8] Indeed, slogans crafted by the propaganda machine flew around the country like biblical proverbs. There were even some for Hoover's Food Administration: "If U fast U beat U boats" and "Serve beans, by all means" and "Wheatless days in America make sleepless nights in Germany." Or, at its most direct and simplest, "Pray hard, work hard, sleep hard, and play hard. Do it all courageously and cheerfully."[9]

Yet, even with Creel's energy and innovative genius, the emphasis on projecting a positive message was not enough. Although Creel had been a vocal critic of censorship, the CPI early on took steps to limit the spread of information that could be deemed "defeatist" or "unpatriotic." It began with setting voluntary guidelines for news media— guidelines that became increasingly nonvoluntary, or compulsory. That pointed the way to the passage, on June 15, 1917, of the Espionage Act, which was aimed ostensibly at halting the activity of German spies but which actually gave government officials wide latitude in limiting the spread of undesirable opinions—otherwise known as limiting free speech.

This suited Wilson. On April 16, he had warned his fellow Americans that "failing to bear true allegiance to the United States" had consequences. He pointed out that the Constitution defined treason as "levying war" against the United States or "in adhering to their enemies, giving them aid and comfort" (Article III, Section 3). The U.S. Criminal Code included under the definition of giving aid and comfort "the performance of any act or the publication of statements or information which will give or supply *in any way* aid and comfort," regardless of intent. Wilson concluded: "I hereby proclaim and warn all citizens of the United States and all aliens, owing allegiance to the United States, to abstain from committing any and all acts which would constitute a violation of any of the laws herein set forth."[10] How far was he willing to go to suppress activity, including speeches and publications, he considered treasonous? The Espionage Act gave him and his attorney general, Thomas Gregory, a fierce Texas Progressive, the opportunity to push the envelope.

The case that summer involved the radical labor union the Industrial Workers of the World. Founded in 1905, the IWW, or "Wobblies," as they were known, had a history of provoking labor violence, including participating in the murder of half a dozen policemen during the bloody Pressed Steel Car Company strike in Pennsylvania in 1909. The IWW had tried unsuccessfully to organize strikes on both coasts in 1916; the attempts had cost it members, until its numbers shrank to fewer than four hundred.

The coming of war, however, revived the IWW's fortunes. Its numbers swelled into the tens of thousands, but when it tried to organize strikes against the war mobilization, the members and their president, Bill Haywood, found themselves on the receiving end of the violence, by angry miners in the West. In Montana, IWW organizer Frank Little was lynched, and in Bisbee, Arizona, twelve hundred striking copper miners who had joined the IWW were loaded onto cattle cars and shipped to the middle of the New Mexico desert, where they were dumped without food or water.[11]

Copper was one of the vital strategic metals for the war effort, and Bernard Baruch of the War Industries Board was determined not to let any strike interfere with the flow of copper to American munitions factories. Baruch and mine owner John D. Ryan found a ready ally in the Citizens Protective League, an offshoot of the American Protective League, a semi-vigilante group that sprang up in May 1917 to root out spies and traitors in the nation's midst, and that wasn't afraid to go where legal authorities feared to tread. By June, the APL had grown to a quarter million members; with the support and connivance of Attorney General Gregory, it became the unofficial enforcement arm of the Espionage Act.[12]

Under siege from Wilson, the APL, the Justice Department, and statutory law, the IWW didn't stand a chance. When Bill Haywood wrote to Wilson protesting the Bisbee incident, Wilson contemptuously handed the letter to Gregory, saying Haywood was only aiming to be a "martyr," and adding in his own letter to American Federation of Labor (AFL) president Samuel Gompers, "[W]e must oppose at home the organized and individual efforts of these dangerous elements who hide disloyalty behind a screen of specious and evasive phrases."[13]

With Wilson's approval, Gregory set out to destroy the IWW once and for all. On September 5, investigators raided IWW offices in thirty-three cities, looking for evidence of the group's having received covert German financial support. When none was found, Gregory's attorneys sifted through the mountains of files, memos, and diaries until they had found enough evidence to support charges of sedition under the ever-useful Espionage Act. Three weeks later, on September 28—just as Douglas Haig was getting ready to renew his attack along the Ypres Salient—no fewer than 166 IWW organizers were indicted on charges relating to the Espionage Act and other laws. When their case went to trial the next year, many drew sentences of twenty years' imprisonment.

They were the lucky ones. In Tulsa, Oklahoma, local authorities turned over seventeen Wobblies to the Ku Klux Klan, who tarred and feathered them. Their crime? Not having bought Liberty Bonds. When the IWW men were on trial for their "crime," five people testified on their behalf; they wound up being tarred and feathered, too.[14]

By 1918, the IWW and the entire radical labor movement were on the run. Yet Wilson did not think of himself as antilabor. He had signed an eight-hour-workday bill during his first term, and that November, he was the first president to address a labor union convention, telling those assembled for the AFL meeting in Buffalo, "[W]hile we are fighting for freedom, we must see . . . that labor is free [at home] . . . I am with you if you are with me."[15] In the aftermath of the Bisbee incident, Wilson appointed a commission, headed by a young Harvard Law professor named Felix Frankfurter, to figure out how to prevent future labor clashes. Inevitably, a new federal bureau came into existence, the National War Labor Board, made up of labor and industry leaders and co-chaired by former president William H. Taft, to deal with the problem.[16]

All the same, radicals don't easily tolerate the presence of other radicals, and Wilson *was* radical in his vision of an America marching in lockstep into war with a unity of industry, government, and labor that would brook no opposition or dissent—a vision that later would be known as corporatism, or even fascism.[17]

Trotsky and Lenin shared aspects of that vision. Later, they would put in place a version in Russia that would make Wilson's look remarkably laissez-faire. In 1917, what separated them, and American radicals and socialists like Bill Haywood from Wilson was the issue of the war. For Wilson, it was going to serve as a springboard to a bright new future. For them, it would be more of the same: capitalism oppressing, cheating, and killing the masses, not in factories or mines this time but on the battlefield.

America's entry into World War I, in other words, was more than a point of arrival in world history. It was also a point of departure—one at which Wilson, for all his liberal Progressivism, parted company with those who had, in many ways, a vision of America similar to his domestically, but who saw in the intervention on the side of the Allies a great and catastrophic leap into the dark unknown, one that we are still coming to grips with today.[18]

Of course, given the IWW's violent record, someone could make the argument that the Wobblies were simply getting as good as they gave. That rationalization didn't apply to Socialist Party leader Eugene V. Debs. No apostle of violence, the former presidential candidate saw his outspoken opposition to the war run afoul of provisions of the popularly known "Sedition Act," a rider to the Espionage Act. The Sedition Act, which Wilson signed on May 16, 1918, made it illegal to speak, print, write, or publish any "disloyal, profane, scurrilous, or abusive language" about the government, the Constitution, the military, or the flag—certainly the single most restrictive gag on free speech and freedom of the press in U.S. history.

Wilson's postmaster general, Albert Burleson, had already de-

clared war on the Socialist Party by yanking second-class postal rates
for a series of socialist-minded periodicals, including *The Masses*, the
Milwaukee Leader, the *New York Call*, and the paper Trotsky had written for, the *Forward*.[19] Soon delivery stopped altogether. In October
1917, *Masses* editor Max Eastman found himself indicted under the Espionage Act, along with cartoonist Art Young and a fellow editor, a
twentysomething Harvard graduate named John Reed, who would
soon earn his place in Lenin's world as well as Wilson's.

Eastman, Young, and Reed's trial ended in acquittal, but with
the passage of the Sedition Act, the government tried again in September 1918. Again, the editorial team was acquitted, but *The Masses*
was forced to close its doors. With Eastman clearly in the crosshairs,
Debs's indictment was almost inevitable. In the end, Debs would
draw a ten-year sentence for making a single antidraft speech. Wilson
ignored several appeals by prominent figures to lift or at least moderate the sentence. The next time Debs ran for president, in 1920, it
would be from behind bars, as Convict No. 9653 in the Atlanta Federal
Penitentiary.

If Wilson had some lingering sympathy for those on his left—
when he received letters from his friend Amos Pinchot protesting the
indictment of Max Eastman, he forwarded them on to Attorney General Gregory with a note that read, "[H]is letter, I must admit, made
some impression upon me"—his feelings toward German Americans
ran in a very different direction.

In August, in response to a plea from the pope for considering a
negotiated peace, Wilson laid out his view of Germany itself in a single blistering sentence:

> The object of this war is to deliver the free peoples of the world
> from the menace of a vast military establishment controlled by
> an irresponsible government, which, having secretly planned
> to dominate the world . . . chose its own time for the war, deliv-
> ered its blow fiercely and suddenly, stopped at no barrier either
> of law or mercy, swept a whole continent within the tide of

blood, not the blood of soldiers only but the blood of innocent women and children and also of the helpless poor, and now stands balked but not defeated, the enemy of four-fifths [of] the world.[20]

His secretary of state hailed the statement with these fulsome sentiments: "You have again written a declaration of human liberty . . . You are blazing a new path, and the world must follow, or be lost again in the meshes of unrighteous intrigue."

Unfortunately, the path Wilson was blazing also burned through the country's 8.3 million–strong German American community with ugly and, eventually, fatal consequences. Groups such as the APL began to target German American churches, schools, societies, and newspapers as tools of the Kaiser. There were also public calls to toss out German-language instruction from schools and to ban "all disloyal teachers." Some states banned the teaching of German in private and public schools alike. One publication stated, "Any language which produces a people of ruthless conquistadors such as now exists in Germany is not a fit language to teach clean and pure American boys and girls."

Another semi-vigilante group, the American Defense Society, advocated the public burning of German-language books and campaigned to change the names of cities, streets, parks, and schools in America to the names of Belgian and French communities destroyed in the war. Germantown, Nebraska, became Garland, in memory of a local boy killed in the fighting in France. East Germantown, Indiana, became Pershing; Berlin, Iowa, changed its name to Lincoln. A Michigan congressman even introduced a bill that would have required such name changes nationwide.

Germanophobia soon grew to ridiculous levels. The names of German foods disappeared from restaurant menus. Sauerkraut became "Liberty cabbage"; hamburger became "Liberty steak."

There was a campaign to exclude the work of German composers such as Beethoven and Bach from the repertoire of American community orchestras. In July 1918, South Dakota even prohibited the use of the German language over the telephone.[21]

This last rule reflected a fear of German espionage that, it is worth bearing in mind, was very realistic. In 1915, the Secret Service had unearthed a covert industrial spy network operating at the behest of a German commercial attaché named Heinrich Albert. In 1916, bombs set by German agents exploded in two factories in New Jersey. Both blasts were efforts to interrupt the flow of munitions and raw materials to the Allies, when America was still neutral.[22] But with the coming of war for the United States and the steady drumbeat of anti-German propaganda, people were seeing German spies around every corner and under every bed—especially German American beds. President Wilson himself raised the issue in his Flag Day speech on June 14, 1917: "The military masters of Germany have filled our unsuspecting communities with vicious spies and conspirators and have sought to corrupt the opinion of our people . . . [These persons] seek to undermine the Government with false professions of loyalty to its principles."[23]

With a commander in chief handing out a general license to hunt for spies, it's not surprising Americans responded. German American churches were especially singled out as agents of German imperialism, since so many maintained close ties with their denominations in the mother country. So were German American publications. With the passage, on October 6, 1917, of the Trading with the Enemy Act, which aimed to curb any commercial transactions with Germany, all German-language newspapers in the United States were required to give English translations of anything they printed about the government.[24] Many newsstands refused to carry German-language papers; paperboys refused to deliver them. Meanwhile, in just a year, the number of German-language publications in America plummeted from 537 to 278.[25]

Likewise, harassment of individual German Americans became commonplace. Employers would get anonymous phone calls asking if they still had "that German spy" on the payroll. Someone seen reading a German-language newspaper or book on a train or trolley would garner insults or even get spat upon. Just having a German surname could be enough to start the American Protective League on its own private investigation into a person's background and business. When a German American vacationing in Florida was caught unprepared by a cold snap and exclaimed within hearing of witnesses, "[D]amn such a country as this," he was arrested for having violated the Espionage Act.[*]

Not surprisingly, acts of violence increased dramatically during the winter months, reaching a climax in the spring of 1918. In Pensacola, Florida, a German American was severely flogged by a citizens' group. He was forced to shout, "To hell with the Kaiser," and then was ordered to leave the state. In Avoca, Pennsylvania, an Austrian American was accused of criticizing the Red Cross. A group of vigilantes tied him up, hoisted him thirty feet in the air, and blasted him with water from a fire hose for a full hour. In Oakland, California, a German American tailor was nearly lynched by a local organization called the Knights of Liberty. In Tulsa, Oklahoma, where IWW members had been tarred and feathered, a German American resident received the same treatment, was lashed fifty times, and was forced to leave the city. Several Lutheran pastors were whipped for having delivered sermons in German.

The worst case was the fate of Robert Prager, on April 5, 1918, in Collinsville, Illinois. Born in Germany but having immigrated to America in 1905, Prager strongly identified with his adopted country.

---

[*] Of all the German Americans, no group was more persecuted than the Mennonites. As members of a pacifist sect, they refused to participate in the draft on religious grounds. The U.S. government, however, denied their exemption. In the end, 130 "refuseniks" were court-martialed and sentenced to ten to thirty years at Leavenworth. Four of the Mennonites were placed in solitary confinement at Alcatraz, denied adequate food and drink, and required to stand all day with their arms chained to bars above their heads. Forced to sleep on cold, damp stone floors, two of them died from pneumonia.

He immediately applied for citizenship and tried in vain to join the navy. Instead, he wound up with a job in a coal mine in southern Illinois. At the time, a rumor was circulating in the town that German agents were going to blow up the mine with miners still in it. Several local German Americans came under suspicion and were forced to publicly declare their loyalty and to kiss the American flag.

Although he had been in the country since 1905, Prager was soon a target. After work on the evening of April 3, a group of drunken miners seized him and paraded him through the streets of Maryville. They denounced him as a German spy and told him to leave town. Prager refused, and instead posted around town copies of a statement he had typed up, declaring his loyalty to America but also voicing a complaint that the local union was denying him membership and thus keeping him from earning a living. That was a mistake—his fellow miners turned on him in defense of their union as well as their country. The next day, April 4, they searched out Prager, stripped him down to his underwear, and then frog-marched him, barefoot and draped in the American flag, through the streets of Collinsville. At the center of town, the furious mob demanded that he sing "The Star-Spangled Banner." Prager admitted he didn't know the words, but he desperately broke into another patriotic song as the crowd jeered and grew uglier.

Now the Collinsville police intervened. They managed to extract Prager from the mob and take him to the police station, where they hid him in the basement. The angry crowd simply followed them to the station, swarmed in, and dragged Prager back outside. Someone suggested he deserved a good tarring and feathering, but no one could find the right materials. So, they decided that the next best thing was to tie him to a tree, where he stood helpless in the headlights of three automobiles.

Then, out of the darkness, someone came forward with a noose made from a towrope and looped it around Prager's neck. According to witnesses, one of the crowd, a veteran named Riegel, shouted,

"Come on, fellas, we're all in on this, let's not have any slackers here," as fifteen men rushed forward to grab the end of the rope. With a collective heave, they hoisted Prager into the air.

Prager kicked and twisted on the rope, but to everyone's disappointment, he failed to die. They lowered him to the ground—not to release him, but to try again. Before they did, though, they gave the hapless German immigrant permission to write a good-bye letter to his parents. He begged to be allowed to pray, asking forgiveness for his sins. Then, once again stating his loyalty to America, he shrugged aside his captors and strode back to the tree and the waiting noose. As more than two hundred persons looked on, Robert Prager said his last words: "All right, boys, go ahead and kill me, but wrap me in the flag when you bury me." Then, yanked into the air by the neck, he died.[26]

The lynching stunned the nation. Theodore Roosevelt denounced it in no uncertain terms, as did Henry Cabot Lodge. As for Woodrow Wilson, it took until the end of July for him to issue a statement in which he decried "the mob spirit which has recently . . . shown its head among us" and said that lynching was "a blow at the heart of ordered law and humane justice." He also drew a direct parallel between the lynching of Prager and the behavior of Germany, which "has made lynchers of her armies"—words that would seem aimed to intensify hatred of German Americans rather than to defuse it.[27] Indeed, many defended the mob, saying they had been forced to do what they did because Congress was failing to punish disloyalty, including disloyal utterances (something Prager had not in fact made). Bowing to the ensuing pressure, Attorney General Gregory asked for requisite changes to the law. Congress responded by amending the Espionage Act with the Sedition Act, which now made it a crime even to utter statements deemed disloyal or to give aid and comfort to the enemy.

As for the Prager case, twelve persons were eventually charged with his murder. The trial took three days. The defense presented its case in six hours, and concluded with the spurious argument that

Prager was a suspected German spy and that the lynching had been justifiable under "unwritten law." After deliberating for forty-five minutes, the jury found all the defendants "not guilty."†

There is no doubt that Woodrow Wilson was unforgivably silent on the mass persecution of German Americans thanks to the war fever he and his fellow Progressives had stirred up. It is also true that his Republican opponents took a similarly strong stand on the need for unity and suppression of dissent. Theodore Roosevelt supported banning teaching the German language from schools and applauded the IWW "deportation" in Bisbee, although he roundly condemned the lynching of Robert Prager.[28] Yet the men who were the fiercest advocates of suspending normal civil liberties and who took the most draconian actions in that regard—Attorney General Gregory; Postmaster General Burleson; and, later, Attorney General A. Mitchell Palmer—were also among the most foursquare Progressives of Wilson's camp. Their actions highlight the curious self-righteousness of the American Progressive mind, and the belief among Progressives that their views once arrived at were beyond criticism; as with Wilson, opposition itself became a sign of disloyalty, even of evil.[29]

This was even more so in wartime, when the desires of the individual by necessity normally have to yield to the needs of the whole, but with Wilson's own Hegelian twist: that achieving such national unity is a sign of a world-historical leader.

"Leadership does not always wear the harness of compromise," Wilson had written as far back as 1890. "Once and again one of those great influences which we call a *cause* arises in the midst of a nation. Men of strenuous minds and high ideals come forward, with a sort of gentle majesty, as champions . . . Masses come over [to] the side of the reform. Resistance is left to the minority, and such as will not be convinced are crushed."[30]

Wilson clearly saw himself as such a man, one of "strenuous mind and high ideals" coming to the nation's rescue in a time of crisis and

† Prager was, however, buried in an American flag, as he had requested.

war, a man who spoke of "a new principle for a new age" and who was leading "a great, free, democratic nation" to its destiny. (Another was Abraham Lincoln, whom Wilson saw as his model war president.) Bringing the country together as a global force for good was also clearly Wilson's ultimate goal in mobilizing the nation for the war— the crusade, almost—to come.

The one problem was: it wasn't working.

* * *

AS THE FALL of 1917 moved on into winter, mobilization wasn't moving anywhere.

The U.S. Shipping Board had spent half a billion dollars but hadn't built a single ship. A similar Aircraft Board had spent even more and hadn't launched a single plane. The War Industries Board had turned out to be nothing more than a title and a suite of offices; it couldn't sign a contract or revise an existing one held by the War Department or the navy. Stories were coming out from army training camps of high rates of sickness, absenteeism, and shortages of everything from food and medicine to weapons and ammunition.[31]

It was turning out that much of the administrative machinery Wilson had put in place to organize mobilization was faulty and badly conceived. It was also split by personal feuds and rivalries. The Shipping Board, for example, was bogged down in an argument between a member of its board, William Denman, and Gen. George Goethals of the board's Emergency Fleet Corporation over what kinds of merchant ships to build. Should they be made of steel, which was more durable but in demand for other war materials, or of wood? The argument went back and forth. Then Goethals, who favored steel and felt he was losing the argument, turned to the newspapers for support. The Hearst syndicate ran a series of exposés of how Denman, who favored wood, was poised to profit from his connections with certain California timber businesses. It was a less than edifying spectacle, and in the end, Wilson had to ask for the resignations of both Denman and Goethals—and not a ship was built.[32]

No one was more disgusted, or frustrated, by how things were going than Henry Cabot Lodge. He blamed Wilson's failure to get the country mobilized for war months or even years before, as well as incompetence in the present. "The utter failure in making preparation," he wrote to Roosevelt, "and the wanton waste of the time which has elapsed since the beginning of the war in 1914 have thrown us into the war with the work of years to be done in a few months."

Another major problem was Wilson's approach to contracts with private business. "The primary object of the administration," Lodge said, "appears to be to cut all the industries down to the barest living profit, and yet to the earning of our industries, both agricultural and industrial, we must look for our taxes and our loans." He concluded bitterly, "[W]e cannot carry on a war against American business and a war against Germany at the same time."[33]

From Lodge's point of view, a good example of the chaos was what was happening with the manufacture of machine guns. The army had decided to stop making the Lewis gun, a British design, and to substitute an American-made design from gun maker John Browning. That was on June 17, Lodge told Roosevelt; six months later, not a single gun had been manufactured. "The English are using 70,000 Lewis guns at this moment," Lodge reported. "[The army] could have turned out Lewis guns with great rapidity. Apparently our War Department thinks it is better to have no guns unless they get what they deem to be perfect. To my commonplace mind," Lodge added sarcastically, "some gun is better than no gun."[34]

The problem of trying to do too much in too short a time with too many rules and regulations extended across the whole range of war matériel. Even though U.S. industry had been supplying the needs of the Allies almost since the war began, those needs had largely been raw materials, explosives and ammunition, and foodstuffs. Most companies had no experience making artillery pieces, machine guns, naval guns, army trucks, tanks, or airplanes, let alone in quantity. Even Detroit, the vaunted center of the fast-growing and innovative automobile industry, Wilson's equivalent of Silicon Valley, made no sizable contribution to the mobilization—certainly not by comparison with its later contribution in World War II.[35] Henry Ford, for example, had promised thousands of tanks coming out of his new factory at River Rouge. The war ended long before any were made.

This failure left its mark on the U.S. war effort right down to the end of the war. Real weapons tended to be made by European firms; American soldiers would go into action using British-made machine guns, while being supported by American artillery officers firing French-made mortars and guns and American pilots, such as Eddie Rickenbacker, flying French-made airplanes. Indeed, three out of every four planes flown by the U.S. Army Air Service would be French built.[36] Meanwhile, by the end of November 1917, eight months after Wilson had declared war, there were only 125,000 American troops in France instead of the one million he had promised—and of those, only two divisions were truly ready to fight at the front. Henry Cabot Lodge summed up the general feeling in Congress when he said, "We cannot beat the Kaiser by standing silently by Wilson."[37]

Then came the railroad debacle.

In July, Wilson had created the Railroad War Board to oversee the shipment of strategic materials around the country. The trouble started when the board ordered the tagging of certain items, creating tie-ups and bottlenecks that virtually shut down the railroads on the East Coast. By the fall, chaos gripped the nation's railroads, its economic lifeline but also the lifeline of the entire war mobilization effort. The various railroads said they wouldn't cooperate; the unions threatened to strike. Cars carrying food, fuel, industrial supplies, and raw materials were stalled across the country. Coal cars carrying the fuel that powered 90 percent of America's factories and electric plants, and most Americans' homes, choked the railroad sidings and marshaling yards of every major city. It was looking to be a very chilly winter.[38]

For months, the crisis continued as the country's ability to keep Americans clothed, fed, and warm—let alone to supply and equip its rapidly growing armed forces—seemed in doubt. Finally, on the day after Christmas, Wilson used the authority he'd been given by the

Army Appropriations Act on August 29, 1916, to nationalize the railroads. The U.S. Railroad Administration was set up, with Wilson's son-in-law, Secretary of the Treasury William McAdoo, as director general of railroads. Only streetcars and suburban commuter rails were exempt from the sweeping executive act.

That did it, as far as Congress was concerned. Fed up, Henry Cabot Lodge and Sen. George Chamberlain put together legislation to take control of the war mobilization effort away from Wilson and hand it to a three-man War Cabinet of distinguished citizens. As the year ended, the battle was on, and Wilson was fighting to keep control of the federal government—and of the war effort he had begun so hopefully (some would say arrogantly) back in April.

His mood was still defiant, despite the many missteps and failures. When he delivered his annual address to a sullen, resentful Congress, on December 4, 1917, he spoke of the forces of opposition—in his mind, still the equivalent of disloyalty, even treason.

"I hear the voices of dissent—who does not? I hear the criticism and the clamor of the noisily thoughtless and troublesome. I also see men here and there fling themselves in impotent disloyalty against the calm, indomitable power of the nation . . . They do not touch the heart of anything. They may safely be left to strut their uneasy hour and be forgotten."[39]

Maybe so, but catastrophic events were unfolding in Russia that would have a profound impact on where Wilson thought the war, now *his* war, was going. Those events would force him to pivot politically as well as diplomatically and open another unmarked door, one that led to a future even he could not conceive.

* * *

IT WAS NOT as if Wilson had not had ample warning of what was happening, or that it might turn out very badly if he failed to act.

Soon after the collapse of the Kerensky Offensive, Wilson's adviser Colonel House had written an urgent note to his friend the president, making it plain that the fate of Russia was now in his hands and no one else's. House had passed along an August 5 note regarding a visit by the British ambassador in Petrograd, Sir George Buchanan, with Russian foreign minister Mikhail Tereshchenko. Buchanan found Tereshchenko "despondent" over conditions on the front. The ambassador himself was "entirely at a loss to see how the Russian army is to be kept in existence and to be properly supplied," let alone to participate in any future offensive against the Germans. Given the coup Lenin and the Bolsheviks had nearly pulled off, it was also becoming clear that the existence of the Russian government itself might be in peril.

The president faced "one of the great cris[e]s that the world has ever known," House wrote. The time had come for a bold move toward peace, House proposed. "It is more important . . . that Russia should weld itself into a virile Republic than it is that Germany should be beaten to its knees." House worried that if the disintegration of Russia continued, Germany might "be able to dominate Russia both politically and economically. Then the clock of progress would indeed be set back."

On the other hand, if a constitutional democracy could be "firmly established" in Russia, in House's view, "German autocracy would be compelled to yield to a representative government within a very few years." House believed that the Germans "do understand what we mean by representative government, and they are eager for it." And with democracy, Germany could "return to the brotherhood of nations," and the world would know lasting peace.

Therefore, if the United States used its position to press for an immediate peace, with a face-saving mechanism regarding Alsace-Lorraine to placate French feelings, it might be possible to save the Kerensky government and democracy in Russia. The Russian ambassador had told House as much on August 19: "that success or failure in Russia may depend on your answer." What House was telling his president was that the time was coming when Wilson would have to choose between sustaining the forces for war or sustaining the forces of democracy, including in America. He could no longer do both.

"The war in America is not popular," House warned prophetically. "It will become increasingly unpopular as time goes on. If a peace could be made this winter, the United States would be at the apex of power." House hoped the president "would not lose this great opportunity." Either way, he knew "that you will meet it with that fine spirit of courage and democracy which has become synonymous with your name."[40]

Here House was mistaken. His president met his proposal instead with the spirit of inflexibility and commitment that went with his being, in Wilson's own words, the man of "strenuous mind and high ideals" he aspired to be: one who committed himself and the nation to the greatest cause in its history, a cause from which there was no going back. Wilson's mission now was *not* saving Russian democracy; it was defeating Germany, the outlaw nation, and pressing the war forward to the conclusion he desired, a great peace conference at which the sources of all the world's conflicts and wars would finally be resolved.

If such a mission was unpopular with the American people, so be it. After all, as Wilson had written, a world-historical leader does not listen to popular opinion or the polls. That August, Wilson had already waved away one plea for reviving the idea of peace without victory, from the pope in the Vatican. He was quite content to wave away another, from Petrograd.

House's plan died without another sound.

Yet, in retrospect, we can see that the stakes were higher in the Russian case. Suppose Wilson had been convinced that House was right; suppose he had used America's financial leverage to force the Allies to the peace table; suppose he had sent a note to Matthias Erzberger and the Reichstag endorsing their resolution on peace negotiations; suppose Kerensky had been able to announce to the Petrograd Soviet that an armistice was pending and the end of the war was in the offing—could that have saved the Russian republic? It's hard to say. The forces for chaos and disorder were already far advanced in Russia by the end of the summer; a civil war between the Provisional

Government and forces determined to put Nicholas II back on the throne was certainly not out of the question. Yet if Wilson had met Kerensky halfway, we can begin to see the outlines of a very different future for Russia, and the world, after 1917—a future where tens of millions of human beings lived to the end of their natural days, instead of dying in civil wars and gulags or by starvation and the firing squad.

But this is fantasy, not history. In the event, Wilson said no to House's offer. The war was going ahead as planned. In his April 2 address, Wilson had said that "the world must be made safe for democracy." Four months later, this no longer included Russia. What followed in that country was therefore at least to some degree Wilson's responsibility—all because of the road to peace not taken.

RUSSIA ON THE BRINK

The course of events compels the revolution "to concentrate all its forces of destruction" against the state power, and to set itself the aim, not of improving the state machine, but of smashing and destroying it.
—LENIN, *State and Revolution*, 1917

PETROGRAD

I N THE WEEKS following the Bolsheviks' failed coup, the new prime minister, Kerensky, focused his attention on protecting the new republic from its enemies. The problem was that he was looking the wrong way.

Having defeated Lenin and broken the Bolshevik movement, Kerensky was inclined to be generous to his former foes. Trotsky, Kamenev, and the others ensconced in prison faced no trial or consequences, let alone a firing squad. In a few weeks, they would be released. Kerensky's attitude was *pas d'ennemis à gauche* ("no enemies to the left"), even for those radical Marxists who had nearly brought Russian democracy crashing to the ground.

What worried Kerensky was a possible threat from the right, not the left. As he told the Ispolkom on July 26, they must not "with their actions inspire the forces of the counterrevolution," and "any attempt to restore the Russian monarchic regime will be suppressed in the most decisive, pitiless manner." The man who in his mind increasingly embodied that threat was not the czar but, rather, the man Kerensky himself had put in charge of the war, Gen. Lavr Kornilov.

Later, his name would be steeped in the deepest, darkest dye for his role as a leader of the anti-Communist White forces in the Russian Civil War. But in August 1917, there was no one more likely to pull together the Russian army and the collapsing front than Kornilov. Unlike Kerensky—or Lenin or Trotsky, for that matter—Kornilov came from peasant stock; his father was a farmer and soldier, his mother a housekeeper. Kornilov's courage was legendary; respect from his troops was without question.[1] When he accepted command from Kerensky on August 1, the general laid down four conditions. The first was that he owed responsibility to his conscience and the nation. The second was that no one was to interfere with his orders or appointments, not even the all-powerful Petrograd Soviet. The third was that to restore order in the army, he would be free to apply his own disciplinary measures, including the death penalty for disobedience or desertion. The fourth was that the Provisional Government accept without question his recommendations on how to fight the war.

The very fact that a Russian general was still talking about fighting, let alone winning, the war against Germany and Austria must have been astonishing, possibly even refreshing. Kerensky, however, sensed a challenge to his own authority and prestige. If he had a fatal weakness, it was an unwillingness to share center stage with anyone, even a general who could turn impending defeat into victory—or at least stalemate. But he had no choice: since the Bolsheviks' failed coup, everything now depended on Kornilov's bringing the army back on the side of the government. After five days of negotiations, the two struck a deal. But if Kerensky had to choose between his new commander in chief and holding together the socialist coalition that underpinned his premiership, he would have to make the hard choice and push Kornilov out.

For Lenin, in hiding in Finland, it was a grim August and September. At the end of July, he penned "Lessons of the Revolution," his postmortem of the failed coup in July. "It is clear that the first phase of our revolution has failed," he wrote. Yet "[t]he old tyranny is coming back. The death penalty is being introduced for the soldiers at the front"—his reluctant nod to Kornilov's new order in the Russian army. "Workers' newspapers are closed down without trial. Bolsheviks are arrested, often without any charge or upon blatantly trumped-up charges"—ignoring the fact that he had left Trotsky, Kamenev, and the others to their fate at the hands of the police while he skipped across the border.[2] It was a contrast in fates that those he had abandoned in Petrograd were aware of. Leon Trotsky in his jail cell remarked to a comrade, "Perhaps we made a mistake. We should have tried to take power." It was a veiled rebuke of Lenin, who had lost his nerve at the last minute while the rest of his conspirators paid the price.[3]

So, what did Lenin learn from his experience? Next time, he would have to make sure that the armed forces were either a reliable ally or totally impotent; he would ignore his weaker and less unscrupulous opponents; and he would take steps to ensure that the Russian public that mattered most, the inhabitants of Petrograd, were either fully on board with a revolutionary takeover or at least acquiescent in a full-dress Bolshevik coup.

As Lenin regained his nerve, *State and Revolution* evolved from a last will and testament into a guide to future revolutionary strategy, in case the Provisional Government gave him another shot. Its overall theme is that all governments, even those such as the Provisional Government or the future government of Russia that the Constituent Assembly would embody, served only the interests of the bourgeoisie. The issue was not who controlled a government, but how "to *smash* it," he said, quoting Marx. "Marx's idea is that the working class must *break up*, *smash* the 'ready-made machinery,' and not confine itself merely to laying hold of it."[4]

So, what would take its place? Lenin was insistent that, under the dictatorship of the proletariat—or, to use the new term he would use, *communism*—the normal institutions of the "parasitic state," the legacy of bourgeois capitalism, would wither away. Under this new order, the dictatorship of the proletariat, the will of the working class, would rule instead of the organs of the state. Even so, even on the verge of the new, more just and egalitarian order, Lenin foresaw that "in the transition from capitalism to communism, repression is still necessary, but it is already the repression of the exploiters by the majority of the exploited." That meant "a special machine of repression" would still be needed, even after the abolition of capitalism and all its works.[5] A place marker had been laid down in *State and Revolution* for what would become the Cheka and the KGB, a means to enforce utopia in the teeth of those who might still oppose its noble goals, even after the architects of utopia have taken power.

That place marker was a measure not just of Lenin's fanatical devotion to his Marxist revolutionary vision no matter the cost, but also of his desperation after his failed coup. In an earlier essay, he made it clear that "all hopes for the peaceful evolution of the Russian Revolution have disappeared without trace." All he needed now, he believed, was the chance for a rematch. That must have seemed a bizarre fantasy coming from a man hiding out in obscurity in a Finnish farmhouse. Then, improbably enough, Kerensky and Kornilov gave him that chance.

It was a busy August in Petrograd. Besides finding a way to halt the relentless German advance through Eastern Galicia toward Riga and the Baltic provinces, the main order of business was preparing the way for elections for the Constituent Assembly, set in August for November 25. When Kerensky called a State Conference in Moscow to rally public opinion, what was supposed to be a display of political unity suddenly fractured. General Kornilov was the other featured personality. When Kerensky appeared, there was polite applause from Socialist Revolutionaries, Mensheviks, and other parties on the left. When Kornilov made his entrance, a cordon of soldiers literally carried him into the hall on their shoulders as the parties on the right roared and shouted their approval.[6]

The battle lines between Kerensky and Kornilov had been drawn. In Kerensky's mind, then and later, that line was ideological. He saw himself as representing the forces of democracy and progress; Kornilov, the forces of reaction and counterrevolution. (As for the Bolsheviks, they were the "party of the political rabble.") In his memoirs, Kerensky would refer to the general as "that unsuccessful Russian Napoleon," the man who had halted the French Revolution in midstream in order to install himself in power.[7]

But Kerensky had read his history almost too well. His knowledge of the French Revolution had taught him that the most effective opponents of revolution came from the political right. What the Provisional Government and the future of Russian democracy had to fear most, he believed, was the threat of counterrevolution, led by an authoritarian general such as Kornilov. As self-declared custodian of the revolution, Kerensky saw his job, following the State Congress, as heading Kornilov off at the counterrevolutionary pass. It was a foolish and, in many ways, tragic mistake. By rounding on Kornilov, Russia's prime minister made an enemy of the one man who could have helped him prevent what was coming.

On September 3, the Germans marched virtually unopposed into Riga, a little more than three hundred miles from Petrograd. The Kerensky Offensive unwittingly opened the door to a German triumph in the east. Before the Russian army could rally itself to face the enemy, Germany would virtually be at the gates of the capital.

That was the final straw for Kornilov. Already there was talk of a possible new Bolshevik coup, to coincide with the German offensive.[8] Prime Minister Kerensky sent an urgent message, asking if Kornilov would be prepared to send troops to put down a Bolshevik revolt. Kornilov said yes; he had even been approached by officers who told him they had two thousand loyal troops in Petrograd ready to deal with any trouble Lenin and his henchmen might try to stir up. Kornilov, however, was conflicted. On the one hand, Kerensky needed his help and his troops. On the other, Kornilov knew that the prime minister was working behind the scenes to deprive him of any authority over the Petrograd Military District, for fear the general might be planning to seize power. A dangerous and complex game was being

played out, one in which Kerensky and Kornilov were both jockey-
ing for ultimate control over the capital. After some initial hesitation,
Kornilov decided it was time to cut the political Gordian knot and
take power himself in the name of Russia.

Yet, on September 8, Kerensky had already made his move. He
sprang a trap by telling the press that Kornilov was marching on the
capital to topple the Provisional Government.[9] Enraged by an accusation he saw as patently, even deliberately false, Kornilov lashed out.
He dismissed Kerensky's charge as "an out-and-out lie" and then issued a call to the public himself: "Russian people! Our great homeland is dying! . . . I[,] General Kornilov, the son of a Cossack peasant,
declare to each and all that I personally desire nothing but to save
Great Russia. I swear to lead the people through victory over the enemy to the Constituent Assembly, where it will decide its own destiny
and choose its new political system."[10]

If this was Kerensky's plan all along, it worked perfectly. Kornilov's appeal was a brazen challenge to both the Provisional Government and the Supreme Soviet. Kerensky took the opportunity to
order all other military commanders to disregard Kornilov's orders,
which they did. If there was a plot by Kornilov to seize power, it was
a singularly small and inept one. There then followed three awkward
days when, in order to hold the Russian army together, Kerensky had
to keep in supreme command a man whom he had publicly accused
of treason, because no one else was willing to take that brutal and
thankless job.

Finally, on September 14, General Alekseev—the man who had
convinced Nicholas II to surrender his office—arrived at Mogilev to
persuade Kornilov to do the same, and to assume command himself. Somewhat to everyone's surprise, Kornilov meekly accepted his
arrest—his wife had taken away his revolver for fear he might shoot
himself.

Kornilov's coup, if ever there was one, was over, but the army had
lost its one strong figure not tainted by the failed policies of the past,
while Kerensky was now doubly discredited. First, there had been the

stupendous failure of the July offensive; now there was the arrest of the commander in chief he himself had appointed.

Worse was to come. As historian Richard Pipes writes, "in September and October, Russia drifted rudderless," while German armies moved ever closer. The stage was set for someone more determined and more ruthless than either Kornilov or Kerensky to assume power.

At the end of October, that someone was Lenin.

* * *

LENIN WAS DELIGHTED by the falling-out between Kornilov and Kerensky. It restored his sense of confidence that he alone held the key to power in Russia, and that violent insurrection was the only way to crack the lock. As late as September 1, Lenin was working on an article stating that he was ready to accept a compromise: the Bolsheviks would stick to nonviolent political tactics as long as the "moderates" were willing to form a government "wholly and exclusively responsible to the soviets."[11]

Lenin could now throw aside any lingering thought of compromise. It was time to strike. He had his own historical parallel in mind: the Paris Commune that seized power from the French government in 1871. "The Bolsheviks, to put it bluntly, hold ten times more 'trumps' than the [Paris] Commune did," he had written on September 16, in a memo urging some compromise with the mainstream political parties.[12] Now, after Kornilov's arrest, he fired off a message to the Bolshevik Central Committee on September 25: "Taking power *immediately* both in Moscow and [Petrograd] (it doesn't matter who goes first; perhaps even Moscow can do it), we will *absolutely and undoubtedly* be victorious."

Since the summer, the Bolsheviks had benefited from the fact that Russian voters (who now included women as well as all men) were becoming fed up with serial failure at the top. In desperation, they were turning to the Bolsheviks, the one party untainted by participation in a failing, flailing government. Votes in the Petrograd Municipal Council in August reflected this, as the Bolshevik share climbed from barely a fifth to a third. In Moscow in September, while the share of votes for the Socialist Revolutionaries and Mensheviks plummeted, those for the conservative Kadets and the Bolsheviks surged, from 17.2 to 31.5 percent and 11.7 to 49.5 percent, respectively.[13]

Part of this was Lenin's softening of the Bolshevik message since July. The apocalyptic side of his vision, the picture of violent world revolution and class war, had been set aside. Instead, he was speaking of the "withering away of the state" under communism, as if the transition from capitalism and bourgeois democracy to the dictatorship of the proletariat would be a gradual, almost peaceful evolution instead of the violent smashing of the state he envisioned in *State and Revolution*. Nonetheless, it also owed its success to the powerful simplicity of Lenin's Bolshevik slogan, "Peace, Land, Bread." By October 1917, with no end in sight for either the war or the food shortages, large numbers of frustrated Russians were ready for a change.

They were going to get more than they had ever bargained for.

On September 14, the elections in the Petrograd Soviet gave a majority to the Bolsheviks for the first time. Yet when Lenin's letter arrived urging immediate revolution, the members of the Central Committee were appalled. Both Trotsky and Kamenev, having been released from prison by the Kerensky government (a move it would bitterly regret in a few weeks' time), were present when the letter was read. Both realized that the call for immediate revolution would be a disaster, and the committee ordered the letter burned (all copies except one, which survives), lest it trigger fresh arrests by the government. No one except Lenin truly believed revolution at this stage was possible or even, in the minds of some, such as Zinoviev and Kamenev, desirable. What was needed was an outside catalyst, something that would rally public opinion to the Bolshevik side while also betraying the fatal weakness of the government.[14]

In fact, that had already happened, on September 15, when the gates of Kresty Prison swung open and Leon Trotsky walked away a free man.

Prison had done him good—it was a time of rest and routine after the frenzy of the summer. For the next month, he, not Lenin, would be the public face of the Bolshevik cause in Petrograd. His name appeared at the top of the Central Committee masthead; he secured a spot on the editorial board of *Pravda*. In the eyes of his admirers in Petrograd that fall (these admirers included a young American named John Reed, who had arrived in the capital days earlier), the story of the October Revolution in Russia was as much about Trotsky as about Lenin.

There was good reason for this. With his penetrating eye, Trotsky zeroed in on the fallacy that still held back the other members of the Central Committee: their belief that if the Bolsheviks were to gain a foothold in power, some arrangement of power sharing with the other socialist parties in the All-Russian Soviet was needed.

Trotsky, like Lenin, didn't want a foothold; he wanted the whole thing. He also understood firsthand, as Lenin did by instinct, that none of the organs of governance in Russia had the capacity or the will to stand in the way of a handful of determined revolutionaries backed by their armed thugs.

So, while Lenin was still out of action in Finland, Trotsky detached the Bolsheviks from all other government organs and parties with the single exception of the All-Russian Central Executive Committee, which he knew would be useful in rubber-stamping a Bolshevik takeover. For example, Kamenev and others had looked forward to Bolshevik participation in the Democratic Conference that Kerensky had summoned to Petrograd to serve as a pre-parliament before the election of the Constituent Assembly. Trotsky, however, scornfully rejected the notion of Bolsheviks seating themselves next to the other, discredited socialist parties, and he secured Central Committee approval for pulling out of Kerensky's staged confab.

There were still two challenges looming on the horizon. The first would be the meeting of a Second Congress of Soviets, slated for sometime in the fall. It was bound to position itself in rivalry to the Provisional Government, as the First Congress had done in June, and could pose a problem for a Bolshevik takeover. But the situation had changed since June, to the Bolsheviks' advantage; they were now poised to send a sizable contingent of deputies to the Second Congress. It was the Mensheviks and Socialist Revolutionaries who had the most to fear from a Second Congress, where their influence was bound to be diminished. So, it was with great reluctance that the Menshevik-dominated Bureau of the Ispolkom finally yielded to Bolshevik pressure and agreed to summoning a Second Congress on November 2. Its agenda was supposed to be strictly limited to putting together legislative proposals for the coming Constituent Assembly.[15] But many Bolsheviks, including Trotsky, saw the Second Congress as the perfect launching pad for their seizure of power.

Yet it was the Constituent Assembly that was the real threat—or, from the perspective of Russian democracy, the one real hope. Elected by universal suffrage, with a mandate to create a genuine constitutional republic, it might fill the looming political vacuum that the Bolsheviks needed in order to grab power. When Lenin wrote on September 26, "History won't forgive us if we don't seize power now," it was also because he knew that if the Constituent Assembly managed to take power first, the tide of Russian history would run irrevocably against a Bolshevik Revolution.[16]

Time was running out in other ways, too. On September 19, German forces began operations against a series of fortified islands in the Gulf of Riga. If those fell, the Germans would be in a position to launch amphibious landings behind Russian lines; the collapse of the entire front could be imminent. Then it would be the Germans, not the Bolsheviks, who controlled events in the capital, including the fate of the Provisional Government. It really was necessary to speed up the timetable: and here Trotsky found one more tool at his disposal.

As the news from Riga got worse, Mensheviks and Socialist Revolutionaries in the Petrograd Soviet began to worry that the city's army garrison might not be able to summon enough troops to stop the Germans if they advanced on the capital. They called for a new independent body to coordinate military activity around Petrograd, to be under the control of the Petrograd Soviet rather than the army's Military Staff.

Trotsky, now chairman of the Petrograd Soviet, quickly agreed to participate. On October 29, the Soviet approved creation of the Military Revolutionary Committee. Trotsky soon made sure that loyal Bolsheviks were installed in its key posts, and then went to key army units to tell them that only the Bolsheviks would make sure they were never sent to the front. That was a definite morale boost for soldiers who had lost faith in the war months before. Trotsky also urged them to transfer their allegiance from the Provisional Government to the Petrograd Soviet, which meant, for all practical purposes, the Bolsheviks, Trotsky, and Lenin.[17]

Lenin himself was now the one piece missing from a successful putsch, and on either October 7 or October 8, he left Helsinki for a safe house on the Finnish-Russian border, at Vyborg. Once again, he traveled with a forged passport and in disguise, this time with a wig and glasses as a Finnish pastor of the Lutheran Church. Before leaving, he fired off to the Bolshevik Central Committee one last letter, titled "The Crisis Has Ripened." (In fact, nothing had ripened except the Bolsheviks' leverage for seizing power.) It urged action: "To pass up such a moment and 'await' the Congress of Soviets"—the Second Congress was due to take its seats in less than a month—"is *complete idiocy* or *complete treason.*"[18]

The moment for revolution was now.

As if on Lenin's cue, on October 16 the Russian General Staff ordered the evacuation of the one remaining fortress between the Germans and the capital. German forces would soon be less than 225 miles from Petrograd. This sent up a storm of consternation in the government. Kerensky and others decided they needed to start preparing to move the government from Petrograd to Moscow; the Germans could conceivably be on the outskirts of the capital in less than a week.[19]

The Ispolkom, however, said no. With the Bolsheviks leading the charge, it declared that evacuation plans were only a ploy on

the government's part to escape the influence of the revolutionary masses, and to abjectly surrender the capital to the advancing
Germans. Trotsky persuaded the Soldiers' Section of the Soviet to
condemn the government's plans: the resolution called on Kerensky
and his colleagues either to surrender to Germany or to give way to
a new government. Alarmed and cowed by the unexpected storm of
criticism, the Provisional Government gave way. It abandoned any
evacuation plans and instead immediately ordered units from the
Petrograd garrison to the front, for a last stand against the advancing Germans.

In retrospect, it's hard to say which decision by the government
was more foolish: yielding to the pressure to stay in a city that might,
in a matter of days, be occupied by a foreign army, or commanding
soldiers who were used to disobeying orders to risk their lives in a
hopeless fight in a war they resolutely opposed.

At the urging of the Bolsheviks, the garrison, of course, refused
to go. The issue went over to the Ispolkom, where the Bolsheviks,
again led by Trotsky, presented a "compromise." When the Mensheviks proposed setting up a Committee of Revolutionary Defense, or
CRD, to organize resistance in the city against the German invader, a
body that the soldiers might be more inclined to obey than their own
officers, Trotsky did one better: he renamed the CRD as the Revolutionary Committee of Defense and ordered it to defend the city from
the "domestic enemy" as well—meaning the Provisional Government. The way to do this was to detach command of all military units
around Petrograd from the Military Staff and make the Petrograd Soviet the final authority in whose name the Revolutionary Committee
of Defense would act. Trotsky did not need to add that this ensured
that the Soviet's Bolshevik majority would have the upper hand in
deciding how and when the troops would be used, if ever.

Without thinking, the Ispolkom said yes. Later, Trotsky noted
gleefully that it was the vote of October 22 that finally sealed the fate
of the Provisional Government.[20] Military units garrisoning the capital could now be officially used against the government, instead of

protecting it. But there was still one more thing needed to pull off the coup: the Bolsheviks had to decide to act.

This was where Lenin had failed back in July; now he was in a very different mood. When he appeared before his comrades on October 23, the first time he had been seen in public in more than four months, he was like a man possessed. The meeting of the Central Committee took place in the Petersburg Side apartment of Galina Flaxerman, wife of leftist Menshevik and Lenin acquaintance Nikolai Sukhanov. Lenin's appearance startled everyone. Shorn of his characteristic goatee and dressed as a Lutheran pastor with a silver-white wig, he looked more like an actor in a regional theater troupe than a revolutionary hero—an impression made more absurd by the fact that his wig kept slipping off as he spoke. He had to reach up constantly with one hand to shove it back into place.[21]

If his appearance seemed comical, his words were not. The time had come for revolution, he thundered. "Now is the moment for seizing power, or never . . . It is senseless to wait for the Constituent Assembly that will obviously not be on our side."

Nor was he worried that if their plan failed, they couldn't seize control of Russia. "The goal was not just to seize power at the center, or even end the war with Germany," he had written to Petrograd's leading Bolshevik organizer, Alexander Shliapnikov. The real goal was simply to destroy the status quo and plunge Russia into chaos and conflict. "The essence of our work, which must be persistent, systematic, and perhaps extremely long-term, is to aim for the transformation of the war into a civil war. When that will happen is another question . . . [but] we must wait for the moment to ripen, and systematically force it to open."[22]

Therefore, when Trotsky raised the issue of waiting until the next meeting of the Second Congress of Soviets, now scheduled for November 7, where the Bolsheviks would have an elected majority, Lenin waved the objection away. "This holds no interest for me whatever," he said irritably. "Of what importance is it? Will it even take place? And what can it accomplish even if it does meet? It is necessary to *tear out* power . . . That date may serve at best as camouflage, but the uprising must be carried out earlier and independently of the Congress of Soviets."

He pounded the table. "The party must seize power, arms in hand, and then we will talk of the Congress of Soviets."[23]

Battered and bullied, the other members of the Central Committee no longer had the willpower to resist their overbearing leader. By dawn, the resolution had passed, 10 votes to 2. Those against were Zinoviev and Kamenev. They still felt that triggering a revolution now, without some kind of popular endorsement, however contrived or phony, would be a mistake. They said as much in a letter they sent out afterward to Bolshevik chapters around the country, adding that Lenin's assertion that a Bolshevik Revolution in Russia would trigger a worldwide workers' revolt was at best an unproved assumption. When Lenin learned of the letter, his rage was considerable; he denounced them both as traitors. In the end, Zinoviev and Kamenev went along with the rest; like the others, they were more afraid of defying Lenin than they were of the consequences of another failed coup—even though if it failed this time, it would almost certainly put them all in front of a firing squad.

Overnight, the scene switched back to the Ispolkom and the All-Russian Soviet. On October 29, in a closed-door session, Trotsky's plan for handing command of the city's military forces to a single committee passed unanimously, with only two Menshevik deputies dissenting. Now renamed the Military Revolutionary Committee, or MRC, this executive body was quickly packed with Bolshevik members, with Trotsky at its head.

Everything was now in place for a bid for power. All that remained was a pretext for launching it. For Lenin's and Trotsky's goal was not just to take power from the Provisional Government *and* the Soviet and its executive body, the Ispolkom. It was also to find a way to make taking power look like a defensive move, as if the Bolsheviks were taking preventive action to protect the All-Russian Soviet from the Provisional Government.

The government soon obliged. When members of the Military Staff learned of the existence of the Military Revolutionary Committee, they were outraged. On November 4, the Military Staff issued a stern ultimatum to the Soviet: revoke the committee or face "decisive measures." The next night, the government ordered the shutting down of the two Bolshevik dailies, *Pravda* and *Soldat*; and troops were ordered to protect key points in the capital, including the Winter Palace.[24]

That night, Kerensky was feeling confident. For weeks, he had been expecting another Bolshevik coup; in many ways, he was actually hoping for one, so that he could crush the Bolsheviks once and for all. He had already dealt with Kornilov and the counterrevolutionary right; now it was the turn of the Bolsheviks and the radical left. To British ambassador George Buchanan, Kerensky kept saying, "I only wish that [the Bolsheviks] would come out, and I will then put them down."

The next day, November 6, he had his wish.

In the early morning hours, people looked out their windows to see troops pouring out to take command of key points in the city, including the Winter Palace. Other soldiers were sent to raise the drawbridges across the Neva, so that workers could not march into the city center. Others took over the offices of *Pravda* and *Soldat* and shut down the presses, while still others set out to round up and arrest members of the Military Revolutionary Committee. By 2:30 in the afternoon, the streets of Petrograd were deserted. The government was closing down the city, and was putting the lid on any incipient revolution.

This was exactly what Lenin and the Bolsheviks were hoping for. That evening, the MRC issued its own statement, claiming that far from planning to stage an uprising, it was actually protecting "the interests of the Petrograd garrison and democracy" against the malign forces of counterrevolution, namely, Kerensky and the government.

Later, Lenin arrived at MRC headquarters, his face heavily bandaged as a disguise. He had been captured by a government patrol, but he pretended to be falling-down drunk, and they laughed and let him go. Now that he heard what was happening, he could not conceal his pleasure and excitement.

"Oh, that is gooood," he said, rubbing his hands together and walking up and down the room, beaming. "That is verrry good."[25]

That night, Trotsky and the MRC sprang into action. At one post after another, the guards the government had assigned were told they were dismissed and should go home; those who didn't were immediately disarmed and sent on their way. In the darkness, one by one, the city's most vital centers were taken over by troops loyal to the Bolsheviks: railroad stations, post offices, telephone offices, banks, and bridges. It was an entirely bloodless coup, run like clockwork. It was clear that the Bolsheviks now controlled all law and order in the Russian capital.

Only the Winter Palace was left. Kerensky, his face a mask of "suffering and controlled fear," as one eyewitness remembered, was absorbing what was happening. He had called all his frontline commanders to plead for troops and help; every one of them turned him down. Almost comically, a two-man delegation from the Soviet appeared at 9:00 p.m., to protest the government's "reactionary" measures. The threat of a Bolshevik takeover was exaggerated, they said. Kerensky, who knew the truth, threw them out.

He and the government had lost; Lenin, Trotsky, and the Bolsheviks had won. The next morning, November 7, at nine o'clock, he slipped out the back of the Winter Palace in the disguise of a Serbian officer and, in a borrowed car, drove through the gates, past both his guards and those of the Bolsheviks, and left the city.

The car was flying an American flag.

WASHINGTON, RAPALLO, BERLIN

THE NEWS OF the Bolshevik coup sent shock waves across Europe, and into the White House. Wilson got the news just when plans for delivering help and supplies to Russia were taking final shape. With his usual optimism, he refused to be discouraged, even though the democratic Russian government that he and the Allies had counted on was gone. On the contrary, as he remarked to Congressman Frank Clark, "I have not lost faith in the Russian outcome by any means. Russia, like France in a past century, will no doubt have to go through deep waters[,] but she will come out upon firm land on the other side, and her great people, for they are a great people, will in my opinion take their proper place in the world."[26]

Wilson saw Lenin and the Bolshevik revolutionaries in Petrograd through his own Progressive prism: "as an extreme form of democratic anti-imperialist idealism," as one expert has explained it, "whose radical energies might be guided by rational argument" into embracing Wilson's globalist agenda, and therefore sustaining the war effort.[27] Even Lenin's talk of a separate peace with Germany did not worry Wilson.

He conveyed the same hopeful view when he addressed the American Federation of Labor on November 12:

> May I not say that it is amazing to me that any group of persons should be so ill-informed as to suppose, as some groups in Russia apparently suppose, that any reforms planned in the interest of the people can live in the presence of a Germany powerful enough to undermine or overthrow them by intrigue or force? Any body of free men that compounds with the present German Government is compounding for its own destruction.[28]

In other words, since Lenin and his allies were "free men" planning reforms in the interests of the Russian people, they would realize that any peace with Germany meant the doom of their regime. Wilson was certain that such a peace would not happen.

The reaction in the other Allied capitals was far more muted, and for good reason. The Allied leaders were gathering that same week in Rapallo, Italy, in their last joint strategic conference without the Americans.

The mood was grim, even before the unwelcome news came from Petrograd. On October 24, German armies had smashed the Italians at Caporetto, where thirty-five divisions of Austrians and Germans overwhelmed thirty-four divisions of Italian troops. The spearhead of the assault was the Alpine Division, led by one Capt. Erwin Rommel. Advancing through Italian lines obscured in rain and mist, Rommel's men were able to sweep past Italian strongholds and create havoc in the enemy's rear, capturing artillery pieces and dozens of prisoners without losing a single man. The next day, Rommel even caught an entire Italian detachment in the act of bathing.[29]

"The further we penetrated into the hostile positions," he recalled later, "the less prepared were the garrisons for our arrival, and the easier the fighting."[30] Rommel's infiltration tactics were in fact a foretaste of the tactics he would employ twenty-three years later, in France, and a year after that, in the Western Desert—those crucial days on the Caporetto front saw the birth of blitzkrieg as well as the collapse of Italy's will to fight on.

As German and Austrian units moved into the gap Rommel had created, one Italian formation after another became demoralized and fell back. On October 25, the Italian general in charge, Luigi Cadorna, had no choice but to order a retreat. In no time, retreat turned into rout—one vividly described by an American volunteer ambulance driver serving with the Italian army named Ernest Hemingway, in his novel *A Farewell to Arms*. Before it was over, on November 9, the Italian line had dropped back more than sixty miles, to the River Piave, just north of Venice. There was considerable fear that the city of canals would itself fall into German hands. In the end, though Venice was saved, forty thousand Italian troops were killed or wounded and a quarter of a million were taken prisoner—and another four hundred thousand deserted. General Cadorna was dismissed.

For a few weeks in November, it seemed that German forces under Gen. Otto von Below were about to drive another Allied country out of the war, just as Germany had driven Romania out the year before—and just as it was threatening to do with Russia now. When the Rapallo conference began, preventing Italy's collapse had been the urgent priority. Before it ended, figuring out how to keep Russia in the war was added to the same list.

To Lloyd George, the fall of Kerensky came as no surprise.[31] The British prime minister had even flirted with a plan to abandon Russia to the Germans in exchange for peace in the west, until Foreign Minister Balfour and the rest of the War Cabinet talked him out of it. The question in his mind, and in the minds of others in the British government, was what to do if Lenin went ahead with his threat to sign a separate peace. There was talk of securing the military supplies stockpiled at Murmansk and Archangel from the other Allies, to keep them from falling into German hands—the first hint that Russia's allies might enter the country to help it fight on. Otherwise, Lloyd George's instinct, and that of his colleagues, was to avoid doing anything to antagonize or alienate the new Bolshevik government, in case it could be brought around to listen to reason. As a goodwill gesture, two Bolshevik agents who had been detained in London were sent back to Russia.[32]

The attitude in France was very different. On November 13, French prime minister Paul Painlevé suffered a major defeat in the Chamber of Deputies and resigned. French president Raymond Poincaré appointed in his place a man whom he despised but who he knew was fully committed to the war: Georges Clemenceau. When he first appeared in front of the chamber, Clemenceau spoke in Churchillian terms: "You ask me for my policy. It is to wage war. Home policy? I wage war. Foreign policy? I wage war. All the time, in every sphere, I wage war." The man who would be Woodrow Wilson's fiercest friend when the Allies gathered to impose peace in Paris in 1919 was the man most determined to see Germany defeated—and the man most hostile to the Bolsheviks and all they represented (one reason France's Socialists refused to join his government).

In Clemenceau's mind, Lenin's proposal to sign a peace with Germany was morally as well as politically nothing less than an act of betrayal. France also held 80 percent of Russia's external debt and

28 percent of Russia's overseas investment. A Russia that felt free to abandon the war was also a Russia willing to abandon its other commitments to France; Clemenceau was determined not to let the ally that had balanced German power by dividing its attention slip away without a fight. But what leverage he could bring to bear was still unclear.

Instead, it would take a man with a mind not so far from Lenin's finally to show France, and the Allies, the way to deal decisively with Bolshevik Russia—namely, Woodrow Wilson.

As for the reaction in Berlin, it was muted elation. The fall of Kerensky not only signaled the termination of Russia's participation in the war, a major triumph at any time, but also opened the way for Germany to extend its territorial conquests in the east: if Lenin kept his word and wound up the war, it would leave Germany as the dominant power in eastern as well as Central Europe.

Anyway, the last thing Ludendorff and the German General Staff worried about was who governed in Petrograd. The possibility that Lenin's workers' revolution would spread from Russia and trigger insurrections that would shake Germany to its foundations and preempt any hope for ultimate victory was as remote as that of Lenin and his colleagues landing on the moon.

Yet, less than a year later, this was exactly what would happen.

PETROGRAD, NOVEMBER 7–8

"THURSDAY, NOVEMBER 8. Dawn broke on a city in the wildest excitement and confusion, a whole nation heaving up in long hissing swell of storm."

These are the words of John Reed, who had arrived in September, in time to be caught up in the action of the Bolshevik Revolution, which he would immortalize, and glamorize, in his memoir of those tempestuous days, *Ten Days That Shook the World*. For the young radical American, it was a heady experience, as expressed in his hyperbolic title. Yet for those who were seizing power, the possibility that it might be suddenly and catastrophically reversed never left them, and dogged their every step, including Lenin's.

The putative leader of the revolution finally turned up, between 8:00 and 9:00 a.m. on November 7, at the Bolshevik headquarters, still in disguise. Many didn't recognize him until he drew up a chair, pulled out a pencil, and began composing a notice for public broadcast:

> TO THE CITIZENS OF RUSSIA! The Provisional Government has been deposed. Government authority has passed into the hands of the organ of the Petrograd Soviet of Workers' and Soldiers' Deputies, the Military Revolutionary Committee, which stands at the head of the Petrograd proletariat and garrison.
>
> The task for which the people have been struggling—the immediate offer of a democratic peace, the abolition of landlord property in land, worker control over production, the creation of a Soviet government—this task is assured.
>
> Long Live the Revolution of Workers, Soldiers, and Peasants![33]

Lenin signed it in the name of the Military Revolutionary Committee—of which he was not actually a member. Trotsky was, however, and when he caught sight of Lenin, he found him giddy with excitement. "Es schwindet!" he exclaimed in German, making a whirling motion with his hand. The experience of going from hunted fugitive to power holder literally overnight was indeed dizzying, almost overwhelming.[34]

They had seized control of the capital virtually without a shot being fired. (Things would be different in Moscow, when the coup spread there and triggered savage fighting.) There was still the Winter Palace to deal with, though. Both men were reluctant to summon the Second Soviet Congress, which was slated to start that day, while the Winter Palace, defended by a detachment of women soldiers from the First Petrograd Women's Battalion, still held out against the coup. So, Trotsky had to bluff his way through his initial meeting with the Petrograd Soviet that afternoon, when he brought it news of what had happened.

"In the name of the Military Revolutionary Committee, I declare that the Provisional Government has ceased to exist." When someone protested that he was jumping ahead of the coming Congress, Trotsky scornfully shouted back, "The will of the All-Russian Congress of Soviets has been predetermined by the enormous feat of the uprising of Petrograd workers and soldiers which occurred last night." Of course, there was no "uprising," but no one dared to disagree, especially when the building was surrounded by and filled with soldiers with bayonets.[35]

Lenin made a brief appearance in front of the Petrograd Soviet, to hail "the worldwide socialist revolution" and to convey a sense of confidence that not everyone in the room was feeling. Then he retired to take a series of catnaps, as the Congress meeting was postponed hour by hour—while the Winter Palace still sat silent and defiant. Five thousand sailors from Kronstadt arrived outside its gates, but showed no inclination to take the palace by storm. A few shots from inside had them retreating back down the street.

Holding the palace were a handful of army cadets and 137 enlistees from an all-women unit, the First Petrograd Women's Battalion, which had formed in emulation of the First Russian Women's Battalion, the so-called Battalion of Death, which had actually fought at the front on the Kerensky Offensive.

Finally, at 6:30 p.m., the MRC gave the palace's occupants an ultimatum to surrender or face bombardment from the cruiser *Aurora* and from guns in the Peter and Paul Fortress, now firmly in Bolshevik hands. At 9:00 p.m., the *Aurora* fired a blank salvo—a gesture that quickly passed into legend. Then the troops moved in.

John Reed was there when they did. Earlier, he had been out in the Nevsky Prospekt, "where the whole city seemed to be promenading," he later wrote. "On every corner immense crowds were massed around a core of hot discussion," while some shook their fists and howled epithets at soldiers lounging on street corners as armored cars raced up and down the street covered with huge red letters: R.S.D.R.P., the initials of the Bolshevik Party.[36] Later, Reed bumped into Kamenev carrying copies of the Petrograd Soviet's endorsement of the revolution.

"You consider it won then?" a breathless Reed asked.

Kamenev shrugged. "There is so much to do," he replied. "Horribly much. It is just beginning."[37]

There was, for example, the Winter Palace, where Reed joined the surging troops. "Carried along by the eager wave of men we were swept into the right-wing entrance, opening to a great bare vaulted room . . ." A row of wooden crates blocked the doorway, which the soldiers quickly knocked to pieces with their rifle butts.

"All out! All out!" a soldier and an officer, members of the Red Guards (the paramilitary units raised from the various workers' soviets that had become Lenin's bodyguards and Bolshevik militias, and his armed alternative to relying on the regular army), shouted down the corridor. The young cadets assigned to guard the palace came out in groups of three or four, and were quickly disarmed, as were the women soldiers (several of whom were later raped or threatened with sexual violence). "Counterrevolutionaries! Enemies of the people!" some shouted at them, making the prisoners fear for their lives. Then others demanded, "Now, will you take up arms against the People anymore?"

"No, no," the cadets said emphatically. Then they were let go.[38]

By midnight, it was all over. A total of five people had been killed and several more wounded, most from stray bullets. The ensuing mob stole everything from the Winter Palace that wasn't nailed down, "statuettes, bottles of ink . . . bed spreads with the Imperial monogram, candles, a small oil-painting, desk blotters, gold-handled swords, cakes of soap, clothes of every description, blankets."[39]

By 2:00 a.m., remaining members of the government were locked up under guard in the Peter and Paul Fortress. They were lucky to be alive, and were nearly lynched by the mob as they passed through the gates.

November 8 saw the streets returning to normal life, with street-cars running and restaurants open, and kiosks selling newspapers—including *Pravda* again. Things were anything but normal at the Smolny Institute, a former girls' academy where the Soviet Congress had finally opened. Its numbers were much reduced. Menshevik and Socialist Revolutionary delegates refused to participate; so did peasant organizations and army committees, condemning the Congress as unauthorized and urging a boycott by the nation's soviets. The Ispolkom issued its own statement, saying it regarded the meeting of the Congress as "not having taken place" and condemning it as "a private gathering of Bolshevik delegates."[40]

None of that mattered to Lenin and Trotsky. With two-thirds of the delegates firmly in their control, they pushed through their principal agenda items: the Decree on Land and the Decree on Peace.

The first ordered the nationalization of all land in Russia and the transfer of ownership to the state until it decided how to distribute it to the various peasant communities. Land held privately by peasant proprietors was exempt from confiscation, however—a brazen appeal for peasant support.

The Decree on Peace was an appeal to all belligerents to open negotiations for a "democratic" peace without annexations or reparations, and according to the principle of "the right to self-determination"—in short, the Petrograd formula adopted by the now deposed Provisional Government and Kerensky. It also proposed an immediate three-month armistice.

"We want a just peace, we are not afraid of a revolutionary war," Lenin told the thronging delegates, some six hundred fifty strong, who, from time to time, erupted with applause like rolling thunder. "Probably the imperialist governments will not answer our appeal." He warned that if they did not accept, the revolution was prepared to fight on. But Lenin was sure that once "the German proletariat" learned of the peace offer, revolution would break out in Germany. The war would soon come to an end.

No Bolshevik proposal, not even the Decree on Land, was more calculated to rally Russian public support to the coup. At 10:35 that evening, Kamenev called for a final vote. One lone hand shot up opposing the Decree on Peace, but its owner was quickly shouted down. The final vote was unanimous; Lenin's proposal to end the war had passed.

John Reed was in the room and watched the euphoric pandemonium that erupted. He saw an old soldier sobbing with relief, while a young man, his face shining, kept saying over and over, "The war is ended! The war is ended!" Someone called out for a moment of remembrance of those who had died for liberty, the ones who had died in prison or in exile, as well as those gunned down by czarist troops in the streets, as the crowd began singing the solemn "Funeral March":

The time will come when your surrendered life will count.
The time is near, when tyranny falls the people will rise, great and
    free![41]

The third order of business was choosing a new government, dubbed the Council of People's Commissars. It was to serve as the *new* Provisional Government until the Constituent Assembly met. The commissars all had virtually the same posts as the old Provisional Government's Cabinet, with one significant exception: the new post of chairman (not commissar) for nationality affairs.

In short order, the Congress elected all Bolsheviks as commissars.

Lenin was elected chairman. Trotsky took over foreign affairs; internal affairs went to Alexei Rykov, a friend of Kamenev's and one of the original holdouts against the coup. A trio of lesser names—Antonov-Ovseyenko, Krylenko, and Dybenko—took over the war and navy slots, a sure sign that Lenin and Trotsky would exercise final authority over whatever decisions were made about the army and navy. Labor went to Alexander G. Shliapnikov, and Anatoly V. Lunacharsky became commissar of enlightenment.

The newest post, chairman for nationality affairs, went to the man who had been largely behind the scenes during the coup of the day before, but who was Lenin's trusted adviser on all matters relating to Russia's ethnic minorities, the Georgian former theology student turned bank robber Joseph Stalin.

That post marked the beginning of Stalin's rise to power, a rise that would eventually eclipse and obliterate everyone else in the Bolshevik leadership with the exception of Lenin himself. In fact, of the fifteen original members of the Commissars' Committee, twelve would later be executed or murdered on Stalin's orders, including Leon Trotsky.

The delegates in the room were wrong. The tyranny and the bloodshed were just beginning.

HINGE OF FATES

*The moral climax of this the culminating and final
war for human liberty has come.*
—WOODROW WILSON, JANUARY 8, 1918

CAMBRAI, NOVEMBER 20–NOVEMBER 30

THAT NOVEMBER, RUSSIA wasn't the only place witnessing a revolution.

On September 20, Douglas Haig renewed his offensive along the Ypres Salient. The new man he had put in charge of the operation, Gen. Sir Herbert Plumer, one of the best and most innovative of Britain's generals, made steady progress through October, until the weather turned again. On November 8, Haig's chief of staff, Gen. Sir Launcelot Kiggell, paid a visit to the front for the first time. His car became stuck in the mud that Allied troops were trying to advance through, without success. "Good God," he exclaimed, "did we really send men to fight in that?" Kiggell burst into tears. His driver merely remarked stoically, "It's worse further up."[1]

The Passchendaele offensive ended that day. British forces had suffered a quarter million casualties, with 53,000 dead. The battle's lasting monument was not the collapse of the German right flank (although the Germans had suffered horrific losses, especially in the last phase of the campaign), but the Commonwealth War Graves Cemetery, the largest in the world. It is the dismal monument to a three-year failed strategy for fighting a European land war.[2]

That same day, the bigwigs in Rapallo had decided to create an Allied Supreme War Council to coordinate the rest of the war. Gen. Ferdinand Foch would be the chairman. Scholar and iconoclast, Foch had served as a private in the Franco-Prussian War and was France's foremost advocate of the attack-no-matter-what doctrine that had opened the war in 1914, with disastrous results.

That failed doctrine, however, had led in 1916 to an abrupt shift in Foch's thinking. He saw clearly that trenches, barbed wire, and machine guns made conventional offensive strategies—waves of soldiers going over the top behind a steady barrage of artillery shells—obsolete. With Joffre and Nivelle advocating continuing the conventional offensive approach, Foch found his advice disregarded. Yet in the aftermath of the French army mutinies and the dismal failure of Britain's Passchendaele offensive, Ferdinand Foch was suddenly the right man in the right place at the right hour to take supreme command of both armies.[3]

As "generalissimo," Foch sought a new way of thinking about offensive warfare to overcome the defense's built-in edge. His moment came on November 20—just as Lenin and the new committee of commissars were trying to consolidate their rule and deciding how to approach Berlin with an offer to end the war.

The moment came at Cambrai, fifty-five miles south of the Commonwealth graveyard at Passchendaele. On November 20, no fewer than 380 British tanks rolled forward from British lines without a sustained preliminary artillery bombardment. Tanks had been tried in the attacks in Passchendaele, but the thick mud simply bogged them down. The hard, chalky surfaces around Cambrai suited them much better. There was no need to send men ahead to cut the extensive lines of barbed wire while being exposed to machine-gun fire. The tanks simply rolled over the barbed wire without stopping, then rolled over the first German line of trenches, then the next, and then the next. By 9:00 a.m., they had advanced five miles, with columns of infantry following dutifully behind. A hole five miles wide and four miles deep had opened in the German lines—the breakthrough every general since 1914 had dreamed of—all at the cost of fifteen hundred British casualties, and resulting from the capture of ten thousand bewildered Germans and the expending of two hundred artillery pieces.

This victory for British arms encouraged the government, for the first and only time in the war, to order church bells rung across London.[4] The exhilaration, however, was short-lived. The unprecedented breakthrough meant there was no precedent for how to exploit it. Cavalry poured into the gap, including famous Indian army regiments such as Hodson's Horse, where they faced steady slaughter from German machine guns as Ludendorff sped reinforcements to plug the gap.[5]

By November 21, Ludendorff had four divisions holding the line and another five entering the sector. The British tanks were taking hits from German artillery and antitank ammunition—the first of its kind. Meanwhile, German airplanes regularly swooped in to pound and strafe British troops, the first example of air interdiction in warfare. On November 23, the attack stalled. A week later, twenty German divisions counterattacked. The tanks proved unable to provide any effective defense to the swarming, surging German infantry advancing under a combination barrage of high-explosive and gas shells. The British lost almost all the ground they had gained ten days before. Forty-four thousand British troops were dead or wounded, and there were fifty-three thousand German casualties. Another promising offensive had launched, and failed.[6]

The failure of Cambrai was deeply disquieting—and not just because the tanks hadn't made the definitive, decisive stroke their advocates had hoped for. German soldiers whom the British and French had captured included men from the 107th Division, which had recently been fighting in Russia. The Germans were transferring men from the Eastern to the Western Front. If Russia left the war altogether, as its new Bolshevik government was threatening, no fewer than forty new German divisions would be available to tip the balance in the west.[7]

The Allies were going to need the Americans even more desperately than before.

WASHINGTON

BUT WHERE WERE the Americans?

Since the summer, Allied planning had assumed there would be one million American soldiers on French soil as 1918 began.[8] As November ended, however, the total was still barely 125,000 men, the effective equivalent of ten French or British infantry divisions. That might be a useful reserve, but it was hardly a force prepared to turn the balance on the battlefield. Besides, of those, barely half were ready for combat—and when American troops first went into the line on October 26, in a quiet French sector, their baptism of fire had been a disaster.[9] In addition, the Americans had no logistical, supply, or transport organization. The entire American Expeditionary Force had fewer than thirty trucks. Instead, they had to beg, borrow, and, in some cases, steal the vehicles, horses, ammunition, and even guns they needed to maintain themselves as a fighting force.

Meanwhile, President Wilson was largely oblivious to all these problems. His focus was still trying to get the Entente powers to embrace his globalist vision, and to give up on those terms of peace that conformed to their own petty national interests. That was not easy, as Colonel House discovered in a series of discussions with high-level British and French officials that fall. Both London and Paris wanted the dispatch of an American War Mission to Europe; this could help to coordinate U.S. and Allied strategy and the joint development of resources ranging from munitions to merchant shipping. Wilson, however, was strongly opposed to shifting the center of gravity for America's share of the war from Washington to London and Paris. He was determined to maintain his independence, no matter how much confusion it might cause in the joint war effort—even regarding how and when American forces would be committed into action. It wasn't until late October that Wilson yielded to the inevitable and allowed

House and a team of military and civilian officials to head across the Atlantic to coordinate mobilization plans.[10]

They arrived at Plymouth, England, in time to confront two disasters: first, the Italians' defeat at Caporetto, and then the Bolsheviks' coup and offer of a separate peace to Germany. House's meeting with Lloyd George led in turn to two pressing demands from the British prime minister: first, to send as many American troops as possible as soon as possible, and second, to ship the six hundred thousand tons of supplies to Britain that Wilson had promised for that year. Conversations with French officials, including the new prime minister, Clemenceau, reiterated the same points.[11] As for Russia, everyone was in despair over how to keep that original member of the Entente committed to fighting on when every signal from the new government in Petrograd indicated the opposite.

But as the start of the first inter-Allied conference loomed, scheduled for December 1 in Paris, another issue raised its head, one that would be ultimately as important as what to do about Russia, although no one realized it at the time: whether to detach Austria from its German ally and bring it to a separate peace.

VIENNA

IN 1917, THE Austro-Hungarian Empire was a great polyglot ant heap of nations, ethnicities, and religions. It was the accretion of five centuries of conquests, marriages, and dynastic alliances. Germans (less than one-quarter of the empire's population), Hungarians (one-fifth of the population), Czechs, Poles, Ruthenes (or Ukrainians), Romanians, Croats, Serbs, Slovenes, Italians, and Jews—what held them all together was loyalty to the ruling Habsburg dynasty, loyalty that, in many cases, dated back to the fifteenth century. Habsburg rule had survived the Reformation and multiple Turkish invasions; it had survived the French Revolution and Napoleon, and the revolutions of 1848. But it could not survive 1917 and the test of modern war, or the forces of nationalism the war unleashed.

Austria had started the war in July 1914 in the hope of teaching recalcitrant Serbia a lesson. Instead, Russian and then German mobilization had pulled Austria-Hungary into the greatest war in European history, one for which it was totally unprepared.

As late as 1903, Austrians spent more on beer and wine than, and as much on tobacco as, the government spent on defense. Austria spent less per capita on the military than either Russia or Italy.[12] A massive military buildup followed until 1914, yet Austria still went to war with fewer infantry battalions than it had in 1866 (even though its population was now twice the size) and with some artillery dating back to 1861.

The lack of preparation, and lack of enthusiasm for war on the part of Austria's Slavic minorities, made itself felt almost from the start. By 1915, the empire's armies in the east were in an extended state of collapse; within a year, its armies would require help from German formation in order to stand up to the Russians—or, a year later, the Italians.

That same year, 1916, Emperor Franz Josef, the man who had held the empire together, died. He had been emperor since 1848, and no inhabitant of Austria-Hungary under the age of seventy could remember any other ruler. Franz Josef once told Theodore Roosevelt, "You see in me the last monarch of the old school."[13] With his death, his nephew Archduke Charles took the throne. Fifty-seven years his junior, Charles was honest, earnest, a man of honor and integrity—and therefore totally unfit to deal with the events that followed.

The war had broken the empire's economy. As early as May 1915, the capital, Vienna, saw its first food riots, as housewives attacked and then looted stores. By the autumn, the capital had run out of flour, potatoes, and animal fats.[14] From that point on, the specter of starvation stalked a monarchy whose newspapers brought daily reports of fresh disasters from every front. As enthusiasm for war plummeted in Vienna, Prague, Budapest, and every other major city in the empire, only Germany's iron grip on its foundering ally kept Austria in the fight.

By the spring of 1917, the misery wrought by hunger, inflation, and the breakdown of normal social life was even worse than in Germany, and had reached crisis proportions. That March, it forced Emperor Charles to put out the first secret peace feelers to the Allies, in the hope that peace might save his crumbling empire.

The first instinct of the French and British was to do nothing. Neither was fighting Austria; on the contrary, they saw its continued collapse as a way to hamper, even cripple, their real foe, Germany, in the way that a wounded comrade carried on his back will burden a soldier trying to fight. Indeed, that was the chief reason they had put self-determination for the peoples of the Habsburg Empire on the list of war ends they had sent to President Wilson on January 10.[15]

They also sensed that the death of Franz Josef had loosened whatever ties of loyalty millions of Hungarians, Czechs, and Croats might have felt for the empire—while the misery of war would make them desperate to seize their own destinies as free and independent nations, possibly even as allies of the Entente powers. If Franz Josef had bothered to ask for a separate peace, he might have had a more favorable hearing, but Charles, fearful of German retribution, refused to take a step that did not involve Berlin.

The conscientious Charles did what he could. In May, he summoned the Reichsrat, the sham parliament once used by his predecessors to forestall nationalist movements in the empire. Now Charles offered generous concessions to those national groups like the Czechs and Slovaks, but they came too late. Everyone sensed the impending doom of the five-hundred-year-old Habsburg monarchy and waited breathlessly for its final collapse.

Then, after dragging out their answer for several months, London and Paris finally gave Charles a thumbs-down. Now, with no options left but with America and Woodrow Wilson fully involved in the war, Charles decided to take his case to the Idealist-in-Chief, Wilson himself.

This involved a series of secret soundings, first to the British and then to President Wilson. Some notes went into specific terms for a negotiated peace, including settling the claims to autonomy from Austria-Hungary's various ethnic nationalities and France's and Italy's respective territorial claims against both Austria and Germany.

Although discussions dragged on into the following year, it was obvious, as December wound down, that these talks were headed nowhere. Since Austria still refused to detach its fortunes from those of Germany, "all plans for peace negotiations with Austria were doomed to failure," House noted later.[16] For the last emperor of the Habsburgs, it meant the doom of his throne as well. Waves of civic disorder and strikes, even in Vienna, were now the norm. Any remaining central imperial authority had collapsed. All it would take for the entire ramshackle empire to fly apart would be one major incident.

Still, as 1917 ended, it was common knowledge in and out of Austria-Hungary that Habsburg rule over central and southern Europe was coming to an end. But no one could have known that the tipping point would come not in Austria, or Hungary or Bohemia, but in a remote railway station in Siberia, near the Russian village of Chelyabinsk.

PETROGRAD

MEANWHILE, LENIN'S REVOLUTION was busy consolidating its grip outside Petrograd.

It almost didn't happen in Moscow, largely because the Bolsheviks there were not as committed to the coup as their Petrograd brethren, and they allowed their main objective, the city's Kremlin, to fall into the hands of troops still loyal to the government. On November 12 and 13, there was fierce street-to-street fighting, as loyalist and Bolshevik troops slugged it out for control of the fifteenth-century fortress. On November 15, however, Moscow's mayor and its Committee of Public Safety ordered troops to lay down their arms, and handed over power to the Moscow Soviet's Revolutionary Committee—which meant the Bolsheviks. From that point on, Moscow would become Lenin's most secure stronghold after Petrograd.

Elsewhere in Russia, the Bolshevik seizure of power had an easier time. Most local soviets were already dominated by their Bolshevik members, or had been intimidated into obedience. In some cases, the Bolsheviks formed coalitions with Left Socialist Revolutionary or even Menshevik allies, to proclaim the revolution; in others, they simply expelled any competitors and took over for themselves.[17] In this way, city after city came under the sway of Lenin and the Council of People's Commissars. By late November, they controlled most of Great Russia, the heart of the Russian Empire. Not bad for a political party that numbered only 23,000 members in February 1917; by that November, however, its ranks had swollen to between 600,000 and 700,000.

Still, in a vast country of more than 100 million inhabitants, its position of power remained precarious, especially with Lenin's chief rival, Alexander Kerensky, on the loose.

And where was Kerensky? After leaving the Winter Palace and Petrograd, he had traveled to Pskov, headquarters of the Northern Front. There he had pleaded with troops to accompany him back to Petrograd, to put down the Bolshevik revolt while it was in its infancy. The only troops available, however, flatly refused; as it happened, they were the same men of the Third Cossack Corps whom Kerensky had accused of backing Kornilov's coup. They hated Kerensky for casting this blot on their honor, which had led their commander to commit suicide. Forced to turn elsewhere for help, Kerensky drove off.[18]

Yet, for almost a week, with communication broken down everywhere, rumors continued to swirl that Kerensky might be headed back to Petrograd at the head of an armed column. Lenin and Trotsky held back from taking any major steps toward consolidating their power and destroying their rivals, in case Kerensky led a government advance and they needed help from the Mensheviks and others to repel it.

Lenin and Nadezhda were now living in the Smolny Institute, the former girls' academy with its elegant Palladian facade, in a two-bedroom apartment on its ground floor. It was hardly a domestic sanctuary. Trotsky and his family lived in the apartment opposite, which meant the two leaders could regularly get together for nonstop strategizing at every hour of the day or night. Troops of people's commissars and Red Guards trudged up and down the corridor outside, their boots ringing in the tiled hallway.

Lenin's office on the second floor in the north wing, No. 81, was also a scene of unending commotion, as he was regularly besieged by visitors and his Bolshevik colleagues, to whom he enjoyed making an impromptu speech in the anteroom. His meals were spartan, sometimes only a heel of bread and a plate of pickled herring, when he ate at all. His health was also increasingly precarious, with bouts of headaches and insomnia.

But he was living on the fumes of revolution, and sitting astride the main artery of power in Petrograd and Russia. The Bolshevik Central Committee, the Military Revolutionary Committee, the Petrograd Soviet, and the Central Executive Committee of the Congress of Soviets (the Council of People's Commissars, of which he was chairman)—all were a short stroll away.[19]

Besides, the Smolny Institute was a defensible position in case fighting broke out, or Kerensky came back with reinforcements. But Kerensky did not come back. He had managed to rally enough troops to take Tsarskoye Selo, the czar's former palace, but they were crushed by Red Guards the next day at Pulkovo, and Kerensky narrowly escaped. Now it was Kerensky, not Lenin, who was the hunted man, on the run and fleeing for the border. And once it became clear that there was no Kerensky on the way, no armed column coming to rescue the government, Lenin and Trotsky felt relaxed enough to impose their own brand of revolution on Petrograd and the rest of Russia, with the Bolshevik-dominated soviets around the country as their tool for enforcement—the first true totalitarian regime in history.

On November 11, a meeting of the Military Revolutionary Committee mentioned the need to fight against the "enemies of the people." On November 26, the MRC decreed that "high-ranking functionaries in state administration, banks, the treasury, the railways, and the post and telegraph offices are all sabotaging the measures of the Bolshevik government. Henceforth, such individuals are to be described as 'enemies of the people,'" and they would be named in newspapers and public places. The war on "enemies of the people," whether the case was proved or not, had begun—and it had likewise begun on those suspected of "sabotage, speculation, and opportunism."[20]

At the same time, the MRC was going through a transformation, from a committee dedicated to coordinating military defense of the capital into a bureaucratic apparatus for state security across Russia. In no time, it had an established network of more than one thousand commissars installed in military units, local soviets, government agencies, and even neighborhood communities, to enforce political loyalty to the regime and ideological solidarity with its Marxist goals—what would come to be called "political correctness." The MRC was originally made up of sixty members, forty-eight of whom were dedicated Bolsheviks. Later, the MRC's head, Pavel Lazimir, turned control over to his most trusted assistant, a forty-year-old perennial political prisoner who knew the ways of the czar's Okhrana secret police almost as well as its own agents did. His name was Felix Dzerzhinsky, and he had been instrumental in planning and executing the MRC's initial coup on November 6.

Dzerzhinsky understood better than anyone else that the MRC, in its new role, could serve as "the iron fist of the proletariat," in Lenin's phrase, crushing any and all opposition—the predecessor of the Cheka and the KGB.[21]

On November 17, Lenin organized his first purge of those people's commissars who still held out for cooperation with other political parties. He forced the resignation of Kamenev from the Central Executive Committee; Alexei Rykov and three other people's commissars were pushed out, as well as several lower-level deputy commissars. Together they penned a protest, calling for a Soviet government that would embrace all existing parties of the left, including the Mensheviks and Socialist Revolutionaries. "We believe that there is only one alternative to this" inclusive Soviet regime, they wrote, "the maintenance of an exclusive Bolshevik Government by means of political terror. This is the path taken by the Council of People's Commissars. We cannot and do not want to go this way."[22]

But Lenin did, and now this was all that mattered—and political terror was exactly what he had in mind.

That same day, he and the remaining people's commissars spawned the Food Committee, to seize food needed at Petrograd and the front. This would be the standard leverage for the new Bolshevik regime, with a brutally simple choice: obey or starve.

That night, Trotsky proposed laws reining in freedom of the press, in the name of the proletariat. "The monopoly of the press by the bourgeoisie must be suppressed," he told a skeptical Petrograd Soviet. "Otherwise it isn't worthwhile for us to take the power . . . The power of the Soviets should confiscate all print shops." When there was grumbling about this unexpected restriction—"Confiscate the printing shop of *Pravda*," someone bawled out—Lenin stepped in to clinch the argument.

"The civil war is not yet finished," he declared in a calm, unemotional voice, his brow deeply furrowed; "the enemy is still with us: consequently it is impossible to abolish the measures of repression against [the] press." He added menacingly that "to tolerate the bourgeois newspapers would mean to cease being a Socialist." Already everyone knew what that meant. The Central Executive Committee approved Lenin's proposal 34 to 24. Many resigned in protest; but as with the resignation of Rykov and the others from the Council of People's Commissars, the disappearance of opposition only sharpened the point of the Leninist spear.[23]

On November 23 came the creation of a Military Investigation Commission to root out "counterrevolutionary" officers and government officials accused of "sabotage"—words that would echo and haunt Russia for the next two decades.[24] Then, on December 20, Lenin authorized the setting up of a separate Emergency Committee, headed by Felix Dzerzhinsky, to root out individuals and groups trying "to undermine the measures the government is taking with a view to a socialist transformation of society," as Lenin put it. It was from that moment that the Cheka (so called from the Russian pronunciation of its acronym), later the OGPU, and still later the KGB, the most infamous secret police in the world, were born.

Yet all these steps were only part of a much larger and more important process. This was the concentration of all executive and legislative authority in the hands of a single party, the Bolshevik Party—soon to become the Communist Party. This was done not by substituting the party organization *for* the government, or by imposing party authority *over* the government, but by combining the two and making sure that everyone occupying the highest rungs of authority, such as the Council of People's Commissars, also held the highest offices inside the Bolshevik Party. To be part of government required being a ranking member of the party; likewise, being a member of the party meant having direct access to the leading executive, legislative, and judicial posts in the country.

As historian Richard Pipes notes, this arrangement is often described as a one-party state; a better term might be *dual state*, in which the government is a mirror image of the dominant political party in terms of office and personnel, and vice versa.[25] Lenin's Russia was the first. Mussolini's Italy soon followed; then Hitler's Germany. The dual-state model persists today in Communist China, North Korea, and Castro's Cuba. It is the essential foundation of the totalitarian state. In the months of November and December 1917, therefore, Lenin blazed a trail that would be followed and built upon by many others.

All the same, there was one obstacle to the consolidation of the Bolshevik Revolution that even Lenin had not yet stopped: the elections for the Constituent Assembly in the last week of November.

With every part of Russia participating, including women (something that couldn't yet happen in Woodrow Wilson's America or Clemenceau's France or Lloyd George's Britain), it was the biggest democratic election in history. Almost three times more Russians voted in November 1917 than Americans in the 1916 presidential election.[26] And the results were devastating for the Bolsheviks.

The Socialist Revolutionaries, Kerensky's old party, gained 38 percent of the vote; the Bolsheviks, less than 25 percent. Combined with
the Mensheviks, Constitutional Democrats, lesser socialist and non-
socialist parties, plus the Ukrainian nationalists, who were mainly
SRs, the opponents of the Bolshevik Revolution were poised to command 56 percent of the votes in the Constituent Assembly. The Bolsheviks had exactly 175 of 715 seats—hardly a position from which to
dominate the proceedings.[27]

Yet Lenin took some comfort in the results. The Bolshevik delegates would come overwhelmingly from the major cities, industrial
areas, and military garrisons (although in Petrograd and Moscow, the
conservative Kadets ran a close second, gaining 26.2 percent and 34.2
percent, respectively). If power truly comes from the barrel of a gun,
to borrow a phrase from a later master of the dual state, Mao Zedong,
Lenin still had his finger on the trigger, especially in the capital. His
best bet, however, was to defuse the authority of the Constituent Assembly before it even met.

The first tactic was to delay the Assembly's opening. The official
date was to be December 11; after several votes and inquiries, the
Council of People's Commissars ordered the Constituent Assembly's
electoral commission to hand over its records, on the grounds that
there had been electoral "abuses." The commission refused; its members were arrested.

In the end, the first meeting of the Assembly was put off until early
January, but not before Lenin had its most conservative party, the Kadet Party, outlawed as "enemies of the people." At the same time, the
Kadets' two newspapers were stormed by Bolshevik mobs and shut
down. Lenin ordered the leading Kadet politicians arrested as "leaders of civil war against the Revolution."[28]

Neither the Mensheviks nor the SRs made any protest at this
clearly repressive political action—even though they could well have
been next. Lenin did not care either way. Their time would come
later; for now, his message had been broadcast loud and clear. No
one, absolutely no one, would be allowed to stand in the way of his

vision for the revolution in Russia—not the political opposition, not the Constituent Assembly, and not the Russian people themselves. "In times of revolution," he had written back in July, it "is not enough to ascertain the 'will of the majority'—no, one must *be stronger* at the decisive moment at the decisive place, and *win*."[29] They were words Wilson at his most critical moments would have endorsed, but not under such circumstances. Nonetheless, Lenin was staking everything to win, and starting in December 1917, everything holding up the Bolshevik regime depended on a single desperate roll of the political dice.

That came on December 2, when representatives of the Bolshevik government arrived at the Polish fortress town of Brest-Litovsk, to meet with representatives from Germany, Austria, Bulgaria, and Turkey to arrive at a final peace treaty.

Back in the spring, Lenin had been savage in his denunciation of the Provisional Government for its "Petrograd formula" and its offer to reach a separate peace with Germany. Now he realized that unless he signed an armistice with the Central powers, his chances of holding on to power were nearly zero. Formal opposition to the Bolshevik regime was still nascent, but its roots ran deep in rural Russia and in the literally thousands of peasant communities from Ukraine to Siberia. The vote for the Constituent Assembly showed that if a determined leader such as Kerensky or Kornilov decided to rally patriotic feeling across the country, that feeling could turn against the German invader as well as Lenin's Bolshevik accomplices. Lenin had to bring about peace, at any price, before it was too late for the rest of his program to take root.

His offer to Germany to reach an agreement had gone out on November 21; for the Germans, this moment was exactly what they had been hoping for. Their master plan to send Lenin to Petrograd to take Russia out of the war was paying off even better than they had imagined. But they had their own reasons for seeking an end to the fighting on the Eastern Front. Industrial unrest was growing; starvation was looming. An immediate peace in the east would mean not only being able to shift German armies west, for a final knockout offensive before the Americans truly arrived, but also gaining access to the rich agricultural lands of the Ukraine, if Lenin was willing to deal. No wonder Berlin replied to the offer to meet in Brest-Litovsk by saying Germany would consider any terms Lenin felt comfortable enough to advance.[30] The reaction in London and Paris to the news of Brest-Litovsk was predictably incandescent. But before December 2, the British and French had other things to think about, as did Woodrow Wilson. This was Lenin's fault, and Trotsky's.

As they set to work turning Russia upside down, they had decided it was time to blow up Russia's international relations, in preparation for the world revolution both Lenin and Trotsky were counting on.

It took two steps to light the fuse. The first came on November 15, when Lenin and his henchman Stalin released their Declaration of the Rights of the Peoples of Russia, which granted Russians "free self-determination, including the right of separation and the formation of an independent state." It was a domestic as well as a diplomatic bombshell, imposed with no consultation with any government body. With astonished eagerness, one former province of the Russian Empire declared its independence. Finland started the flight for the exits, on December 6; Lithuania was next, on December 11. Latvia, Ukraine, Estonia, Transcaucasia (on April 22, 1918), and Poland (on November 3 of that year) followed suit. In a few months starting in December 1917, the future northeastern Europe took geographic shape, looking largely as it does today.

What in the world was Lenin thinking? Many in and outside Russia must have wondered, including members of the Council of People's Commissars, which was not consulted. Yet there was a method to Lenin's madness, or what seemed like madness at the time: allowing the Russian Empire to fall to pieces. His initial goal was to speed up the process of disintegration of the old Russian system and the status quo; if Faust's Mephistopheles was right and "everything that exists deserves to be destroyed" (Karl Marx's favorite quotation), then the destruction of the Russian Empire as the Bolsheviks inherited it had to be the top priority.

There was a larger, hidden agenda for Lenin, though. Since the earliest days of the revolution, he had seen separatist nationalism, such as that of the Irish Easter Rebellion, as a tool for promoting chaos and world revolution. His hope was not that setting free the non-Russian peoples of the empire would lead to a new regional order; he foresaw that it would lead to a new *disorder*, to riots, wars, uprisings, and massacres, which would smash the existing capitalist system beyond recognition. The weaker that system was, the stronger the Bolsheviks would become. Out of the resulting chaos would come opportunities for the new government in Petrograd that would extend and consolidate its power—at the expense of everyone else.

The Declaration also threw down the self-determination gauntlet to the other Allied powers. *You speak of self-determination of peoples*, Lenin and Stalin were saying to them and to Woodrow Wilson. *We are actually daring to do something about it.* In that sense, it was the perfect complement to the other gauntlet the new regime threw down, on November 22.

This move was pure Leon Trotsky. As commissar for foreign affairs, he had access to the recent archives of the czarist Foreign Ministry, including its relations with the other Entente powers. As he leafed through the documents in his spare time, Trotsky realized that they contained political dynamite.

There were copies of the secret Treaty of London, signed in 1915 in order to entice Italy to join the war against its former allies of the Central powers, with promises of land to be taken from Austria-Hungary and given to Italy, with whole non-Italian populations in the Tirol and Balkans to be transferred to rule by Rome. So much for self-determination.

There was a secret agreement among the Entente powers to give Constantinople to Russia along with the Dardanelles Strait. There was also the Sykes-Picot Agreement of 1916, by which Britain and France had agreed to break up the Turkish Empire in the eastern Mediterranean and Arabian Peninsula, without a single word of consultation with the peoples living there—another egregious violation of the principle of self-determination, all with the knowledge of both the czar and Kerensky's Provisional Government.

There were other secret agreements, diplomatic cables, and memorandums that no one except the authors had known about. Trotsky asked himself what to do with them. At last he decided he would publish them, make them available to the Russian public and publics around the world, including those of the signatories, so that everyone could see the shameless backdoor dealings that constituted the alliance that advertised itself as the forces of civilization.

"In publishing the secret diplomatic documents from the foreign policy archives of Tsarism and of the bourgeois coalition Governments of the first seven months of the revolution, we are carrying out the undertaking which we made when our party was in opposition," Trotsky wrote in his introduction to the published secret treaties.

"Secret diplomacy is a necessary tool for a propertied minority which is compelled to deceive the majority in order to subject it to its interests," he continued. "Imperialism, with its dark plans of conquest and its robber alliances and deals, developed the system of secret diplomacy to the highest level . . . The Russian people, and the peoples of Europe and the whole world, should learn the documentary truth about the plans forged in secret by the financiers and industrialists together with their parliamentary and diplomatic agents."

He added: "The abolition of secret diplomacy is the primary condition for an honest, popular, truly democratic foreign policy . . . The workers' and peasants' Government abolishes secret diplomacy and its intrigues, codes, and lies. We have nothing to hide. Our program expresses the ardent wishes of millions of workers, soldiers, and peasants. We want the rule of capital to be overthrown as soon as possible. In exposing to the entire world the work of the ruling classes, as expressed in the secret diplomatic documents, we address the workers with the call which forms the unchangeable foundation of our foreign policy: 'Proletarians of all countries, unite!'"[31]

The treaties were published in the pages of the Bolshevik newspaper *Izvestia* on November 23, 1917, in Russian. The publication of the treaties and coded diplomatic telegrams might not have caused a worldwide sensation if the *Manchester Guardian* hadn't gotten wind of what was happening and begun publishing the translations in English starting on December 12. Their exposure to the public set off shock waves across Europe (although French censors kept most of the details under tight wraps) and in the United States.[32] Suddenly, the Allies' high-minded statements about why they were fighting Germany in the "war for civilization," and their supposed desire to free subject peoples living under tyranny, seemed a hypocritical sham. The inter-Allied conference being held in London at the same time, the very first attended by the United States, was already unable to agree on a new joint statement of war aims.[33] Now the release of the secret treaties added to the confusion and the loss of overall direction.

Three days after the *Manchester Guardian*'s revelations, Germany and Russia signed an armistice. The entire course of the war was again up in the air. David Lloyd George and Georges Clemenceau were hopelessly divided as to what to do next. If anyone was going to find a new direction for joint Allied policy in the wake of these sensational revelations, and define America's role in determining that policy, it was going to have to be Woodrow Wilson.

WASHINGTON

IT WAS NOW up to President Wilson to answer the challenge that Lenin had given to the Allies and, one could say, to the future of the world.

Contrary to some historians' views, Wilson's instinct was *not* to confront Lenin head-on; to counter the Bolshevik message with an American one, there was no desire to create "a Lenin-Wilson dialectic" that would set the stage for the American-Soviet rivalry of the Cold War.[34] On the contrary, Wilson's feelings toward the Bolshevik leadership were still friendly and hopeful. The glowing vision he had expressed to Congressman Clark earlier that fall, that "Russia, like France in the past century, . . . will in my opinion take [its] proper

place in the world," remained undimmed. He saw Lenin and the Bolsheviks as essentially liberals who had temporarily lost their way and
embraced extremism, but who would eventually return to the democratic course charted by the revolution in March. On December 4,
he told a joint session of Congress that the Allies should have made
clear their opposition to all forms of tyranny and their support for
freedom: "I cannot help thinking that if they had been made plain at
the very outset the sympathy and enthusiasm of the Russian people
might have been once for all enlisted on the side of the allies, suspicion and distrust swept away, and a real and last union of purpose
effected."

He added that "had they believed these things at the very moment
of their revolution . . . the sad reverses which have recently marked
the progress of their affairs toward an ordered and stable government
of free men might have been avoided."[35]

It was not the last time a well-meaning American Progressive
would express the view that if only we made our good intentions
plain, the opposition of our foes would melt away. But coming from
Wilson, it was an extraordinarily obtuse statement. It was Wilson
whom Colonel House had urged to reach out to the Provisional Government back in August, when it might have made a difference, and
to talk about the possibility of peace, and Wilson had said no. For
his own high-minded reason Wilson had missed the moment, a moment when a western-style parliamentary democracy under Kerensky might have taken root in the Russian political soil. Now he and
the rest of the world would have to deal with a dedicated Marxist revolutionary regime, one committed to revolution abroad and political
terror at home.

Yet Wilson was not discouraged. Even the release of the secret
treaty documents, maliciously meant to damage the Allied cause, did
not deter him. He believed that a rapprochement with Lenin was still
possible. What truly worried him was not that the Bolsheviks would
spread worldwide revolution, but that they would allow Germany to
dominate Russia's future. "Lenine [sic] and Trotsky sounded like op-

era bouffe," he told a Cabinet meeting on November 27, "talking of armistice with Germany when a child would know Germany would control and Dominate and destroy any chance for the democracy they desire."[36] In short, Wilson refused to take the November revolution seriously. He remained convinced that the Bolshevik clique's ultimate objective was democracy as well as peace. But he did see an opportunity to use the release of the secret documents to formulate his own vision of where victory in this long war would take the world and, in the process, to convince Lenin and his cohort to rejoin the effort for victory.

On December 18, Wilson told House that he intended to "formulate the war aims of the United States." If the Allies meeting in London could not agree on what they were fighting for, then Wilson would do it for them. His closest aide was astonished at the speed with which the president reached his decision. House admitted, "I never knew a man who did things so casually. We did not discuss the matter more than ten or fifteen minutes when he decided he would take the action."

It was also a strange time for doing this. The war mobilization effort was at its nadir. The War Industries Board was in a state of helpless confusion; the railways crisis was at its height, prompting Wilson to nationalize the railroads the day after Christmas (see chapter 10). Congress was still looking for ways to displace the president from his war-making powers altogether, and to install "three distinguished citizens" to run the war instead (two of them, without doubt, would be his adversaries Theodore Roosevelt and Henry Cabot Lodge). Nonetheless, for the next two weeks, his mind was entirely focused on "remaking the map of the world, as we would have it"—or, rather, as Woodrow Wilson would have it. His ideas took the form of a speech to a joint session of Congress set for January 8.

To help in this mammoth mental undertaking, Wilson had a memorandum prepared by a trio of young Progressive intellectuals—Walter Lippmann, David Hunter Miller, and Sidney Edward Mezes—who were tasked back in September with examining the various possible final peace arrangements, based on the facts on the ground but also on the broader principles that Wilson had already articulated going back to his "Peace Without Victory" speech of nearly a year ago, on January 22, 1917. He had asked Colonel House to coordinate the effort, and offered to pay for the work of "the Inquiry," as the study group came to be known, out of his own presidential budget. House gave him the final memorandum on December 23, and Wilson immediately set to work.[37]

Certain unshakable principles were uppermost in his mind. One was freedom of the seas; democracy was a second; a third was "self-determination"—according to House's diary, the president became quite crestfallen when he learned that British prime minister Lloyd George had given a speech the previous year using the term, which Wilson feared had stolen his thunder. Yet now another principle for the list of principles, or points, Wilson was compiling would come shining through: open diplomacy. Interestingly, it was Colonel House who argued most strongly for including this point. "I told [Wilson] there was nothing he could do that would better please the American people and the democracies of the world, and that it was right and must be the diplomacy of the future."[38]

The inclusion of "open diplomacy" would also be a stinging rebuke to the Bolsheviks. They would not be the only government to abolish "secret diplomacy and its intrigues, codes, and lies" or that had "nothing to hide." Now the rest of the world, led by the United States, would follow the same path: "open covenants openly arrived at" was the way Wilson would ultimately frame it when he finished his speech—a comprehensive list of the principles the civilized world must adhere to in order to end this war and avoid all similar wars in the future, summarized in fourteen points.

The speech, delivered to Congress on January 8, 1918, is one of the classics of American foreign policy and the climax of the Wilsonian vision of the future. In Wilson's mind, it finally closed the book on a discredited international past and pointed the way to a new world in which war, injustice, and tyranny would wither away and die. It embodied a utopianism at least as soaring and far-reaching as Lenin's, one that reached out to the Bolsheviks as possible future partners in establishing peace, freedom, and democracy throughout the world.

Certainly, Russia was very much on Wilson's mind when he wrote the speech. In the waning days of 1917, his personal emissary to Russia, Edgar Sisson, had sent a telegram to Washington that read in part: "If the President will restate anti-imperialist war aims and democratic peace requirements of America, I can get it fed into Germany in great quantities . . . and can utilize Russian version potently in army and elsewhere"—in order, it was hoped, to derail continuing negotiations in Brest-Litovsk.[39]

That was exactly what Wilson proceeded to do. He began by referring to the peace negotiations in Brest, noting that the "Russian representatives" had "insisted, very justly, very wisely, and in the true spirit of modern democracy, that the conferences they have been holding with the Teutonic and Turkish statesmen should be held within open, not closed doors."

So, Lenin, Trotsky, and the Bolsheviks were still, in Wilson's mind, genuine but misguided democrats. In laying "our whole thought and purpose before the world, not in general terms only, but each time with sufficient definition to make it clear what sort of definitive terms of settlement must necessarily spring out of them," he hoped that they would come around to the Allied side, as would the rest of the peoples of the world, leaving only Germany and the Central powers out in the cold.

With that, he laid out the principles on which the future was to be built.

The first was "open covenants of peace, openly arrived at"—in other words, no more secret diplomacy or treaties. The second was "absolute freedom of navigation upon the seas," a rebuke to Britain's naval blockade as well as to Germany's submarine warfare.

The third was "the removal, so far as possible, of all economic barriers and the establishment of an equality of trade conditions among all the nations"—a commitment to the universal principle, if not to the empirical reality, of international free trade.

The fourth pushed for a reduction in world armaments, while the fifth stressed "a free, open-minded, and absolutely impartial adjustment of all colonial claims, based upon a strict observance of the principle that in determining all such questions of sovereignty the interests of the populations concerned must have equal weight with" the claims of the governments in question: a rather watered-down version of the right of self-determination—the term appears nowhere in the entire speech—especially since colonies in Africa and Asia were the last place Wilson or anyone else envisaged self-determination applying.

The sixth returned to Russia, calling for "the evacuation of all Russian territory," meaning a total German withdrawal, "and such a settlement of all questions affecting Russia" in ways that would get Russia "an unhampered and unembarrassed opportunity for the independent determination of her own political development." Here Wilson took the opportunity for a fresh digression in praise of Lenin and the Bolsheviks, calling them "the true spirit of democracy" and lauding their statement "of what is right, of what is humane, and honorable for them to accept . . . with frankness, a largeness of view, a generosity of spirit, and a universal human sympathy, which must challenge the admiration of every friend of mankind."

Indeed, Wilson's enthusiastic words led one New York columnist to conclude that the administration was about to extend diplomatic recognition to the Bolshevik regime.[40] Not quite: Wilson's worry that Lenin might still strike a unilateral peace settlement with Berlin that would leave Russia's erstwhile allies in the lurch and turn Russia into a permanent German satellite stayed his hand from that ultimate gesture. But if any country came out of his Fourteen Points speech with its reputation burnished and enhanced, it was Russia, specifically Lenin's Russia—even as it was on the verge of dashing every one of Wilson's hopes.

After that dramatic celebration of the Bolshevik Revolution,

Wilson's next seven points were rather anticlimactic. Each was a nod to the stated war aims and interests of his other allies; they absorbed little of his own attention. Belgium had to be restored to independence (point seven); all French territory had to be restored and Alsace-Lorraine given back to France (point eight); the borders of Italy needed to be adjusted along lines of ethnic nationality (point nine).

Point ten stated that the peoples of Austria-Hungary should be given "the freest opportunity of autonomous development," a sure sign that Wilson was endorsing the breakup of the Habsburg monarchy. Eleven touched on the fate of Romania, Serbia, Montenegro, and other Balkan states; point twelve ensured the continued sovereignty of Turkey but also the breakup of its Middle East empire; point thirteen endorsed the creation of an independent Poland.

But point fourteen saved the best, and biggest, for last. It was a rousing call for "a general association of nations" created by "specific covenants"—Wilson's use of the term *covenants*, borrowed from the Presbyterian Church, is striking—in order to guarantee the "political independence and territorial integrity of great and small nations alike." This was his beloved League of Nations, now inserted as one of the goals for which the war was being fought, and part of the foundation on which a lasting peace would be made. Nothing was said about preventing future wars or guaranteeing collective security; those tasks for the League of Nations would occur to Wilson later. For now, in the opening days of 1918, it was enough that the League represented as fundamental a part of a future world order as national self-determination (as noted above, a term that appears nowhere in the speech) or transparency in diplomacy.

Then Wilson summed up his vision. "An evident principle runs through the whole program I have outlined. It is the principle of justice to all peoples and nationalities, and their right to live on equal terms of liberty and safety with one another." He closed on an even more sublime note: "The people of the United States could act upon no other principle; and to the vindication of this principle they are ready to devote their lives, their honor, and everything they possess.

The moral climax of this the culminating and final war for human liberty has come."

In Wilson's mind, he had retaken the moral high ground that he had temporarily lost by allowing the United States to become involved in the war—a high ground that had nearly been captured by Lenin and the Bolsheviks. Certainly, the reaction to the speech was overwhelmingly positive, in both Allied and neutral quarters. British prime minister Lloyd George dubbed it "a magnificent pronouncement," and the *Times* of London called Wilson "the greatest American president since Abraham Lincoln."[41] In the avalanche of praise, those who may have felt the Fourteen Points reflected more starry-eyed idealism than grounded good sense, including Senate Republicans, chose to remain largely silent—as did the Germans.

The time when such a speech could have moved a majority in the Reichstag (for example, during the summer) was long past. Ludendorff and the generals were now firmly in charge, and racing toward their own deadline. This was a peace to be imposed on the Bolsheviks that would have nothing to do with the ideals in the Fourteen Points, and then the wholesale transfer of German armies from east to west, for a final, Götterdämmerung-like push.

By contrast, nowhere was the reception to Wilson's speech more favorable than in Russia and among members of the Bolshevik government. Lenin immediately took it as an endorsement for the Bolshevik regime, and ordered it translated into Russian and posted all over Petrograd. He also sent it off to Trotsky, now in Brest-Litovsk, as a token of their success in getting the imperialists to quarrel with one another.[42]

Still, Lenin was mistaken if he thought he had successfully pulled the revolutionary wool over Wilson's eyes. In early December, Wilson had a series of meetings with Secretary of State Lansing, a man who saw the world through a lens very different from that represented by the Fourteen Points. Lansing had convinced Wilson that recognition of the Bolshevik regime had to be out of the question: a government that had imposed itself by force, including the shooting of political opponents, as American observers in Petrograd and Moscow had reported, could not have normal diplomatic relations with an America dedicated "to the supremacy of the popular will operating through liberal institutions." Lansing had also encouraged Wilson to think about alternatives to the Bolsheviks; there were already armies taking shape in the interior of Russia ready to fight the Leninists for control, armies to which secret aid could be sent—and which could bring Russia back into the fight against Germany.[43]

In short, already at the end of 1917, an alternative American policy was taking shape, one of intervention against the Leninist regime. Its goal wasn't to crush Bolshevism; it was to prevent a German hegemony in eastern Europe. In the context of 1917 and how the war was going, it was sound thinking. The Fourteen Points may have expressed naive, pie-in-the-sky idealism, but they did not mean Wilson had taken complete leave of geopolitical reality. In regard to Russia, he would be coming back to that reality in less than six months—with fateful consequences both for Russia and for his own presidency.

LONDON AND JERUSALEM

THE FATE OF the war and, with it, of the world increasingly hinged on what happened in two capitals, one in Russia and the other in the United States. Yet before 1917 was out, one of the old powers managed to make one last contribution to the birth of the new world disorder— although largely as a result of Wilson's *inaction* on the issue.

The issue at stake was the fate of the Turkish Empire, the weakest and least populous of the Central powers, and the most polyglot and heterogeneous of all. Eighteen million Turks, Greeks, Jews, Arabs, Kurds, and Armenians practicing fifteen different religions lived jammed together—in some places, like Jerusalem and Damascus, living together in the same city—as subjects of an empire stretching from the most eastern tip of Europe to the border of Iran and the southernmost tip of the Arabian Peninsula on the Red Sea. This was the shrunken remnant of an Ottoman territory that just thirty years earlier had extended across much of the Balkans and North Africa, and an empire that most diplomats had long designated as "the sick man of Europe."

By 1914, that empire was barely on life support. Germany's alliance with Turkey that year had been an afterthought by Berlin, done on the fly in the opening months of the war as a way to discomfit the British in the eastern Mediterranean—and with the Gallipoli debacle, a useful diversion of British and French resources in the second year of war.

The Allies had taken Turkey much more seriously. A series of secret treaties had divided up Turkish territory among the Entente powers, in the likely event that the pressure of modern war collapsed Ottoman rule—the same treaties Leon Trotsky had exposed to the world.[44] Yet while the French waited for the spoils of their eventual victory in the Middle East, the British took a more active role. A British army moved into Mesopotamia, where the fighting went badly against them at first but then improved; a British agent named T. E. Lawrence co-opted the revolt against Ottoman rule begun by Arab Bedouin tribes and, in July 1917, captured the Turkish fortress at Aqaba, on the Red Sea—winning worldwide celebrity as Lawrence of Arabia.

Nonetheless, there was a feeling in Whitehall that something else had to be done to speed the collapse of the Turkish war effort, something that would coincide with the new emphasis on national self-determination—something, indeed, that would appeal to Woodrow Wilson's altruistic side but that would also forestall Lenin's abandonment of any Russian claims to Constantinople and the Black Sea straits, which would have made Britain's takeover of the Turkish Middle East look like unilateral imperialism.

What the Foreign Office found was the Zionist cause. Since 1914, Jewish Zionist nationalists had been urging both the United States and Britain to act as their protector.[45] Then the war brought a sudden change of allegiance. The Zionist movement, headquartered in Germany, declared itself neutral. Jewish communities in the United States and in the rest of Europe were delighted when German armies drove the czar's troops out of western Poland, promising an end to a regime of brutal pogroms. Even the negotiations at Brest-Litovsk seemed to promise a new era of liberation for Polish as well as Russian Jews under a German dispensation.

It was to head off this pro-German Jewish sentiment that, in August 1917, the British Foreign Office asked a group of Zionist intellectuals living in London and led by Chaim Weizmann to draft a declaration in support of a Jewish national home in Palestine, a strategically crucial part of the Turkish Empire.

There were other reasons to endorse Jewish nationalism besides undermining Turkish rule. The members of the British Cabinet thought they could read the influence of American Jews on their national politics, including Jewish support for Woodrow Wilson, who was sympathetic to the Zionist cause. Winning over American Jews, the Cabinet believed, would help bring Wilson along in the war effort—just as winning over Russian Jews would weaken their support for the Bolshevik government.

It was a complicated political calculation, which Wilson almost upset that August when he proved uninterested in supporting the push for a Jewish homeland. The British Cabinet pulled back; it was not until October that the issue came up again, with Foreign Secretary Balfour penning a brief declaration announcing Britain's support for a Jewish "national home" in Palestine. The Cabinet approved, and on November 2, 1917, the declaration was forwarded to Lord Rothschild, the presumed leader of Anglo Jewry, for his approval.[46]

Then, on December 9, events on the ground took a hand in forcing a British decision. A British army marched into Jerusalem, ending Muslim control of the city for the first time since the Crusades. This also signaled the demise of Turkish rule in the Middle East. What would take its place? The Balfour Declaration, which had been largely aspirational, was now positioned to become reality. Lloyd George, with his biblical upbringing, was stirred by the capture of Jerusalem by British general Edmund Allenby—the man who had earlier taken Vimy Ridge. "The capture of Jerusalem has made a most profound impression throughout the world," Lloyd George told a jubilant House of Commons on December 20. "Mesopotamia and Palestine, which have been the cradle and the shrine of civilization, will remain [so] for many ages to come."[47]

The fall of Jerusalem meant nothing to the Germans, but to the Turkish government it was nothing less than catastrophe. The ruler in Constantinople had been exposed as impotent to resist the forces of the modern world; the end of the Ottoman Empire and the rise of modern Turkey were already appearing on the horizon. At the same time, it opened a new chapter in the history of British rule in the Near East, one that would be marked not by triumph but by constant pain and tribulation.

As for the eastern Mediterranean, a way of life that had prevailed under Muslim rulers for more than a thousand years—with a brief interruption during the Crusades—was coming to an end. Now instead of living side by side in subjection to a distant imperial government, Arab and Jew would begin to seek their own destinies as peoples in the new age of national self-determination—destinies that more and more brought them into conflict.

Taken together, the Balfour Declaration and the collapse of Ottoman rule marked the beginning of an entirely new Middle East, the one we are still living with today. They are the last two events of 1917 that contributed directly to the new world disorder Lenin and Wilson were setting in motion.

1918: WAR AND PEACE AND WAR AGAIN

Our only choice now is civil war . . . Long live civil war!
—LEON TROTSKY, APRIL 1918

PETROGRAD, JANUARY–MARCH

THE SOVIET REGIME has acted in the way all revolutionary prole-
tariats should act; it has made a clean break with bourgeois justice, which is an instrument of the oppressive classes." This was
Lenin speaking to a workers' assembly in Petrograd in early January
1918. This was a self-confident Lenin who now bestrode the stage,
gesticulating and glancing fiercely from left to right as the workers
stared, hanging on his every word.

Lenin had good reason to feel confident. Barely two months after
seizing power, the Bolsheviks now controlled most of the north and
center of Russia as far as mid-Volga, in addition to cities farther south,
such as Baku, in the Caucasus—the heart of Russia's oil industry, still
one of the largest in the world—and Tashkent, in central Asia.[1]

The possibility that former prime minister Kerensky might rally
Russian resistance to the new regime had evaporated almost over-
night. The only people to take up arms against Lenin's government
were a tiny force of three thousand volunteers under the command of
Generals Kornilov and Alekseev, in Cossack territory along the Don.
(The Cossacks were freeholder farmers, and rightly feared that the
Bolsheviks would strip them of their landholdings.)

Nonetheless, large stretches of rural Russia were still outside

Lenin's control. Those areas were crucial to the Bolsheviks' promise of bread for Russia's hungry urban masses. Likewise, sections of Russian urban society, ranging from offices and factories to schools and universities, still eluded Lenin's increasingly totalitarian grasp. Bringing both those groups to heel, eliminating any possible alternative to Bolshevik rule: that would be Lenin's agenda now.

"Soldiers and workers must understand that no one will help them unless they help themselves," Lenin continued, his head and eyes darting from one side of the crowd to the other. "If the masses do not rise up spontaneously, none of this will lead to anything . . . For as long as we fail to treat speculators the way they deserve—a bullet in the head—we will not get anywhere at all!"[2] Trotsky had delivered a similar warning to the Central Executive Committee of the Soviets back on December 14, 1917: "In less than a month, terror is going to take extremely violent forms, just as it did during the French Revolution." A bullet in the head; a "revolutionary terror of the masses"—both Lenin and Trotsky would make those promises come horrifyingly true.

Years later, apologists for Lenin and Trotsky would insist that the terrible things that would happen to Communist Russia (the gulags, the Great Purge, the Great Famine) were really all the fault of Comrade Joseph Stalin. If Lenin or Trotsky had been able to stay in charge, goes the argument, things would have turned out differently.

In fact, it was Lenin and Trotsky who set up the totalitarian apparatus Stalin would use to impose his one-man rule—and they knew exactly what it would be used to do. They, not Stalin, were the architects of the Red Terror, and the "war communism" that followed. It was Lenin, not Stalin, who turned his utopian dream of a new Communist global order into a living nightmare.

One of his tools for accomplishing this goal was the Cheka, under Felix (Feliks) Dzerzhinsky. Lenin knew perfectly well that with the Cheka, he had spawned the Bolshevik version of the Okhrana, the czarist secret police. As he told his secretary, Vladimir Bonch-Bruevich, he needed to find "our own Fouquier-Tinville, to combat the counterrevolutionary rabble"—referring to Antoine-Quentin Fouquier-Tinville, the dreaded head of the French police during the Reign of Terror. He had no doubts about the man he chose to head it. "It's Feliks who spent the most time behind bars of the czarist prisons" of all the Bolsheviks, Lenin had said with a grim smile, "and who had the most contact with the Okhrana. He knows what he's doing!"

So he did—in his first speech as head of the "commission," Dzerzhinsky spelled out his agenda for the war against counterrevolution: "Do not imagine, comrades, that I am simply looking for a revolutionary form of justice. We have no concern about justice at this hour! We are at war, on the front where the enemy is advancing, and the fight is to the death."[3]

All this at a time when the Bolsheviks faced no meaningful opposition. Nonetheless, the combination of orchestrated street violence and vigilante justice by Red Guards, beginning in January 1918, in which individuals branded as "bourgeois" or "saboteurs" were summarily shot or beaten to death, and the deployment of Dzerzhinsky's "hard men without pity" to root out suspected counterrevolutionaries (meaning anyone who resisted or even doubted the Bolshevik program) defined the future contours of Soviet revolutionary terror.

Yet the single most important, immediate step for eliminating any alternative to Lenin's regime was breaking the Constituent Assembly. The Assembly was slated to meet at long last on January 18, 1918. The Bolshevik campaign against Russia's first truly representative institution went all the way back to the elections in November 1917 when, on the opening day of the Petrograd election, armed mobs smashed the editorial offices of the conservative Kadet newspaper, and the Constitutional Democratic Party found itself outlawed and its leading members described by Lenin as "leaders of the civil war against the Revolution."[4]

Then, on the day after Christmas 1917, Lenin had published a crucial article in *Pravda* entitled "Theses on the Constituent Assembly." It was, as historian Richard Pipes puts it, "a death sentence on the Assembly." Lenin made it clear that anyone who still supported the Constituent Assembly "signifies betrayal of the cause of the proletariat and a transition to the point of view of the bourgeoisie." In short, support of the Constituent Assembly was tantamount to treason.

Yet there were still those who had the courage to press ahead—even though, on the eve of its convocation, the Central Executive Committee officially adopted a resolution by Comrade Zinoviev that the slogan "All power to the Constituent Assembly" actually meant "Down with the Soviets." The day the meeting opened, two hundred deputies threaded their way through a dense row of hostile Red Guards, Bolshevik-led soldiers, and demonstrators to the Tauride Palace, where "the entire square of Tauride Palace was filled with artillery, machine guns, field kitchens . . . Machine gun cartridge belts were piled up pell-mell."⁵

Meanwhile, Lenin himself appeared at the head of a military column, as if the 463 deputies and their families posed a physical threat to the government. In fact, Lenin personally supervised what happened over the next nine hours. Despite their puny numbers and the massive propaganda campaign being waged against them, he knew the members of the Constituent Assembly represented the most serious political challenge yet to the legitimacy of his regime—especially since the Bolsheviks had endorsed it themselves just before their coup. He was "excited and pale as a corpse," his secretary remembered. "In this extreme white paleness of his face and neck, his head appeared even larger, his eyes were distended and aflame, burning with a steady fire."⁶

Deputies were frisked and searched before being allowed to enter the Tauride. It was not until the streets around the palace were cleared of any pro–Constituent Assembly demonstrators and the Bolsheviks were firmly in control that Lenin permitted the Assembly to begin. Four hundred sixty-three deputies, of whom 136 were Bolsheviks, officially opened proceedings in the first steps toward creating a constitution for the Russian republic.

Within minutes, the Bolsheviks gutted the entire program with a simple but brilliant act of subterfuge. A Bolshevik-sponsored resolution to renounce the Constituent Assembly's legislative powers was voted upon and defeated, with every Bolshevik deputy voting in favor. The Bolsheviks then staged a walkout, making it appear that Lenin's warning had been correct: the Assembly was a counterrevolutionary scheme to snatch power away from the soviets and their official representatives, the Central Executive Committee and Lenin.

With the Bolsheviks gone, the deputies at least could get some business done. They elected Viktor Chernov, the Socialist Revolutionary leader, as their president. Despite continuing Red intimidation and catcalls, with Lenin himself glowering down from the balcony, one deputy after another spoke about his hope of resurrecting the liberal-democratic process that had been derailed since November 1917 and warned that if the Bolsheviks destroyed the Constituent Assembly, the result would almost certainly be civil war.

The deputies voted for an egalitarian land reform plan, the dream of agrarian reformers for more than a century. Then, as the doors closed that evening, Viktor Chernov solemnly proclaimed the birth of the "Russian Democratic Federated Republic."

Those doors would never reopen. Instead, the next morning, armed Red Guards kept them locked as *Pravda* denounced Chernov and the other deputies in banner headlines: "THE HIRELINGS OF BANKERS, CAPITALISTS, AND LANDLORDS" and "SLAVES OF THE AMERICAN DOLLAR." That same morning, the Central Executive Committee issued its own resolution permanently dissolving the Constituent Assembly.[7]

The last hope for a government of the Russian people, by the Russian people, and for the Russian people was dead. It was killed as much by the indifference of Wilson and the Allies as by the machinations of Lenin and his supporters. Lenin, for one, was elated, and relieved. To have attended even one meeting of the Constituent Assembly, he wrote afterward, was like being in a nightmare. "It was terrible! To be transported from the world of living people into the company of corpses, to breathe the odor of the dead, to hear those mummies with their empty . . . phrases, to hear Chernov and Tsereteli, was simply intolerable." Even worse, "It was as though his-

tory had accidentally . . . turned its clock back, and January 1918 became May or June 1917!"[8]

It was not the past but the future that Lenin was looking toward,
and there, the company of corpses would soon be real enough. On the
twenty-first, he summoned the Third Congress of Soviets, this one
even tamer than the last—94 percent of the seats were reserved for
the Bolsheviks and their Left Socialist Revolutionary allies—which
duly proclaimed that the official government was now "the Federation of Soviet Republics," and Russia itself the "Russian Soviet Socialist Republic." Trotsky and Lenin both made it clear that the new
nation had been born on the bones of the Constituent Assembly.

"We have trodden underfoot the principles of Democracy for the
sake of the loftier principles of Social Revolution," Trotsky said. "We
are against oppression, but we will not yield our power without a
ruthless struggle."

Lenin was grimmer and more forthright. "Yes, we *are* oppres-
sors," he said. Just how true that was, the Russian people would soon
find out.[9]

Yet, even now, Lenin sensed that his position was still precarious. The cities were still starving; transportation and communications were largely broken down, except for what the government
could confiscate for itself. The next month, February, brought a fresh
emergency. On the eleventh, the Germans, fed up with the stalled
discussions at Brest-Litovsk, resumed their offensive. Lenin's regime
officially declared the nation in danger and announced that "all enemy agents, speculators, hooligans, counterrevolutionary agitators,
and German spies will be shot on sight"—the official beginning of
the Red Terror. That week also saw the creation of the Red Army to
defend the regime, with Trotsky named as its commander in chief.

Still, the key to securing the regime was a final peace with Germany. And here everything hinged on what was happening in Brest-
Litovsk.

It was not until March 3, after two and a half months of negotiation, that a final treaty was signed between Russia and the Cen-

tral powers. For any Russian patriot, its terms were catastrophic. At one stroke of a pen, the treaty stripped away the Romanov dynasty's western conquests for the last two hundred years. The Baltic states, Poland, Ukraine—all gone. A new map of eastern Europe had taken shape, one that bears a striking resemblance to the present map.

What had taken so long? At first, the talks at Brest-Litovsk had gone remarkably well. Both sides, for example, had agreed to uphold the original Petrograd formula for peace (self-determination, no annexations, no indemnities) that had underpinned the armistice. Then, on Christmas Day, they issued a joint communiqué announcing a further agreement on the withdrawal of all forces from contested regions in Russia. It really did seem to signal an end to hostilities in the east. Huge crowds began to assemble in the streets of Vienna in anticipation.[10]

Statesmen and diplomats in Paris, London, and Washington felt the same anticipation, but with a sense of dread rather than hope. Having Russia in the war had been a disappointment, even a burden, to its Allies, but it was better than having to face all Germany's armed might. Even Wilson's praise of the Bolsheviks' peace efforts in his Fourteen Points speech was based on his expectation that he could dissuade them from signing a separate peace by offering them a fair and just comprehensive one.

In January, however, things began to stall. The Russians assumed that by the Christmas agreement, Germany had agreed to pull out from all parts of the former Russian Empire, including the Baltics and Ukraine. The Germans had no such intention. In their mind, Lenin's December 15 declaration giving those regions the right of self-determination meant that these territories no longer belonged to Russia. Besides, the Germans worried that if the Bolsheviks realized the true extent of the territories they were surrendering (representing one-quarter of Russia's population and one-third of its agricultural base), they would disavow the entire process, and any agreement would be a dead letter.

This was particularly true for the Ukraine. Its rich grain-producing lands would be essential for the Bolsheviks to feed Russia's hungry masses, and its industries produced 75 percent of Russia's iron and 60 percent of its steel. That would be just as vital for any postwar recovery, collectivized or not. A government based in Kiev that was independent of Petrograd could well spell the end of Lenin's promised bread, and of the future of the Russian economy. At the same time, a Kiev-based government *dependent* on Germany and German arms for survival could easily supply the same needs for the German Reich.

Visionaries in Berlin and at the bargaining table could see the outline of a future German hegemony extending across eastern Europe and the Baltic, with tame governments headquartered in Kiev, Warsaw, Riga, and the other national capitals providing Germany with food, cheap labor, Baltic naval bases, and opportunities for German colonial settlement.[11]

A later generation in Germany would have a term for this vision: *Lebensraum*. And so, at the negotiating table at Brest-Litovsk a dream of German eastern domination, even an eastern empire, took shape, one that an Austrian-born corporal currently serving in the army would turn into a race-based vision of his own when he became chancellor just fifteen years later—and which he, Adolf Hitler, would generate a new world war to achieve.

For the time being, however, the Germans' plans were frustrated by the Russians' refusal to sign the final document. That refusal solidified at the end of January with the arrival of a new chief negotiator, Leon Trotsky.

Trotsky stalled day after day by launching philosophical discussions with the German negotiators. He hectored them with arguments about the origins of political power; what did "the will of the people" really mean? At one point, he said that the violence the Bolshevik regime was applying to its opponents was no different from the violence that capitalist governments used to oppress their working class in order to stay in power. It was the kind of specious moral equivalence that intellectuals would use when comparing the Soviet Union with its democratic foes for the next seven decades.[12] "The violence is supported by millions of workers and peasants and that is directed against a minority which seeks to keep the people in servitude, this violence is a holy and historically progressive violence."

The Kaiser himself wrote in the margin of the transcript of the discussion, "For us the opposite!"[13]

Yet Trotsky was doing more than conducting a seminar on Marxist dialectic. He was waiting for the workers' revolution to take hold in Germany and Austria; then there would be no need to sign a peace treaty. And indeed, a wave of strikes did hit Vienna and then Germany in January—but then they died away. Finally, on February 10, with Lenin's approval, Trotsky played his last card: the Russian government would cease fighting but would sign no treaty. "No war, no peace." The Germans lost all patience and declared the armistice over. German troops resumed their march eastward. Now there really was nothing between them and the capital except open space.

A frustrated Trotsky returned to Petrograd, where the government was preparing to evacuate to Moscow as the German army moved ever closer. Most of the Central Committee members wanted to stand and fight, but there was no Russian army anymore to fight. "They have voted with their feet by running away," Lenin said sardonically.[14] The government was in worse shape than Kerensky's when faced with the same situation. In sheer desperation, Trotsky turned to Russia's erstwhile allies, the Entente powers. What could they do to help Russia stand against the Germans?

That startling request put London and Paris in a very tough spot. Neither they nor Washington had recognized the Bolshevik government, and they weren't about to recognize it. They had plenty to be sore about. On February 3, the Central Executive Committee, at Lenin's urging, had repudiated the entirety of Russia's foreign debt, from both the war and before the war: almost nine billion dollars, of which nearly four billion had been formally guaranteed by the French and British governments. An apoplectic London denounced the move as unprecedented, an attack on "the very foundations of international law." Lenin shrugged it off as money owed by one capitalist government to others, a debt that had been "long since redeemed" by the blood of the Russian people.[15]

Nonetheless, the Allies were willing at least to consider helping out the Bolsheviks at the last minute. The problem was that they had no troops to send; they needed every soldier to meet the massive German offensive in the west that they knew was coming. When they offered to send Japanese troops, who were close by and could land at Vladivostok, Trotsky and Lenin recoiled as if the Allies had offered to sell them Liberty Bonds. The prospect of the Japanese occupying Vladivostok and maritime Siberia was, if anything, even worse than the thought of being overrun by the Germans.

There was no alternative, Lenin realized, but peace at any price. Bolshevik delegates returned to Brest-Litovsk and signed the formal treaty without even reading it. Lenin still had a fight on his hands, though—first, with his fellow Bolsheviks and, then, in the Third Congress of Soviets. On March 7, 1918, he forced the treaty through a deeply reluctant Congress of the Bolshevik Party. Russia had never lost a war before; even now, there were Bolsheviks who were not willing to start a precedent. (One of them, interestingly, was Trotsky, who abstained from the final vote.)

"The revolution is not a pleasure trip!" Lenin bellowed. "The path of revolution leads over thorns and briars. Wade up to the knees in filth, if need be, crawling on our bellies through dirt and dung to communism, then in this fight we will win." He had made this speech on February 23, when the Bolshevik Committee had to accede to new German demands at Brest-Litovsk. But the same arguments applied now, even as German planes were dropping bombs on Petrograd.[16]

On March 14, the government moved the capital to Moscow, where it remains today. From the Kremlin, Lenin used all the leverage at his disposal to jam the treaty through the Russian Congress of Soviets. He called on Russia "to size up in full, to the very bottom, the abyss of defeat, partition, enslavement, and humiliation into which we have been thrown"—in other words, by the czarist and then the Provisional Government. Once reconstruction was complete, he argued, Russia would "arise anew from enslavement to independence." In the meantime, ratification of the Treaty of Brest-Litovsk was the only option.

The Bolsheviks voted yes, not surprisingly, but the Left Socialist Revolutionaries voted strongly no, while Left Communists (another far-left splinter group) abstained and walked out. The battle lines of a future civil war were drawn over Brest-Litovsk. These were not simply Bolshevik Reds versus Czarist Whites, but Russian patriots versus those whom they saw as traitors to Mother Russia and cat's-paws of Prussian militarism, namely Lenin and his Bolsheviks.

Now the diplomatic ball passed into the Germans' court. On March 17, a delegation of German landowners from Latvia formally asked the Kaiser to become their archduke. The unveiling of a future German Empire in the east had begun. Five days later, the Reichstag reluctantly signed on to the Brest-Litovsk Treaty—reluctantly because the advocates of a larger, comprehensive peace saw prospects for such a peace vanishing with a bilateral treaty with Russia. Conservatives were pleased. Gustav Stresemann said scornfully, "I do not believe in Wilson's universal League of Nations; I believe that after the conclusion of peace [with Russia] it will burst like a soap bubble."[17] Just six months later, he would have reason to regret that statement. In the meantime, on March 22, the Reichstag approved the treaty, while the entire Social Democratic Party, once keen supporters of Germany's war effort, abstained.

Not that it mattered. On the day before, March 21, the greatest offensive of the war had begun.

PARIS AND NORTHEAST FRANCE, MARCH 21–JULY 15

ON THE TWENTY-FIRST, the predawn sky lit up over a fifty-mile front as six thousand German guns, the biggest artillery concentration of the entire war, poured out a bombardment of shrapnel, high explosives, and chemical weapons. The early morning mist turned green with phosgene, chlorine, and mustard gas.

A young German lieutenant remembered the moment when his men waited to attack. "The decisive battle, the last charge, was here," Ernst Jünger would write. "Here the fate of nations would be decided, what was at stake was the fate of the world. I sensed the weight of the hour, and I think everyone felt the individual in them dissolve, and fear depart."[18]

Then, at 9:40 precisely, seventy-six German divisions, many of them fresh from victory over Russia on the Eastern Front, erupted from their trenches and poured out toward the Allied lines between La Bassée, France, in the south of the front, and Diksmuide, Belgium, in the north, where the British Fifth Army had only twenty-eight divisions. Only an hour after the attack began, the Germans had opened a chasm almost twelve miles wide in the British lines; by noon, they had reached the Fifth Army's main battle line, where opposition was fierce but increasingly desperate. That afternoon, resistance all but collapsed. In a single day, the war in the west had taken a dangerous new turn.[19]

This was a very different kind of offensive from its many predecessors. The tens of thousands of German soldiers going over the top had all been trained in the quick-infiltration tactics pioneered the year before by young officers such as Erwin Rommel and regularized, in a pamphlet published on New Year's Day 1918 with the title *The Attack in Position Warfare*, by a captain on Ludendorff's staff named Hermann Geyer. Backed by artillery-fire control perfected on the Eastern Front and interdiction from the air by hundreds of planes at a time— another first for the German army—the German infantrymen practiced a new kind of tactic, one of fast infiltration followed by teams of more heavily equipped troops bringing up light artillery to hold and extend each break in the enemy lines. The infantrymen also had a new name, *Stosstruppen*, or "Stormtroopers," the fighting men of the future.

Behind them was also a massive mobilization effort, which Ludendorff had code-named "the Amerika program." The idea was to turn out as many airplanes, machine guns, tanks, and artillery pieces and shells as possible, and to move men and equipment from the Eastern Front to the Western—all in order to hit the Allies before the American industrial production behemoth could counterbalance German strength in equipment and numbers. In the end, Ludendorff was wrong. America's industrial mobilization was running too slowly to affect the outcome of the war. When U.S. Army captain Eddie Rickenbacker made his first solo flight over German lines that March, he would be flying a French, not an American, plane. Still, the presence of the United States in the strategic balance was already affecting how not just the Allies thought about how to fight a major land war but the enemy as well.[20]

Over the next four days, Germany's Stormtroopers opened a hole forty miles wide and forty miles deep. The swift advance was pushing the British to the brink of collapse, and with them, the entire Allied cause. An emergency meeting was held at Doullens, near Amiens— once the anchor of the Allied rear but now only twenty miles from the German spearhead. It was attended by France's president and prime minister and leading British and French generals. When the conversation paused, the participants could hear the German guns in the distance.[21] To some at the table, the rumble must have sounded like the crack of doom. It was the worst crisis France and Britain had faced since the initial German attack in 1914.

This time, however, the Allies had the Americans with them. There were not the droves of men, ammunition, and equipment they had counted on when Woodrow Wilson sent the United States into war almost a year earlier, but there were a quarter million fresh American troops, with more on the way. By the end of April, there would be nearly half a million[22]—not enough to turn the war around, perhaps, but enough to help Foch, Pétain, and Haig stem the German tide and, when the opportunity came, begin to reverse it.

In fact, the German tide was already ebbing. For Ludendorff's men, the same old problem had reasserted itself. An army on the attack, no matter how successful, depended on a single axis of advance. An army on the defensive could quickly move troops from a variety of points to stem any breakthrough. Now this happened again. By April 10, the Germans had forced the British to evacuate Messines, the scene of Britain's great success in June 1917. On April 11, they took Armentières. British general Douglas Haig gave a special order to his beleaguered men: "There is no other course open to us but to fight it out. Every position must be held to the last man: there must be no retirement. With our backs to the wall and believing in the justice of our cause each one of us must fight on to the end."[23]

Yet two days later, a relieved Ferdinand Foch told Haig that the German offensive had spent itself. Foch was right. Exhaustion had set in among the German ranks; discipline was breaking down as starving soldiers scrambled for food and other supplies. As April ended, the entire offensive had stalled.

Then Ludendorff regrouped, recovered, and, on May 27, launched the last massive offensive of the war. That day, fourteen German divisions broke through on the Aisne River, where the Nivelle Offensive had failed a year earlier, and advanced ten miles in one day, the biggest single move since the frantic days of August 1914. By June, Paris was being threatened. A massive German gun nicknamed Big Bertha rained shells on the helpless populace from a distance of twenty-three miles. If Paris fell, Allied commanders knew, the war would be all but over.

But once again, Ludendorff's offensive ran out of steam. The French commander in chief, Ferdinand Foch, was able to commit his reserves, including the Americans. Pershing had hoped that he would be able to operate American forces independently, as the British army had done. But the crisis left him and Wilson no choice but to submit the American Expeditionary Force to Foch's command. Very soon, far from cracking the front wide open, the Germans found they had put themselves into a cul-de-sac. Once the front stabilized, it would simply be a matter of the Allies closing the bag around an exhausted and disorganized German army.

So, Ludendorff and the German High Command braced themselves for one final big push with no fewer than fifty-two divisions.

It was to take place to the north and west of Reims, the burial place
of French kings since Clovis. They sprang the attack on July 15. This
time, the Allied command knew it was coming, and had American
divisions in the line to blunt the spearhead. German gains were minimal. When French and British forces moved forward to try to snap off
the salient, the Germans sullenly pulled back across the Marne. Paris
was safe, and now, for the very first time, the Allies under Ferdinand
Foch could put together a joint strategy to break the German army
once and for all.

Before they could, though, all attention had swiveled eastward, to
a remote corner of Siberia where the future of the Bolshevik Revolution, and the future of Central Europe, was suddenly in doubt.

VLADIVOSTOK AND WASHINGTON, APRIL–JULY

IT WAS ALEXANDER Kerensky's final blow to the Bolshevik
regime—an unexpected blow but one that brought Lenin's regime
to the very brink of collapse. In August 1917, in order to shore up Russia's sagging front, Kerensky had allowed Czech nationalist activist
Tomáš Masaryk to raise a volunteer army drawing on prisoners of
war from the ethnic minorities of Austria-Hungary who wanted freedom from the Habsburg monarchy. The result was the Czech Legion,
a 47,000-strong force made up of Czechs and Slovaks. In September
they were rushed to fight the Germans at the front, where they served
with matchless courage and determination.

Then came the Brest-Litovsk Treaty. The Bolshevik regime had
no more use for the Czech Legion and took steps to repatriate them.
This made the Czech legionnaires uneasy. The Bolshevik threat to
take away their weapons, leaving them defenseless in a foreign land,
was bad enough. But now they were to be grouped together with all
the other Austrian POWs (many of whom saw the Czech Legion as
traitors) for shipment back to Austria-Hungary.

On May 14, 1918, thousands of released prisoners gathered at the
remote Siberian railway station at Chelyabinsk, including soldiers

of the Czech Legion. Feelings ran high. When an angry Hungarian POW hurled a chunk of metal at one of the Czechs standing on the Chelyabinsk rail platform, badly wounding him, the Czechs lashed out. In the midst of the pandemonium, the Hungarian assailant was killed by the legionnaires. Ironically, the dead soldier was of Czech descent.[24]

When news of the incident at Chelyabinsk reached Moscow, the reaction was extreme. Lenin, Trotsky, and the Soviet commissar for nationality affairs, Joseph Stalin, immediately decided that the Czech Legion now represented a mortal threat to the revolution and ordered the unit disarmed and destroyed.

But members of the Czech Legion quickly turned the tables on their former captors. Within a matter of weeks, their ranks had swollen to more than sixty thousand as they seized control of the entire Trans-Siberian Railway from Samara to Irkutsk, including its major cities, while the Bolsheviks watched, helpless to stop them.

It was at this point that the Allies, including a very reluctant Woodrow Wilson, decided they would have to intervene militarily in Russia.

Various legends surround this extraordinary episode, which ended with more than 180,000 American, British, French, and Japanese troops remaining in Russia for more than a year. The first was the story propagated by Lenin himself, days after the Czech Legion took charge of the Trans-Siberian Railway: that the Czech soldiers had been bought by French and British imperialists for fifteen million rubles to fight against the Soviet regime. It was true that foreign money was given to the Czech Legion, including eighty thousand pounds from the British government and (what Lenin did not know) more than a million rubles from the French War Ministry, before the Bolsheviks seized power. Yet the money had been funneled to the Legion to fight the Habsburgs, not Lenin, and it was done at the behest of Masaryk—the same Masaryk who had raised the Czech Legion to fight for Russia in the first place, and who would carry out a vital mission for President Wilson the following year. Overall, the Czech

Legion got far more support from the Bolshevik government than it ever did from the Entente powers. As historian John Bradley states, "It is clear that the Allies had little control over the money paid to the Czechs; in fact they had little control over the Czechs or their movements," then or later.

In fact, Trotsky himself had tried to recruit the Czechs to form the core of a reborn Russian army, but the legionnaires had refused. Prior to May 14, they were determined that if they were to do any more fighting, it would be to liberate their homeland from the Austrians.[25]

The second legend is that the Allies decided to intervene themselves in order to crush the Bolshevik menace. In fact, the real objective was to help the Bolsheviks fight the Germans, and somehow to keep Russia in the war. In February 1918, there were even noises from various Allied agents in Russia that if the Allies recognized Lenin's regime, he would join the war effort. All over Russia, French engineers and demolition experts were helping the retreating Russians to blow up railway lines to slow the German advance.

Then March brought the collision of two traumatic events: the ratification of the Brest-Litovsk Treaty and the Ludendorff Offensive. As April dawned, it seemed that Germany was about to win decisively on two fronts at once. The Allies were desperate. Bolshevik control in Siberia was limited, and progressing slowly. If Allied troops could somehow make a stand, perhaps patriotic Russians would rally and prevent the country's complete capitulation to the German juggernaut. Thus far, the Czech Legion was not even on their agenda.[26]

On April 5, the first Allied soldiers—Japanese soldiers, as it happened—disembarked on Russian soil at Vladivostok, while a detachment of British sailors landed from the cruiser HMS *Suffolk* to guard the British embassy. The operation was the brainchild of the two officers on the scene, Adm. Kato Kanji and the *Suffolk*'s skipper, Capt. Christopher R. Payne. Their goal was to protect their respective nations' citizens in the Russian port city: a Japanese civilian had been murdered days before. Yet their presence also reflected the forward direction of Allied policy—that is, until the governments in London and Tokyo ordered the two men to reembark and leave Russian soil.

The reason was President Woodrow Wilson. He considered military intervention in Russia as distasteful as the British and French considered it necessary. To Wilson, it smacked of the kind of imperialism that his Fourteen Points had relegated to the historical garbage heap. In fact, when the Japanese had tried the same thing back in December 1917, again ostensibly to protect Japanese citizens in Vladivostok, Secretary Lansing read them the riot act, and an American warship appeared in Vladivostok Harbor to warn the Japanese off, much to the relief of the Russian inhabitants.

Four months later, in April 1918, Wilson's anger was palpable when he learned what Tokyo and London were up to. On March 14, he had told the Bolsheviks that no Japanese intervention would happen as long as he was president. In April, his displeasure nipped the joint British-Japanese action in the bud. In less than a month, the Japanese were gone from the streets of Vladivostok, and the Japanese foreign minister who had sanctioned the move was fired. "The US government holds the key to the situation," Wilson bluntly told the British diplomat Sir William Wiseman. "The Japanese government will not intervene" again unless Washington (meaning Wilson) gave the go-ahead.[27]

An urgent problem remained, however: how to persuade or cajole Lenin and Trotsky into reversing themselves on war with Germany. Trotsky and Lenin were by no means unequivocal on that point; Trotsky himself had indicated that the government would rather go down fighting than have Japanese occupying Russian territory. Wilson took that as an opening. For several weeks, he and Trotsky engaged in a peculiar Kabuki dance in which both worked to keep Japan out of Russia—Trotsky because he feared and loathed Japan's imperial ambitions, Wilson because he hoped keeping the Japanese out would encourage Moscow to bring in the other Allies instead. A note from Trotsky at the end of April indicating that Moscow would indeed wel-

come Allied intervention put Wilson in a jubilant mood. He declared
that the invitation had "changed everything."

The truth was that it had changed nothing. On May 4, Trotsky
made it clear he never intended to invite the Allies for a major operation. He said Moscow was prepared to accept Allied troops landing
at Murmansk, Archangel, and remote corners of the Far East if the
Allies pledged that those troops would never be used to topple the
Bolshevik regime.[28]

The "invitation" clearly had been a bluff, to forestall any Japanese
landing. But the clarification did help Wilson make up his mind. He
was still opposed to any landing in Siberia, but if Allied troops in
Murmansk and Archangel could prevent valuable war matériel from
falling into German hands, he was prepared to endorse taking action. Wilson's last reservation against Allied intervention had been
removed. Now it was just a question of when London and Paris were
prepared to redeem the offer.

Meanwhile, Lenin approached the Americans with a bizarre offer
of his own. He had had a conversation with the Red Cross's representative in Moscow, Col. Raymond Robins, who had been a keen
advocate of a U.S.-Bolshevik rapprochement for months. Now Lenin
told him that Germany's own domestic problems meant that after
the war it could never be Russia's primary industrial partner, as it had
been before the war.

"Only America can become that country," Lenin declared to an
astonished Robins. Russia would need new railway equipment, mining and farm machinery, and a host of infrastructure projects, including electricity generation. In exchange, the United States could be
looking at three billion in annual exports from Russia, including oil,
manganese, platinum, and access to Russia's huge fur industry. His
mouth watering, Robins shot back to Washington that Russia's reconstruction would be the "largest economic and cultural enterprise
remaining [in] the world," and warned that if the Americans did not
get in there first, the Germans would.[29]

For a few tantalizing days in May, then, the world rocked on its hinges at the prospect of a future U.S.-Russian consortium dominating the postwar world. Yet Wilson said no. He stated that Robins was someone "in whom I have no confidence whatever," and refused to meet him, then or later. So, Wilson once again missed a historic opportunity to change the future direction of Russia: the first time was when he abandoned Kerensky and the Provisional Government to their fate, and the second was now, when he bypassed the chance to turn American industry and ingenuity loose on the development of Russia's vast resources.

How sincere Lenin's offer to Wilson was is anyone's guess. On the other hand, with German troops in Kiev and German and Finnish armies only a few miles from Petrograd, the Bolsheviks' situation was just desperate enough that it might have been worth a try.

Wilson, however, did not bite—and days later, he would make a third fateful choice regarding Russia, when Professor Masaryk arrived in Washington on May 9. Masaryk had been in contact with the rebels of the Czech Legion, who still held a commanding position in central Siberia. He told Wilson he was willing to convince the legion's leaders to abandon their march to Vladivostok and ports home, and to remain astride the Trans-Siberian Railway in order to support Allied efforts to secure Murmansk and Archangel. He stressed that the goal was to keep Russians fighting Germans, not fighting the Bolsheviks. Indeed, he urged the president to recognize Lenin's regime.

But in exchange for resurrecting the Eastern Front, Masaryk wanted a favor: Wilson's endorsement of the nationalist aspirations of the peoples of the Habsburg Empire, including the Czechs and Slovaks. Wilson agreed. Secretary Lansing had been urging America to support the stranded Czech Legion, both against the Germans *and* as a standard-bearer for the Czech and Slovak cause. On June 26, Wilson replied, "I agree with you that we can no longer respect or regard the integrity of the artificial Austrian Empire." At one stroke, he had linked Allied intervention in Russia to the fate of the Czech Legion, and vice versa, and had pulled apart the four-hundred-year-old "artificial" Habsburg Empire.[30]

In this way, two former professors, one American and one Czech, managed to set in motion the machinery for intervention in Russia—and distantly to set the stage for the Cold War.

Britain and France endorsed Czech independence on June 30. They recognized Professor Masaryk and his National Council "as trustee of the future Czechoslovak government," and cited the "sentiments and high ideals expressed by President Wilson" as their inspiration—which had now unexpectedly committed him to the move he had been putting off for months. One week later, on July 6, Wilson announced that the Allied intervention in support of the Czech Legion would take place in Siberia and involve two contingents of seven thousand troops, to be supplied by the United States and Japan.

Official American recognition of Czechoslovakia did not come until September 3, but by then the die had already been cast. Together with Italy's recognition in April of the South Slav independence movement (the future founding fathers of the new nation of Yugoslavia), Wilson had ensured that a new constellation of nations would arise from the wreckage of the Habsburg Empire—ones that would become the cockpit of turmoil and instability over the next two decades.[31]

The United States (in the person of Wilson) was now in the habit of dictating unilaterally what happened in the world without asking anyone's consent, and then letting its Allies catch up. Wilson added another condition: that intervention would take place to allow the Czech Legion to pass unmolested to Vladivostok, nothing more. There would be no effort to intervene against the Germans, let alone topple Lenin's Bolsheviks as Germany's de facto puppet regime. The aim was entirely humanitarian; any effect on the strategic balance in the east was purely coincidental.[32]

No one was more furious at Wilson's decision than British prime minister Lloyd George. He realized at once that the intervention would be just enough to provoke the Bolsheviks into hostile action, but not enough to do them any significant damage. Lloyd George was more and more convinced that leaving Lenin in power would be a mistake. Under Lenin and his increasingly repressive regime, Russia was bound to be reduced to a German satellite. The future of the entire postwar order hovered in the balance.

"Unless by the end of war Russia is settled on liberal, progressive and democratic lines," he prophesied, "the peace of the world" would be forever in doubt. But, he added bitterly, "we can do nothing without the U.S."[33]

Here Lloyd George was admitting nothing more than reality. As another saddened British observer, Bruce Lockhart, later put it, Wilson's decision "was a paralytic half-measure, which in the circumstances amounted to a crime."[34] Yet the time had passed when other nations could check Woodrow Wilson if he decided to commit a crime or a major folly on the grounds that it adhered to his Fourteen Points.

Meanwhile, Lenin had raised the stakes again. On July 14, he ordered the murder of the deposed czar and his entire family in their dacha in Siberia, where they were living in quiet retirement. Lenin was taking no chances that a living Nicholas would be a rallying point for a growing anti-Bolshevik insurgency. He also made sure there were no physical remains to be treated as relics and ordered the bodies burned before they were buried in an abandoned gold mine outside Kipriaki, a village north of Ekaterinburg. Stories circulated later that the czar's four daughters were raped before being killed. These seem to have been untrue, but there was physical evidence that their bodies, and that of the czarina, were ghoulishly groped by their killers before they were immolated and then dumped in their mineshaft resting place.[35]

Lenin also began calling for a "merciless mass terror against kulaks [landowning peasants], priests, and White guards," with "concentration camps" for rounding up "unreliable elements"—the first glimmerings of the Soviet gulag. He was now also positioning the Bolshevik regime firmly in the German camp, against the intervening Allies. Worried about British and American intentions, Lenin's personal envoy asked the German ambassador for German troops to cordon off the Allies in Murmansk.[36]

In short, the die had been cast by both sides, and the Allies had no choice but to go where it landed.

WESTERN FRONT, AUGUST 8–NOVEMBER 11

IF IT WAS Lenin who had enabled Germany's triumph in the east, it was Wilson who secured its doom in the west.

On July 22, Ludendorff had ordered a pullback from the Marne Salient. From that day until the end of the war, Germany found itself permanently on the defensive. Two days later, Foch unveiled his master strategy for encircling the German line. The British would strike from the north, operating out of the Ypres Salient; the Americans, who now numbered over one million men, would move from the south from Verdun. The French would apply steady pressure along the center, which would tie down the bulk of German forces while the other two closed the circle.

The German army would be steadily squeezed to death.

The British attack got under way on the morning of August 8, 1918. The main thrust would be through Amiens and was led by the British Fourth Army under the command of Sir Henry Rawlinson. Only 20,000 men guarded the Germans' main defensive positions; they were outnumbered six to one. The British, backed by Australian and Canadian divisions, used 465 tanks in the attack, along with more than 2,000 artillery pieces and some 800 aircraft. The lesson of Cambrai had been learned at last. The British advanced six miles in what Ludendorff later said was "the blackest day of the German army," not because the army was routed or its spirit broken, but because after suffering some 175,000 casualties during the entire offensive since March, it was back virtually to where it had started.

Before the sun had set, the Allies had punctured German lines around the Somme with a fifteen-mile-long gap. Of the 27,000 German casualties, an unprecedented proportion (12,000) had surrendered to the enemy. Though the Allies at Amiens failed to continue their impressive success in the days following August 8, the damage had been done. "We have reached the limits of our capacity," Kaiser Wilhelm II told Ludendorff on that "black day." "The war must be ended."[37]

A badly shaken Ludendorff had to agree. Negotiation was the only way out of complete collapse now. The one remaining mission of the German army was holding on until the last possible minute, in order to gain the best possible advantage at the bargaining table. It was no longer going to be easy holding on, however. The Germans were about to be hit by a series of short, sharp shock attacks, one after another, that left what was the most professional and feared military force in the world reeling like a battered prizefighter trying desperately to stay on his feet.

On August 10, the French Third Army struck at the German lines; on August 17, it was the turn of France's Tenth Army. Fresh British attacks came on August 21 and 26. Then, on September 12, the American Expeditionary Force (AEF) launched its first independent operation. It had proved its worth in earlier operations—for instance, in June, when American marines fought a savage and costly battle at Belleau Wood. When the French local commander telephoned the colonel in charge of the Marine Corps brigade, Wendell C. Neville, to ask why his men were dropping back—the French general was misinformed—Neville gave an answer that passed into legend: "Retreat? Hell, we just got here."

No one doubted the bravery of American troops. Haig's view was that the average American soldier was "keen and eager to learn," although he thought his senior officers were "ignorant of their duties."[38] But that September, the Americans showed they had learned from the French and British, and could do them one better. Their September 12 operation at Saint-Mihiel pitted nine American divisions against seven German; the AEF made its objectives in less than twenty-four hours.

On September 26, the fighting got fiercer. In the Argonne For-

est, the Americans hit some of the Germans' most heavily fortified points, which had layer after layer of staked barbed wire and
concrete-reinforced entrenchments studded with machine-gun nests.
The Americans came on in the old style, and were repelled in the
old style—with horrific results. By October 4, the AEF had suffered
more than seventy-five thousand combat casualties, a grim harvest
highlighted by individual acts of bravery, but one that did not suggest
that the Americans would do any better than their allies unless they
abandoned the failed tactics of the past.[39]

Still, overall, Foch's offensive had done its job. Although the Allies
had failed to break the German line, Ludendorff was now convinced
that eventually they would break it. On September 29, he told the Kaiser it was time to insist on an immediate armistice. The general did
not see this as a gesture of surrender—far from it. An armistice would
give Germany time to regroup, to rearm, to shorten its line again. But
to convince the Allies that Germany was in earnest, there would have
to be some cosmetic changes at the top. The Kaiser agreed. Germany
would get a new chancellor, Prince Max of Baden, a man of liberal
reputation. The Social Democrats were invited to join the government. Restrictions on press freedom were lifted. Very suddenly, Germany began to look like a liberal-democratic nation, all in order to
court the favor of the Allies—and of Woodrow Wilson.

Prince Max was certainly the man to do it. Conscientious, upright,
a certified moderate in his politics, and a key figure in the German
Red Cross, he was reputed to be an opponent of Ludendorff and Hindenburg. He also took seriously his assignment to arrange an armistice. On October 4, the day after he became chancellor, he sent a
request for an immediate armistice—not to the Allied commander
in chief, Foch; not to Lloyd George or Clemenceau, the leaders of the
two remaining Entente powers that Germany had been fighting since
1914; but to President Woodrow Wilson.

The note asked for peace negotiations on the basis of the Fourteen
Points, to which the German government now gave its assent. When
the note reached Washington, the reaction in the Senate and House

was sheer rage. The Germans were playing the president and America for fools. Unconditional surrender was the only option for the Kaiser's government. Henry Cabot Lodge was particularly bitter. "I cannot but feel a painful anxiety as to what effect this note will have upon the Allies, upon our armies, upon the soldiers who are fighting and dying and conquering in order to crush 'The Thing' with which the President is opening a discussion." Privately, Lodge added, "The thing to do is to lick Germany and tell her what arrangements we are going to make."[40]

But Wilson was deaf to these appeals. Max von Baden's note did the job for which it was intended. In a single simple paragraph, Germany had raised itself to the same high moral ground as Wilson. The other Allies, after all, had still not accepted his Fourteen Points as the basis of a negotiated peace (nor had Congress or the American people, for that matter). But after nearly twenty months, the dream of "peace without victory" had never passed from Wilson's mind. He still regretted that America had had to become a belligerent in this conflict, even as an Associated Power. Now Max von Baden's note was giving him an exit door.

It was an opportunity to turn the war into a visionary crusade for peace and democracy, after all.

Still, he gave the new German chancellor a cautious reply. He wanted to be sure that the prince was serious about endorsing the Fourteen Points and not "speaking merely for the constituted authorities of the Empire who have so far conducted the war."[41] On October 12, Berlin sent a note assuring the president that both the German government and the German people endorsed the Fourteen Points. Wilson was now prepared to accept the Germans at their word, and to propose an immediate armistice.

The reaction from Britain and France can be guessed at. Yet this turn of events was in many ways their own fault. They had put the war aims in terms of national self-determination and making the world safe for democracy and had called the conflict a war to end all wars. If Wilson took them at their word, and the Germans acceded, they had nothing to complain about. So, the discussion now shifted to the terms of the armistice, rather than to its necessity or wisdom.

Then events overtook the mutual idealism. On October 12, the same day Berlin responded to Wilson, a German U-boat sank the liner RMS *Leinster* on its way between Ireland and England. Four hundred fifty innocent passengers died, many of them Americans. Wilson was outraged, as were others. "Brutes they are," British foreign minister Balfour said, referring to the Germans, "and brutes they remain."[42]

But Wilson was still not ready to give up on the Germans. He sent a stern note, requiring Berlin to abandon submarine warfare at once and stating that the military commanders on the ground would be responsible for arranging the terms of the armistice. He added that he wanted more evidence that Berlin's sudden conversion to liberal democracy was genuine.[43]

At that moment, Max von Baden and the other civilians now in the government realized that the jig was up. Ludendorff's bluff had been called. There was no choice now but to accept all of Wilson's conditions. Ludendorff and the generals objected, insisting that Germany could still win. A clear-eyed Max von Baden overruled them. It was one of the most perceptive decisions of the war, and one of the very few from the German side. Baden did what Bethmann-Hollweg had more than once wanted but failed to do: he asserted civilian authority over Germany's military—just too late to prevent the loss of five million German lives. Ironically, it was Wilson's schoolmasterly intransigence, backed by an American army that was now more than a million strong, that finally forced Germany's hand.

On October 20, Germany formally accepted Wilson's terms. Wilson was still unhappy about Germany's semi-defensive tone, however. After consulting with his Cabinet, he said that Germany must make one more sacrifice for principle: the Kaiser must resign. "[T]he Government of the United States cannot deal with any but veritable representatives of the German people."[44] Almost incredibly, that was exactly what happened next, although it took Field Marshal Hindenburg to convince Wilhelm II to lay down his crown—in a frank discussion as traumatic and painful as the one that had led Czar Nicholas II to lay down his.

By now, Germany had fallen into virtual chaos. When the Naval High Command ordered a final general sortie against the British fleet on October 30—what many sailors and officers suspected was a suicide mission—the fleet rose up in mutiny. By November, the uprising had moved to the naval base at Kiel. Almost by the hour, it spread through northern Germany and into the Rhineland. Strikes proliferated; workers formed councils with the now sinister name of workers' soviets. Rebellious soldiers set up machine-gun nests on street corners. On November 7, crowds in Munich proclaimed a republic. For anyone who had been in Petrograd a year or so before, the scene must have been depressingly (or excitingly) familiar.[45]

Germany was in full revolt. At headquarters, Hindenburg told Kaiser Wilhelm II that he could no longer guarantee his safety. Gen. Wilhelm Groener, who had replaced Ludendorff on October 26, finally told his monarch, "The army will march home in peace and order . . . but not under the command of Your Majesty, for it no longer stands behind Your Majesty." The Kaiser bowed to the inevitable, and abdicated. Shortly afterward, he was on his way to exile in Holland.[46]

Before that, the other Central powers had capitulated. Bulgaria had signed an armistice on September 29. Turkey signed its surrender on October 30, after British troops occupied Damascus. A British fleet sailed through the Dardanelles, taking control of the capital, Constantinople. There was still a sultan, and still a Turkish army, but for all intents and purposes, after five hundred years of existence, the Ottoman Empire had passed into history.

Austria-Hungary had also asked to negotiate peace with Wilson on the basis of the Fourteen Points. Wilson soon found there was no longer any government to negotiate with. The subject nations were pulling the empire apart, each declaring its independence, starting with the Czechs and Slovaks. The map of central and southern Europe was suddenly and catastrophically remade, as the Austrian army hastily signed an armistice on November 3, before it, too, vanished into history.

Little more than a week later, it was Germany's turn.

On November 8, the German delegation for the armistice arrived at the appointed place in the forest of Compiègne, led by the former Social Democratic renegade, now a member of the new German government, Matthias Erzberger. If anyone on the German side represented Wilsonism at its most high-minded, it was Erzberger; his book *The League of Nations: The Way to the World's Peace* had just been finished in August. He was also a critic of the Brest-Litovsk Treaty, which he did not feel went far enough to protect the rights of self-determination for Poland, Ukraine, and the Baltic states—not against Lenin's Bolsheviks but against his own countrymen. Erzberger was not the only German liberal to feel that the signing of the armistice marked not just the end of the fighting, but also a new era in European and world relations. As for the other participants, French and British, they were simply eager to conclude the world's bloodiest war.

There was only one major dissenter on the need for an armistice: Gen. John J. Pershing. He saw no reason to stop the forward advance against a retreating enemy. He had suffered terrible casualties in the Argonne, but he still had more than a million men, fresh and well equipped, to throw into the fight. Pershing was of one mind with Roosevelt and Henry Cabot Lodge: he wanted to force Germany to surrender unconditionally, by driving its forces all the way to Berlin, if necessary. Also, by next year, America would be carrying the brunt of the war, and could dictate the final terms of victory to Germany and the Entente powers alike.[47]

Such a proposition had no appeal to London or Paris, but the British and the French had their own reasons for wanting to stop the fighting. Of course they wanted Germany defeated, but their most important goals—for Britain, surrender of the German High Seas Fleet; for France, return of Alsace and Lorraine and neutralization of the Rhineland—could all be accomplished through an armistice, which could be signed now. What Germany would be willing to sign when Allied troops were on its soil, or even what government there would be to sign it if the war dragged on, was a question no British or French diplomat cared to contemplate. Right now, there was a democratic government in Berlin willing to renounce all its conquests east and west, and to relinquish huge stockpiles of arms, making a renewal of war all but impossible.

So the armistice ceremony went forward.

It was held in Marshal Ferdinand Foch's private railway car on a siding deep in the woods of Compiègne, which Foch figured would keep away nosy journalists and angry French demonstrators. Erzberger arrived with representatives from the German navy and army, and the Foreign Ministry. Britain was represented by three British naval officers, including First Sea Lord Rosslyn Wemyss—an indication of which armed service had the most at stake in the armistice agreement. France was represented by Marshal Foch and an aide, Gen. Maxime Weygand.

As it happened, there was no American representative at the signing, but not because of any disapproval on Pershing's or even Wilson's part. It was simply Wilson's way of separating America as an Associated Power from its Entente allies. In Wilson's mind, the signing represented the defeat not simply of Germany but of an entire way of organizing the world. Balance of power, armed alliances, secret treaties, "might makes right"—all these assumptions would now be thrown out. A new world order based on self-determination, peace, and democracy would take their place. When the Allies met later in Paris for the final peace treaty with Germany, Wilson told reporters, "I will say to them, if necessary, that we are gathered together, not as masters of anyone, but [as] representatives of a new world met together to determine the greatest peace of all time."[48]

All the same, there were hard angles even with this armistice. For one thing, it did not go into effect at the time of its signing on November 8. Fighting would cease only at the eleventh minute of the eleventh hour of November 11, almost three days hence. In the meantime, the Allied armies would continue to roll back the German army, in order to gain the best possible advantage. More men would die, thousands of men, in the final hours of the conflict—more than would die on both sides on D-day.

For another, Germany renounced the Treaty of Brest-Litovsk. This not only meant abandoning its gains in the east, but also reopened the issue of Russia's status as a belligerent, and as a formal ally of the other Entente powers. Indeed, as one war was ending, another was beginning.

On September 4, the first American troops had disembarked at Archangel under the command of Maj. Gen. Frederick C. Poole. They were mostly young recruits from the 339th Infantry, many of whom had been struck down by the Spanish influenza that was already sweeping across Europe and would very soon sweep around the world, adding its own weighty death toll to the one from the war. In October and November, thousands of other troops poured in from other nations. In addition to the 180,000 Allied troops—Americans, British, Japanese, French, Italians, Greeks, Serbs, and the indomitable Czech Legion—as 1918 ended, there were 300,000 anti-Bolshevik Russian troops now actively engaged in operations against Trotsky's Red Army. The aims of the intervening Allies remained confused. Some wanted troops there to make sure the Germans departed; others (such as Britain's minister of munitions, Winston Churchill) wanted to topple Lenin's regime as that of an international pariah; still others wanted simply to set up a quarantine zone to keep Bolshevism from spreading to a Europe deep in postwar turmoil—a *cordon sanitaire*, as the French put it.

In any case, as its leading historian has concluded, the intervention in Russia "damaged everybody and profited no one."[49] Above all, it provided an excuse for Lenin and his cohort to characterize their opponents in the growing civil war as puppets of the foreign bourgeoisie and to double down on their own oppressive control over Russia. Wilson's "paralytic half-measure," which started the whole thing, would indeed pass into history as a "crime," as Bruce Lockhart warned—one for which the Russian people paid the highest price.

But the new German government had no time to worry about these events thousands of miles away from Berlin. It was too busy staving off its own Bolshevik Revolution in the streets, and wondering how it was going to feed its population, even with the war ended. This was the other hard angle of the armistice—in fact, the hardest of all: the British naval blockade would remain in place until a final peace. Even though the guns were at last silent, starvation would continue to stalk the German people.

No condition of signing embittered Erzberger more than the blockade. Still, he signed the armistice. After he did, he handed Foch a declaration that ended, "A nation of seventy million suffers, but does not die." Foch read it, folded it up, and announced, "Très bien," and then left the railway carriage without shaking hands. Dawn was just coming up from behind the trees.[50]

Yet darkness, and bitterness, would linger. This would be the last legacy to spring out of the forest at Compiègne. General Pershing's instinct to press forward to make Germany surrender unconditionally had been disregarded, most significantly by his own president. Disarming Germany at the moment seemed enough. But Pershing had warned, "There can be no conclusion of this war until Germany is brought to her knees." In the end, he was more right than he knew.

In years to come, a still-standing Germany would revive and return triumphantly to the same woods in Compiègne in 1940 and the same railway carriage, this time to force France to sign an armistice. And the French general presiding over that defeat would be the same Maxime Weygand who had witnessed the original signing twenty-two years earlier, a man older and sadder but unfortunately not wiser.

It was three o'clock in the morning at the White House when Wilson got the news that the armistice had been signed. He and Edith Wilson stood mute, stunned, and "unable to grasp the significance of the words," she remembered. Three days earlier, Wilson had received another cable, this one from Colonel House in London: "We have won a great diplomatic victory in getting the Allies to accept the principles laid down in your January eighth speech," House wrote, referring to the Fourteen Points. Everyone now, it seemed, was ready to occupy the same moral playing field.

Woodrow Wilson was moved to biblical eloquence. "A supreme moment of history has come," he said solemnly to Edith. "The eyes of the people have been opened and they see. The hand of God is laid upon the nations."[31]

But the hand of Congress had also laid itself upon Woodrow Wilson. The same day House's note was sent, Wilson had suffered a sweeping defeat in the midterm election by the Republicans. He had sown bitterness among his political opponents the previous year and was about to reap the political whirlwind.

Also, it turned out, the eyes of the people had not been opened quite as wide as he thought.

14

1919: GRAND ILLUSIONS

WOODROW WILSON:
*. . . is Australia still prepared to defy the appeal of
the whole civilized world?*

PRIME MINISTER WILLIAM MORRIS HUGHES:
That's about the size of it, President Wilson.

LONDON AND WASHINGTON

ON THE MORNING of November 11, 1918, a young English clerk named Harold Nicolson was working in a basement room in the Foreign Office. Only a few months before, it had served as a shelter during German air raids. Now the bombers were gone.

Nicolson's job was to prepare documents for the upcoming Peace Conference, which the Allied combatants, at President Wilson's urging, had agreed would follow on Germany's signature of the impending armistice.

Nicolson had gone upstairs to the Map Room when he noticed a commotion in the street below, just opposite the prime minister's residence at Number 10. "A group of people stood in the roadway," Nicolson remembered later, "and there were some half a dozen policemen. It was 10:55 a.m."

At that moment, Lloyd George opened the front door and waved his arms outward at the people in the street. "At eleven o'clock this morning the war will be over," he joyfully announced to no one in particular.

People stepped forward to congratulate him and pat him on the back. But Lloyd George only waved them off and smiled, and retreated back inside. Soon, people were running from all directions toward the prime minister's house, and Downing Street was blocked by a surging crowd. "There was no cheering." Minutes later, Lloyd George appeared again at the garden gate, just to wave—there didn't seem to be words to describe the feelings that surged through him and through London and the rest of Britain. Later, when Nicolson left the office, he found that "the whole of London had gone mad," but it was that initial moment of Lloyd George's spontaneous joy that stuck with him fifteen years later.[1]

Britain had suffered much in the Great War. Not as much as France or Germany perhaps, but its 750,000 dead represented twice the deaths it would suffer in World War II—and more than six times the deaths the United States had suffered in little more than a year. Yet Nicolson knew that the United States would be the dominant voice in the Peace Conference to come. Although Nicolson was a well-educated and patriotic Briton, that was fine with him—and for millions of other Britons and Europeans in November 1918.

Nicolson had first learned about Wilson shortly after the former head of Princeton University became president of the United States, in the late autumn of 1913. In the last autumn before the world changed forever, Nicolson had been having lunch in Constantinople with the new American ambassador there, Henry Morgenthau. When Wilson's name came up, Morgenthau suddenly leaped up and went into his study. He came out with one of Wilson's books. "If you really wish to learn the lesson of Wilsonism," the ambassador said, "then read this book."

Nicolson was struck by the word *Wilsonism*. Here was a president who had become an "ism" before he had even finished a year in office. Nicolson noted that Morgenthau himself was a convert to Wilsonism—"there was a note of religious fervor" in the ambassador's words about his president—and after reading Wilson's book, Nicolson became a convert, too.

"In the main tenets of his political philosophy I believed with fervent credulity," Nicolson wrote later. Nicolson came to believe with Wilson that "the standard of political and international conduct should be as high, as sensitive, as the standard of personal conduct." Nicolson added:

> I shared with him a hatred of violence in any form, and a loath-ing of despotism in any form. I conceived, as he conceived, that this hatred was common to the great mass of humanity, and that in the new world this dumb force of popular sentiment could be rendered the controlling power in human destiny. "The new things in the world," proclaimed President Wilson on June 5, 1914, "are the things that are divorced from force. They are the moral compulsions of the human conscience."[2]

Even after four years of almost unimaginable violence, Nicol-son still believed in Wilson's powerful, high-minded message. As he set out two months later to take his place with the British staff at the Peace Conference in Paris, he took with him Wilson's Fourteen Points "the way a fervent Catholic might bring along his catechism."

He was not alone in this. For many on two continents after the war, Wilson seemed both prophet and savior. They revered him both for prompting America's entry into the war and for his vision, which they believed would rebuild the world. If the Fourteen Points were the catechism, then the Peace Conference meeting at the Quai d'Or-say in Paris was to be the service where they would be consecrated.

Or so many like Nicholson thought. The reality turned out, per-haps inevitably, to be very different.

There have been many books on the 1919 Paris Peace Conference, including an international best seller. But Nicolson's personal account, published in 1933, holds a particular fascination. It's what the Germans would call a *Bildungsroman*. It is a narrative of a young man steeped in Wilsonism who became intimately involved in the conference and who learned that his hero was not the man he thought he was. He also learned that the principles that Woodrow Wilson espoused were not quite as pure or as disinterested as their advocate—or, more accurately, the young man's prophet, as Nicolson had branded Wilson—liked to pretend. The Paris Peace Conference in fact turned out to be a chamber of grand illusions, and not only for the president of the United States.

That, however, was not where everything started—especially for Woodrow Wilson.

The armistice and the end of the fighting gave him a jubilant, almost frantic energy—a new sense of possibilities for a sixty-one-year-old who was far from the peak of his powers. The war had taken a heavy toll. His secretaries and staff all noticed that he had seemed increasingly tired as 1918 waned; his voice became weak and faded in and out, and he had trouble remembering names and dates. In front of a public audience, though, he could still rise to new, almost biblical heights, which might have reminded old friends of his Presbyterian minister father.

Wilson would need that revivalist fervor at the Paris Peace Conference. The strain of making war would be nothing compared with the strain of making peace. There, the victors would assemble to put together a final settlement in the wake of the armistice signed on November 8. They would devise the formula for the postwar organization on which Wilson had placed his hopes for the future: the League of Nations.

All in all, Wilson had set his postwar goals almost unimaginably high. "The whole world must be in on all measures designed to end wars for all time," he declared.[3] In a speech on the Fourth of July, he had proclaimed that the war's inevitable end had to signal "the destruction of every arbitrary power anywhere [or] its reduction to virtual impotence." He had also spoken in soaring tones of hearing "the voices that speak the utter longing of oppressed and helpless people all over the world," people who were waiting for the "great hosts of liberty [who were] going to set them free, to set their minds free, set their lives free, set their children free."[4]

Wilson had no doubt as to who was going to lead those hosts of liberty in the confab in Paris. Yet not everyone shared that confidence in the U.S. president, including many Americans.

In May 1918, he had happily told an audience, "Not a hundred years of peace could have knitted this nation together as a single year of war has knitted it together."[5] He was mistaken, and the proof came in the November midterm elections. Wilson chose to dub them the most important "our country has ever faced or is likely to face in our time." He told the American people, "If you have approved of my leadership and wish me to continue to be your unembarrassed spokesman in affairs at home and abroad," then the way to show it was to return Democratic majorities in both the House and the Senate.

It was a challenge as well as a heartfelt appeal. The American people replied with a resounding "No, thanks." In the first election in which senators could be elected by the popular vote under the Seventeenth Amendment, Republicans picked up six Senate seats, which gave them a two-vote majority. In the House, the GOP won twenty-five seats, which gave them control of the lower chamber as well. Whatever peace treaty Wilson managed to negotiate with the Allies, it would now have to pass muster with a Senate controlled by the opposition party. The bitterness with which Wilson had fought against Republicans, and particularly Henry Cabot Lodge, for one and a half presidential terms especially, would now come back to haunt him. Lodge would be the new Senate majority leader—and if ever in American politics an irresistible force (Wilson) was about to hit an immovable object (Lodge), this was that moment.

Wilson was unfazed. On the same day as the election, his adviser Edward House told him that the British and French had agreed to the Fourteen Points as the basis for the conference. It was a signal victory for Wilsonism, and for the president's hopes for the transformational nature of this peace summit (although it turned out to be a hollower victory than he realized then). On November 13, he reached another major decision: he would go to Paris himself.

This was unprecedented: no American president had ever left the

United States during his term of office. Criticism came thundering down from various quarters, including from Republicans: with Wilson on the other side of the Atlantic, who would be in charge of the government if there was a crisis? Wilson shook off the critics, as he always did—"a little band of wilful men representing no opinion but their own," as he once called them—but there were other, more prudent reasons for not going. By going to the Peace Conference in person, he shed his status as the outsider, the most powerful man in the world, who could step in and straighten things out if the negotiations wound up in a mess. Now if they became a mess, Wilson would have to bear the responsibility along with everyone else.

But Wilson ignored the advice to be cautious. In his increasingly messianic mood, he knew there would be no failure in Paris, not while he was there.

Then came a second decision. As Wilson put together his team of fellow delegates for the conference—the ubiquitous Edward House; Secretary of State Lansing; his military representative on the Supreme War Council, Gen. Tasker Bliss; and retired diplomat Henry White—he deliberately excluded any Republican leaders. It was bitter payback for the harsh attacks by Roosevelt and Lodge—"he is a good hater," as Wilson's friend and press secretary Ray Stannard Baker admitted later.[6] It was also a major blunder. By being excluded from any role or consultation, the Republicans were also freed of any joint responsibility for what happened in Paris. The treaty Wilson brought back to Washington would be his work and his alone.

He was quite prepared for that, even eager. But even he sensed he was leaving a hornet's nest behind him in the Senate. Before he left for Paris, he delivered his annual message to Congress. He quoted from Shakespeare's *Henry V* in describing how American troops had turned the tide against Germany: "Back, back, back for their enemies, always back, never again forward!" He spoke of "great days of completed achievement," and of his plan to "translate into action the great ideals for which America has striven."

He also added an almost plaintive note: "May I not hope, Gentlemen of the Congress, that in the delicate tasks I shall have to perform on the other side of the sea . . . I may have the encouragement and added strength of your united support?"[7] The response from the assembled congressmen and senators was chilly—"an ice bath," one observer called it. One of the senators there, Henry Ashurst of Arizona, said that "the applause was meager; his message was long, and surely he must have felt the chilliness of his reception." It got worse in the following days. Senate Republicans passed a resolution formally protesting President Wilson's decision to go abroad, and calling for Vice President Thomas Marshall to take power during Wilson's absence. It was a nonbinding resolution but a shot across the president's bow nonetheless.[8]

In Hoboken, New Jersey, at midnight on December 3, 1918, Wilson and his entourage boarded the USS *George Washington* (ironically, a former German liner impounded after America's declaration of war) for the voyage across the Atlantic. Not far away, in a New York City hospital, Theodore Roosevelt lay in the grip of a mortal illness. Among his last words was a public statement denouncing the Fourteen Points and urging Britain to take the lead in stripping Germany of its power. "Let us dictate peace by the hammering guns," he said in the waning days of the November midterm campaign, "not chat about peace to the accompaniment of the clicking of typewriters," a clearly dismissive reference to Wilson.[9] With Roosevelt's last blessing, a great battle was looming between two different ways of seeing the war, and the world. Henry Cabot Lodge and his fellow Republicans would be on one side. They would also have important support from many other countries attending the Paris conference.

Wilson would be on the other. By the time the conference was over, he would be almost alone.

Wilson's own mood began to darken as the USS *George Washington* left its moorings and headed out to sea. The task ahead was mammoth; the obstacles were many. He would be meeting his Allied counterparts for the first time. Delegates from twenty-seven countries, some of which had not even existed a year before, would be there, along with hundreds of experts and scholars ready to redraw the map of Europe and the world. Would his Fourteen Points really be enough of a political and moral compass for an undertaking such as this?

One of those on board with him was George Creel, the redoubtable head of the Committee of Public Information and Wilson's right-hand man in getting the American public geared up for war and for the magnificent peace to follow. "You know, and I know," Wilson confided to him, "that these ancient wrongs, these present unhappinesses, are not to be remedied in a day or with a wave of the hand. What I seem to see—with all my heart I hope I am wrong—is a tragedy of disappointment."

He also said to Creel, "I am wondering whether you have not unconsciously spun a net for me from which there is no escape."[10] He may have been referring to the expectations his propaganda expert had raised in the American public. But it could have been Wilson's admonition to himself.

Meanwhile, the USS *George Washington* sailed quietly on.

PETROGRAD

THERE WAS ONE major combatant, and one major leader, who would not be attending in Paris. The combatant was Russia and the leader was Lenin. Lenin's betrayal of the other Allies in signing a separate peace at Brest-Litovsk had not been forgotten; his brutal murder of the Romanov family had put him and the Bolsheviks beyond the civilized pale. No invitation to attend was forthcoming, and none was expected. As 1918 drew to an end, any intelligent and informed observer had to conclude that Lenin's Bolshevik Russia not only was an illegal regime but also would be a short-lived one.

On November 18, 1918, Adm. Alexander Kolchak, hero of the Russo-Japanese War, a dedicated anti-Bolshevik and the man whom Alexander Kerensky had tried unsuccessfully to convince to assume command of the Provisional Government's armed forces, declared himself supreme ruler of Russia from his capital in Omsk, in Western

Siberia—not too far from where Wilson and the Allies were building up their forces.

It was the worst possible news for Lenin, who controlled barely half of Russia's prewar population. Finland, Ukraine, Poland, the Baltic region, Transcaucasia, central Asia, and Siberia were all either independent states or under the control of the Whites.[11] In fact, as 1919 began, Lenin's regime was coming under military assault from three directions at once: from Kolchak's forces operating from Western Siberia; from forces led by Gen. Anton Denikin operating in Southern Russia; and from Gen. Nikolai Yudenich's army based in Estonia with two hundred thousand troops and six British tanks—while Vladivostok had been transformed into virtually an alternative Russian capital. An alliance between the Whites and the Allies was slow to form but difficult to avoid. The first troops to disembark in Archangel and Vladivostok had expected to be fighting Germans; then Germans and Bolsheviks, as the government in Moscow seemed poised to become Berlin's ally. Now, with Germany's surrender, there were only Bolsheviks to fight—and anti-Bolshevik insurgents to supply and support.

Since the summer, also, the new Red Army had been steadily wilting under the pressure. At first its commander in chief, Trotsky, had taken stiff measures to keep units from deserting, including shooting political commissars of units that cracked. When that did no good, he fell back on installing "barrier troops" behind the front lines, with orders to shoot anyone who fled the fighting.

The real problem through most of that fall of 1918, though, was that Lenin himself was almost entirely out of action, thanks to an assassination attempt that had left two bullets in his body and brought him within inches of death—and nearly shortened the history of communism by three-quarters of a century.

Not surprisingly, Lenin had been the object of assassination attempts before. He was the most revered but also the most hated figure in Russia, and the single most powerful man in the government, so a host of political factions, from czarists and renegade Old Believers at one end to Mensheviks and Socialist Revolutionaries at the other, wanted him dead. In July 1918, he had been driving to the Smolny Institute after a speech when two armed men stepped into the street and opened fire on his Rolls-Royce limousine. His German friend Fritz Platten threw himself across Lenin's body to protect him from being hit. Lenin escaped unwounded, but Platten took a bullet in the hand.[12]

The next time, Lenin was not so lucky. On August 30, he was planning to give two open-air speeches in Moscow. His sister Maria Illichna begged him not to go. There were rumors circulating that the head of the Petrograd Cheka had been assassinated. Lenin might be next. He shrugged off her worries and set forth without a bodyguard and with only his chauffeur, Stepan Gil. His first speech was to be at the Grain Commodity Exchange, in the Basmannyi District; he then went to the Mikhelson Factory, where an audience heard him give his usual speech denouncing bourgeois democracy.[13]

As he left the factory and stepped into the courtyard to board his car, an angry woman stopped him. She complained that bread coming in from the countryside was still being confiscated at railroad stations, following Bolshevik ration regulations. Lenin told her that orders had been issued to stop the practice, and he then put his foot on the Rolls-Royce's running board.

Suddenly, another woman, dressed in work clothes, sprang forward with a pistol and shot him three times.

One bullet went through his left shoulder blade and was wedged near the collarbone on his right side. The second bullet was far more damaging, striking him where the jaw meets the neck, near the left carotid artery. Another inch or two on either side, and the bullet would have left him completely paralyzed or severed the artery, leaving him to bleed to death in minutes.

As it was, the wounds were serious enough to make doctors worry about his survival. They discovered that one of the bullets had punctured a lung; when she heard this, Nadezhda, who had been summoned from a meeting at Moscow University, assumed he was going to die.[14] Even Lenin at one point asked, "Is the end near?" But he was tougher than the doctors thought. He insisted the wounds were not painful and urged them to leave the bullets in place. By the next day, it was clear he would pull through.

As for the assassin, she was soon caught, and faced a five-hour interrogation by the Cheka. It turned out her name was Fanya ("Fannie") Kaplan and she was an anarchist. Ironically, she had served a long sentence in Siberia before the war for trying to kill a czarist official. In her mind, Lenin represented the same kind of tyranny. "I shot Lenin because I believe him to be a traitor," she told her interrogators. "By living long he postpones the idea of socialism for decades to come." She expressed sympathy for the People's Army of Komuch, a thirty-strong force of anti-Bolshevik troops allied with the Czech Legion, and said she supported an alliance with Britain and France against the Germans. But she also swore that she'd acted alone, without accomplices, and she refused to say where she'd gotten the gun.[15]

On September 3, she was taken out to a courtyard adjoining the Kremlin and unceremoniously shot.

All at once, the failed assassination attempt made even Lenin's closest followers begin to see him in a new, almost messianic light: as the intrepid leader miraculously spared death to carry forward the revolution. "It was Fannie Kaplan's shots," writes historian Richard Pipes, "that opened the floodgates of Leninist hagiography . . . It was as if God Himself intended Lenin to live and his cause to triumph." The references to God were not accidental. Zinoviev began to describe Lenin as "apostle of world Communism" and "leader by the grace of God."[16] In fact, that September marked the start of a Lenin cult of personality that would spread with religious fervor and imagery for the next four years, and culminate in Lenin's immortal enshrinement in a tomb on Red Square.

As for the still-living Lenin, doctors advised him to take rest and quiet away from Moscow. They found a mansion near Gorky, where he spent September recuperating, reading, and writing. The literary fruit of his convalescence was *Proletarian Revolution and the Renegade Kautsky*, a tedious diatribe against an obscure German Marxist theorist that contains only one memorable phrase: "Dictatorship is the power relying upon force unbound by any laws."[17] That was precisely the kind of unbridled dictatorship of the proletariat Lenin intended to impose on the rest of Russia from that point on.

He returned to Moscow on October 27, and attended his first meeting of the Central Committee two days later. The long-term impact of the assassination attempt was to unleash a mass purge of enemies of the revolution, real and imagined, later to be known as the Red Terror. For the time being, however, Lenin's most urgent concern was dealing with the White insurgency before it could destroy him and the Soviet regime.

Like Wilson, Lenin knew he was no war leader. As with Wilson, his strength lay in inspiring speeches, a grand utopian vision, and a ruthless brushing aside of objections or of those who opposed him, a power struggle in which any scruple gave way to expediency. Therefore, the devising of a military strategy and organizing an army were tasks he was happy to leave to Trotsky. In the course of the war that followed, even in its darkest hours, when Moscow itself might fall, he never visited the troops at the front or sat with his generals to learn how they were going to prevent the regime from collapsing.

Instead, he remained focused on the political organization of the Bolshevik, now Soviet, regime. One of the steps was to split the Central Executive Committee into two subcommittees: the Organizational Bureau, or Orgburo; and the Political Bureau, known forever after as the Politburo. Set up in January 1919, the Politburo became the true wielder of power in the new Soviet state. All the other committees and organizations, including the Central Committee, now danced to the commands of the Politburo and its most powerful figure, who was unchallengeably Lenin.[18]

Yet Lenin's chief political strategy in those crucial winter months of 1918–19 was to wait—wait for the world revolution to catch up with events in Russia; wait for the inevitable workers' revolts to smash the Western imperialists and consign his enemies to the ash heap of history, as Marx himself would have put it.

He did not have to wait long. On New Year's Day 1919, two German Marxist organizers, Karl Liebknecht and Rosa Luxemburg, formed the first German Communist Party, and on January 5, they attempted to seize control of Berlin by force. For ten days, the German capital was convulsed by fighting in the streets, as German troops had to blast their way into the Reich Chancellery.[19]

Then, as suddenly as it started, the Communist revolt was stamped out, and Liebknecht and Luxemburg were brutally killed. A week later, Germans went to the polls to cast their vote for a new Constituent Assembly. Eighty-three percent of German adults, men and women, cast their votes—but not for revolution. They threw their support behind the Social Democratic Party, now the standard-bearer of German liberal democracy. Germany's right wing, heirs to Bismarck and Bethmann-Hollweg, netted barely 15 percent.[20] The new German republic's course was set toward constitutional democracy. Unlike in Russia, no German Lenin arose to grab the political controls and drag the nation down the Communist path, and no Trotsky to turn revolutionary rhetoric into military action.

Instead, communism in Marx's homeland died an ignoble and unceremonious death. There would be a brief flicker of the Leninist spirit in March, when extremists seized control of Munich and announced a Soviet Republic, and a bigger one in Hungary that month, when a former Hungarian POW of the Russians turned Communist organizer named Béla Kun grabbed precarious power in Budapest. Kun raised his own Red Army and set off to spread the revolution into neighboring Romania; he even hoped eventually to link up with Trotsky's Red Army. Kun's terror squads, nicknamed "Lenin's boys," roamed the streets of Budapest murdering anyone identified as a counterrevolutionary, while Kun ordered the arrest of five thousand Hungarian Jews as symbols of capitalism, confiscated their property, and threw them out of Hungary.

Then the Béla Kun nightmare soon came to an abrupt end. Romanian troops soundly crushed Kun's forces in July, and he fled the Hungarian capital on August 1.

His Soviet Republic had lasted exactly 133 days. German authorities had restored order in Munich long before, so even though Lenin had enough hope to call the first Communist International in Moscow that March, to oversee the coming world workers' revolution, after a few shots, Kun's revolution died with barely a whimper.[21]

If the Bolshevik regime was going to survive, then, it was going to have to rely on its own resources. By June 1919, those resources looked precariously slim. In the first two months of the year, White forces had driven the Red Army out of Latvia and Estonia. On March 13, Admiral Kolchak's forces retook Ufa and pushed steadily westward, until the Red Army, under its ablest commander, Gen. Mikhail Tukhachevsky, checked its advance and recaptured most of the lost territory.

More serious was the White drive up from the south, under General Denikin, whose soldiers expelled Red troops from the Crimea and Odessa region. By mid-June, the Whites were in control of Kharkov, Belgorod, and Tsaritsyn. On June 20, Denikin began preparing his troops for the final, decisive assault on Moscow.[22]

Lenin could feel the fate of his regime, and his own grand vision, teetering in the balance. He sent a desperate, furious note to the Revolutionary-Military Soviet, which was preparing an offensive against Kolchak's army from its base in, of all places, Lenin's hometown, Simbirsk. "If we don't conquer the Urals by winter," it read, "I consider the death of the Revolution inevitable."[23]

There were many that summer who would have agreed. As for Lenin's hopes for a new world order based on his revolutionary Mparxist vision, these had clearly faded if not disappeared. If any new world order was going to arise, it looked like it would have to do so in Paris.

PARIS

THE GREETING WILSON received the moment he stepped off the USS *George Washington* and onto French soil did much to restore his mood. At the anchorage at Brest, virtually the entire population of the city had turned out to shower flowers in the American president's path. On the train ride from Brest to Paris, through the Brittany country-side, the entire route was lined by men, women, and children raising their hats and caps in salute as the train passed.[24]

In Paris, the reception, as one longtime American resident put it, was "the most remarkable demonstration of enthusiasm and affection on the part of the Parisians that I have ever heard of, let alone seen"— far more than the rapturous welcome Pershing and the first elements of the AEF had received. To Frenchmen and millions of other Euro-peans, Wilson was more than their savior in the war. He was the mes-siah who would give them and the rest of the world a new peaceful order. The reception was the same in London when Wilson made a state visit a few days later; and in Italy during the first week in Janu-ary. Everything reinforced Wilson's view that this was his moment to lead the peoples of the world, like Moses, to a new Promised Land.

As he told the assembled guests at a magnificent dinner at Lon-don's Guildhall, the Allied soldiers had "fought to do away with an old order and to establish a new one" without "that unstable thing which we used to call the 'balance of power.'" He added that "the men who have fought in this war . . . were determined that this sort of thing should end now and forever." He told American soldiers when he addressed them shortly after arriving, "This being a people's war . . . it must be a people's peace."[25]

Yet what precisely did that mean? If there were no balance of power, what would take its place? That's what the hundreds of experts traveling with him on the *George Washington* had wanted to know. It came as a surprise to some of them to learn that, for their great leader, the contours of this new order, of the coming Promised Land, were still vague in his mind.

It was the young diplomat William Bullitt (who, as it happened, had just returned from Russia, where he had been a keen advocate of cooperation with Lenin and the Bolsheviks) who suggested to Wilson that "he ought to call together the members of the Inquiry and other important people on board and explain to [them] the spirit in which he was approaching the conference." Wilson seemed surprised; the idea of informing his own staff of his plans had never occurred to him. He had not brought his Cabinet into his plans to declare war; why should his entourage for the Peace Conference be any different? Still, he gave way. Midway across the Atlantic, he and his inner circle sat down for an hour on shipboard. One astonished member of the group stated later that it was the first time they had heard in any detail his ideas for arranging the peace of the world.[26]

What they heard was not particularly impressive.

For example, Wilson was not very clear what he meant by self-determination. Did it mean democratic self-government? Could any people who decided to declare themselves a nation-state be said to be exercising the right of self-determination? Did it refer to "a race, a territorial area, or a community?" Lansing wanted to know. Wilson was maddeningly vague. He apologized, saying that his ideas "weren't very good but he thought them better than anything else he had heard."

He added, "You tell me what's right and I'll fight for it." They had thought it was supposed to be the other way around, but said nothing.

One thing in Wilson's mind *was* clear: "[T]he men whom we were about to deal with did not represent their own people." That was an astonishing thing to say about Lloyd George and Clemenceau, both of whom owed their office to their nations' voters, or even about the representatives from countries such as Japan and China. But with a new, luminous future about to unfold, Wilson saw all his fellow leaders as men representing an obsolete past. His worry was how to argue his case with old-fashioned statesmen like these. "What means, Mr. Seymour," Wilson said, addressing Charles Seymour, chief of the Austro-Hungarian Division of the American Commission to Negotiate Peace, "can be utilized to bring pressure upon these people in the interests of justice?" No one in the stateroom seemed to have a clear answer, least of all Wilson.[27]

Wilson did have a moment of self-doubt. "If it doesn't work right," he said, "the world will raise hell." If that happened, he added with a sheepish smile, he intended to go off and hide, maybe in a remote spot such as Guam.[28] With reporters on board afterward, however, the president was more confident, even cocky. He told them he would tell the other Allies that "we are gathered together, not as the masters of anyone, but as representatives of a new world met together to determine the greatest peace of all time." Once they realized he was serious, he said, "I think we can come to an agreement promptly."[29]

All the same, the day they landed, Wilson sensed the stakes involved. "If we do not heed the mandates of mankind," he told the assembled throng of reporters, "we shall make ourselves the most conspicuous and deserved failures in the history of the world."[30] With that, he went off to do combat with his imagined adversaries, including his own Allied leaders.

The conference convened at 3:15 p.m. on January 18, 1919, in a plenary session hosted by French president Poincaré. After one speech after another, when the first day's meeting adjourned, French politician Jules Cambon turned to one of the British delegates, Ian Malcolm. "You know what's going to result from this conference?" Cambon said. "Une improvisation." Nicolson, who was listening, wrote angrily in his diary, "Cynical old man."[31]

Cambon turned out to be right. It may have been the most disorganized peace conference ever. Wilson had prepared no agenda, no order of priorities, no system of agreement. Proceedings were supposed to be conducted by the Council of Ten—two delegates from each Great Power: Britain, France, Italy, Japan, and the United States. Very quickly, however, the Council of Ten got shoved aside to make room for the Big Four: Lloyd George, Clemenceau, Italian prime minister Vittorio Emanuele Orlando, and Wilson. They had no time or inclination to focus on any specific agenda. Each of their meetings for the next four months—the Big Four also formed the Supreme War Council, which still had to make key decisions for the Allies at a time when the war was still officially on, armistice or no armistice— jumped from one topic to another, almost at random, as secretaries wrote furiously to keep track of major decisions that often affected the future of millions of people, even tens of millions, at home and in the far corners of the world.

The four men were distracted, were overworked, and found very little in common. They also weren't together as a foursome very often. Wilson had to return to the United States to preside over the reopening of Congress. Lloyd George returned often to London to oversee political crises there, traveling by boat and train, which usually took an entire day. Orlando was also sometimes obliged to go home. On February 19, an ultranationalist, Émile Cottin, shot Clemenceau, leaving him severely wounded. That took him out of action for several weeks, when some of the Supreme War Council's most important decisions were being made—including decisions on Russia.[32]

All the same there was more common ground among the four Allied leaders than Wilson perhaps cared to admit. There is no doubt that Wilson stood apart from the others in his idealistic approach to world politics and his rejection of "outdated" concepts such as the balance of power. Clemenceau, for one, wasn't buying it. "There is an old system of alliances called the Balance of Power," he told the Chamber of Deputies the day after Wilson gave a speech in London about the importance of the future League of Nations. "[T]his system of alliances, which I do not renounce, will be my guiding thought at the Peace Conference." The deputies stood and cheered. They and Clemenceau, like Lloyd George and his British constituents, had been through too much to put their faith in a handful of high sentiments and a world organization that didn't yet exist.[33]

Clemenceau found Wilson astonishingly ignorant of Europe and Europeans, and of how very different the world they inhabited was from his study at the White House or his lecture hall at Princeton. "He believed you could do everything by formulas and fourteen points. God Himself was content with ten commandments," the French statesman concluded sardonically. Clemenceau once remarked, "I find myself between Jesus Christ on the one hand, and Napoleon Bonaparte on the other."[34] "Bonaparte" was a reference to Lloyd George; everyone knew who Clemenceau was comparing to Jesus Christ.

In the end, "I don't think he is a bad man," Clemenceau would sometimes say of Wilson, "but I have not yet made up my mind as to how much of him is good."[35] It was a judgment with which an increasingly disillusioned Harold Macmillan and other acolytes of "Wilsonism" were coming to share, as their hopes for their hero to lead the Peace Conference to a bright, shining, new world order, began to unravel.

Later, the debacle that arose from the Paris Peace Conference and the Treaty of Versailles with Germany would be blamed on leaders other than Wilson. John Maynard Keynes, for example, in his highly influential *Economic Consequences of the Peace*, would paint a compelling picture of sophisticated and unscrupulous European leaders beguiling and manipulating a gullible and naive President Wilson. Wilson's American admirers, such as biographer Ray Stannard Baker, would extend that picture into a black-and-white photograph with an evil, corrupt Europe on one side and a high-minded but innocent Woodrow Wilson (and America) on the other.

In fact, both Clemenceau and Lloyd George were far more sympathetic to Wilson's position than the history books suggest. Clemenceau, for one, was certainly a believer in an old-fashioned balance of power—and was committed above all to breaking Germany's ability ever again to make war or threaten France. But he also sincerely believed that France's future was in cooperation with its Anglo-Saxon allies the United States and the United Kingdom. He told the Chamber of Deputies in December 1918, "For this Entente, I shall make every sacrifice."[36] He had lived in the United States, spoke fluent English, and had an American wife. He (far more than Wilson) was a deep admirer of Abraham Lincoln, in whose army he had almost served during the Civil War. But he was also prepared to face reality.

"Please do not misunderstand me," he once told Wilson. "We too came into the world with the noble instincts and the lofty aspirations which you express so often and so eloquently. We have become what we are because we have been shaped by the rough hand of the world in which we have to live and we have survived only because we are a tough bunch."[37] Being tough with the Germans made Clemenceau the great villain to those who criticized the Versailles Treaty. But he sacrificed much to get the agreement past his countrymen, who wanted far more. At least one of them had been prepared to kill him for it. If any single leader gave Wilson the treaty he wanted to take back with him to the United States, it was Clemenceau.

The same was pretty much true of Lloyd George. Right after the war, he spoke of squeezing the German orange "until the pips squeak," meaning insisting on financial reparations. He was also responsible for maintaining, even after the armistice, the punitive British naval blockade, which kept Germany perpetually on the brink of starvation (although the supposedly high-minded humanitarian liberal Wilson never objected to the blockade). Yet, once Britain's key requirement for peace, the internment of the German High Seas Fleet, was taken care of, Lloyd George was willing to take steps to salve the feelings of Germany, the same Germany that had sunk British merchant ships without mercy and terror-bombed London.

For example, when the creation of a new, independent Poland involved lavish losses of German territory, it was Lloyd George who insisted there be a plebiscite in Silesia before the territory was handed over to the Poles. (The Germans won the plebiscite, but Poland got Silesia anyway.) He also stood against handing over the port of Danzig, which was overwhelmingly German in population but whose major access to the Baltic Sea Poland said it needed. As a result, Danzig became a free city instead, independent of Poland but economically integrated into the Polish economy. It seemed like a good idea at the time, but by trying to do Germany justice after the First World War, Lloyd George, without knowing it, had helped to set the detonator for the Second.

As for Italian prime minister Orlando, his entire focus was on his own borders, and what Italy was owed by previous agreements. As far as Germany and the future of the world were concerned, he couldn't have cared less. He would have signed anything Wilson had crafted, as long as the terms of the London Treaty, which had drawn Italy into the war, were observed.

It was Wilson and Wilson alone who was the source of the problems that haunted the Peace Conference and, afterward, the Treaty of Versailles. His unabashed admirer, British Foreign Office employee Harold Nicolson, watched from a front-row seat as, week by week, month by month, his hero suffered political, even moral, collapse. There were many reasons for this, Nicolson later reasoned. There was Wilson's overweening spiritual arrogance, which Nicolson saw as part of the president's Presbyterian inheritance. There was Wilson's thin-skinned response to the slightest criticism or opposition, but above all, there was, as Wilson himself admitted, the American president's "one-track mind."

This intellectual disability "rendered him blindly impervious, not merely to human character but also to shades of difference. He possessed no gift for differentiation, no capacity for adjustment to circumstances. It was his spiritual and mental rigidity that proved his undoing."[38]

Like many high-minded people, Wilson, when faced with opposition that he considered evil but which refused to yield to his arguments, felt no compunction about simply crossing his arms and refusing to play the game.

Early on, for example, there was the issue of what to do about Germany's former colonies in Africa and the South Pacific. Australia wanted New Guinea; South Africa wanted former German South Western Africa (today Namibia); New Zealand was after former German Samoa. Wilson was shocked. He was opposed to any settlement that involved the annexation of Germany's former possessions, but he had no better idea of what should happen to these lands—especially those in Africa and Micronesia, where the assumption of the "white man's burden" still applied. Eventually, the Big Four arrived at the concept of the mandate: passing stewardship of non-European territories to the Great Powers for a limited period, one that would be ratified by the future League of Nations. Mandates were largely a fiction, of course. The distinction between "mandate" and "colony," especially in highly colonized Africa, was meaningless. But the idea provided a fig leaf for Wilson's insistence that the Paris conference not become the tool of European imperialism. France and Britain accepted Wilson's phony compromise.

Australia, South Africa, and New Zealand did not. They rejected the notion of getting a mandate for the territories they saw as necessary for protecting their national interests—in the case of South Western Africa, adjoining territory. Wilson was horrified. He assumed that evil old Great Powers might want colonies; but Australia, South Africa, and New Zealand were freshly minted republics, democracies by their lights and Wilson's—of course, blacks had no vote in South Africa, but in effect many of them had no vote in Wilson's America, either—and therefore his allies.

A discussion of this issue with Australian prime minister William Hughes exploded into a heated argument. Hughes viewed Wilson with nothing short of contempt; he thought Wilson's high-minded idealism a lot of humbug, and dismissed the League of Nations as the president's toy: "He won't be happy until he gets it,"* Hughes would say with disgust.[39] He also noted, as others did, that Wilsonism had been repudiated in the last American election. Hughes found it "intolerable," he said at a British Cabinet meeting in December— Australia, like South Africa, had a seat in Lloyd George's expanded War Cabinet—"for President Wilson to tell us that the world is to be saved on his terms." Australia, for one, wasn't going to stand for it.[40]

So, when Wilson rose up in indignation as they discussed the issue of New Guinea and asked archly, "Am I to understand that if the whole civilized world asks Australia to agree to a mandate in respect of these islands, is Australia still prepared to defy the appeal of the whole civilized world?" Hughes's answer was prompt and forthright. "That's about the size of it, President Wilson." Prime Minister William Mass†ey of New Zealand grunted his agreement.[41]

---

* I have changed the tense of the sentence, but not its meaning.

In the end, a compromise was struck. The mandates were split into three groups: former Turkish colonies in the Middle East, which were judged close to running their own affairs, were A class; colonies in places such as Africa, where the mandate power would run things, were B class; and C-class territories were those close to or adjoining the mandate powers, which would administer the areas and peoples living in them as their own national territory. It was this C class into which Australia, South Africa, and New Zealand were judged to fall, so the issue went away. But the whole mandate system was clearly a face-saving farce, and in places such as the Middle East, where France received a mandate for Syria and Britain for Palestine, it sowed the seeds of much trouble later on.*

Then there was Italy and the question of Trieste. To get the Italians to switch sides and join the Entente powers during the war, France, Britain, and Russia had signed the Treaty of London, which promised Italy a wide swath of Mediterranean islands and territory in the Balkans, including the important port of Trieste and sizable portions of the Austrian Tirol, in the Alps. The Treaty of London was precisely the kind of Bismarckian balance-of-paper diplomacy President Wilson most despised: arranged in secret, involving annexations from other countries with no consideration of the feelings or wishes of the people living there (a quarter million German-speakers, in the case of the Tirol), all in order to further a war. But Britain and France had put their names, and national honor, to the treaty; their ally Italy arrived at the Peace Conference expecting to see that pledge redeemed. It was, as Harold Nicolson observed, a clear case of the clash between the "old diplomacy" and the new, based on the Fourteen Points. "Here, if ever, was the opportunity for the Prophet of the new World to enforce his message upon the old."[42]

---

* All the receivers of mandates agreed to what would eventually be confirmed in the League of Nations in 1920. The very last mandate, that of Palau, did not officially run out until 1994, when the tiny island nation became independent.

Yet Wilson did not do this. "He failed us," Nicolson wrote later. "We ceased, from that moment, to believe that President Wilson was the Prophet whom we had followed."

Wilson started well. On January 13, he informed Italian prime minister Orlando that, in his mind, the Treaty of London was all but dead (although it is not entirely clear if Wilson had even read the text of the treaty).[43] Unfazed, Orlando used the conversation to reaffirm his own personal commitment to Wilsonism, but warned that Italy had been placed in a difficult position with the collapse of Austria-Hungary. Annexation of the Tirol became a matter not of imperialist greed but of national security; surely the United States could understand that, given its own interests in the Western Hemisphere. Here Italy offered a deal. It would support exempting the Monroe Doctrine (the U.S. policy of opposing European colonialism and intervention in the Americas) from the Covenant of the League of Nations, an exception Wilson himself supported. Wilson would find no better friend and supporter for the League of Nations he wanted than Italy, Orlando averred, if the American president could see his way clear on the Tirol and the Brenner, a mountain pass through the Alps forming the border separating Italy and Austria.[44]

And so, Wilson did. And "if Wilson could swallow the Brenner," Nicolson noted sourly, "he would swallow anything." One by one, Italy's claims under the Treaty of London (Dalmatia, Istria, a protectorate over Albania, Rhodes, and eleven other islands in the Dodecanese entirely populated by Greeks) were established and validated. Clemenceau and Lloyd George were inclined to say nothing; they left it up to Wilson to draw the line with Orlando, which Wilson did not. He did, however, finally balk at Fiume. One of the new states recognized by the conference, Yugoslavia, claimed it as well. Fiume's population was largely South Slav; by the principle of self-determination, it belonged to Yugoslavia. Italy, however, was an Allied Power and threatened to walk out if the Yugoslavs won the argument. Wilson tried to go over the heads of Italian leaders and speak directly to the Italian people—and got a faceful of nationalist backlash instead. On

April 19, the Italians did walk out of the Peace Conference. Wilson had suffered his most serious rebuke.[45]

In the end, the Paris Peace Conference could not arrive at a solution for Fiume. It was left to Rome and Belgrade to sort out, which they did, to no one's ultimate satisfaction. The Fiume issue did, however, mobilize two new voices for Italian nationalism. One was the poet and soldier of fortune Gabriele D'Annunzio; at one point, he would lead an armed revolt to seize Fiume for Italy. The other was a socialist journalist named Benito Mussolini. He had experienced first-hand the disastrous retreat from Caporetto in 1917; he would spend the rest of his political career determined never again to let Italy be humiliated on the international stage. The political party he would head, and its Blackshirts and Fascists, found a spark in the battle over Fiume and in Wilson's cavalier treatment of Italy, including, at one point, his halting of famine-relief shipments to the country. Mussolini would be a powerful example of how the events of 1917 shaped the future—and of the unexpected product of a failed and increasingly bankrupt Wilsonism.

The same was true in the case of Japan and China. Japan had proved itself America's indispensable ally in the Siberian expedition. It had also provided aid to Britain and France from the other side of the world, including loaning money when those financially strapped nations were at their most desperate.[46] Then, in January 1917, Japan also sent a flotilla of destroyers to help deal with the Austro-German submarine threat (more than two hundred Japanese sailors died fighting the U-boat menace, thousands of miles from their Pacific home). In gratitude, the Entente powers secretly agreed to let Japan take over German's treaty rights in the Shandong Peninsula, in China—a move that set the stage for a long and dismal future for China, and for East Asia more generally.

But it wasn't just Britain and France that agreed to let the Japanese take over. The government of Chinese premier Gen. Duan Qirui, in Peking, also signed on. The deal would have allowed Japan to maintain a garrison in Shandong in exchange for its support for revising the entire structure of unfair treaties with China.[47] And because Japan had also agreed to Wilson's Fourteen Points, its delegates arrived in Paris assuming they were in a strong position both to get what they wanted for Japan and also to act as the conscience of Asia—a strong enough position, in fact, to ask the Peace Conference to insert in the Covenant of the League of Nations then being drafted a clause embracing the principle of racial equality. The Japanese saw this as a way to assert their own equality with the Western Allies, that is, as a Great Power, but also to boost their position as defender of China's interests and to offset their image as imperial aggressor.

Yet to a generation of westerners reared on white supremacist dogmas and Darwinism, the clause seemed to offer a dangerous precedent. Such a clause might apply to the Japanese, British foreign minister Balfour pointed out, but what about central Africa?[48] The proposal went nowhere.

At the end of March, as the conference was entering the home stretch, the Japanese delegation tried offering a watered-down version of the League agreement. It, too, failed to pass muster, with Wilson casting the final veto. This led Japan to threaten to leave the conference altogether, unless its participants recognized Japan's rights in Shandong according to Japan's agreement with Peking. The Chinese delegates complained that they had signed the agreement under duress. As one of Japan's delegates scoffed to U.S. secretary of state Lansing, it was "ridiculous for a nation of 400 millions to go around complaining that they had signed a treaty under duress."[49]

In the end, the Japanese won their concession. On April 22, in one of the conference's last acts, Wilson and the others had to inform the Chinese delegation that the Allied powers were bound by the prior treaty. The result was a double disaster. The Chinese delegates refused to sign the final treaty, and left Paris in high dudgeon. When the news reached China, anti-Western and anti-Japanese riots exploded across the country. On May 4, some five thousand Chinese students stormed into Tiananmen Square in Peking to protest the Treaty of

Versailles. The so-called May Fourth Movement set the stage for decades of turmoil and collapse at the center in China, and led to civil war and, ultimately, war with Japan.[50]

As for Japan, the rejection of the racial equality clause and, by implication, of Japan's status as a Great Power equal to France or Britain doomed those Japanese politicians arguing for an accommodationist, pro-Western slant to their country's foreign policy, especially toward the United States. The forces of the militaristic right in Japan took heart from the setback, just as the extreme nationalists in Italy had done with Fiume. The roots of a future war were planted that fateful spring; Wilson's failure to support Japan's highest aspirations would end with bombs dropped on Pearl Harbor.

And so it went, with one issue after another. Some discussions, such as that over the borders for the new Czechoslovakia (Professor Masaryk's great dream), went relatively well; many others, such as those concerning the borders of Poland and the mandate for Syria, did not. Most important, the number of violations of the Fourteen Points kept mounting. Having conceded on one or two, Wilson seemed to see no point in not conceding on almost all of them.

He convinced himself by reasoning that he could make these concessions because he was now staking everything on his League of Nations. This had become the remaining Holy Grail of his failed crusade. Whatever injustices or inequities had to be tolerated to arrive at a final peace treaty, they could all be corrected by the League of Nations—or so he believed. And the Holy of Holies of the League would be its Covenant, the document that dictated the basic principles that this gathering of all nations would commit itself to observing in its future deliberations. That the Fourteen Points would themselves be at the heart of that Covenant, Wilson did not doubt from the moment he set foot in Paris.

On April 28, nine days after the Italian delegation walked out and after Wilson had made his concession on Shandong, the conference met in a plenary session to review the revised League of Nations Covenant. Wilson was speaking when observers noticed that he seemed unusually lackluster and muted; his presentation included several factual errors that caused him to start over.

That morning, something was wrong. Wilson had been signing documents with his usual strong hand. By afternoon, however, the handwriting had deteriorated; it "became more heavily slanted to the right," his biographer, Arthur Link, noticed in reviewing the documents half a century later; "[it] was more and more heavily inked, and became almost grotesque."[51]

Others noticed a physical change. The U.S. secretary of war, Newton Baker, noted that "the left side of his face twitched sharply, drawing down the under lid of his eye." Later, Wilson had trouble recalling in the afternoon what he, Lloyd George, and Clemenceau had discussed in the morning. As April turned into May, others described his forgetfulness, his irritability, and a growing "suspicion bordering on paranoia."[52]

Did Wilson suffer a stroke on that day in late April? The evidence strongly suggests he did. It may not have been severe enough to render him unable to attend meetings or to cause him to withdraw from public settings, but that he was physically and mentally a different man after the date seems indisputable. If it was a stroke, it would leave him impaired just when he most needed his strength.

For one thing, there were still the Germans to deal with.

The German delegation, led by a clutch of Social Democratic politicians, arrived in Paris in early May. They expected to be treated, especially by Wilson, as a fellow democratic nation, there to negotiate a final equitable peace. Instead, to their shock and humiliation, they were received as a beaten adversary to be punished and reduced to impotence, while Wilson sat mutely by, doing nothing.

On May 7, the very day of the fourth anniversary of the sinking of the *Lusitania*, the German delegates were escorted into the Hall of Mirrors at Palace of Versailles and presented with a peace treaty to sign. The venue was an additional humiliation. The Hall of Mirrors was where the German Empire had been proclaimed in 1871, following Germany's triumph in the Franco-Prussian War. Now there was a peace treaty that overturned the earlier triumph by restoring to France the two eastern provinces it had lost in the war, Alsace and Lorraine, and depriving Germany of the Saarland and of control over its Rhineland. The national shame of France was at last vindicated, with interest.

The loss of Alsace and Lorraine was in fact the least of it. The treaty, comprising 15 parts and 440 articles, committed Germany to an army of a maximum of 100,000 men; it prohibited Germany from ever having a navy or an air force—and certainly from having any submarines.

The treaty moved Germany's western frontier sharply eastward, with an Allied occupation of the Rhineland and of the Rhine bridge-heads, and sliced away large sections of territory on its eastern border to give to Poland. In all, Germany lost 13 percent of its territory, and one out of every ten Germans now belonged to another country. These losses hardly justified the German foreign minister's bitter riposte that the treaty could be summed up in four words: "Germany renounces its existence." But it was a shock to a country that thought it had preserved itself by agreeing to end the war and embrace Wilsonism. Instead, the war, and the memory of how it ended, would be there to haunt Germany for a generation to come.[53]

This was because the treaty also imposed on Germany an admission of sole guilt for having caused the war—it was the only combatant forced to admit guilt at all. There was also a clause imposing major financial reparations, for amounts as yet unspecified. Nonetheless, by signing the treaty, Germany would be admitting its liability for those reparations whatever the final amount.

The conferees gave the German delegates two weeks to read and sign. To encourage them to cooperate, in the five months since the armistice, Britain's naval blockade had remained in force, keeping German shop shelves bare and German children's stomachs rumbling. At first, the German delegates' instinct was *not* to sign, blockade or no blockade. But that would mean a renewal of the war when the armistice expired in June. It was true that Germany was in a stronger position in May 1919 than it had been when the armistice was signed the prior November. Large chunks of the Allied armies had been demobilized and sent home, including the bulk of American troops. The possibility of resuming the war might cause a backlash from war-weary publics in the United States as well as in Britain and France. But when Germany's new leaders asked whether German armies could retake the field, Ludendorff's successor, General Groener, said no. There was no alternative; Germany had to sign the treaty, however humiliating and discouraging for the future it was.[54]

The one person Germany could have appealed to was Woodrow Wilson, but his mind was closed to any compromise. There were many in Paris, such as Harold Nicolson, who saw the treaty as a stark betrayal of Wilson's Fourteen Points, the supposed bedrock of Wilsonism and the new order to come. Yet when General Smuts and even Lloyd George asked Wilson to reconsider, to revise the treaty so Germany could sign it in good conscience, he brusquely brushed them away.

"We ought not to be sentimental," he told them. "Personally I do not want to soften the terms for Germany. I think that it is a good thing for the world and for Germany that the terms should be hard, so that Germany may now know what an unjust war means."

Then he lashed out at his critics with real fury. "The time to consider all these questions was when we were writing the treaty . . . It makes me a little tired of people to come and say now that they are afraid the Germans won't sign, and their fear is based upon things that they insisted upon at the time of the writing of the treaty; that makes me very sick!"[55]

This was a new, more frightening Woodrow Wilson: angry, petulant, nearing the end of his tether. So, the critics backed off. On June 28, as scheduled, the Germans came back to the Hall of Mirrors to sign.

Harold Nicolson was there to watch the ceremony. The Hall of Mirrors was jammed with humanity, but "the silence is terrifying," he recorded in his diary. The Germans "keep their eyes from those two thousand staring eyes, fixed upon the ceiling. They are deathly pale." After the documents were signed, "we kept our seats while the Germans were conducted like prisoners from the dock, their eyes still fixed upon some distant point on the horizon." That night, after the celebrations throughout Paris, Nicolson went to bed "sick of life."[56]

He was also thoroughly sick of Wilson. Many were. The U.S. president's consent to the Versailles Treaty did more to damage his reputation among his fellow liberals than anything else he did that crucial year. It also sowed the seeds for a bitterness among Germans that would ripen into the political movement that led to Adolf Hitler and World War II.

*   *   *

MEANWHILE, THE RUSSIAN Civil War was reaching its climax.

September 1, 1919, was the high-tide mark of the White advance. The White armies had momentum, but they were overextended. Most important, they were critically low on supplies and ammunition, thanks to the Allies. Allied support for the White cause had all but evaporated. Once a final peace loomed with Germany, the one power everyone feared, the original rationale behind intervention in Russia faded. Only a handful of Western politicians, such as Winston Churchill, saw what was coming. They urged converting Wilson's equivocal interventionist strategy into an all-out thrust into the Bolshevik regime. Clemenceau, man of the left though he was, agreed. But he was helpless to turn the Supreme War Council into a crusade against Lenin.

Churchill knew that Wilson was not his only chief impediment to an all-out Allied war against the Soviet regime. The desire to avoid another general conflict, on the heels of the world's worst, was general. The Allies failed to understand how momentum from a victory from one war can carry over to another—if it is pressed home in time. Nonetheless, in February 1919, a hopeful Churchill stopped in Paris to put his case to the Allied delegates, but Lloyd George said no.[57] Instead, the Allies began a steady pullback, even when the anti-

Bolshevik Whites seemed on the verge of success. The rationale for withdrawal took on added weight that fall, with the excuse that Allied troops should not get trapped by the Siberian winter.

The Whites had also lost the war for hearts and minds. Wherever they drove out the Reds, the locals welcomed them with open arms. But the Russian populace soon learned that Kolchak's and Denikin's soldiers could be as brutal and as mercenary as the Reds—perhaps because they were just as hungry. Deserted by the Allies, divided by their respective leaders' ambitions, and reckless about building popular support, the Whites were in the losing corner in this war. Only mistakes by the Reds could save their cause, and there were few such mistakes after the summer of 1919.

In fact, Lenin reinforced the ruthless approach he had taken when the fighting broke out—what would be called war communism. It was buttressed by two major measures: The first, in May 1918, gave extraordinary powers to the People's Commissariat for Food to requisition any and all foodstuffs the regime required, regardless from whom and for what purpose. The second measure, which passed the Central Committee on June 11, 1918, replaced the rural soviets that had been the formal basis of the Bolshevik regime with select peasant committees that were more obedient to the regime and more willing to take drastic action to provide the food the government required, even with increasing force and brutality.[58]

The reaction to the two draconian laws was immediate and intense. There were 245 peasant uprisings in 1918 within Bolshevik-controlled territory, and 99 in the first seven months of 1919. Agricultural output in Russia fell to roughly half that of 1913. The specter of widespread famine now haunted the nation, yet the fighting was only intensifying.[59]

September saw the last White offensive, along the Tobol front. On October 14, the Reds launched a decisive counterattack, while White forces fell back. Five days later, Trotsky rebuffed the most serious challenge to the regime, directed at Petrograd and coming from Estonia. Gen. Nikolai Yudenich led two hundred thousand men and six British tanks into the attack, and on October 19, they were in the outskirts of the former capital.

Trotsky himself took personal charge of the defenses—"We will not give up Petrograd!" was his slogan—saying that he would "defend Petrograd to the last ounce of blood," while funneling Red reinforcements until they outnumbered Yudenich's troops three to one. Comrade Stalin was also there, using masses of Petrograd civilians to act as human shields to prevent White soldiers from firing on Red troops.[60] Sensing defeat, Yudenich's men fell back in the direction of Estonia. Petrograd had been saved, Trotsky was a national hero, and the Red cause had its first decisive success.

The second came on October 24, when Tukhachevsky crushed Gen. Konstantin Mamontov's forces in a large-scale, brutal battle. The remainder of October and November saw one Red victory after another, as the White cause approached its final doom.

Fighting would go on into 1920, but the main issue had been decided. Lenin had won the Russian Civil War, and his enemies, despite Western backing, had lost. Weighing the reasons for the Bolshevik success, Britain's last general on the spot and former victor at Arras, Sir Henry Rawlinson, put it baldly: "They know what they want and are working hard to get it." That, in fact, summed up Lenin's entire career. It was a ruthless commitment he had communicated to all his followers since the revolution began, and the result was that Russia was finally theirs.

The cost was staggering. The civil war Lenin had invited left more than one million dead, at least half a million from the Red Terror alone. Social order had broken down throughout the country; famine stared Russia in the face. An internal Cheka memo of December 1919 noted, "The food crisis has gone from bad to worse, and the working masses are starving. They no longer have the physical strength necessary to continue working, and more and more often they are absent simply as a result of the combining effects of cold and hunger."[61]

Still, Lenin could be satisfied. His power over Russia, or what was left of it after the Brest-Litovsk Treaty, was now unquestioned. His political rivals on the right had long since been defeated, arrested, or, like Kerensky, driven into exile. The Socialist Revolutionaries were on the run, as were the Mensheviks. Their roundups, arrests, and trials would begin the next year. The turn of the Bolsheviks' only ally in the civil war, the Left Socialist Revolutionaries, would come next.

Meanwhile, the Cheka, under the loyal Dzerzhinsky, had now infiltrated itself into every aspect of Russian life. The secret functionaries who made up "the iron fist of the proletariat" would grow to a quarter of a million by 1921. Their raison d'être was stated with arrogant bluntness by Dzerzhinsky's lieutenant in the Ukraine, Martin I. Latsis:

> We are exterminating the bourgeoisie as a class. We are not looking for evidence or witnesses to reveal deeds or words against the Soviet power. The first question we ask is—to what class does he belong, what are his origins, upbringing, education or profession? These questions define the fate of the accused. This is the essence of the Red Terror.[62]

Latsis's and Dzerzhinsky's chief tool (and Lenin's) for crushing out Russia's bourgeois class was the Red Army bullet and the Cheka concentration camp, the direct ancestor of Stalin's gulag. After the laws of 1918, it was steadily mushrooming into a fixture of Soviet life. Within two years, its unwilling population of counterrevolutionaries, saboteurs, and other class enemies would swell by the tens of thousands— and the camps would spread across the bleak landscape of Siberia year by year.

Even more important from the point of view of continuity of the regime, Lenin had no serious rivals within the Bolshevik elite, not even the hero of the civil war, Leon Trotsky. On the contrary, ever since Fannie Kaplan's poorly directed bullets missed their mark, Le-

---

* Latsis would himself be shot during the purge of 1938—another victim of the police state he helped establish.

nin had become a sacrosanct, Christlike figure of deliverance. What Wilson aspired to be, to be hailed as the savior of his people and the light of humanity, Lenin had already achieved, but through unbelievable brutality and ruthlessness, and in a broken, starving country.

It was a fate that other, later Communist leaders would know, from Stalin and Mao Zedong to Fidel Castro and Kim Il-Sung. Lenin at least had the ruthless honesty to acknowledge the truth about what had happened and what would come next. In a statement in 1919, he posed the present and future in no uncertain terms: "We recognize neither freedom, nor equality, nor labor democracy if they are opposed to the interests of the emancipation of labor from the oppression of capital," meaning opposed to the Communist Party. Later, he would even insist that "revolutionary violence" was necessary "against the faltering and unrestrained elements of the toiling masses themselves."[63] Thanks to the Cheka and Trotsky's victorious Red Army, he also had the means to enforce it.

This above all separated Lenin and Wilson. The Russian at least was willing to confront what realizing his dream would cost him, his people, and the world. Wilson never was. Lenin's grasp of the hideous truth enabled him to gain a level of power no despot in modern history had ever enjoyed.

Deceived by his ideals, Wilson never grasped that truth. That ultimately redeems his legacy, even today. Yet it also means that, confronted by one of history's greatest monstrosities, Wilson led the West in throwing away its one great chance to prevent it.

LAST ACT

We cannot turn back . . . The light streams upon the
path ahead, and nowhere else.
—WOODROW WILSON, JULY 10, 1919

WILSON AND HIS entourage celebrated the Fourth of July on the voyage home. To the others, he seemed tired; Edith had to struggle to get him to go for walks on the deck. The strain of the last six months was visible; she and the president's staff could see the effects of his hypertension in his face and body, and noticed his constant need for breaks.[1]

Yet his mood was upbeat. Arriving at Hoboken, he was greeted by enormous crowds both at the dock and as he made his way to City Hall in New York for a meeting with the mayor. He boarded the train for Washington that afternoon and got into Union Station at midnight. There he found a similar crowd of well-wishers. It was a revived, confident Woodrow Wilson who walked down the aisle of the Senate two days later, with Senate majority leader Henry Cabot Lodge at his side.

Yet he was in for the fight of his life.

He had had a foretaste of what was coming when he returned briefly to Washington from Paris in March, to open the new Congress. On February 23 he had arrived in Boston, where he addressed a rally of seven thousand supporters and spoke passionately of the American soldiers he had met in France. They had, he said, "a religious fervor. They were not like any of the other soldiers. They had a vision; they had a dream, they turned the whole tide of battle; and it never came back."[2] None of this was strictly true. There were plenty of American soldiers who had fought because they had to, and who would come home with anything but religious fervor—except for a fervent wish never to go to war again. If anyone had a religious, almost millennialist vision of what the war had meant and what the future must be, it was certainly Wilson—and he was determined to turn the tide of battle on one remaining issue, the centerpiece of his Fourteen Points: the League of Nations.

The statement laying out the organization and the principles of the League, known in appropriately Presbyterian terms as the League Covenant, was itself a product entirely of Wilson's vision, if not much else. The first draft he presented to the conference in Paris had been heavy on aspirations and light on details. The British and the French had offered their own ideas. Clemenceau, Foch, and the French leadership foresaw a League that would guarantee peace through armed force, especially against Germany, by means of a system of standing military arrangements that largely maintained the wartime alliance. It bore a close resemblance to today's North Atlantic Treaty Organization, or NATO.[3]

The British had prepared a carefully organized memorandum (far more than Wilson had done) composed by two quasi-pacifists, Walter Phillimore and Robert Cecil (Lord Cecil), son of the great prime minister Lord Salisbury. Cecil had none of his father's grasp of realpolitik but plenty of his own evangelical sanctimony, which grafted well onto Wilson's. He saw a League that would rely entirely on consultation, discussion, and moral force to rein in aggression by any of its members. He felt horror at the thought of using physical or military force. "Without the hope that [the League] was to establish a better international system, I should be a pacifist."[4]

Wilson was willing to borrow many, if not most, of Cecil's and Phillimore's ideas. The first full draft of the Covenant was ready on February 13. Its broad outlines are familiar from today's United Nations. There would be a General Assembly made up of all member nations, and an Executive Council where the Big Five (the Big Four plus Japan) would hold a slight majority—the ancestor of the United Nations Security Council. There was a provision for League-armed forces, but no compulsory arbitration or provisions for forced disarmament. All League members were sworn to respect one another's independence and territorial boundaries—an echo of one of the Fourteen Points. Most decisions by the General Assembly would have to be unanimous, in order to prevent the Great Powers from being swamped by the lesser ones.

The Covenant also set up a court of international justice; contained provisions against slavery and arms trafficking; and set up an International Labor Organization—all music to the ears of Progressives and humanitarians everywhere. Wilson was also delighted that the Covenant had come to exactly twenty-six articles, twice thirteen—thirteen being his personal lucky number.[5]

That, however, was not the primary reason he fought off any and all attempts to amend the Covenant, such as Japan's racial equality clause or French efforts to include a clause regarding military force against recalcitrant members. When the Covenant passed in a plenary session on February 14, he announced, "Many terrible things have come out of this war, but some very beautiful things have come out of it," including his League. He was determined that the Republican majority he would meet with in Congress should have no opportunities to alter or deface the Covenant that he and the Peace Conference had finally arrived at.[6]

The Republicans, however, were ready and waiting for him. They had gotten wind of what was coming and wanted to force a special session of Congress, after Wilson left for France, to debate the League at length. Wilson turned down their request. (As president, only he had the authority to call a special session.) He was determined that Congress not meet until he returned to the United States at the end of the conference, when he would have both a peace treaty and the League Covenant to present as a package.

On March 28, he did sit down to a dinner with congressional leaders, including the new Senate majority leader, Henry Cabot Lodge. Wilson fended off one question after another about the League: whether it would violate U.S. sovereignty; whether a member nation would be free to leave it; and whether the United States must send troops to Europe or some other place as part of a League of Nations mandate.[7]

Wilson replied to all of them that "in his opinion this nation would relinquish some sovereignty," but it would do so "for the good of the world," and that every other nation in the League would have to make the same sacrifice. He said that any member could leave if it took "the proper steps," and that sending troops would not be mandatory under the League Covenant—in his opinion.[8]

Two days later, it was Lodge's turn in the Senate. Everyone hates war, the senator stated at the start, and therefore it was time to lay aside the argument that if men differed over how to prevent one, then the other side must necessarily be against peace. He went on solemnly, "No question has ever confronted the United States Senate which equals in importance that which is involved in the league of nations . . . There should be no undue haste in considering it . . ."

Right now, he averred, "it seems to have been very hastily drafted, and the result is crudeness and looseness of expression, unintentional, I hope." There was no clear clause about voluntary withdrawal from the League, despite what the president had said. Every clause, including the one regarding leaving the League, seemed to be open to conflicting interpretations. All these would have to be straightened out and clarified before the Senate put its stamp of approval on the treaty.

Then the Senate majority leader closed on the heart of the matter. In joining this League, he said, "We abandon entirely by the proposed constitution the policy laid down by [George] Washington in the Farewell Address and the Monroe Doctrine . . . Washington declared against permanent alliances. He did not close the door on temporary alliances for particular purposes." The entry into the Great War had been such an alliance. But now "the Washington policy is to be en-

tirely laid aside and we are to enter upon a permanent and indissolu-
ble alliance . . . Let us not overlook the profound gravity of this step."

He made some suggestions for changes, including adding a clause
to protect the Monroe Doctrine as part of traditional U.S. policy and
changing Article 10, which obliged the United States to "guarantee
the territorial integrity and political independence" of other League
members—which could only mean committing beforehand to the
use of force in conflicts and in places unknown.

Lodge added that he was not ruling out the United States' joining
an organization such as a League of Nations, but as far as the current
version went, "we are asked to abandon the policies which we have
adhered to during all our life as a Nation"—and that, he believed, the
Senate should not do.[9]

When he learned of Lodge's speech, Wilson's fury was overwhelming. He told a meeting of the Democratic National Committee that their Republican opponents were "blind and little provincial
people, they are the littlest and most contemptible . . . They are going
to have the most conspicuously contemptible names in history . . . If
I did not despise them, I would feel sorry for them." He furiously set
to work to use every tool at his disposal, including appealing directly
to the American people, to defeat them. The promise of this League
was, he declared, nothing less than "an international miracle."[10]

The Republicans shrugged off Wilson's rage. On March 2, Lodge
and Senators Frank Brandegee and Philander Knox circulated a pe-
tition among their colleagues denouncing the League. Forty senators, all but one of them Republicans, signed what became known as
Lodge's Round Robin. Forty did not represent a Senate majority by
any means, but it was not a good send-off as Wilson headed back to
France.

Worse was to come on the other side of the Atlantic. One of Wilson's most important arguments was that his League was inseparable
from the peace treaty. When he got back to Paris on March 13, he
learned, to his shock, that this was exactly what Edward House had
been working to undo. Lloyd George and Clemenceau had learned

about the Round Robin and had decided it was time to take a fresh look at Wilson's "toy," as Australian prime minister Hughes had branded it.

The other members of the Big Four began pushing for a preliminary peace treaty with Germany first; only then would they take up the League. It was actually a good idea, one that, if implemented, could have prevented the long delays that complicated relations with the Germans later on. Wilson, however, would have none of it. When he learned that House had been involved in these discussions, which included raising the issue of creating a separate republic for the German Rhineland (one of France's pet projects), Wilson exploded.

Edith saw him right afterward. "He seemed to have aged ten years," she remembered. "He smiled bitterly. 'House has given away everything I had won before we left Paris. He has compromised on every side, and so I have to start all over again.'"[11]

So, he did, and hammered and cajoled the French and British delegations into accepting once again the linkage between endorsing the League and agreeing to the peace treaty. Yet the bond of trust between Wilson and House had been shattered beyond repair. His most important and sensible associate, especially in dealing with the other Allies, was now permanently sidelined, at a time when Wilson's own physical and mental health was increasingly in doubt. On May 30, House noted in his diary, "I seldom or never have a chance to talk to him seriously . . . he is practically out from under my influence." Many of the troubles that came during the rest of the conference, including those with Italy and Japan, might have been avoided if House had been able to offer advice and counsel that Wilson was willing to accept—but which more and more he was not.

House's sidelining actually gave the other leaders in the Big Four, including Lloyd George, some additional leverage with Wilson. In the last two months of the conference, whenever they wanted to wring a concession from Wilson on some point, they would threaten to revisit the question of the League Covenant. Instead of holding the Allies hostage to the League of Nations, as he had hoped, Wilson was now the hostage. And because he was staking everything on his hope that a future League of Nations would set straight all the problems and inconsistencies left unresolved by the Peace Conference, including the treaty with Germany—even though, inexplicably, Germany was denied membership in the League—the future of his new world order was being held hostage as well.

Nonetheless, the Wilson who strode down the aisle of the Senate chamber on July 10, 1919, was ready to do battle. With the consent of the Allies, he had made some cosmetic changes to the League Covenant. The Senate was not going to accept any of these, especially since the exemption of the Monroe Doctrine from League jurisdiction was still missing from the document. But against the U.S. Senate, Wilson firmly believed he had the moral force of the planet behind him, and he would prevail.

"The treaty constitutes nothing less than a world settlement," he told the assembled senators. It was the direct fruit of America's entry into the world war, an act that decisively turned the tide of the conflict but that sprang from "a different footing from every other nation's . . . We entered it, not because our material interests were directly threatened or because any special treaty obligations to which we were parties had been violated, but only because we saw the supremacy, and even the validity, of right everywhere put in jeopardy," and freedom imperiled by aggression and tyranny. "We entered the war as the disinterested champions of right," he reminded his audience, "and we interested ourselves in the terms of the peace in no other capacity."

It was precisely to protect the supremacy of right that the treaty before them had been crafted, Wilson averred. It was "not exactly what we would have written" if left to ourselves, but it still represented a transformative departure from everything that had come before.

"War had lain at the heart of every arrangement of Europe—of every arrangement of the world—that preceded the war. Restive peoples . . . knew that no old policy meant anything else but force,

force—always force. And they knew that it was intolerable." Wilson glossed over the fact that the old arrangement had managed to keep Europe out of a general war for nearly a century, but his mind was focused not on history but on the future.

He conceded that "it was not easy to graft the new order of ideas upon the old," in the drafting of the treaty. "Some of the fruits of the grafting may, I fear, for a time be bitter." Nonetheless, "every true heart in the world . . . demanded that, *at whatever the cost of independent action*, every government that took thought for its people or for justice or for ordered freedom should lend itself to a new purpose and utterly destroy the old order of international politics . . ."

It was important that America, and the Senate, not disappoint them. He added dramatically, "Shall we or any other free people hesitate to accept this great duty? Dare we reject it and break the heart of the world?"

He concluded that "a new role and a new responsibility have come to this great nation that we honor and which we would all wish to lift to yet higher levels of service and achievement."

Wilson's speeches usually included something that astonished (or appalled) his audience, but nothing prepared the Senate for what he said next. Wilson suddenly pushed aside his prepared text, lifted his eyes, and intoned a peroration like none an American president had ever given.

"The stage is set, the destiny disclosed. It has come about by no plan of our conceiving, but by the hand of God who has led us into this way. We cannot turn back . . . The light streams upon the path ahead, and nowhere else."[12]

It was a bizarre speech, even for Woodrow Wilson, and utterly out of step with the occasion. Even Wilson's supporters in the chamber, such as Arizona senator Henry Ashurst, were stunned by its misplaced religiosity and bad poetry. Ashurst wrote later, "Wilson's speech was as if the head of a great Corporation, after committing his company to enormous undertakings, when called upon to render a statement as to the meanings and extent of the obligations he had incurred, should arise before the Board of Directors and tunefully read Longfellow's Psalm of Life."[13]

Ashurst noted mournfully that "League opponents were in a state of felicity"; they sensed that Wilson had blown it. They may also have been rather miffed at his effort at emotional blackmail. Wilson was implying that to say no to the treaty, and to the League of Nations, would be to betray America's highest responsibilities as a nation to the world—and break the world's heart. But many senators were asking, "What about our responsibilities to America?" And if refusing to consent to a treaty that was flawed, badly conceived, and in many ways unjust was a betrayal of American boys' sacrifice on the battlefield, then why had we sent them there in the first place?

That question would arise in most Americans' minds later, especially when their boys came home with stories of how much they had sacrificed, and how little had been gained. For now, senators were focused on the immediate issue at hand: could they give their consent to a treaty that left important questions unanswered—questions the president seemed unable to answer himself? House had warned Wilson that "a fight was the last thing to be brought about, and then only when it cannot be avoided." Perhaps Wilson listened to House on this occasion, because on July 15, he agreed to meet with individual senators every day from ten o'clock to noon, to address their concerns and allay their fears. The first meetings went well; then, on the nineteenth, a Saturday, he and Edith set out on a cruise on the Potomac on the presidential yacht, the *Mayflower*.

It went very badly. Wilson became profoundly ill and spent the entire two-day cruise flat on his back in his cabin. He spent another day in bed after they got back.[14] His doctor Cary Grayson told the press it was a bout of dysentery. In retrospect, there can be no doubt Wilson had suffered a second stroke, more serious than the one in late April. In a day or two, he began meeting with senators in the Oval Office, but anyone who spoke to him or simply looked at him could see he was a man stretched to the end of his physical and mental powers.

Yet the battle over the League was just getting started. On August 1,

Henry Cabot Lodge's hearings in the Senate Foreign Relations Committee began. In the coming bruising battle over the fate of the treaty, not only in the Senate but in the court of American public opinion, Lodge had lost his most influential and steadfast ally. Theodore Roosevelt had died on January 6, quietly, in his sleep, at Sagamore Hill. (Roosevelt's son Archibald had telegraphed to his brothers and sisters, "The old lion is dead.") Lodge attended the funeral at Oyster Bay, along with William Howard Taft and the Republicans' presidential candidate in 1916, Charles Evans Hughes. None of them commanded the national, let alone international, respect Roosevelt had, especially on an issue such as the League of Nations, though Taft was a League supporter.

Roosevelt had been opposed not to a League of Nations, but just to a Wilsonian one. He had warned that America could never again "completely withdraw into its shell" and that consultation with other nations would help avert future wars. But the League he had foreseen was one that would be "an addition to, and in no sense a substitute for the preparedness of our own strength for our own defense." He saw the Great Powers acting in concert, introducing "some kind of police system in the weak and disorderly countries at their thresholds," while the United States tended to the Western Hemisphere. Above all, he had written after the armistice, "let us with deep seriousness ponder every promise we make *so as to be sure our own people will fulfill it.*"[15]

Now Roosevelt was gone. But Henry Cabot Lodge had other weapons in his own political arsenal. He knew more about foreign affairs than any other American politician, far more than Wilson. He also had an unexpected ally in William Borah, the Republican senator from Idaho. A rock-ribbed isolationist and Progressive, Borah had vigorously opposed the war but was also opposed to the League of Nations—so much so that he had refused to attend Wilson's at-home dinner on March 28. Although he and Lodge disagreed on just about everything, their shared opposition to the League allowed the Senate majority leader to strike a deal. He convinced Borah it would be impossible to defeat the League in a straight up-or-down vote. Too many wavering Republicans who disliked this or that aspect of the treaty but were afraid to oppose it outright would end up voting for it.

Yet if Borah and his allies agreed to support a series of amendments (or reservations, as Lodge called them) aimed at protecting U.S. interests and still didn't like the results, they would be free to vote against it. Borah signed on.[16] This ensured that those opposed to the League would have not only enough Republican votes to carry almost all of Lodge's proposed reservations, but also Borah's oratorical skills—the Idaho senator was a well-known spellbinder—coming up in support at every step. Borah was not as important an ally as TR would have been, but he filled the gap nicely.

Lodge's other ally was Wilson himself. In the Senate, "there were not a few who . . . shared Lodge's personal distaste for Wilsonian rhetoric" and for the president's high-handed approach to politics, which had alienated almost as many Democrats as Republicans.[17] For six long years, they had endured his often arrogant treatment of them, and his behaving as if the House and Senate did not exist. Even the Democrats who would dutifully cast their votes with their president were, many of them, not entirely with him in spirit. If the defeat of the treaty and of the League ended up being a humiliating one for Wilson as well, not many tears would be shed in the Senate cloakroom.

For now, Lodge's main problem, in fact, was not so much Wilson as the American public. Polls showed they strongly supported the League of Nations. Lodge figured he knew why: "knowing nothing of the details," the average man assumed "since the principle was good the plan was also." This was what Lodge set out to disprove in his hearings.

One of his first witnesses was Secretary of State Lansing, who powerfully, though unintentionally, helped Lodge's cause. Wilson had left Lansing out in the hallway during the months of negotiations in Paris, largely because he did not trust him—in some ways, correctly: Lansing was no fan of the League of Nations. Lodge's probing questions exposed how little America's own secretary of state knew about what the League Covenant meant at key points, or how specific articles and subsequent modifications of the treaty had been arrived at. Lodge called it a "pathetic exhibition," and wrote to his daughter, "What do you suppose Lansing did while he was in Paris?" Clearly, he did not oversee his country's foreign affairs—and if anyone was responsible for this dereliction of duty, it was not Lansing but Wilson.[18]

The administration's case for the League of Nations went downhill from there. The committee asked for documents and papers relating to the Paris conference, which Wilson had offered to surrender in his July 10 speech but which he now resolutely refused to hand over—or delayed so long in producing that committee members, even Democrats, had to shrug their shoulders in frustration. The committee also heard from delegations from Italian American, Irish American, African American, and even Swedish American groups protesting one aspect of the Covenant or another. (Rejection of the racial equality clause was a particularly bitter grievance for members of the newly formed National Association for the Advancement of Colored People and their spokesman, W. E. B. Du Bois.) Meanwhile, Lodge fought to bring along wavering Republicans who liked the idea of a League and were prepared to vote for this one, even though they had one minor reservation or another.

Finally, on August 14, feeling that he was ready to go on the offensive, Lodge wrote to Wilson asking for a meeting at the White House. Somewhat to his surprise, Wilson immediately agreed, and on the morning of August 19, he and Lodge and the other members of the Foreign Relations Committee, including Idaho's William Borah, met in the East Room.

It was a strange gathering. No detail of the meeting was kept secret, any more than the meeting itself. Stenographers took down every word and carried the results out to reporters jammed in the hall, who in turn broadcast them around the country.[19] Wilson was in an increasingly uncompromising mood, one not helped by the constant headaches and the feeling of exhaustion that dogged him almost daily. He assumed that Lodge's concerns about the Monroe Doctrine exception and the procedure for withdrawal from the League had been covered by the changes he had made in Paris—they had not, as he would find out later—and so steered discussion away from those points. On the issue of reservations—in Lodge's opinion, these were better than amendments because they would not require changing the pact, but would merely register America's formal exception to certain provisions, even when it had passed—Wilson said he had no objections, either, provided such reservations weren't "embodied in the instrument of ratification," which would have required review by the Allies all over again.

The real issue, however, boiled down to the by-now-notorious Article 10, the Covenant's final word on collective security, or Wilson's belief that any attack on a member of the League should be viewed as an attack on all, and should be treated as such.

Article 10 read as follows: "The Members of the League undertake to respect and preserve as against external aggression the territorial integrity and existing political independence of all Members of the League. In case of any such aggression or in case of any threat or danger of such aggression the Council shall advise upon the means by which this obligation shall be fulfilled."[20]

No issue was bound to arouse more hostility from the other men in the East Room. Wilson saw Article 10 as the way to replace the "balance of power" with what he called a "community of power." It not only proposed that if any member of the League were attacked, everyone should view the threat in the same way: as an attack on a peaceful and just world order. It also required every member to make the same sacrifice in terms of committing military force, if the League council so deemed it.

This could mean, for example, that if Yugoslavia found itself attacked by Italy, or China by Japan, the League could order the U.S. Marines to the rescue if it decided that was the most effective response—even if the United States had no dog in that fight, as Senator Borah might have put it.

Wilson impatiently waved their objections away. Article 10 "is in no respect of doubtful meaning when read in the light of the covenant as a whole," he airily said. "The council of the league can only 'advise upon' the measures by which the obligations of that great article are to be given effect to." Military participation for an individual country such as the United States would be a matter of "a moral, not a legal, obligation."[21]

This answer seemed even more confusing than the original article. Sitting there in the East Room, Wilson himself could not clearly explain the difference between a moral and a legal obligation in international affairs (except that the latter came with some kind of sanction, whereas the former did not); nor could he explain what he meant by the council's giving "advice" regarding what actions would discharge that obligation under Article 10. That was exactly what worried men such as Borah and Lodge. It sounded a lot like signing a blank check on future American military action, with no clear answer as to what would happen if the United States decided to say no. And if the United States (or any other League member) could say no with impunity, which was what Wilson seemed to imply, then what was the point of Article 10 in the first place?

The arguments ran on and on, politely and without rancor, but by the time the August 19 meeting broke up, it was obvious that there was no room for compromise on either side. Two great and ultimately incompatible visions of the United States' present and future role in the world were on a direct collision course.

One vision—Wilson's vision—was of the United States subordinating its own national interests to an institution representing the larger global community, for the sake of peace and security, while retaining its leadership by moral example. The other was of the United States, for all its moral exceptionalism as the world's standard-bearer of liberty, being essentially a Great Power like other Great Powers, with vital national interests to protect and defend—in conjunction and alliance with other nations if possible, but by acting alone if necessary.

One side, Wilson's side, saw the traditional balance of power between nation-states as a formula for protecting tyrannical and unjust political systems and as the chief source of conflict among nations—as witnessed by the Great War just fought. For Lodge and his friend and mentor the late Theodore Roosevelt, that balance of power preserved the peace among nations. It was when one power tried to overthrow that balance, as Germany did in 1914 (and would do again in 1939), that wars broke out and violence and injustice spread themselves across the landscape, as other nations rose up to defend their interests by any means necessary. This was why both Lodge and Roosevelt had supported going to war on the side of the Allies almost at once— because they saw a German-dominated Europe as more hazardous to U.S. interests than one in which the traditional balance of power was maintained.

Yet that was precisely why Wilson had *refused* to go to war. To act in that manner was to act as other nations did, which was exactly what America's destiny forbade it to do. If America acted like others (France and Britain, for example), then "all the fame of America would be gone, and all her power dissipated." Instead, "we set this Nation up to make men free, and we did not confine our conception and purpose to America, and now we will make men free."[22]

It was on this same point that Wilson's vision and Lenin's startingly agreed. Both conceived of a new international order that transcended the boundaries of traditional politics and of history. One was founded on a universal commitment to freedom for all peoples everywhere; the other on a world proletarian revolution that would eliminate all injustice forever.

But both new orders, they believed, would be inevitably imposed on others by the forces of history, whether people wanted their lives transformed or not. The force of history as Hegel and then Marx had formulated it was not a force that can be resisted; it was a power that both Lenin and Wilson believed they had personified, and which gave their actions a singular rightness that no opponent could or should dare to oppose.

Yet each man had been forced to make moral choices that contradicted his universal vision. To bring peace to the world, Wilson had been forced to go to war; to bring freedom to the proletariat, Lenin had enslaved everyone else, and eventually the proletariat as well. In 1917, both men had decided to step outside the normal course of events and act according to their own visions of reality. In the aftermath, however, that normal course of events had come back to bite them—for Lenin, in the Russian Civil War; for Wilson, in the battle over the League of Nations.

Lenin had endured his greatest trial in 1918–19 and escaped destruction by the skin of his teeth. Now it was Wilson's turn to undergo the fiery trial, at the hands of the U.S. Senate.

Nonetheless, one ineluctable fact was that America *had* gone to war in 1917, and had radically changed the character of the war from a bout between European Great Powers into an international crusade for freedom and justice. As the Democratic leader in the Senate put it, "Internationalism has come" for America; "we must choose what form the internationalism is to take."[23] It is impossible to say now, one hundred years later, which side was ultimately right and which wrong about when America should have gone to war, and why. Wilson had asked for war, and had gotten it on terms both sides could accept.

Now the two great visions for America were on a collision course once again, in the aftermath of war and in considering America's relationship with the League of Nations. And as the summer of 1919 turned into fall, both sides gathered their forces for the final showdown.

On Lodge's side, his hearings that August had shifted the public mood. Former president William Howard Taft, previously one of the League's biggest supporters, now came out in favor of reservations. A few days before the White House conference, Lodge gave a speech on the League and the treaty in the Senate that packed the visitors' gallery. Nearly every sentence drew wild cheers, with ladies waving their handkerchiefs and a group of marines banging their helmets on their chairs. Even the press gallery cheered Lodge on. Whenever a pro-League Democrat rose to pose a question, he was met by hisses and boos. This marked a sea change. The media, as well as other senators, watched and digested what they saw and heard.[24]

By August 20, Lodge was feeling confident that more than a third of the senators, in addition to his allies among the hard-core opponents of the League, would vote against the treaty if the reservations weren't included. If a vote came up on Wilson's treaty, it would go down to a crushing defeat. It was now up to Wilson to give ground if he wanted the League of Nations saved.

Wilson, however, was not a man who gave ground easily. He heard the bad news coming out of the Senate, even from his own supporters, and, on August 27, announced he was going on a cross-country speaking tour to arouse the American people to the importance of supporting the League, and to put pressure on senators in their home states. Both Edith Wilson and Dr. Grayson were appalled by the decision. They knew the true state of the president's health, even though the press and the public were still in the dark. But Wilson refused to reconsider. "I have to go," he told Grayson in the end.

The tour would begin in Columbus, Ohio. It would head out to the West Coast and back, and would include several stops in California. Thirty-three stops were planned across the country, with a major speech, sometimes two speeches, in each. No president, not even Theodore Roosevelt, had ever done a whistle-stop tour quite like this one—certainly not a president with one or possibly two strokes on his medical chart. But Wilson felt this was his destiny, even if it cost him his life.[25]

On the evening of September 2, 1919, Wilson arrived at Washington, DC's, Union Station. His private railway car, named the *Mayflower* like his presidential yacht, was waiting for him. His aide Joe Tumulty had planned the itinerary down to the last stop. The tour would last twenty-seven days, and would take Wilson all the way from Columbus, Ohio, to the Pacific Coast. He was skipping the South, where his word as Democratic president was law, League or no League. He would also bypass the Northeast, which was Lodge's and the GOP's stronghold. Instead, he intended to take the fight to the stronghold of the uncommitted, the land that stretched across the Midwest and the Great Plains and was represented by a bevy of wavering senators.

How many votes he expected to get by doing the tour, no one could guess, not even Wilson. He had written years before, "[T]he Senate is not so immediately sensitive to [public] opinion" as the House of Representatives, "and is apt to grow, if anything, more stiff if pressure of that kind is brought to bear upon it."[26] Yet it was the only Plan B he had.

As the presidential train pulled out of the station, Henry Cabot Lodge's puzzled but wry reaction was: "The only people who have the vote on the treaty are here in the Senate."[27] He was more prescient than Wilson's devoted admirers were willing to admit.

* * *

TO THE REPORTERS on the train, President Woodrow Wilson seemed in excellent health and in good trim, as he had always been. Only his wife, Edith; his doctor, Grayson; and Joe Tumulty, his political Cagliostro, knew the truth—but they also knew Wilson could not quit, not now.

Each stop became another Station of the Cross, another ordeal to be endured.

Certainly, the first, in Columbus, did nothing to lift anyone's mood. The crowd at the station was apathetic and sparse. Barely a fifth of the seats in the reviewing stand (which had a two-thousand-seat capacity) were filled.[28]

Things went better at the hired hall. Wilson wore a dark gray suit as he gave a lackluster speech to a packed audience. He was there, he said, to inform the American public "concerning those affairs of the world which now need to be settled." He added, "[T]he only people I owe any report to are you and the other citizens of the United States." It was a theme he would return to again and again: he owed nothing to the U.S. Senate; his obligation was only to the American people as they existed in his grand vision.

In Indianapolis, things went still better, but Wilson's voice seemed strained—as did his message. He said it was time for his critics "to put up or shut up." It wasn't until he reached St. Louis that he hit his stride.

The event was more like those of his two presidential campaigns than a public appearance by a semi-invalid. He jubilantly toured the city for three hours, and at the Coliseum, where he had been nominated for the presidency for the second time, he received an ovation many considered the biggest in the history of the city.

He offered strong meat to an enthusiastic crowd. He said if the treaty and the League were defeated, he would have to go back to the doughboys who had fought in France and tell them, "'Boys, I told you before you went across the seas that this war was a war against wars, and I did my best to fulfill the promise, but I am obliged to come to you in mortification and shame and say I have not been able to fulfill the promise. You are betrayed. You fought for something that you did not get.'" The crowd went wild.

Then came Kansas City and Des Moines (September 6), Omaha and Sioux Falls (September 8). In Kansas City, he savagely lashed out at Lodge and other opponents of the League as "men who think only of some immediate advantage to themselves." He gained satisfaction in thinking that "when at last in the annals of mankind, they are gibbeted, they will regret that the gibbet is so high."[29]

Kansas City marked the high point of the tour. From there, the speeches (often two a day, with an hour or more allotted for each) steadily degenerated into off-script rants. For the first time in his life, Wilson had run out of things to say. He tried to gain control of his message. One reporter saw the president "pounding strenuously on his typewriter" as the train pulled out of Kansas City. But usually he produced no useful notes. He was just an angry, increasingly sick man pulling out of his head whatever arguments he could remember.[30]

In Des Moines, for example, he told the crowd that America was headed "to those distant heights upon which will shine at last the serene light of justice, suffusing a whole world in blissful peace"— jejune rhetoric even for him.[31] Then the telegraph brought two hammer blows. The first was that Henry Cabot Lodge was presenting the Foreign Relations Committee's report on the League to the full Senate. There were four reservations to the treaty—these included the all-important Article 10—and no fewer than forty-five amendments. Whatever happened on the rest of the tour, Wilson would still be headed back to a mammoth fight in the Senate.

The second blow was William Bullitt's testimony before the committee, quoting Secretary Lansing saying that the League of Nations was useless and that if the senators had any sense, they would defeat it. The testimony made headlines across the country, including some in Bismarck, North Dakota, where Wilson's train had stopped. Wilson's rage against what he saw as Lansing's betrayal was fierce: "Think of it! This from a man whom I raised from the level of a subordinate to the great office of Secretary of State of the United States. My God! I did not think it was possible for Lansing to act in this way."[32]

First House, then Lansing, plus the once loyal Bullitt, who testified after resigning from his post in Paris in protest against the treaty—the emerging trail of betrayal added to Wilson's headaches, which now lasted for days at a time. In Idaho, William Borah's home state, the president got some more encouraging news: the governor of Massachusetts, Calvin Coolidge, had just fired Boston's striking police force. Although Coolidge was a Republican, Wilson applauded his bold action and implied it was a tribute to the fight that Wilson was making for the League of Nations. A strange tribute, perhaps, but the president's inclination now, in the words of biographer August Heckscher, was that "all troublesome or evil things seemed to spring from uncertainty over the outcome of the League; all good things, from the prospect of its favorable conclusion."[33]

When the train reached the Pacific Coast, Wilson appeared to find at last the favorable crowds he had been looking for. "The spirit of the crowd seemed at times akin to fanaticism," observed the *New York Times*. "The throngs . . . joined in a continuous and riotous uproar." There was an emotional moment when Wilson, bareheaded, reviewed the Pacific Fleet from the forward turret of the battleship *Oregon*.

In Portland that September 14, a Sunday and a day of rest, the president could pause and reflect. He had completed about half of his thirty-three planned stops. His health was precarious, but the crowds had been supportive, if not overwhelming in number, and the press coverage favorable and respectful. Yet he could not sleep: an "extremely troublesome" cough and the same persistent headache kept him awake almost all night.

California was Hiram Johnson territory. A Progressive Republican and an isolationist, Johnson was a fierce critic of the League and the treaty generally. Californians didn't care for the Shandong settlement in favor of the Japanese. Californians of Irish descent didn't like the fact that Britain's dominions, but not Ireland, would have votes in the League. The visit to the state was a low point for Wilson, physically and intellectually. A splitting headache in San Francisco left him almost unable to speak. Later, on September 19, he told an audience in San Diego that "the heart of humanity beats in [the Covenant]." If America didn't join the League, it would be "a death warrant" for its children, who would die in the next war.[34]

Then there were Los Angeles (September 20), Sacramento (September 21), Reno (September 22), and Las Vegas (September 23). Every stop left the president of the United States more exhausted and disoriented than the last. But Salt Lake City was where things really began to go wrong.

The Mormon Tabernacle on September 24 was stiflingly hot; even Edith nearly passed out from the "fetid air." When the crowd, however well meaning, cheered as Wilson read Lodge's reservation on Article 10, he completely lost his temper. "Now wait a minute!" he roared at the startled crowd. "You want to applaud that!"[35]

Cheyenne, Wyoming, and Denver, Colorado, saw him barely able to stand, let alone speak. Then the president's train pulled into the station in Pueblo, Colorado. Wilson was on the verge of collapse but still spoke in a hoarse voice to those who had come to hear him. He referred to the children of the next generation, to the American soldiers who had served and died in France, and to seeing Frenchwomen putting flowers on their graves. Then he said this: "I believe men will see the truth, eye to eye and face to face. There is one thing that the

American people always rise to and extend their hand to, and that is the truth of justice and of liberty and of peace."[36]

It was his last public speech. Twenty miles outside Pueblo, Dr. Grayson asked for the train to stop. President Wilson was clearly in deep distress. He told his doctor he had such a headache that he could barely see. Grayson hoped a walk in the open air would help him recover his breath and his wits. The two walked for almost an hour. Wilson met a farmer, who gave him a head of cabbage and some apples; they spied a young veteran in a private's uniform, and Wilson stopped to chat with the soldier and his family.[37]

They boarded the train again, and it headed down the track for a brief stop at Rocky Ford. Wilson did not feel up to speaking; he did stand and wave as they headed out of Rocky Ford and into the early evening sunlight.

That night "was the longest and most heart-breaking of my life," Edith Wilson later recalled. Wilson felt sick, very sick, and was in intense pain. He finally fell asleep, but then sat bolt upright at 5:30 a.m.

Wichita was the next stop—ironically, the hometown of his old rival William Jennings Bryan. Wilson gamely dressed and shaved, but after several minutes, it was clear he was not up to speaking to the crowd outside the train station. "I don't seem to realize it," he then confessed to Tumulty, "but I seem to have gone to pieces." Then he burst into tears.[38]

Wilson broke off the rest of the speaking tour and with its shades drawn, the presidential train headed back to Washington at top speed.

*   *   *

MEANWHILE, IN THE Capitol, Henry Cabot Lodge was marshaling his forces to compel Wilson to give way on the League of Nations.

He had already proposed making substantial changes to the treaty. One was dropping the language that transferred Germany's treaty rights in Shandong to Japan, and substituting China instead— ironically, a move that reinforced the principle of "self-determination." Lodge himself was deeply suspicious of Japan's ambitions regarding

China, and Asia generally. "Their oral promises are worthless . . . They are the Prussia of the East. Their culture is German, their ambitions are German . . . You might as well argue that Belgium ought to be handed over to France and Britain because France and England rescued Belgium from Germany."[39]

Another change was adding language that exempted the Americas from the collective security requirements that would have violated the Monroe Doctrine. Wilson's earlier change—"nothing but a mere mention of the name [Monroe Doctrine]," as Lodge put it—was less than adequate; there could be no ambiguity about the United States' right to enforce its own interests in its own hemisphere. There was even an amendment, led by Sen. Hiram Johnson, to give the United States six votes in the League General Assembly as a counterweight to the provision that gave League votes to Britain's dominions, including Canada and Australia.

All these amendments went down to defeat in the Senate, as Democrats and moderate pro-League Republicans came together to say no. But like the chess master who sacrifices his queen in order to get to checkmate on the next move, Lodge knew what he was doing. "I never expected to carry the amendments," he privately told one of his nephews.[40] With the amendments out of the way, the Senate could now move on to the reservations: these lay at the heart of Lodge's strategy. Amendments changing the language of the Covenant and treaty would have required renegotiating with the other Allies—a highly unlikely possibility, and one that, it is important to note, would have killed the treaty and the League of Nations outright, which was never Lodge's goal.

Inclusion of the reservations, however, would make it possible to get enough votes for ratification. "What I fear," Lodge wrote to his ally and Roosevelt's former secretary of war Elihu Root, "is that if we do not make the reservations strong and effective . . . the whole may be killed on the floor of the Senate. You may not realize how strong the feeling has grown against it . . . I want reasonable reservations but strong and efficient ones."[41]

The initiative was now firmly in Lodge's hands. With masterly and exquisite skill, he had managed to keep the Republicans united behind his reservations strategy. For Democrats who still supported Wilson's vision of the League without changes, such as their leader Sen. Gilbert Hitchcock, what they needed now was for their president to show the same degree of skill and strategy in heading off the Republicans.

That was precisely what they would not get, for the next two crucial months.

The president's train returned to Union Station on Sunday morning, September 28. Although his daughter Margaret and a crowd of one thousand people were waiting for him, none of them knew what had happened in Pueblo. Wilson managed to walk to his car without help, and bowed and waved stiffly to the cheering throng. In the White House, "he wandered like a ghost between the study at one end of the hall and my room at the other," Edith recalled. "The awful pain in his head that drove him back and forth was too acute to permit work."[42] For four days he stayed in the residential quarters of the White House, seeing no one and unable to conduct any business. Then, on October 1, he suddenly seemed better than he had in days. He read aloud to the family from the Bible. The next morning, when he awoke, however, he confessed he had no feeling at all in his left hand. He asked Edith to help him walk to the bathroom.

On the way, he collapsed and fell to the floor. Edith screamed for Dr. Grayson. Together they brought the president back to his bed. Woodrow Wilson was paralyzed along his entire left side. The White House's chief usher, Ike Hoover, caught a glimpse of him later that day, stretched out on the Lincoln bed. "He looked as if dead. There was no sign of life. His face bore a long cut above the temple" from his fall, "from which signs of blood were still evident."[43]

This was the stroke that now left the nation without a functioning president for more than a year, and left Senate Democrats leaderless and rudderless as the final votes for the League of Nations approached.

Throughout October, as Lodge's Foreign Relations Committee

voted on one reservation after another, particularly the reservation on Article 10, Woodrow Wilson was completely bedridden, unable to see anyone except his wife and doctor—or, rather, doctors, as a serious prostate infection had been found that threatened to kill the invalided president. On October 24, the committee submitted a total of fourteen reservations to the full Senate—and yet nothing was coming from the Oval Office or the White House.

It was not until November 7 that Edith Wilson finally permitted Senator Hitchcock to meet with the president. Wilson was still clearly paralyzed on his left side; his mouth worked with difficulty. Hitchcock was wary about mentioning Lodge's name, for fear that it would provoke a fresh emotional outburst from the president, even another stroke. He carefully laid out what the Democrats could still do to stop Lodge from getting his victory. Lodge had his majority to pass the reservations; the Democrats, however, had enough votes to prevent the required two-thirds majority needed to ratify a treaty. Should the Democrats let the treaty with reservations go down to defeat, Hitchcock now asked Wilson, or should they compromise and accept some reservations in order to get the treaty approved—and if so, which ones?

Wilson refused to consider any compromise. "Let Lodge compromise," he mumbled.

"Well, of course, he must compromise also," Hitchcock replied, "but we might well hold out the olive branch."

"Let Lodge hold out the olive branch," Wilson finally barked. And that was that.[44]

With the final vote on the treaty and the reservations to take place in less than a week, Hitchcock realized that the person he needed to talk some sense into wasn't the president, but the president's wife, who was constantly at his side and was still compos mentis. On November 13, he penned a note to Edith Wilson laying out a last-minute strategy for saving the treaty, and Wilson's League.

"One by one we are voting on the Lodge reservations," he informed her. "The Republicans are supporting these reservations solidly." The plan was for Democrats to offer a resolution to pass the treaty without reservations. "We shall be beaten on that and shall then offer interpretative reservations to take the place of the drastic reservations proposed by Lodge." They would lose those as well, but once Lodge's treaty plus reservations failed to get the needed two-thirds majority, the Democrats would revive their version of the compromise. Republicans would either have to vote for the compromise or go home and face an angry constituency wondering what had happened to the peace treaty.[45]

It wasn't much of a plan, but at least it was a plan. Yet there was no reply from the White House. On November 15, Hitchcock asked for some sign that the president accepted the Democrats' strategy. In response, Edith wrote on the envelope that the president would be willing to sign on to Hitchcock's watered-down version of Lodge's reservation on Article 10; but when they met again, for the last time, on November 17 (two days before the vote), Wilson was adamant about opposing any acceptance of Lodge's version (which was actually almost indistinguishable from Hitchcock's) or any of the other reservations, which now numbered fifteen.

"If the Republicans are bent on defeating this Treaty," he said in a quavering voice, "I want the vote of each Republican and Democrat recorded, because they will have to answer to the country in the future for their acts. They must answer to the people." Wilson said he knew he was a sick man, but "if I have breath enough in my body to carry on this fight, I shall do this . . ." He then added with real venom, "I will get their political scalps."[46]

In short, Wilson had ruled out any compromise. To make sure of it, he signed a letter drafted by Hitchcock the next day stating that "the friends and supporters of the treaty will vote against the Lodge resolution of reservation."

On November 19, the predictable happened. Lodge and the Republicans defeated the Democrats' compromise reservations one by one. Then Lodge called for a vote on the treaty with his reservations. It went to defeat, failing to get a two-thirds majority. Then he held a vote on the treaty *without* the reservations. It, too, went down to defeat.

The treaty was dead, as was American participation in the League of Nations. It was a crushing defeat for Wilson, and Henry Cabot Lodge had no doubt as to whose doorstep the failure belonged on.

"He would not consult, he would not compromise," Lodge later wrote; "he would not consider any change of meaning or consequence." He added, "If Wilson had not written his letter to the Democratic caucus, calling on them to kill the treaty rather than accept the reservations, the treaty would have been ratified on the 19th of November. There would have been enough Democrats voting with us to have done it. *It was killed by Wilson.*"[47]

It's hard to disagree with Lodge's postmortem. Wilson's antipathy and bitterness toward Lodge and the Republicans had blinded him to what the implications would be if the treaty and the League did indeed fail to gain the two-thirds majority. The defeat resounded around the world; it left the Allies high and dry, and the future of America's relations with the world uncertain. But Wilson was too sick and too mentally and emotionally unbalanced to fully grasp what had happened.

That was not entirely the end of the story. On December 17, Wilson roused himself to put forward one of the most extraordinary proposals any president had ever made to Congress. He suggested that the fifty-six senators who opposed him resign and run for reelection in a special election, as a way to test their vote on the League against public opinion. Wilson was so convinced that the American people would support him—he still saw himself as their champion and spokesman—that he made a wager: "if all [the anti-League senators] or a majority of them are reelected, I will resign the presidency."[48]

The plan was never made public. Even if it had been, Lodge and the others would have recognized it for what it was: a mad scheme by a man who had now completely lost touch with reality, just as he had lost control of the presidency. By now, Edith Wilson was signing all Wilson's bills and holding all his Cabinet meetings. From this point on, she was in fact acting as president, while she and the doctors, in the most elaborate and successful cover-up in presidential history, continued to maintain the fiction that Wilson was still functioning as chief executive.[49]

If Wilson had given up, the Democrats had not. The following January, they tried to reach an agreement with Lodge to revive the League and the treaty in a compromise form, with appropriate reservations. Lodge was open to the idea, but when Senate Democrats approached Wilson, now a virtual recluse with a long white beard, he fought the plan with all his remaining strength. Barely able to remain alert and conscious more than ten minutes at a time, he rallied enough to issue a statement condemning the compromise as a nullification of the entire treaty.

In the end, twenty-one Democratic senators bucked their president and voted with Republicans for the treaty with reservations on March 19, 1920. That was still seven votes shy of the two-thirds needed, and so the treaty, and American participation in the League of Nations, passed into history. Lodge pronounced the League "as dead as Marley's Ghost." Republican presidential candidate Warren G. Harding added, in a swipe at Wilson and the Democrats' past, "dead as slavery."[50]

So was the presidency of Woodrow Wilson. That November, Democrats would go down to a crushing defeat at the polls, with the election of a new Republican president, Warren G. Harding—largely out of bitterness over the war and where Wilsonism had led the country. As Eugene Debs, still sitting in his jail cell at the Atlanta Federal Penitentiary, wrote, "No man in public life in American history ever retired so thoroughly discredited, so scathingly rebuked, so overwhelmingly impeached and repudiated as Woodrow Wilson."[51]

Discredited and repudiated, yes. Defeated and forgotten, no—as the next century would show.

CONCLUSION

I am, it seems, immensely guilty before the workers
of Russia.
—LENIN, DECEMBER 26, 1923

O N MAY 25, 1922, Lenin suffered a massive stroke, eerily similar
to the one Wilson suffered on his return from his speaking tour
in 1919. As with Wilson, the stroke paralyzed an entire side of
Lenin's body, but in his case the right instead of the left. And like Wilson, Lenin would be helpless over the following months as control
over his legacy slipped out of his hands.

Yet, unlike Wilson's, the stroke hit Lenin when he seemed at the
very height of his personal power. He had no more rivals or opposition. The Whites' fleeing supreme ruler of Russia, Admiral Kolchak,
had been captured on January 14, 1920, and shot, his body dumped
under the ice of a frozen Siberian river. There had been a real scare
in March 1921, when sailors at Kronstadt naval base, the same men
who had put Lenin in power in November 1917, rose up in armed revolt against the regime. They demanded reforms such as the freeing
of all political prisoners, the abolishing of secret police control of all
army and naval units, and freedom for Russia's peasants to "do as
they please with their land"—in effect, an end to everything Lenin
and the Central Committee had imposed since the revolution.[1] For a
few short weeks, the Communist regime (as it was now increasingly
called) seemed once again in peril. Then Marshal Tukhachevsky and
his troops stormed the fortress, and the sailors involved in the revolt
were captured and executed.

For Lenin, the Kronstadt mutiny was the excuse to wipe out any remaining sources of opposition. He presented the Kronstadt sailors as agents of White and counterrevolutionary forces and denounced all those who were not members of the Communist Party as "nothing else but Mensheviks and Socialist Revolutionaries dressed up in modern, Kronstadt, non-party attire."[2] There was a roundup of remaining Socialist Revolutionaries and a trial for treason in 1921—the first of the "show trials" that would be a hallmark of the Soviet regime. There was no trial for the Mensheviks, but by then they had simply ceased to exist. Any survivors had joined Alexander Kerensky, Viktor Chernov, Nikolai Chkheidze, General Denikin, and the tens of thousands of other Russians (czarists; democrats; Socialist Revolutionaries; princes and princesses; and musicians and artists such as Sergei Rachmaninoff, George Balanchine, Marc Chagall, and Igor Stravinsky) who would now spend the rest of their lives as "White" Russian exiles and émigrés.

By the time of his stroke, Lenin "had systematically constructed, in all its essentials, the most carefully engineered apparatus of state tyranny the world had ever seen."[3] It included the power of the Cheka (which had carried out some fifty thousand death sentences by the start of 1921) to punish "the helping in any way" of opposition to the Communist regime in thought, word, or deed—a license for terror that, as Lenin told his minister of justice just days before his stroke, "must be formulated as wide as possible."[4] It even included the power of the Central Committee to sentence to death anyone in the country, including members of the Central Committee.

Yet this was absolute power over a country in ruins. A third of Russia's prewar landmass was gone; so was a quarter of its population, having vanished into the new nations created after Brest-Litovsk, including Poland and the Baltic states. The economy had been wrecked almost beyond recognition. Industrial production had fallen to 10 percent of prewar levels; Russian manufactured-goods production stood at 12.9 percent of what it had been in 1913. Production of cast iron, for example, was less than 2.5 percent of the total in 1913. The ruble was worth 1 percent of its prewar value.

Russia's major cities stood deserted. Three-quarters of the population of Petrograd and almost half that of Moscow had fled or been killed. Russia's agriculture sector had completely collapsed. For the first time since the 1880s, famine stalked the land. During the winter of 1921–22, no fewer than three million Russians died of starvation.

Not all these statistics can be blamed on the Great War or the Russian Civil War. The root cause was Lenin's failed crash program of mass collectivization as part of "war communism," which had led to chaos in the villages and on factory floors. As 1921 began, Lenin and Russia were staring catastrophe in the face. With extreme reluctance, therefore, in March 1921, Lenin was forced to backtrack on collectivization with his New Economic Policy, or NEP, which allowed a return to some private holdings and to limited market forces in order to prevent widespread famine—although repression and mass arrests of recalcitrant workers and miners continued.[5]

It was still not enough. In desperation, Communist Russia turned to, of all places, the United States and the new Republican administration of Warren G. Harding. Herbert Hoover—the man who had fed Belgium's wartime refugees, had overseen America's food supply for Woodrow Wilson, and was now feeding postwar Germany and Europe as head of the American Relief Administration—directed millions of tons of food from U.S. farmers to Russia, and saved Lenin's regime from collapse. The system Lenin most despised, American capitalism, had rescued the system he had created to stamp it out, Soviet communism. The irony was lost on him, and probably also on Hoover (who would be the American president in less than half a decade), but it should not be lost on anyone else.

A desperate Lenin also turned to Germany. "Yes, learn from the Germans!" he wrote in one of his final publications, *On Left Infantilism and the Petty Bourgeois Spirit*.[6] He had in mind "the state capitalism of the Germans," their version of war communism that the generals had imposed in 1917. Ludendorff had saved Lenin once, by sending him to Russia to stir up revolution. Lenin hoped he could save him again by providing a model for how to organize a command economy. He even called himself and Ludendorff "two separate halves of socialism, side by side." He began bringing German industrial experts to Russia, and at Rapallo in 1922, the pariah nations of Europe, Russia and Germany, signed a nonaggression pact. It was the start of a diplomatic path that would lead ultimately to the Nazi-Soviet Nonaggression Pact.

The reality of communism's failure, however, and the tactical retreat to NEP reinforced Lenin's growing emotional outbursts at friends and colleagues alike, and fed the problems stemming from his declining health. Doctors worked around the clock to figure out why Lenin seemed more and more exhausted, and why he kept developing illnesses that took him out of action for days, even weeks at a time. Some blamed the toxic effect of Fannie Kaplan's bullet, still imbedded in his neck, which they had considered too dangerous to remove. Others feared the possibility that he might be suffering from tertiary syphilis, although the surviving medical evidence is sketchy and incomplete, probably deliberately so. Others chalked up his health problems to a lifetime of overwork, with a poor diet and inadequate rest.

A more plausible explanation is that Lenin suffered from the same disease as Woodrow Wilson: arterial sclerosis. Lenin's father had died of it in 1886; other members of his family suffered from it, including his sister Anna, who would die of a stroke in 1935.[7]

That spring, however, the doctors opted for the bullet theory, and on April 23, 1922, they performed an operation to remove the foreign body from his neck. They pronounced the operation a success; Lenin told them he felt no pain there for the first time in years. Then, a month later, while he was still recuperating from the operation at his retreat in Gorky, came the stroke, which not only paralyzed his right side but also made him unable to speak.

Recovery would be slow, and in the meantime, the man who would increasingly take charge during Lenin's convalescence would be Joseph Stalin.

That April 4, at the Eleventh Party Congress, Lenin had ceded to his loyal Georgian lieutenant the prize position of general secretary of the Communist Party, with Vyacheslav Molotov and Nikita Khrushchev as Stalin's deputies—the first time that unsavory pair entered into the mainstream of history. Yet the qualities Lenin had most liked in Stalin began to pall on the stricken leader. Lenin began to complain about Stalin's steady accretion of power, which included moving his obedient cronies such as Molotov, Khrushchev, Sergey Kirov, and Lazar Kaganovich into more and more key posts in the regime. But Lenin's own range of motion was diminishing, owing not only to his stroke but also to the fact that, in December 1922, Stalin took personal control of Lenin's recovery, in effect turning him into a prisoner in his own home.

Those who saw Lenin at the Fourth Congress of the Comintern on November 13 were stunned at his appearance. He was now able to walk with assistance, but after a brief speech, "he was completely wet from exhaustion, his shirt was drenched and there were beads of sweat on his forehead."[8] Even Lenin sensed that the end might be near, as Stalin's behavior toward him and Nadya became less and less respectful—at one point, the new general secretary even threatened Lenin's wife with a Cheka investigation for allegedly working for Lenin behind Stalin's back. If another stroke did not bring him down, Lenin was beginning to realize, his once loyal lieutenant might.

The day before Christmas, December 24, 1922, Lenin began dictating his last will and political testament. It is a sobering document. What comes out is not just his growing disillusionment with Stalin as a possible successor, but his dissatisfaction with everyone who would come after Stalin, and everything that he, Lenin, had left behind. He considered Trotsky "the most capable person in the present Central Committee," but "over-preoccupied with the administrative side of things," Lenin's term for the ongoing repression around Russia. Stalin, he felt, had accumulated too much power, "unlimited power," in fact, and "I am not convinced that he will always manage to use this power with sufficient care."

He pondered whether the creation of the Union of Soviet Socialist Republics, which would incorporate Communist-controlled but non-Russian soviet republics such as Georgia and Azerbaijan, was really a good idea. He expressed sorrow that his own Russian ethnic chauvinism had led him to denigrate the possibility of incorporating more non-Russians into the party and giving more freedom to their local soviets—a surprising admission from the man who had preached international revolution all his life.

He also wrote a sentence that began, "I am, it seems, immensely guilty before the workers of Russia"—guilty not of the deaths and massacres and poverty his regime had precipitated, which he largely ignored, but of a badly conceived USSR.[9] About the human costs of his great revolution, Lenin had nothing to say. If his political testament really is, as his biographer Robert Service writes, Lenin's "baring of his soul," it's not hard to conclude that his soul was, to borrow a line of Emily Dickinson's, "Zero at the Bone."

Yet it was Stalin who was most on Lenin's mind. On January 4, Lenin dictated a supplementary paragraph that began, "Stalin is too crude, and this defect which is entirely acceptable in our milieu and in relationships among us as communists, becomes unacceptable in a General Secretary. I therefore propose to comrades that they should devise a means of removing him from this job."[10]

Lenin hoped to be strong enough to read his testament aloud at the Twelfth Party Congress at the end of March, but on March 10 another massive stroke intervened. This one left him almost totally paralyzed and unable to speak; it was two months before his doctors thought it safe even to move him back to Gorky. All the same, the loyal Nadya passed the document on to the party leaders, who did their best to bury it, despite her insistence that delegates to the Congress be allowed to read it.

By then, Lenin's wishes no longer mattered. Trotsky and Stalin were locked in a life-or-death struggle for control of the Soviet Union; neither one wanted any reference to Lenin's political testament to leak out, and both could now safely ignore the stricken architect of the Russian Revolution. Over the next ten months, Lenin was racked by more ministrokes and seizures, more than seven between November and December 1923 alone.[11]

Then, on January 21, 1924, came the last one, as at 6:30 p.m. Lenin breathed his last. The funeral in Moscow was set for January 27, which turned out to be the coldest day of the year. A month later, doctors began the gruesome process of preparing the body—not for burial but for permanent embalmment. Stalin had decided that Lenin should be transformed forever into a mummy on display, a frozen monument to the revolutionary system that he had built and that Stalin, acting as his heir, would lead.

*   *   *

EIGHT DAYS AFTER Lenin's funeral, on February 4, Woodrow Wilson also died of a stroke, in his town house in Kalorama, in Washington, DC, where he had moved after leaving the White House. As with Lenin, his last years had been almost completely a time of convalescence, with only brief public appearances—his final one in 1923, on the anniversary of the armistice. He, too, had published a political last testament, "The Road Away from Revolution," which ran in the *Atlantic Monthly* in August 1923. It had required months of painful effort to compose at his once reliable typewriter, which no longer seemed to respond to the command of his fingers, or in almost illegible scribbles in pencil, which the ever-faithful Edith transcribed.

The most fascinating passage identified Lenin's Russian Revolution as "the outstanding event of its kind in our age."

What gave rise to the Russian Revolution? The answer can only be that it was the product of a whole social system. It was not in fact a sudden thing. It had been gathering head for several generations. It was due to the systematic denial to the great body of Russians of the rights and privileges which all normal men desire and must have if they are to be contented and within reach of happiness. The lives of the great mass of the Russian people contained no opportunities, but were hemmed in by barriers against which they were constantly flinging their spirits, only to fall back bruised and dispirited. Only the powerful were suffered to secure their rights or even to gain access to the means of material success.

In the end, Wilson blamed capitalism for the revolution. The inequities capitalism had unleashed in Russia had caused Russians "to see red," as he put it—perhaps forgetting his own role in denying Russians the means to resist the Bolshevik juggernaut. Indeed, he blamed most of the ills in the modern world on what he saw as unbridled capitalism, but also ended by saying, "[O]ur civilization cannot survive materially until it be redeemed spiritually."[12]

It was a strange admission from the man who had labored so hard, as Lenin had, to change the world through politics, and whose devotion to bringing about a new global order had ended, as Lenin's had, only in leaving behind a nation in far worse shape than it was when he took power. The day he had returned to Washington from Paris in July 1919, race riots in the nation's capital left fifteen dead. In Chicago, similar riots left thirty-eight dead. That summer, twenty-five American cities saw the worst race violence since the Civil War.[13]

At almost the same time, the country was also in the grip of the Red Scare, led by former Progressive labor lawyer and attorney general A. Mitchell Palmer and triggered by a series of terrorist bombings that were blamed on Bolshevik agitation. This led to the worst police repression the United States had seen in its history. On one day, January 2, 1920, police and federal officials rounded up three thousand foreign-born leftists in thirty-three cities. Deportations became America's way of dealing with radical political dissent, and groups such as the IWW found themselves renewed targets of mobs and the police.

The violence and hysteria of the Red Scare compounded an economic depression started by Wilson's Federal Reserve, as it sharply raised interest rates at the war's end to tamp down fears of postwar inflation. "The deflationary impact was drastic," writes economic historian Adam Tooze. "[T]he abrupt tightening of credit tipped the American economy over the cliff."[14] By January 1921, as Warren Harding was preparing to enter the White House, industrial unemployment was estimated at 20 percent. American agriculture was hit by a crisis from which it would not recover for the rest of the century, even after the New Deal's efforts at price supports and government-mandated cuts in farm production.[15] Inflation, followed by deflation and depression, also helped to fuel the revival of extremist groups such as the Ku Klux Klan in the Deep South and the Farm Belt, and created industrial unrest elsewhere, including a strike against U.S. Steel that left twenty dead.

In short, all that Wilson's Progressivism had promised—racial harmony, better pay and a higher standard of living for the average worker and the little guy, a booming but more just economy carefully micromanaged by the experts at the Federal Reserve, and staying out of war—had turned out to be lies. It would take two Republican administrations, under Warren Harding and Calvin Coolidge, to turn America around. By the time Wilson died six months into Coolidge's presidency, his legacy was a wreck. He was a man forsaken by his party and his country.

As for his rival Henry Cabot Lodge, he died of a stroke nine months after Wilson's death, on November 5, 1924. He would be remembered forever as the man who kept the United States out of the League of Nations—when in fact it was Wilson who had made America's entry into the League impossible.

Lenin's rival Alexander Kerensky would live on until June 1970, in the United States. When he died in New York City, Russian Orthodox churches refused to bury him because he had allowed Bolshevism to come to power in 1917—when in fact he had been the last hope for keeping Russia on the road to democracy. Before Kerensky died, a British television interviewer asked him why he never had Lenin arrested or even killed. Kerensky could only answer quietly, "Because I never took him seriously."[16]

Leon Trotsky would be hounded into exile by his rival Stalin in 1928. He would spend the rest of his life trying to raise international awareness of the crimes Joseph Stalin was committing against the Russian people—crimes Trotsky himself would almost certainly have committed if he had won the power struggle after Lenin's death. Twice he managed to escape assassination attempts by Stalin's agents. Then, on August 20, 1940, an assassin found him in Mexico City and murdered him with a blow to the head with an ice pick. More than any other single person, Trotsky had brought the Bolshevik Revolution into reality—without him, Lenin would very likely have lost the Russian Civil War. Trotsky's modest memorial in Mexico City is probably a more appropriate pilgrimage site for anyone still admiring the Bolshevik Revolution than Lenin's grandiose tomb in Moscow's Red Square.

Lenin's other savior, Erich Ludendorff, died of liver cancer on December 20, 1937. Adolf Hitler, Germany's then-chancellor, who had been Ludendorff's protégé in the 1920s, gave him an elaborate state funeral, something Ludendorff had specifically requested not happen. By 1933, Ludendorff had turned against Hitler. On the day Hitler took office as chancellor, Ludendorff sent a telegram to his old commander in chief, field marshal, and now president Hindenburg, warning him, "I solemnly prophesy that this accursed man will cast our Reich into the abyss and bring our nation to inconceivable misery."[17] Thus, the man who had made so many wrong judgments regarding his country—resuming unrestricted submarine warfare in February 1917, launching the final disastrous offensive in March 1918, not to mention letting Lenin and his Bolsheviks return to Russia—finally got one right, but too late to prevent his prediction from coming true.

Theobald von Bethmann-Hollweg died in Switzerland on New Year's Day 1921, a broken man whose only son had been killed in the war that he, more than any other single person, had allowed to happen. Arthur Zimmermann, author of the infamous telegram that finally pushed America into the war, and who authorized Lenin's journey across German territory to the Finland Station, died on June 6, 1940, just as Germany was poised to win the war against France that it had failed to win in 1914.

That war of 1940 would be the undoing of the man who emerged as a national hero of the first one, Marshal Philippe Pétain. Having served as president of the puppet Vichy government following France's catastrophic defeat, he would be sentenced to death after France's liberation in 1945. President Charles de Gaulle commuted the death sentence and allowed Pétain to sit out the rest of his sentence in a prison on the Île d'Yeu, in the Mediterranean, where the man who had saved the French army from collapse in 1917 finally died in July 1951, at age ninety-five.

David Lloyd George lived on to serve his country in the Second World War, before his death on March 26, 1945, on the eve of final victory. As the senior statesman of his Liberal Party in the House of Commons, he gave a pivotal speech that doomed Neville Chamberlain's government in the aftermath of the Norwegian campaign and enabled his lifelong friend Winston Churchill to become prime minister in May 1940.*

By the time Churchill, Franklin Roosevelt, and Joseph Stalin, men who all got their start on the world stage in 1917, assumed their roles as supreme leaders in the next world war, Woodrow Wilson and Lenin had passed into historical memory, if anyone thought of them at all. But the Big Three were actually only dealing with the legacy Wilson and Lenin had left them starting that fateful year—and the new world disorder they had set in motion.

* * *

* As for Nigel de Grey, the man who started it all by decoding the Zimmermann telegram, he never returned to publishing. He stayed on with Naval Intelligence after the Great War, and worked in the deciphering headquarters at Bletchley Park in the next world war. In September 1941, he presented Winston Churchill with some of the first evidence of Hitler's Holocaust from intercepted German radio messages. De Grey died on May 25, 1951, struck down by a sudden heart attack in the middle of Oxford Street in London.

SO, WHO WERE these two extraordinary men, Lenin and Wilson? And what was their legacy?

Both men were visionaries, certainly; utopians, clearly. Both foresaw the need to change the world for the better, by sweeping away everything that seemed to root the present in a corrupt and irredeemable past. Each set his eyes on a bright new future of mankind—two very different futures in many ways, but futures that shared many characteristics.

Both were admirers of the German philosopher Georg Wilhelm Friedrich Hegel, who taught them (in Lenin's case, via his primary intellectual influence, Karl Marx) that all history has an end point, a culmination in human perfection toward which all great thinkers and reformers and other world-historical figures consciously or unconsciously direct their energies to realizing. Indeed, Wilson and Lenin both convinced themselves that making this perfection one's conscious goal ipso facto turned one into a world-historical figure. In their minds, the sacrifices they demanded of themselves, their wives and families, and their fellow human beings, sometimes truly horrific sacrifices, were all worth the final goal: the equivalent of paradise on earth.

And if single-minded determination, inner discipline, and the sheer resolve to bend people and events to one's will are proof that one is prepared to assume that momentous role, then what Lenin and Wilson did in their lifetimes is nothing less than awe inspiring. They stand as living proof of Marshal Ferdinand Foch's words "The most powerful weapon on earth is the human soul on fire."

They were also in their own ways both secular millennialists. They saw the world and mankind around them as fallen, but they believed there was a final, destined golden age of redemption coming—not through a Second Coming of Christ, as conventional Christian millennialists have believed, but through a Final Coming of History, a great convergence of global fire into a single, coherent whole.

Their total commitment to these beliefs certainly made them both self-righteous, usually infuriatingly so. Yet there were also important defferences. Lenin's background and experience made him a more brutal man than Wilson; he was capable of overseeing acts of violence that Wilson would have been horrified to contemplate, let alone commit. Lenin's correspondence is full of references to machine guns, bombs, and shooting and killing opponents; Wilson's is not.[18]

At the same time, both men dismissed those who opposed them as not just wrongheaded or misguided but evil. They could be unbelievably vindictive toward those who they thought were thwarting or betraying them or blocking the path to their chosen paradise on earth. And both could be cunning and unscrupulous when they believed the ends justified the means, as when Lenin happily cooperated with the German government to get himself installed in Russia, and when Wilson was willing to compromise one after another of his Fourteen Points in order to get his League of Nations.

Finally, both were revolutionaries, men who dedicated themselves to overthrowing an existing world system in order to build a new and, in their minds, more perfect system. By and large, they succeeded in overthrowing those old systems, although what they created instead in their lifetimes turned out to be unqualified disasters.

Yet it would be a mistake to see either of them as an unqualified failure. Starting in 1917, Lenin and Wilson left important, lasting achievements, for better *and* for worse, that would shape the next century and beyond and that still animate much of what happens today.

Lenin's achievement actually seems easier to summarize. He left behind the Communist Soviet Union, the single most comprehensively destructive and tyrannical system in human history— destructive not only to those living inside the Soviet Union for the next seventy years, but to those who had the misfortune to live in countries whose leaders were inspired by Lenin's system and by his personal example. Those would come to include Mao Zedong's China, Ho Chi Minh's Vietnam, Kim Il Sung's North Korea, Fidel Castro's Cuba, Daniel Ortega's Nicaragua, and Hugo Chávez's Venezuela, not to mention the countries of eastern and central Europe that were forced to become Soviet satellites after World War II and that had to endure Soviet-style economies, armed forces, and police states until the entire Soviet Empire collapsed in 1989. Lenin's artifact, the Soviet Union itself, died much as it had been born, in a violent coup d'état in the Russian capital in 1992, with Mikhail Gorbachev playing the role of Alexander Kerensky—except that, in this case, Kerensky won. As for the total body count of Lenin's Communist legacy, the best round estimate is one hundred million people.[19]

Lenin's legacy extends beyond the history of communism, however. It was Lenin who made the terms *terror* and *terrorism* part of the global political vocabulary, and who made imposing terror on innocent civilian populations by both official and unofficial means (the thrown hand grenade, the targeted assassination, the taking of hostages, the murder of family members, the car bomb, and the suicide vest) part of the normal revolutionary repertoire. Stalin would use terror to subjugate entire populations (including those of eastern Europe); Mao would do the same in China and Tibet. Both would pass the practice along to others—in Mao's case, to Communist terrorist groups across Asia in the 1950s and '60s; in Stalin's case, and that of his successors, to terrorist groups in the Middle East.[20]

Today's Al Qaeda and ISIS killers are as much Lenin's heirs as Stalin's, Mao's, or Castro's. Their goals are also very similar: the destruction of the existing order, with the aim of imposing a new order—in the case of Al Qaeda and ISIS, one inspired by the Koran and Sharia law rather than by *The Communist Manifesto*, even though, in its broadest outlines, it sometimes doesn't seem so different.

For Lenin, then, a global legacy of permanent violent revolutions and terror.

For Wilson, the legacy looks more complex, but one single, ineluctable fact emerges from what he started in 1917: U.S. global hegemony, right up until today.

Historians and others sometimes like to date the arrival of that U.S. hegemony, of the United States as superpower, as the end of World War II. This is a well-worn misperception and myth. Memoirs such as Dean Acheson's *Present at the Creation*, meaning the creation of the U.S.-led liberal international order that supposedly dominated and stabilized the world after 1945, have compounded that myth. If anything, Acheson, Truman, George Marshall, and the others were latecomers to the feast. It was America's entry into the *First* World War, not the Second, that signaled the arrival of the United States as the single most powerful nation on earth, and that restructured the world system around a new centrifuge of global power.

Compared with its economic and financial dominance, America's military and strategic power was a lesser contribution to that hegemony, at least at first. Although Wilson and Pershing wound up adding nearly two million American soldiers to the military balance on the Western Front, virtually none of them remained in Europe by 1923. Nor is it the case that U.S. membership in the League of Nations could have prevented war in Europe, any more than it could have prevented war in Asia. The United States' distance from Europe ensured that it would exercise almost no direct influence on the tumultuous events that would engulf the Continent over the next two decades, from the rise of Mussolini and Hitler to the outbreak of the next war in 1939, League or no League. If anything, the Soviet Union, for more than two decades after the 1917 revolution a pariah state and also not a member of the League, had a far more decisive impact. For instance, Hitler could not have fought a war against Britain and France if he had not signed a nonaggression pact with Stalin two weeks before he invaded Poland.[21]

Nor were the interwar years a complete waste, as far as the United States was concerned. Contrary to later myth, "American diplomacy was ceaselessly active in European questions" in the Republican 1920s.[22] It was the 1930s of Franklin Roosevelt and the Democrats, who were embarrassed and horrified by Wilson's legacy, that finally firmly shut the door on Europe. By 1933, the issue of reparations was dead. All the former Allies except Finland had defaulted on their debt to the United States, and the United States let it happen. (Also by then, Germany's new chancellor, Adolf Hitler, had made it clear he would not be paying reparations to anybody, treaty or no treaty.)

All the same, by that date the leadership of America in the world financial system, which Woodrow Wilson had made possible and on which the entry into the First World War had put the final seal, was now evident to all, and was permanent. After the 1920 depression, the American industrial economy and trade with the United States had become the sustaining engine of world growth, even in the darkest days of the Great Depression of 1930–32. No country could ever again rise to prominence by ignoring or snubbing American financial interests, or without calculating the United States' economic clout—not even the Soviet Union, whose own rebirth as an industrial economy under Stalin was made possible only by American engineers and business interests, from the United States' iron and steel industry to its mining, oil, and natural gas to its railroads and hydroelectric power grid.

Adolf Hitler realized this, too. After coming to power in 1933, he launched himself in a race to dominate Europe before he believed the United States would—a race he lost during World War Two. It was, in fact, a competition he had no hope of winning, once America's vast economic resources were mobilized for all-out war.[23]

Because it was not until World War II that the military and strategic components of American hegemony came back into line with a world economic order built since 1917 around the United States. In 1945, American troops and naval fleets did not go home; this time they stayed in Europe to meet a new threat, a Soviet Union transformed by war from pariah nation into an economic and strategic superpower; and they stayed in Asia long enough to blunt a Communist push to turn victory in China into a sweep through the Korea Peninsula and then into Indochina and Southeast Asia.

The Soviet Union that dominated and commanded the Communist world in 1945, much as the United States dominated (though it never commanded) the capitalist free world, was, at first glance, a far cry from the one Lenin left when he died in 1924. That Russia had been a bankrupt and virtually failing state, an international outcast unrecognized by no nation except its fellow outcast, Germany, and the hub of an international Communist conspiracy that was as ineffectual as it was despised. In 1945, it was the world's second-largest economy with the world's biggest army and, in terms of sacrifice and gain, the key victor of World War II—and four years later, the world's only nuclear power after the United States. It enjoyed power and reach in Europe and Asia that the czars had only dreamed about, and international communism was becoming an empirical reality, significantly in the most populous nation on earth, China.

Yet this Soviet Union was still very much Lenin's. Much of its vaunted international eminence was transient and illusory, and the result of the complete destruction of its twin nemeses, Nazi Germany and Imperial Japan. It was a brutal police state run by the same narrow and narrow-minded elite who were corrupted but also paralyzed by total power and terrified by any hint of dissent or opposition. It was still an economic basket case, barely able to feed itself, whose relations with its neighbors were characterized by intimidation and terror. In many ways, it's the same Russia that persists today.

Since the Soviet Union now possessed nuclear weapons, however, it was assumed to be a superpower as well. In retrospect, it seems easy to predict who would ultimately win the Cold War. It was much harder for those who lived it to know what the final outcome would be. In the end, of course, after decades of bitter conflict, Wilson's America prevailed over Lenin's Soviet Union. By every measure, that was a better outcome for the world and for the global future. Yet, now, more than twenty years after the end of the Cold War, the same uncertainties that were seen in 1917 and at the dawn of the Cold War have returned. The new world disorder isn't going away anytime soon.

This is because today the United States' status as the dominant global power, Wilson's most lasting legacy, seems threatened once more. Both Russia and China loom large as challengers, on the economic as well as the military and strategic plane; never before, not even in the bleakest days of the Cold War, has the United States' position as leader of the international order been threatened by two powerful rivals at once. There are fierce calls to "make America great again." Whatever the merits of that case, the fact is that the need to build a new, more durable order out of the outmoded old American hegemony has never been greater.

That makes learning the lessons of Wilsonism from one hundred years ago more urgent than ever.

Wilson's initial and biggest mistake may not have been entering the Great War in the first place, as some neo-isolationists like to argue.[24] Rather, his mistake may have been entering it *too late*—when the balance of power had already shifted disastrously against the Entente. If Wilson had entered when Theodore Roosevelt and Henry Cabot Lodge wanted, for example, after the sinking of the *Lusitania* in 1915, instead of in 1917, the war might have ended much earlier and many millions might not have died—and Russia might have had breathing room to carry out the reforms it needed to emerge as a modern democratic nation.

Or, alternatively, if Wilson had used America's financial leverage over Britain and France in January 1917 to force them to the bargaining table instead of scolding them about the need for "peace without victory," he could have achieved much the same result—and not one but two depressions, in 1920 and in 1929–32, could have been avoided.

Still, either option would have demanded that the United States act like a Great Power instead of as a shining light and beacon of humanity, as Wilson wanted. By seeing the world through a utopian lens, one that reflected the world as he wanted it to be instead of as it actually was, Wilson missed more than one historic opportunity, with tragic results—as does every president who makes the same mistake.

Wilson's second blunder was his approach to the issue of the League of Nations—not the concept itself but the existential weight he assigned to it, and to virtually every international agreement he put his name to. He would have been better off listening to Theodore Roosevelt: "I regard the Wilson-Bryan attitude of trusting to fantastic peace treaties, to impossible promises, to all kinds of scraps of paper without any backing in efficient force, as abhorrent." He added,

"A milk-and-water righteousness unbacked by force is to the full as wicked as and even more mischievous than force divorced from righteousness."[25] It's hard to find a better formulation of both Wilson's *and* Lenin's approach to political power.

Roosevelt's friend Henry Cabot Lodge was no enemy of setting up a League of Nations to adjudicate disputes among nations. But he lacked Wilson's fascination with vague commitments and high-minded promises. Instead, Lodge saw an international organization arising from America's wartime alliance with Britain and France, one backed by the American public and by its members' willingness to use military force.[26] It was in fact a vision much closer to France's and Clemenceau's, and it would finally take on flesh and bones with the creation of NATO in 1947—after the world had learned the folly of relying on Wilson's version alone. Over the four decades of the Cold War, it was NATO—not the League's direct heir, the United Nations—that deterred Lenin's legacy of "force divorced from righteousness," and that has kept the peace in Europe until today.

As we've seen, some still blamed the failure of the League, and the disasters of the 1930s, on the United States' failure to join in. Just the opposite is the case. By staying out, the United States paradoxically preserved its role as pure and unsullied global arbiter, much as Wilson would have wished. It was ready to step in as deus ex machina when chaos and tyranny threatened in 1941, and could impose its role as global umpire once again, both in Europe and in Asia this time, when the war was over in 1945.

America learned its lesson after 1945, in the era of the Cold War. It needs to learn it again now, in the era of Vladimir Putin and an aggressive militarized China. The leaders of Russia and China are heirs to Lenin's legacy, who wish to reap the whirlwind of today's global disorder. By disengaging globally, America succeeds only in setting the conditions for the next round of global chaos, and we end up intervening when the stakes are much higher and the forces we confront much deadlier. This is not an argument, however, for acting as "globocop." It is an argument for updating Woodrow Wilson's fundamental legacy with a strong dose of realpolitik of the kind Theodore Roosevelt and Henry Cabot Lodge could have brought if Wilson had been ideologically and temperamentally capable of sharing with others his vision of America's global future.

For the goal of America's relations with others in war and peace is still Woodrow Wilson's: that the mantle of American exceptionalism should serve as the shelter from the storm that Lenin's disciples constantly unleash. That's why, today, Wilson's legacy still is relevant. As Henry Kissinger once wrote, from World War II to the Cold War to the war on terror and beyond, America is still wedded to the role that "Wilson had envisioned for it, as a beacon to follow, and a hope to attain."[27]

It's one an American president ignores at everyone's peril.

ACKNOWLEDGMENTS

THIS BOOK HAS its distant origin in memories of listening to a conversation between Alexander Kerensky and my father in the shadow of Hoover Tower at Stanford University. Who could have imagined that it would take more than fifty years to see that conversation to its completion here in these pages?

My thanks go as always to the staff of Alderman Library at the University of Virginia, but also to the staffs of the Library of Congress; the Woodrow Wilson Presidential Library in Staunton, Virginia; the Hoover Institution at Stanford University; and the Massachusetts State Historical Society.

My Hudson Institute colleagues Chris DeMuth and Scooter Libby, and Alex Pollock of R Street, listened while I described the parameters and themes of the book; their advice and counsel contributed greatly to the final result. My research assistant Idalia Friedson helped to organize and prepare the final version of the footnotes, as did Mark Ashby and Gabriel Davis. And thanks also go to the anonymous intern who tracked down the ever-important but ever-elusive Volume 42 of the *Papers of Woodrow Wilson* at George Washington University.

My gratitude also goes to my agents, Keith Urbahn and Matt Lattimer, of Javelin DC, who embraced the project from the beginning and enthusiastically cheered it on from start to finish. Conversations with my editor at HarperCollins, Eric Nelson, helped to give the book its final shape, and thanks go to him and to his assistant editor, Eric Meyers, for seeing the text through to completion.

Above all, my gratitude goes out to my wonderful wife, Beth, for her advice, support, and patience with a husband who found himself with two full-time jobs—one as Senior Fellow at the Hudson Institute and the other as an author writing a book that devoured many weekends, evenings, and early mornings. This book is gratefully dedicated to her, because without her it could never have been written.

NOTES

PROLOGUE: A WORLD ON FIRE

1. Barbara Tuchman, *The Zimmermann Telegram* (New York: Random House, 1985), 5.
2. Thomas Boghardt, *The Zimmermann Telegram: Intelligence, Diplomacy, and America's Entry into World War I* (Annapolis, MD: Naval Institute Press, 2012), 80–81.
3. "Wilson's First Lusitania Note to Germany," World War I Document Archive, Brigham Young University Library, Provo, UT, last modified June 30, 2009, https://wwi.lib.byu.edu/index.php/Wilson's_First_Lusitania_Note_to_Germany.
4. Arthur Herman, *To Rule the Waves: How the British Navy Shaped the Modern World* (New York: Harper Perennial, 2005), 511.
5. Helen Rappaport, *Conspirator: Lenin in Exile* (New York: Basic Books, 2010), 271–72.
6. V. I. Lenin, *Collected Works* (Moscow: Progress Publishers, 1960), 23:253.
7. Rappaport, *Conspirator: Lenin in Exile*, 280.

PREFACE

1. Arno Mayer, *Wilson vs. Lenin: Political Origins of the New Diplomacy 1917–1918* (New York: Meridian, 1964).
2. "Bismarck's Morality," in A. J. P. Taylor, ed., *Napoleon to Lenin* (New York: Harper & Row, 1966), 85.
3. Quoted in Arnold Wolpers, *Discord and Collaboration* (Baltimore, MD: Johns Hopkins University Press, 1962), 86.

CHAPTER I. THE GERMAN NOTE

1. A. J. P. Taylor, *The First World War: An Illustrated History* (London: Penguin, 2009), 78.
2. Konrad Jarausch, *Out of Ashes: A New History of Europe in the Twentieth Century* (Princeton, NJ: Princeton University Press, 2016), 249.
3. Gerhard Ritter, *The Sword and the Scepter: The Problem of Militarism in Germany* (Coral Gables, FL: University of Miami Press, 1973), 3:246.
4. Taylor, *The First World War*, 96.

5. Ibid., 28–29; Herman, *To Rule the Waves*, 510–11.

6. Adam Tooze, *The Deluge: The Great War, America, and the Remaking of the Global Order, 1916–1931* (London: Penguin, 2014), 37–38.

7. Jarausch, *Out of Ashes*, 289.

8. "Extract from the Speech of Chancellor von Bethmann-Hollweg in the German Reichstag, December 12, 1916," World War I Document Archive, Brigham Young University Library, last modified January 16, 2016, https://wwi.lib.byu.edu/index .php/Extract_from_the_Speech_of_Chancellor_von_Bethmann-Hollweg_in_ the_German_Reichstag,_December_12,_1916.

9. "Peace Note of Germany and Her Allies, December 12, 1916," World War I Document Archive, Brigham Young University Library, last modified January 16, 2016, https://wwi.lib.byu.edu/index.php/Peace_Note_of_Germany_and_Her_Allies,_ December_12,_1916.

10. Taylor, *The First World War*, 98–99.

11. Ibid., 40.

12. John Grigg, *Lloyd George: War Leader 1916–1918* (London: Faber and Faber, 2013), 19.

13. A. J. P. Taylor, *The First World War*, 5.

14. Ibid., 98.

15. Tooze, *The Deluge*, 37.

16. Ibid., 441.

17. Taylor, *Lloyd George: Rise and Fall*, 77.

CHAPTER 2. RUSSIA AND AMERICA CONFRONT A WORLD WAR

1. Alexander Kerensky, *The Crucifixion of Liberty* (Hudson, NY: Periodicals Service Company, 1934), 233.

2. Richard Pipes, *The Russian Revolution* (New York: Vintage, 1991), 191.

3. Ibid., 192.

4. Paul Johnson, *Modern Times: The World from the Twenties to the Nineties* (New York: Harper Perennial Modern Classics, 2001), 14–15.

5. Pipes, *The Russian Revolution*, 216.

6. Norman Stone, *The Eastern Front 1914–17* (London: Penguin, 2008), 134.

7. Nicholas Werth, "Paradoxes and Misunderstandings Surrounding the October Revolution," in Jean-Louis Panne, *The Black Book of Communism: Crimes, Terror, Repression* (Cambridge, MA: Harvard University Press, 1999), 43.

8. Pipes, *The Russian Revolution*, 210–11.

9. Ibid., 224.

10. Bernard Pares, *A History of Russia* (London: Marlboro Books, 1991), 482.

11. Pipes, *The Russian Revolution*, 228.

12. "Speech of Nicolas Pokrovsky, Russian Minister for Foreign Affairs, in the Duma, December 15, 1916," in James Brown Scott, ed., *Official Statements of War Aims and Peace Proposals: December 1916 to November 1918* (Getzville, NY: W.S. Hein, 1921), 9.

13. Ibid., 11.

14. "Durnovo Memorandum," in Pipes, *The Russian Revolution*, 211.

15. Robert Service, *Lenin: A Biography* (Cambridge, MA: Harvard University Press, 2000), 229, 235.

16. Arthur Link, ed., *The Papers of Woodrow Wilson* (Princeton, NJ: Princeton University Press, 1966), 1 (1856–1890): 3–4, 31.

17. "October 3, 1914," in Elting E. Morison, ed., *Letters of Theodore Roosevelt* (Cambridge, MA: Harvard University Press, 1951), 821.

18. "TR to HCL, June 15, 1915," in Theodore Roosevelt and Henry Cabot Lodge, *Selections from the Correspondence of Theodore Roosevelt and Henry Cabot Lodge, 1884–1918* (New York: Scribner's, 1925), 459.

19. "TR to Hugo Munsterberg, October 3, 1914," in Morison, ed., *Letters of Theodore Roosevelt*, Vol. 8, 322–23, and "TR to Rudyard Kipling, November 4, 1914," Ibid., 829–30.

20. "McAdoo to Wilson, August 21, 1915," in Link, ed., *The Papers of Woodrow Wilson*, 34: 275.

21. Link, *The Papers of Woodrow Wilson*, 30: 248–55.

22. Woodrow Wilson, *The Public Papers of Woodrow Wilson*, ed. Ray Stannard Baker and William E. Dodd (New York: Harper and Brothers, 1925–1927), 1: 224–25.

23. Link, *The Papers of Woodrow Wilson*, 32: 41.

24. Quoted in Tooze, *The Deluge*, 45.

25. Link, *The Papers of Woodrow Wilson*, 33: 134.

26. "President Wilson's Peace Note, December 18, 1916," World War I Document Archive, Brigham Young University Library, last modified January 19, 2016, https://wwi.lib.byu.edu/index.php/President_Wilson%27s_Peace_Note,_December_18,_1916.

27. Tooze, *The Deluge*, 52.

28. Ibid., 51.

29. Woodrow Wilson speech to Congress, January 22, 1917, in Link, *The Papers of Woodrow Wilson*, 41: 29.

30. Richard Striner, *Woodrow Wilson and World War I: A Burden Too Great to Bear* (Lanham, MD: Rowman and Littlefield Publishers, 2014), 94.

31. Morison, *Letters of Theodore Roosevelt*, 1162–63.

32. Striner, *Woodrow Wilson and World War I*, 94.

33. John Garraty, *Henry Cabot Lodge: A Biography* (New York: Alfred A. Knopf, 1953), 332.

34. Link, *The Papers of Woodrow Wilson*, 34: 41. Emphasis mine.

35. Tooze, *The Deluge*, 57.

36. Link, *The Papers of Woodrow Wilson*, 41: 51–52.

37. Tooze, *The Deluge*, 55.

38. V. I. Lenin, *Imperialism, the Highest Stage of Capitalism: A Popular Outline* (New York: International Publishers, 1969), 10–11.

39. Ibid., 86–87, 91.

CHAPTER 3. TOMMY AND VOLODYA

1. H. W. Brands, *Woodrow Wilson*, ed. Arthur M. Schlesinger Jr. (New York: Times Books, 2003).

2. Robert Conquest, *V. I. Lenin* (New York: Viking Press, 1972), 51.

3. Brands, *Woodrow Wilson*, 17.

4. Conquest, *V. I. Lenin*, 21.

5. Sigmund Freud and William C. Bullitt, *Woodrow Wilson: A Psychological Study* (Piscataway, NJ: Transaction Publishers, 1998).

6. Link, *The Papers of Woodrow Wilson*, 58: 270–71.

7. Striner, *Woodrow Wilson and World War I*, 10.

8. Link, *The Papers of Woodrow Wilson*, 41: 120.

9. August Heckscher II, *Woodrow Wilson: A Biography* (New York: Scribner's, 1991).

10. Ronald J. Pestritto, *Woodrow Wilson and the Roots of Modern Liberalism* (Lanham, MD: Rowman and Littlefield Publishers, 2005), 13.

11. Ibid., 13; Brands, *Woodrow Wilson*, 11.

12. Conquest, *V. I. Lenin*, 6.

13. Constantin de Grunwald, *Tsar Nicholas I: The Life of an Absolute Monarch* (New York: Macmillan, 1955), 5.

14. Conquest, *V. I. Lenin*, 13.

15. Service, *Lenin: A Biography*, 54–55.

16. Ibid., 60.

17. Ibid., 77–78.

18. Ibid., 112.

19. Ibid., 126.

20. Conquest, *V. I. Lenin*, 31.

21. V. I. Lenin, *Essential Works of Lenin*, Henry Christman, ed. (Mineola, NY: Dover Publications, 1987), 74, 104, 105, 57.

22. Heckscher, *Woodrow Wilson: A Biography*, 139.

23. W. Barksdale Maynard, *Woodrow Wilson: Princeton to the Presidency* (New Haven, CT: Yale University Press, 2008), 71.

24. Ibid., 66; Heckscher, *Woodrow Wilson: A Biography*, 145.

25. Heckscher, *Woodrow Wilson: A Biography*, 199.

26. Striner, *Woodrow Wilson and World War I*, 194.

27. Pestritto, *Woodrow Wilson and the Roots of Modern Liberalism*, 14–19.

28. Ronald J. Pestritto, *Woodrow Wilson: The Essential Political Writings* (Lanham, MD: Lexington Books, 2005).

29. Brands, *Woodrow Wilson*, 17; "Acceptance Speech, September 15, 1910," in Link, *The Papers of Woodrow Wilson*, 21: 91–94.

30. Heckscher, *Woodrow Wilson: A Biography*, 274.

31. "Inaugural Address, March 4, 1913," Link, *The Papers of Woodrow Wilson*, 27: 151–52.

32. Conquest, *V. I. Lenin*, 55–56.

33. Ibid., 39.

34. Rosa Luxemburg, *Leninism or Marxism* (Ann Arbor: University of Michigan Press, 1961).

35. Conquest, *V. I. Lenin*, 50.

36. Service, *Lenin: A Biography*, 186.

37. Conquest, *V. I. Lenin*, 57.

38. Pipes, *The Russian Revolution*, 237.

39. Conquest, *V. I. Lenin*, 61.

40. Ibid., 64.

41. Service, *Lenin: A Biography*, 228.

42. Conquest, *V. I. Lenin*, 69.

CHAPTER 4. NEUTRALITY AT BAY

1. Admiral von Holtzendorff to Field Marshal von Hindenburg, Memo on Unrestricted Submarine Warfare, December 22, 1916, www.gwda.org/naval/holtzendorffmemo.htm.

2. Jarausch, *Out of Ashes*, 299.

3. Ibid., 300.

4. Ibid., 301; Tuchman, *The Zimmermann Telegram*, 129.

5. Link, *The Papers of Woodrow Wilson*, 34: 41.

6. Striner, *Woodrow Wilson and World War I*, 99.

7. Link, *The Papers of Woodrow Wilson*, 41: 87.

8. Ibid., 41: 108–12; *Congressional Record*, February 3, 1917.

9. "TR to HCL, February 12, 1917," in Roosevelt and Lodge, *Selections from the Correspondence of Theodore Roosevelt and Henry Cabot Lodge, 1884–1918*, 494–95.

10. Tuchman, *The Zimmermann Telegram*, 103.

11. Ibid., 138.

12. "Wednesday, January 31, 1917," in Maurice de Paléologue, *An Ambassador's Memoirs*, Brigham Young University Library, trans. F. A. Holt, O.B.E., http://net.lib.byu.edu/estu/wwi/memoir/FrAmbRus/palTC.htm.

13. Ibid., "Monday, February 5, 1917."

14. Ibid., "Thursday, February 8, 1917."

15. Ibid., "Friday, February 9, 1917."

16. Ibid., "Wednesday, February 21, 1917."

17. Tuchman, *The Zimmermann Telegram*, 145–46.

18. Ibid., 107.

19. Link, *The Papers of Woodrow Wilson*, 41: 280–82.

20. Tuchman, *The Zimmermann Telegram*, 152.

21. Ibid., 156–57.

22. Ibid., 160.

23. "HCL to James Ford Rhodes, March 27, 1917," in Henry Cabot Lodge, *Papers of Henry Cabot Lodge, 1890*, Massachusetts Historical Society.

CHAPTER 5. BREAK POINT

1. Pipes, *The Russian Revolution*, 272.

2. "Tuesday, March 6, 1917," in Paléologue, *An Ambassador's Memoirs*.

3. Ibid.

4. Kerensky, *Crucifixion of Liberty*, 261.

5. Pipes, *The Russian Revolution*, 275.

6. "Saturday, March 10, 1917," in Paléologue, *An Ambassador's Memoirs*.

7. Pipes, *The Russian Revolution*, 276.

8. "Saturday, March 10, 1917," in Paléologue, *An Ambassador's Memoirs*.

9. Pipes, *The Russian Revolution*, 281.

10. "Sunday, March 11, 1917," in Paléologue, *An Ambassador's Memoirs*.

11. Pipes, *The Russian Revolution*, 280.

12. "Monday, March 12, 1917," in Paléologue, *An Ambassador's Memoirs*.

13. Pipes, *The Russian Revolution*, 285.

14. Henry Cabot Lodge, "HCL to Roosevelt, March 2, 1917," in *Papers of Henry Cabot Lodge, 1890*, Massachusetts Historical Society.

15. Tuchman, *The Zimmermann Telegram*, 161.

16. Boghardt, *The Zimmermann Telegram*.

17. Tuchman, *The Zimmermann Telegram*, 163.

18. Ibid., 164.

19. "HCL to TR, March 2, 1917," in Roosevelt and Lodge, *Selections from the Correspondence of Theodore Roosevelt and Henry Cabot Lodge, 1884–1918*, 499–500.

20. Tuchman, *The Zimmermann Telegram*, 164.

21. Boghardt, *The Zimmermann Telegram*, 175–76.

22. Heckscher, *Woodrow Wilson: A Biography*, 432.

23. Tuchman, *The Zimmermann Telegram*, 167.

24. Ibid., 168.

25. Heckscher, *Woodrow Wilson: A Biography*, 436–37.

26. Pipes, *The Russian Revolution*, 285.

27. Ibid., 291.

28. Pipes, *The Russian Revolution*, 287. ·

29. Kerensky, *Crucifixion of Liberty*, 270.

30. Pipes, *The Russian Revolution*, 310.

31. Ibid., 312.

32. Nicolas de Basily, *Diplomat of Imperial Russia, 1903–1917* (Stanford, CA: Stanford University Press, 1973), 128.

33. Pipes, *The Russian Revolution*, 317.

34. Ibid., 319.

35. Kerensky, *Crucifixion of Liberty*, 270.

36. Pipes, *The Russian Revolution*, 303.

37. Lenin, *Collected Works*, 23:282, 290–91.

38. Edmund Wilson, *To the Finland Station* (New York: Lightyear Press, 2000), 462.

CHAPTER 6. PRESIDENT WILSON GOES TO WAR; LENIN GOES TO THE FINLAND STATION

1. Norman Saul, *War and Revolution: The United States and Russia (1914–1921)* (Lawrence: University Press of Kansas, 2001), 97–98.

2. Heckscher, *Woodrow Wilson: A Biography*, 437.

3. Ibid.

4. Link, *The Papers of Woodrow Wilson*, 41: 528–29.

5. Service, *Lenin: A Biography*, 249.

6. Mayer, *Wilson vs. Lenin*, 91.

7. Service, *Lenin: A Biography*, 256; Mayer, *Wilson vs. Lenin*, 92.

8. Link, *The Papers of Woodrow Wilson*, 41: 519–27.

9. Ibid., 41, 537–39.

10. Michel Winock, *Clemenceau* (Paris: Tempus Perrin, 2007), 418–19.

11. Link, *The Papers of Woodrow Wilson*, 42: 140–48.

12. Ibid., 41, 483.

13. Striner, *Woodrow Wilson and World War I*, 103.

14. "HCL to TR, April 4, 1917," in Roosevelt and Lodge, *Selections from the Correspondence of Theodore Roosevelt and Henry Cabot Lodge, 1884–1918*, 506–7; Garraty, *Henry Cabot Lodge: A Biography*, 333–34.

15. Wilson, *To the Finland Station*, 464.

16. Rappaport, *Conspirator: Lenin in Exile*, 288.

17. J. Alvarez Del Vayo, *The Last Optimist* (New York: Viking, 1950), 124.

18. Rappaport, *Conspirator: Lenin in Exile*, 291.

19. Service, *Lenin: A Biography*, 257.
20. Ibid.
21. Ibid., 258.
22. Rappaport, *Conspirator: Lenin in Exile*, 294.
23. Wilson, *To the Finland Station*, 469.
24. Z. A. B. Zeman, *Germany and the Revolution in Russia, 1915–1918* (Bethesda, MD: Oxford University Press, 1958), 51.
25. Service, *Lenin: A Biography*, 261.
26. Ibid., 262.
27. Lenin, *Collected Works*, 24:19–26.
28. Service, *Lenin: A Biography*, 266.

CHAPTER 7. RUPTURES, MUTINIES, AND CONVOYS

1. Sir Edward Spears, *Prelude to Victory* (London: J. Cape, 1939), 41.
2. Rod Paschall, *The Defeat of Imperial Germany, 1917–1918* (Chapel Hill, NC: Algonquin Books, 1989), 19.
3. Ibid.; John Keegan, *The First World War* (New York: Vintage, 2000), 322–23.
4. Taylor, *The First World War*, 108.
5. Paschall, *The Defeat of Imperial Germany, 1917–1918*, 38.
6. Keegan, *The First World War*, 325.
7. Alexander McKee, *Vimy Ridge* (London: Endeavour Press, 2016), 116.
8. Paschall, *The Defeat of Imperial Germany, 1917–1918*, 48.
9. Keegan, *The First World War*, 327.
10. Spears, *Prelude to Victory*, 489–90.
11. Keegan, *The First World War*, 314.
12. Spears, *Prelude to Victory*, 493.
13. Paschall, *The Defeat of Imperial Germany, 1917–1918*, 49.
14. Keegan, *The First World War*, 329.
15. Paschall, *The Defeat of Imperial Germany, 1917–1918*, 51.
16. Keegan, *The First World War*, 331.
17. Paschall, *The Defeat of Imperial Germany, 1917–1918*, 51.
18. Taylor, *Lloyd George: Rise and Fall*, 271–74.
19. Taylor, *The First World War*, 54.
20. "Alcohol and the First World War," last modified August 2014, http://spartacus-educational.com/FWWalcohol.htm.
21. Grigg, *Lloyd George: War Leader*, 48.
22. David Lloyd George, *War Memoirs* (London: Odhams Press, 1943), 1223.
23. Tooze, *The Deluge*, 207.
24. Lloyd George, *War Memoirs*, 1234–35.
25. Grigg, *Lloyd George: War Leader*, 50.
26. Herman, *To Rule the Waves*, 512.
27. Grigg, *Lloyd George: War Leader*, 50–51.
28. Burton J. Hendrick and William S. Sims, *The Victory at Sea* (London: J. Murray, 1920); Herman, *To Rule the Waves*, 513.
29. *Naval Investigation, Hearings Before the Subcommittee of the Committee on Naval Affairs*, 66th Cong., 2nd sess., (1921).
30. Taylor, *Lloyd George: Rise and Fall*, 115.

31. Charles Seymour, ed., *The Intimate Papers of Colonel House* (Boston: Houghton Mifflin Company, 1928), 2: 129.

32. Arthur Herman, *Gandhi and Churchill: The Epic Rivalry That Destroyed an Empire and Forged Our Age* (New York: Bantam, 2008).

33. Grigg, *Lloyd George: War Leader*, 188.

34. Ibid., 91.

35. Arthur Herman, *Freedom's Forge: How American Business Produced Victory in World War II* (New York: Random House, 2012).

CHAPTER 8. MR. WILSON'S WAR

1. Seymour, *The Intimate Papers of Colonel House*, 2: 316–17.

2. Arthur Link, *Woodrow Wilson and the Progressive Era* (New York: Harper Torch, 1963), 269n43.

3. Arthur Herman, *Douglas MacArthur: American Warrior* (New York: Random House, 2016), 89.

4. Ibid., 92.

5. A. J. Balfour and Blanche Dugdale, *Chapters of Autobiography* (London: Cassel and Co., 1930), 239.

6. Heckscher, *Woodrow Wilson: A Biography*, 445–46.

7. Balfour and Dugdale, *Chapters of Autobiography*, 201.

8. Joseph Tumulty, *Woodrow Wilson As I Know Him* (Los Angeles: HardPress, 2012), 286–88.

9. Striner, *Woodrow Wilson and World War I*, 110.

10. Ibid.

11. Ibid., 108.

12. Robert Zieger, *America's Great War* (Lanham, MD: Rowman and Littlefield, 2001), 66–67.

13. Paul Koistinen, *Mobilizing for Modern War: The Political Economy of American Warfare, 1865–1919* (Lawrence: University Press of Kansas, 1997), 148.

14. See Arthur Herman, *Freedom's Forge* (New York: Random House, 2012), 81–84.

15. Robert Ferrell, *Woodrow Wilson and World War I* (New York: HarperCollins, 1986), 25.

16. Zieger, *America's Great War*, 57.

17. Ibid., 72.

18. Ibid., 73.

19. See Arthur Schlesinger, *The Crisis of the Old Order* (New York: Mariner Books, 2003), 22.

20. Zieger, *America's Great War*, 75–76.

21. Tooze, *The Deluge*, 206–7.

22. Link, *The Papers of Woodrow Wilson*, 43: 390–91, 424–25.

23. Ibid., 41.

24. Pipes, *The Russian Revolution*, 329.

25. Ibid., 305.

26. Ibid.

27. Ibid., 307.

28. Ibid., 304.

29. Kerensky, *Crucifixion of Liberty*, 285.

30. Alexander Kerensky, *The Catastrophe* (New York: D. Appleton and Company, 1927), 264–69.

31. Kerensky, *Crucifixion of Liberty*, 284.

32. Tooze, *The Deluge*, 76.

33. Link, *The Papers of Woodrow Wilson*, 43: 465–70, 487–89.

34. Ibid., 42, 365–67.

35. Tooze, *The Deluge*, 78.

36. "Kerensky's Address, April 26, 1927," Foreign Language Press Survey, http://flps .newberry.org/article/5423967_3_0872/.

37. Lenin, *Collected Works*, 24:21–26.

38. Tooze, *The Deluge*, 80.

39. Service, *Lenin: A Biography*, 267.

40. Ibid., 271.

41. Tooze, *The Deluge*, 80.

CHAPTER 9. SUMMER OF DISCONTENT

1. Gordon Corrigan, *Mud, Blood and Poppycock: Britain and the Great War* (London: Weidenfeld and Nicolson, 2012), 373.

2. Taylor, *Lloyd George: Rise and Fall*, 120–21.

3. Grigg, *Lloyd George: War Leader*, 247.

4. Taylor, *Lloyd George: Rise and Fall*, 120.

5. Keegan, *The First World War*; Grigg, *Lloyd George: War Leader*, 166–67.

6. Taylor, *Lloyd George: Rise and Fall*, 121.

7. Holger Herwig, *The First World War: Germany and Austria-Hungary 1914–1918* (London: Bloomsbury Academic, 2009), 284, 295.

8. Ibid., 376.

9. Jarausch, *Out of Ashes*, 371; Klaus Epstein, *Matthias Erzberger and the Dilemma of German Democracy* (Munich: Ullstein, 1977).

10. Mayer, *Wilson vs. Lenin*, 130.

11. Herwig, *The First World War*, 374.

12. Tooze, *The Deluge*, 75.

13. Jarausch, *Out of Ashes*, 374.

14. Herwig, *The First World War*, 375.

15. Ibid., 263–64.

16. "The Auxiliary Service Law of December 5, 1916," German History in Documents and Images, http://germanhistorydocs.ghi-dc.org/sub_document.cfm?document_ id=953.

17. Herwig, *The First World War*, 263–64.

18. Ibid.

19. Kerensky, *Crucifixion of Liberty*, 312, 296.

20. Pipes, *The Russian Revolution*, 413.

21. E. H. Wilcox, *Russia's Ruin* (London: Chappell and Hall, 1919), 197.

22. Kerensky, *Crucifixion of Liberty*, 320–27.

23. Keegan, *The First World War*, 338.

24. Service, *Lenin: A Biography*, 159.

25. James Cannon, "Trotsky in America," *International Socialist Review* 21, no. 4 (1960): 99–105.

26. Robert Service, *Trotsky: A Biography* (Cambridge, MA: Belknap Press, 2011), 164.
27. Pipes, *The Russian Revolution*, 421.
28. Service, *Trotsky: A Biography*, 172.
29. Pipes, *The Russian Revolution*, 407.
30. Stefan Possony, *Lenin: The Compulsive Revolutionary* (Washington, DC: Regnery, 1964); Pipes, *The Russian Revolution*, 412.
31. Lenin, *Collected Works*, 25:153–54.
32. Pipes, *The Russian Revolution*, 427.
33. Service, *Trotsky: A Biography*, 174.
34. Pipes, *The Russian Revolution*, 431.
35. Ibid., 432.
36. Leon Trotsky, "Lenin Before October (1924)," *From the Arsenal of Marxism* 13, no. 1 (1952): 11–16.
37. Service, *Lenin: A Biography*, 287–88.
38. Pipes, *The Russian Revolution*, 436.
39. Tooze, *The Deluge*, 78.
40. Corrigan, *Mud, Blood and Poppycock: Britain and the Great War*, 353.
41. Martin Farndale, *History of the Royal Regiment of Artillery* (London: Royal Artillery Institute, 1986), 203.
42. Paschall, *The Defeat of Imperial Germany, 1917–1918*, 70.
43. Keegan, *The First World War*, 365.

CHAPTER 10. AMERICAN LEVIATHAN

1. Johnson, *Modern Times*, 14.
2. Link, *The Papers of Woodrow Wilson*, 38: 577.
3. George Creel, *Wilson and the Issues* (New York: Century Co., 1916).
4. Thomas Fleming, *The Illusion of Victory: America in World War I* (New York: Basic Books, 2008), 93.
5. Paul Berger, "How World War I Shaped Jewish Politics and Identity," *Jewish Forward*, June 25, 2014, http://forward.com/news/200509/how-world-war-i-shaped-jewish-politics-and-identit/.
6. George Creel, *The War, the World, and Wilson* (New York: Harper and Brothers, 1920).
7. Zieger, *America's Great War*, 80.
8. Ibid.
9. Ibid., 74.
10. Link, *The Papers of Woodrow Wilson*, 42: 77–79.
11. Arnold Stead, *Always on Strike: Frank Little and the Western Wobblies* (Chicago: Haymarket Books, 2014).
12. Fleming, *The Illusion of Victory*, 139.
13. Link, *The Papers of Woodrow Wilson*, 44: 101–2; Striner, *Woodrow Wilson and World War I*, 118–19.
14. Franklin Folsom, *America Before Welfare* (New York: NYU Press, 1996).
15. Zieger, *America's Great War*, 118.
16. Joseph A. McCartin, *Labor's Great War: The Struggle for Industrial Democracy and the Origins of Modern American Labor Relations, 1912–1921* (Chapel Hill: University of North Carolina Press, 1998).
17. Johnson, *Modern Times*, 17.

18. For different political perspectives on this, see Jim Powell, *Wilson's War: How Woodrow Wilson's Great Blunder Led to Hitler, Lenin, Stalin, and World War II* (New York: Crown Forum, 2003); and Michael Kazin, *War Against War: The American Fight for Peace, 1914–1918* (New York: Simon and Schuster, 2017).

19. Striner, *Woodrow Wilson and World War I*, 117–18.

20. Link, *The Papers of Woodrow Wilson*, 44: 33–36.

21. Ronald Schaffer, *America in the Great War: The Rise of the War Welfare State* (Bethesda, MD: Oxford University Press, 1994), 20.

22. Fleming, *The Illusion of Victory*, 73–74.

23. Link, *The Papers of Woodrow Wilson*, 42: 498–504.

24. Fleming, *The Illusion of Victory*, 136.

25. Ibid., 405.

26. "The Robert Prager Lynching: Media Reaction," Vancouver Island University, https://web.viu.ca/davies/h324war/prager.lynching.1918.htm.

27. Link, *The Papers of Woodrow Wilson*, 49: 207–9.

28. See Kathleen Dalton, *Theodore Roosevelt: A Strenuous Life* (New York: Vintage Books, 2007), 501.

29. Wayne Wiegand, *"An Active Instrument for Propaganda": The American Public Library During World War I* (Westport, CT: Praeger, 1989), 88.

30. Link, *The Papers of Woodrow Wilson*, 6: 633.

31. Fleming, *The Illusion of Victory*, 173.

32. Ibid., 127.

33. "HCL to TR, August 14, 1917," in Roosevelt and Lodge, *Selections from the Correspondence of Theodore Roosevelt and Henry Cabot Lodge*, 527–28.

34. Ibid., "HCL to TR, December 18, 1917," 530.

35. Herman, *Freedom's Forge*.

36. Tooze, *The Deluge*, 202.

37. Fleming, *The Illusion of Victory*, 173.

38. Zieger, *America's Great War*, 71.

39. Link, *The Papers of Woodrow Wilson*, 45: 195.

40. Ibid., 43: 522–23.

CHAPTER 11. RUSSIA ON THE BRINK

1. Pipes, *The Russian Revolution*, 440.

2. Lenin, *Collected Works*, 25:225.

3. Pipes, *The Russian Revolution*, 431.

4. Lenin, *Collected Works*, 25:414.

5. Ibid., 25:463.

6. Pipes, *The Russian Revolution*, 448–49.

7. Kerensky, *Crucifixion of Liberty*, 351.

8. Pipes, *The Russian Revolution*, 448.

9. Ibid., 459.

10. Ibid., 460.

11. Service, *Lenin: A Biography*, 299–300.

12. Lenin, *Collected Works*, 25:309.

13. Pipes, *The Russian Revolution*, 465–66.

14. Ibid.

15. Ibid., 474.

16. Lenin, *Collected Works*, 26: 186.

17. Service, *Trotsky: A Biography*, 182–84.

18. Lenin, *Collected Works*, 26: 186.

19. Pipes, *The Russian Revolution*, 478.

20. Ibid., 479.

21. Service, *Lenin: A Biography*, 303–4.

22. Panne, *The Black Book of Communism*, 48.

23. Pipes, *The Russian Revolution*, 482.

24. Ibid., 488.

25. Trotsky, "Lenin Before October (1924)," 94.

26. Link, *The Papers of Woodrow Wilson*, 45: 39.

27. N. Gordon Levin Jr., *Woodrow Wilson and World Politics: America's Response to War and Revolution* (Bethesda, MD: Oxford University Press, 1970), 58.

28. Wilson, *The Public Papers of Woodrow Wilson*, 45: 120.

29. Paschall, *The Defeat of Imperial Germany, 1917–1918*, 94.

30. Keegan, *The First World War*, 348.

31. Grigg, *Lloyd George: War Leader*, 298.

32. Ibid., 299.

33. Pipes, *The Russian Revolution*, 459–60.

34. Trotsky, "Lenin Before October (1924)," 77.

35. Pipes, *The Russian Revolution*, 494.

36. John Reed, *Ten Days That Shook the World* (Overland Park, KS: Digireads.com, 2007), 95.

37. Ibid., 97.

38. Ibid., 108–9.

39. Ibid., 109; Pipes, *The Russian Revolution*, 495.

40. Pipes, *The Russian Revolution*, 498.

41. Reed, *Ten Days That Shook the World*, 133–34.

CHAPTER 12. HINGE OF FATES

1. Taylor, *The First World War*, 124.

2. Corrigan, *Mud, Blood and Poppycock: Britain and the Great War*, 354–55.

3. Keegan, *The First World War*, 402–3.

4. Taylor, *The First World War*, 124.

5. Corrigan, *Mud, Blood and Poppycock: Britain and the Great War*, 151–55.

6. Paschall, *The Defeat of Imperial Germany, 1917–1918*, 124–25.

7. Ibid., 120.

8. Tooze, *The Deluge*, 201; D. R. Woodward, *Trial by Friendship: Anglo-American Relations 1917–1918* (Lawrence: University Press of Kentucky, 1987).

9. Paschall, *The Defeat of Imperial Germany, 1917–1918*, 120.

10. Seymour, *The Intimate Papers of Colonel House*, 3:202.

11. Ibid., 257–59.

12. Herwig, *The First World War*, 12.

13. A. J. P. Taylor, *The Habsburg Monarchy, 1809–1918* (Chicago: University of Chicago Press, 1976), 9.

14. Ibid., 274.

15. Cf. chapter 2.

16. Seymour, *The Intimate Papers of Colonel House*, 3:278.

17. Pipes, *The Russian Revolution*, 303.

18. Ibid., 493.

19. Service, *Lenin: A Biography*, 326.

20. Panne, *The Black Book of Communism*, 54–55.

21. Ibid.

22. Pipes, *The Russian Revolution*, 520.

23. Reed, *Ten Days That Shook the World*, 238–39.

24. Panne, *The Black Book of Communism*, 56.

25. Pipes, *The Russian Revolution*, 507.

26. Tooze, *The Deluge*, 85.

27. Pipes, *The Russian Revolution*, 542.

28. Ibid., 544–45.

29. Lenin, *Collected Works*, 25:201.

30. Tooze, *The Deluge*, 112.

31. Leon Trotsky, "Statement on Publication of the Secret Treaties, 22 November 1917," *Collected Writings* 3, no. 2, 64.

32. Mayer, *Wilson vs. Lenin*, 268, 278–79.

33. Seymour, *The Intimate Papers of Colonel House*, 3:285–86.

34. E.g., Mayer, *Wilson vs. Lenin*, 385–86.

35. Link, *The Papers of Woodrow Wilson*, 45: 134.

36. Ibid., 45: 147.

37. Ibid., 44: 120–21.

38. Ibid., 45: 551.

39. John Wheeler-Bennett, *Brest-Litovsk, the Forgotten Peace, March 1918* (New York: W. W. Norton and Co., 1971), 117–20.

40. Tooze, *The Deluge*, 122.

41. Striner, *Woodrow Wilson and World War I*, 136.

42. Betty Unterberger, *The United States, Revolutionary Russia, and the Rise of Czechoslovakia* (College Station: Texas A&M University Press, 2000), 54.

43. Levin, *Woodrow Wilson and World Politics*, 17.

44. Taylor, *The First World War*, 71–72.

45. Tooze, *The Deluge*, 194–95.

46. Ibid., 196.

47. Grigg, *Lloyd George: War Leader*, 343–44.

CHAPTER 13. 1918: WAR AND PEACE AND WAR AGAIN

1. Panne, *The Black Book of Communism*, 60.

2. Ibid., 59.

3. Ibid., 50.

4. Pipes, *The Russian Revolution*, 544.

5. Ibid., 545–46; SR deputy Mark Visniak, quoted in ibid., 550.

6. V. D. Bonch-Bruevich, *The First Days of the October* (Moscow: Progress, 1977), 256.

7. Pipes, *The Russian Revolution*, 554.

8. Tooze, *The Deluge*, 128.

9. Aryadna Tyrkova-Williams, *From Liberty to Brest-Litovsk* (London: Macmillan, 1919), 369.

10. Tooze, *The Deluge*, 115–16.

11. Ibid., 114–15.

12. Wheeler-Bennett, *Brest-Litovsk, the Forgotten Peace*, 161–63.

13. Tooze, *The Deluge*, 126.

14. Taylor, *The First World War*, 137.

15. Tooze, *The Deluge*, 129.

16. Pipes, *The Russian Revolution*, 594.

17. Tooze, *The Deluge*, 139.

18. Ernst Jünger, *Storm of Steel*, trans. Michael Hofmann (New York: Penguin Classics, 2004), 231.

19. Keegan, *The First World War*, 396.

20. Paschall, *The Defeat of Imperial Germany, 1917–1918*, 128–29.

21. Taylor, *The First World War*, 402–3.

22. Corrigan, *Mud, Blood and Poppycock: Britain and the Great War*, 373.

23. "Sir Douglas Haig's 'Backs to the Wall' Order, 11 April 1918," Primary Documents, firstworldwar.com, http://www.firstworldwar.com/source/backstothe wall.htm.

24. Kevin McNamara, *Dreams of a Great Small Nation* (New York: PublicAffairs, 2016), 201.

25. John Bradley, *Russian Revolution* (Wilton, CT: Brompton Books, 1988), 68, 72.

26. Ibid., 32–33.

27. Kennan, *The Decision to Intervene*, 91–92.

28. Bradley, *Russian Revolution*, 35.

29. Tooze, *The Deluge*, 152–53.

30. McNamara, *Dreams of a Great Small Nation*, 242–43; George Kennan, *Russia Leaves the War: Soviet-American Relations, 1917–1920* (Princeton, NJ: Princeton University Press, 1989), 360–62.

31. A. J. P. Taylor, *The Habsburg Monarchy* (London: Hamish Hamilton, 1948), 248–49.

32. Bradley, *Russian Revolution*, 106–7.

33. Tooze, *The Deluge*, 160.

34. Ilya Somin, *Stillborn Crusade: The Tragic Failure of American Intervention in the Russian Civil War, 1918–20* (Piscataway, NJ: Transaction Publishers, 1996), 40.

35. Pipes, *The Russian Revolution*, 776–78.

36. Tooze, *The Deluge*, 165–66.

37. Matthew Hughes and Matthew Seligmann, *Leadership in Conflict, 1914–1918* (Barnsley, UK: Leo Cooper, 2000), 278.

38. Ibid., 163.

39. For background on the Argonne operation, see Robert Farrell, *America's Deadliest Battle: Meuse-Argonne, 1918* (Lawrence: University of Kansas Press, 2007); Herman, *Douglas MacArthur*, 132–35.

40. Garraty, *Henry Cabot Lodge: A Biography*, 341.

41. Link, *The Papers of Woodrow Wilson*, 51: 263–64, 264–65; Striner, *Woodrow Wilson and World War I*, 157.

42. Herman, *To Rule the Waves*, 518.

43. Link, *The Papers of Woodrow Wilson*, 51: 333–34.

44. Striner, *Woodrow Wilson and World War I*, 162.

45. Richard Watt, *The Kings Depart: The Tragedy of Germany: Versailles and the German Revolution* (New York: Simon & Schuster, 1968), 110–11.

46. Gordon Craig, *Politics of the Prussian Army* (Bethesda, MD: Oxford University Press, 1964), 346.

47. A. J. P. Taylor, *Origins of the Second World War* (New York: Simon and Schuster, 1996), 26.

48. Link, *The Papers of Woodrow Wilson*, 53: 531–33.

49. Bradley, *Russian Revolution*, 214.

50. Taylor, *Origins of the Second World War*, 163.

51. Striner, *Woodrow Wilson and World War I*, 169.

CHAPTER 14. 1919: GRAND ILLUSIONS

1. Harold Nicolson, *Peacemaking, 1919* (London: Faber and Faber, 2013), 6–8.

2. Ibid., 36–37.

3. Striner, *Woodrow Wilson and World War I*, 171.

4. Link, *The Papers of Woodrow Wilson*, 48: 57.

5. Striner, *Woodrow Wilson and World War I*, 153.

6. Margaret MacMillan, *Paris 1919: Six Months That Changed the World* (New York: Random House, 2002), 5.

7. Link, *The Papers of Woodrow Wilson*, 53: 285–86.

8. Heckscher, *Woodrow Wilson: A Biography*, 496.

9. Striner, *Woodrow Wilson and World War I*, 165.

10. Creel, *The War, the World, and Wilson*, 163.

11. Pipes, *The Russian Revolution*, 841.

12. Service, *Lenin: A Biography*, 335–36.

13. Ibid., 366; Pipes, *The Russian Revolution*, 806.

14. Service, *Lenin: A Biography*, 368.

15. Pipes, *The Russian Revolution*, 807.

16. Ibid., 813, 811.

17. Service, *Lenin: A Biography*, 376.

18. Johnson, *Modern Times*, 83.

19. Tooze, *The Deluge*, 238.

20. Ibid., 240.

21. Panne, *The Black Book of Communism*, 272–74.

22. Bradley, *Russian Revolution*, 159–61.

23. Service, *Lenin: A Biography*, 392.

24. Heckscher, *Woodrow Wilson: A Biography*, 500.

25. Link, *The Papers of Woodrow Wilson*, 53: 531–33; 505–7.

26. MacMillan, *Paris 1919*, 8.

27. Striner, *Woodrow Wilson and World War I*, 174.

28. MacMillan, *Paris 1919*, 14; Hunter Miller, *Drafting of the Covenant: History* (New York: Johnson Reprint Corporation, 1969), 42; Seymour, *The Intimate Papers of Colonel House*, 23.

29. Striner, *Woodrow Wilson and World War I*, 175.

30. Nicolson, *Peacemaking, 1919*, 196–97.

31. Ibid., 242.

32. Taylor, *Origins of the Second World War*, 167–68.

33. MacMillan, *Paris 1919*, 23.

34. Ibid., 33.

35. Ibid., 33.

36. Taylor, *Origins of the Second World War*, 40.

37. MacMillan, *Paris 1919*, 23.

38. Nicolson, *Peacemaking, 1919*, 198.

39. MacMillan, *Paris 1919*, 93.

40. Striner, *Woodrow Wilson and World War I*, 175.

41. MacMillan, *Paris 1919*, 103–4.

42. Nicolson, *Peacemaking, 1919*, 164.

43. MacMillan, *Paris 1919*, 287; Striner, *Woodrow Wilson and World War I*, 179–80.

44. Heckscher, *Woodrow Wilson: A Biography*, 563–64.

45. MacMillan, *Paris 1919*, 291–92.

46. Tooze, *The Deluge*, 96–97.

47. Ibid., 323.

48. MacMillan, *Paris 1919*, 317.

49. Link, *The Papers of Woodrow Wilson*, 58: 165.

50. MacMillan, *Paris 1919*, 340.

51. Link, *The Papers of Woodrow Wilson*, 58: 607–40.

52. Striner, *Woodrow Wilson and World War I*, 209.

53. MacMillan, *Paris 1919*, 465.

54. Taylor, *Origins of the Second World War*, 174.

55. Link, *The Papers of Woodrow Wilson*, 60: 71, 75–79.

56. Nicolson, *Peacemaking, 1919*, 368–71.

57. Bradley, *Russian Revolution*, 122.

58. Panne, *The Black Book of Communism*, 66.

59. Conquest, *V. I. Lenin*, 96.

60. Service, *Trotsky: A Biography*, 243–44.

61. Panne, *The Black Book of Communism*, 89.

62. Johnson, *Modern Times*, 71.

63. Robert Conquest, *The Great Terror: A Reassessment* (New York: Oxford University Press, 2008), 6.

CHAPTER 15. LAST ACT

1. Heckscher, *Woodrow Wilson: A Biography*, 581.

2. Striner, *Woodrow Wilson and World War I*, 189.

3. Taylor, *Origins of the Second World War*, 168.

4. Johnson, *Modern Times*, 31.

5. MacMillan, *Paris 1919*, 94.

6. Ibid., 95.

7. Thomas Knock, *To End All Wars* (Princeton, NJ: Princeton University Press, 1995), 229.

8. Striner, *Woodrow Wilson and World War I*, 190.

9. Striner, *Woodrow Wilson and World War I*, 192.

10. Link, *The Papers of Woodrow Wilson*, 55: 313.

11. Edith Wilson, *My Memoir* (Indianapolis, IN: Bobbs-Merrill Company, 1939), 245–46.

12. "Address to the Senate on the Versailles Peace Treaty," July 10, 1919, in Link, *The Papers of Woodrow Wilson*, 61.

13. Link, *The Papers of Woodrow Wilson*, 61: 445–46.
14. Heckscher, *Woodrow Wilson: A Biography*, 586–87.
15. Knock, *To End All Wars*, 229.
16. Garraty, *Henry Cabot Lodge: A Biography*, 362.
17. Frederick Lewis Allen, *Only Yesterday: An Informal History of the 1920s* (New York: Harper Perennial Modern Classics, 2010), 24–25.
18. Striner, *Woodrow Wilson and World War I*, 221.
19. Heckscher, *Woodrow Wilson: A Biography*, 587.
20. "Covenant of the League of Nations, 1919–24," Primary Documents, firstworldwar .com, http://www.firstworldwar.com/source/leagueofnations.htm.
21. Striner, *Woodrow Wilson and World War I*, 222.
22. Henry Kissinger, *Diplomacy* (New York: Simon and Schuster, 1994), 50.
23. Knock, *To End All Wars*, 229.
24. Garraty, *Henry Cabot Lodge: A Biography*, 369–70.
25. Gene Smith, *When the Cheering Stopped* (New York: Morrow, 1964), 56.
26. Heckscher, *Woodrow Wilson: A Biography*, 593.
27. Garraty, *Henry Cabot Lodge: A Biography*, 370.
28. Heckscher, *Woodrow Wilson: A Biography*, 596.
29. "An Address in Convention Hall, Kansas City, September 6, 1919," in Link, *The Papers of Woodrow Wilson*, 63: 66–67.
30. Heckscher, *Woodrow Wilson: A Biography*, 597.
31. Striner, *Woodrow Wilson and World War I*, 226.
32. Ibid., 227.
33. Heckscher, *Woodrow Wilson: A Biography*, 603.
34. Ibid., 606; Link, *The Papers of Woodrow Wilson*, 64: 177.
35. Striner, *Woodrow Wilson and World War I*, 228.
36. Link, *The Papers of Woodrow Wilson*, 64: 189; Heckscher, *Woodrow Wilson: A Biography*, 609.
37. Smith, *When the Cheering Stopped*, 78–79; Heckscher, *Woodrow Wilson: A Biography*, 609.
38. Heckscher, *Woodrow Wilson: A Biography*, 610.
39. Garraty, *Henry Cabot Lodge: A Biography*, 374.
40. Ibid., 375.
41. "HCL to Root, September 29, 1919," in Garraty, *Henry Cabot Lodge: A Biography*, 375.
42. Edith Wilson, *My Memoir*, 286–88.
43. Heckscher, *Woodrow Wilson: A Biography*, 612.
44. Garraty, *Henry Cabot Lodge: A Biography*, 378.
45. Link, *The Papers of Woodrow Wilson*, 64: 28–30.
46. Ibid., 64, 44–46.
47. Henry Cabot Lodge, *The Senate and the League of Nations* (New York: Charles Scribner's Sons, 1925), 215–16.
48. Link, *The Papers of Woodrow Wilson*, 64: 199–202.
49. The full story is contained in Gene Smith, *When the Cheering Stopped*, 85–178.
50. Johnson, *Modern Times*, 35.
51. Ibid., 34.

CONCLUSION

1. Johnson, *Modern Times*, 79.
2. Lenin, *Collected Works*, 26:352.
3. Johnson, *Modern Times*, 84.
4. Ibid., 84–85.
5. Panne, *The Black Book of Communism*, 109, 114–15.
6. "Left-wing Communism: An Infantile Disorder," in Lenin, *Collected Works*, Vol. 31, 17–90.
7. Service, *Lenin: A Biography*, 445.
8. Ibid., 457.
9. Ibid., 468–69.
10. "Lenin's Testament," in Lenin, *Collected Works* 36, (1956): 593–611.
11. Service, *Lenin: A Biography*, 477.
12. Heckscher, *Woodrow Wilson: A Biography*, 667.
13. Tooze, *The Deluge*, 339.
14. Ibid., 345.
15. Amity Schlaes, *The Forgotten Man: A New History of the Great Depression* (New York: Harper, 2007).
16. Johnson, *Modern Times*, 739n51.
17. Ian Kershaw, *The "Hitler Myth": Image and Reality in the Third Reich* (Bethesda, MD: Oxford University Press, 2001), 426.
18. Johnson, *Modern Times*, 85.
19. Panne, *The Black Book of Communism*, 9–10.
20. Claire Sterling, *The Terrorist Connection* (New York: Henry Holt and Co., 1981).
21. Taylor, *Origins of the Second World War*, 35.
22. Ibid., 35–36.
23. Adam Tooze, *The Wages of Destruction: The Making and Breaking of the Nazi Economy* (New York: Penguin Books, 2007), 7–11.
24. Powell, *Wilson's War*.
25. Morison, *Letters of Theodore Roosevelt*, 824–25.
26. Tooze, *The Deluge*, 336.
27. Kissinger, *Diplomacy*, 55.

INDEX

submarine warfare, 3, 6, 26–27, 51, 60,
99–100, 109–10, 162, 174, 221, 367
tonnage sunk by, 27, 100, 109, 174
U-boats, 2, 26, 98–99
U-boats, bases, 215
U-boats, fleet, size, 99
U.S. ships or American passengers killed
and, 109–10, 114, 130, 142, 341
Germany
advance into the Baltic, 22
advance into Italy, 276
advance into Poland, 32
advance on Caporetto, Italy, 276
advance on Moscow, 323
advance on Paris, 328–29
advance on Petrograd, 269–70
advance on Riga, 224, 232, 263, 268
Allied blockade of, 23–24
allies of, 21
armistice signed, 343–45
armistice sought from Wilson, Oct. 4,
1918, 339
armistice with Russia, 303
Bethmann-Hollweg negotiated peace
offer (Dec. 12, 1917), 19, 22, 25–26,
28–30, 38, 52–53, 59
Bolshevik takeover in Russia and, 278
Brest-Litovsk peace negotiations,
299–300, 307, 310, 313, 320–23
Brest-Litovsk Treaty, 324–25, 331, 343, 345
British naval blockade of, 23–24, 51, 346,
367, 376
casualties, 20, 167, 341
Central Powers alliance crumbles, 21
codes used by, 1–7
as constitutional democracy, 360
decision for unrestricted submarine
warfare as pivotal, 100
eastern domination and, 322
economic crisis in, 23
Erzberger as war critic, 218
espionage and, 247
Fatherland Party, 221–22
fighting on two fronts, 20, 21, 23
first German Communist Party, 360
food and supplies shortages, 24, 217, 218,
346
future of, 174
Hitler's one-party state, 297
Japanese alliance sought, 111–12

labor strikes in, 217–18, 323, 342
League of Nations and, 389
Lebensraum, 322
Lenin abetted and funded by, 144–47, 159,
228–32, 278
Lenin as Trojan horse for, 154, 299–300
Lenin's request for troops from, 337
Mexico alliance and, 111–12
mobilization of men in, 156
Nazi-Soviet Nonaggression Pact, 414, 425
negotiated peace offers by, 19, 22, 25–26,
28–30, 38, 52–53, 59, 219–20
Paris Peace Conference and, 375–77
Petrograd formula for ending the war
and, 218
Polish independent state strategy, 22–23
post-war revolt, 342, 346
public morale and, 217
size of military, 20
Social Democrats in, 95, 325, 339, 343, 360,
375
strategy for quick strike on France, 19
Treaty of Versailles and, 375–77, 425
war's economic strain on, 6
Wilson and armistice terms, 339–42
Wilson informed of submarine warfare
decision, 101
Wilson's peace note (December 18, 1916)
and, 59, 60
workforce and, 220–21
Zimmerman telegram, 3–7, 105, 110–11,
112, 123–30, 226, 421n
Zionist movement and, 312–13
See also Bethmann-Hollweg, Theobald;
Central Powers; Hindenburg, Paul
von; Ludendorff, Erich; Wilhelm II,
Kaiser; *specific battles; specific military
branches*
Geyer, Hermann, *The Attack in Position
Warfare*, 326
Gibson, Dana, 239
Gil, Stepan, 357
Glass, Carter, 186, 194
Goethals, George, 252
Golitsyn, Nikolai, 122
Gompers, Samuel, 243
Gorbachev, Mikhail, 424
Gordon, John Steele, 196
Gough, Hubert, 234
Gourko, Joseph, 107

ABOUT THE AUTHOR

ARTHUR HERMAN, PHD, is the author of nine books, including the *New York Times* bestseller *How the Scots Invented the Modern World*, which has sold half a million copies worldwide; and *Gandhi and Churchill*, which was a finalist for the 2009 Pulitzer Prize. Among his six other books are *To Rule the Waves: How the British Navy Shaped the Modern World* (HarperCollins, 2004), which was nominated for the United Kingdom's prestigious Mountbatten Maritime Prize; *Freedom's Forge*, named by *The Economist* as one of the Best Books of 2012; and *Douglas MacArthur: American Warrior*. He is a senior fellow at the Hudson Institute in Washington, DC. He writes regularly for the *Wall Street Journal*, the *Wall Street Journal Asia*, and the *Nikkei Asian Review*, and is a contributing editor for *National Review*.

ALSO BY ARTHUR HERMAN

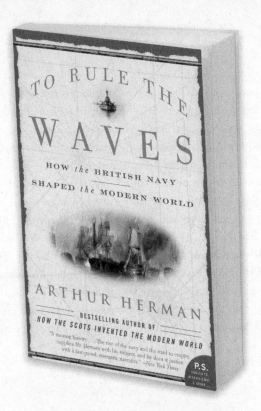

TO RULE THE WAVES
HOW THE BRITISH NAVY SHAPED THE MODERN WORLD
Available in Paperback

"*To Rule the Waves* is a riveting story of some 400 years of British naval mastery that serves as an especially timely reminder that national purpose and unity, coupled with a sense of self-sacrifice and heritage, really do win wars and keep the peace."
—Victor Davis Hanson, author of *Carnage and Culture*
and Senior Fellow, at the Hoover Institution, Stanford University

To Rule the Waves tells the extraordinary story of how the British Royal Navy allowed one nation to rise to a level of power unprecedented in history. From the navy's beginnings under Henry VIII to the age of computer warfare and special ops, historian Arthur Herman tells the spellbinding tale of great battles at sea, heroic sailors, violent conflict, and personal tragedy — of the way one mighty institution forged a nation, an empire, and a new world.